Hank Williams

THE BIOGRAPHY

D064560-4

Also by Colin Escott

Good Rockin' Tonight: Sun Records & the Birth
of Rock & Roll

Hank Williams

THE BIOGRAPHY

COLIN ESCOTT

with George Merritt
and William MacEwen

JE10 '96

Portage County District Library
10482 South Street
Garrettsville, OH 44231-1116

Little, Brown and Company

Boston New York Toronto London

Copyright © 1994, 1995 by Colin Escott

All rights reserved. No part of this book may be reproduced in any form or by any electronic or mechanical means, including information storage and retrieval systems, without permission in writing from the publisher, except by a reviewer who may quote brief passages in a review.

First Paperback Edition

Library of Congress Cataloging-in-Publication Data

Escott, Colin.
    Hank Williams : the biography/Colin Escott with George Merritt
    and William MacEwen. — 1st ed.
        p. cm.
    Discography: p.
    Includes bibliographical references and index.
    ISBN 0-316-24986-6 (HC)   0-316-24938-6 (PB)
        1. Williams, Hank, 1923–1953. 2. Country musicians—United
    States — Biography. I. Merritt, George. II. MacEwen, William.
    III. Title.
    ML420.W55E83   1994
    782.42'1642'092 — dc20
    [B]   93-48092

10 9 8 7 6 5 4 3 2 1

RRD-VA

Published simultaneously in Canada by Little, Brown & Company
(Canada) Limited

Printed in the United States of America

To my father and fondly remembered mother

C.E.

To the memory of Bob McKinnon

G.M.

2104743-6

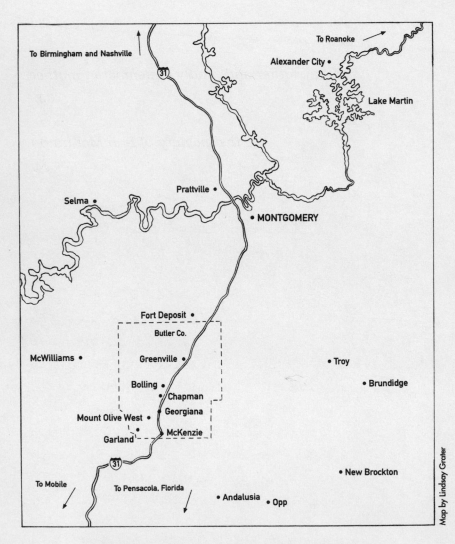

Map by Lindsay Grater

South Central Alabama

CONTENTS

INTRODUCTION

*T*HERE is no business so callous or so quickly forgetful as the music business. This week's Best Bet is next week's unreturned phone call. Even the Singing Nun committed suicide. In part, the nature of the business stems from the contradiction embodied in the very term "music business." "Music" and "business" essentially detest each other and often barely even understand each other.

Hank Williams was an enigma that the business element simply could not unravel. Why couldn't he straighten up and fly right? Why did he have to say those things onstage? Why did he damn one promising opportunity after another? What was the matter with the man? The result was that, in the months before he died, Hank Williams's life was becoming an unreturned phone call, and, if the pace of his hits had slowed up even fractionally, he would have been jettisoned unsentimentally by those who shed copious tears over his remains.

Death is a sound career move if it can be timed right, and Hank Williams's triumph was to avoid growing old disgracefully. Not for Hank the haggard mask of senility. In terms of forging a legend, he could have done no better than to burn out at twenty-nine before his fire grew dim and the face of country music changed. Had he lived, he might have become a poor parody of himself, shamelessly hustling tepid remakes of his greatest hits on cable shows. As it is, his premature death left what is still the most important single body of work in country music, as well as the tantalizing promise of what might have been.

In life Hank Williams defined the argot of contemporary country music; in death he set the standard by which success on every level — even self-destruction — is measured. Several times this year, the hype mill will damn some kid it considers promising by dubbing him "the next Hank Williams," or by seeing in him "shades of Hank Williams." In 1975 Waylon Jennings, then atop the ladder, looked at his life and what it had become and posed the question, "Are You Sure Hank Done It This-a-Way?" In fact, Hank had done it very much that-a-way. Still unable to let go, Waylon recently had another tussle with the legacy. Acknowledging that living as Hank had lived had nearly killed him, a veggie-and-tofu-munching Waylon Jennings declared, "The Hank Williams Syndrome is Dead." For Waylon perhaps. Try telling that to the kid who has just driven his pickup into Nashville with a handful of songs in his guitar case. In a very real sense, The Hank Williams Syndrome *is* country music.

The legend of Hank Williams quickly overtook the man. Odder yet, the legend changed radically over the years. The sainted Hank Williams who presided beatifically over country music in the years immediately after his death barely let alcohol or a cussword pass his lips. Yet by the 1970s and '80s, he was drinking enough to kill fifty men — let alone one rather frail one. Along the way, the living, breathing Hank Williams who once pulled on his boots one at a time got lost. Who was the man behind the grinning rictus of those publicity photos? The grind that made up much of what he did on a day in–day out, year in–year out basis isn't always the stuff of legend. It's emblematic of what has overtaken Hank Williams since his death that when the video for Alan Jackson's "Midnight in Montgomery" was shot, a re-created Hank Williams grave site was used, one somewhat bigger and more unearthly than the real thing.

There is no shortage of Hank Williams stories, many of them Hank-Williams-falling-over-drunk stories. Some of the tales have taken on the power of urban myths; many others have become overblown in the constant retelling. In the process, Dead Hank became like Dead Elvis, a flypaper that attracted myth and misinformation. Dead Hank became the vindicator of anyone who ever fell blind drunk onto the floor. Bobby Lee Springfield caught that view of Hank with "(Now I Know Why) Hank Drank." But was that the same Hank Williams cast by Leonard Cohen as the poet of existential misery ("I said to Hank Williams, 'How lonely does it get?' ")? Or was he the icon of bubba defiance invoked by Kris Kristofferson ("If you don't like Hank Williams, baby, you can kiss my ass.")? Or what about Moe Bandy, who used Hank as the key to understanding the inevitability of screwing up ("You wrote 'Your Cheatin' Heart' about a girl like my first ex-wife. . . . Hank Williams, you wrote my life.")? And still the songs keep coming.

Could Hank Williams really have been all things to all men, or has the lack of knowledge been used as a blank screen onto which fantasies can be projected? Are the simple, manageable images an excuse for not coming to terms with the unwieldy fragmentary nature of a person's life, particularly a life so full of contradictions as Hank Williams's?

The myths and the tales have all been good for the legend, though; the problem is that they would have eventually passed for history unless someone had tried to set the story straight. The number of those who knew Hank Williams diminishes every year, and many of those who remain have condensed their memories to well-rehearsed set pieces. With that in mind, we have tried — inasmuch as it is now possible — to start from scratch in retracing the steps Hank Williams trod. We've also tried to place him in the context of the music industry of *his* day, not ours, and to show how the industry grew around him during the years that he lived.

Hillbilly music was a cottage industry in the late '40s, only recently elevated from folk music played in the small community centers of the rural South. As such, the day-to-day routine of its performers scarcely warranted a mention anywhere. Newspapers, even in southern towns, tended to concentrate on the goings-on among society's grandees. Taken together, both Nashville papers had just four references to Hank Williams before his death. Trade paper coverage was a random affair edited out of New York or Chicago, often with more than a touch of condescension. Radio stations programmed country music in the early morning hours before the network feeds were picked up. Many of Hank Williams's personal appearances were announced only on early morning radio and on posters. Today's standards don't apply: the country musician's life was one lived at a very low level — socially and financially. But, in the year or two immediately before Hank's death, all of that was beginning to change, due in no small measure to Hank himself. Country music began to shake off its regional aspect and began its eternal quest for prime-time programming. The way in which Hank Williams's career meshed with the growth of the country music industry is our subtext here.

Our primary purpose, though, has been to try to reclaim the real Hank Williams from the myth. The true story of his life can't be cast in the hushed and reverential tones that were the norm after he died, but neither can it be the story of the man who "Just Said Yes" for twenty-nine years. Certainly his alcoholism has to be addressed; to do otherwise would be like writing about the *Titanic* without mentioning the iceberg. But there are more important broad and specific questions to be answered in the quest for the Hank Williams who once walked this earth. His was a life that spun quickly out of control. Too quickly he became a candle that burned with no wax to replace what had melted away. It was a tragedy more sordid than ennobling, but Hank Williams's ultimate triumph was that, in trying to conjure up something that would sell a few records tomorrow, he defined the vernacular of contemporary country music, and provided a soundtrack for other peoples' lives without being half-way in control of his own.

Colin Escott
Toronto, Canada
November 1993

Hank Williams

THE BIOGRAPHY

The road to that bright happy region
Is narrow and twisted, they say
But the broad one that leads to perdition
Is posted and blazed all the way.
"The Drifting Cowboy's Dream"
(Unknown)

* *

THE DRIFTING COWBOY'S DREAM

* * * * * * * * * * * * * * * * * *

*T*HE Mount of Olives, which overlooks Jerusalem from the east, will, according to biblical lore, be the gathering place when the dead shall rise upon the Messiah's return. Those buried on the Mount will be the first to rise, and will have pride of place at the Messiah's side. Hank Williams probably learned as much from the Book of Matthew, but if he had ever returned to Mount Olive West, Alabama, he would have seen a red-dirt settlement of half a dozen houses strung along an unpaved road — with not even a crossroads. The few souls who lived there eked out a living as farmers or as indentured employees of the lumber companies that were opening up the dark coniferous forests of southern Alabama.

Hank was the third and last child of Elonzo Huble Williams and his wife, Jessie Lillybelle Skipper Williams. Their first child died soon after birth; their second child, Hank's sister, Irene, was born on August 8, 1922; Hank was born on September 17, 1923. He was meant to be christened Hiram, after King Hiram of Tyre in the Book of Kings, but he was belatedly registered with the Bureau of Vital Statistics as "Hiriam" when he was ten. By then, friends, family, and neighbors were calling him "Harm" or "Skeets." He was born at home in a double-pen log house in Mount Olive West known as the Kendrick Place because it had been built in the late 1800s by a Mr. Wiley Kendrick and his wife, Fanny.

Lon Williams was thirty-one years old when Hank arrived. He was born on December 22, 1891, in Macedonia in Lowndes County, Alabama.

His family came from North Carolina, and the only surviving photo of his grandmother shows a woman with high cheekbones and deep-set eyes. Hank always said he was part Indian, and there was probably some Creek or Cherokee on his father's side. Lon's mother, Anne Autrey Williams, committed suicide when he was six. Lon would tell his children about the time he found his mother dead; sometimes he said she drank rat poison, other times that she hanged herself. Never did he give any indication why. His father, Irvin, moved the family to McWilliams, Alabama, a lumber company town some thirty miles from Greenville. Irvin died in 1909, when Lon was seventeen, but from the time he was twelve, Lon had drifted, working as a water boy, ox-driver, and anything else he could get. He grew up without a father, just as Hank would, and just as Hank Jr., would.

Jessie Lillybelle Skipper was a delicate name for a woman who, had she been a canary, would have sung bass. Born in Butler County on August 12, 1898, Lillie was a large, broad-boned woman, who, according to general consensus, didn't take no crap. Quite what Lon saw in her, or she saw in Lon, is unclear; later in life, neither could mention the other's name without a curse. Lillie ruled every one of her roosts with a steely sense of purpose hardened by having to deal with one feckless, useless man after another. She could be funny, even tender, but always formidably strong-willed, and not much given to self-doubt.

The Skippers lived for a while around Chapman, Alabama, and Lon Williams was probably working near there on a lumber train crew when he met Lillie. She was eighteen, almost a spinster, when they married on November 12, 1916. On July 9, 1918, as the First World War was drawing to a close, Lon was sent to Camp Shelby in Mississippi, then on to France in the 113th Regiment of Engineers, 42nd Division. Shortly after arriving, he got into a fight with another soldier over a French woman. He was struck on the side of his face with a wine bottle and kicked on the side of his head when he was on the ground. He spent about a week in the base hospital before being shipped back to the front. He seemed to have recovered, but he had suffered an injury that would come back to haunt him.

On June 26, 1919, Lon was discharged from Camp Gordon, Georgia, returned to Alabama, and began working for the lumber companies. The company crews would run a narrow-gauge railroad track up to the logging sites, and entire families lived on-site in boxcars for weeks or months at a stretch. Lon drove the log trains, and he worked, as he was fond of saying, "from can to cain't."

When Irene and Hank arrived, though, Lon and Lillie were renting the old Kendrick place for eighty dollars a year, and running a small strawberry farm with a country store on one end of their house. Then a late frost hit, probably in the spring of 1924, and Lon was forced back to work for the lumber companies. He started with Ray Lumber in Atmore, then moved to W. T. Smith. By the time Lillie finally got around to registering Hank's birth in 1934, she stated that Lon was working as an engineer for the lumber companies when Hank was born, which was a few months shy of the truth.

Hank later said that his first recollection was of living in a W. T. Smith boxcar at the McKenzie camp near Chapman. After that, Lon bought a house a mile and a half out of Georgiana and worked on the Ruthven job. Then, in 1927, when Hank was four, he sold the place and bought a house and ten acres in McWilliams, continuing on the Ruthven job for W. T. Smith until 1929. Hank attended first and second grade in McWilliams, another tiny settlement almost entirely dependent upon the lumber business. Every house, every business was built of pine, and every man worked for the lumber companies or for a business that depended on them. The Louisville and Nashville (L&N) Railroad had opened up the town around 1900, and it was as bustling as it ever was when Lon and Lillie moved there, insular and self-contained in the way that communities had to be when the mule was as common a form of transport as the automobile.

One of the last songs that Hank would write was about his father. Situated in Chapman, "The Log Train" was partially out of meter and a predictably sketchy tribute to a man Hank barely remembered from childhood. Figuring that a narrative ballad should have a dramatic outcome, Hank killed off his father in the last verse, and for many years the story circulated that Lon had indeed died when Hank was young, when in fact he outlived both Hank and Lillie by many years.

Hank was his parents' child in every respect. Whether through propinquity or some mystery of DNA, Hank had Lillie's driving ambition, but it would be forever subverted by Lon's tendency to backslide. Later, when he was berated for his drinking, Hank was fond of saying, "If you think I'm a drunk, you shoulda seen my old man." For her part, Lillie saw some of Lon's lack of willpower and sloth in Hank and cursed both men, telling her son that he was no better than his wastrel of a father.

Writing about Hank in a notoriously unreliable biography called *Life Story of Our Hank Williams,* Lillie said that he always liked to sing — but then, so do most children. Looking now down the wrong end of the telescope, it's hard to tell if Hank was the *wunderkind* whose talent was innate, or whether he simply had a bent for music that he nurtured until it became the easiest way he knew of making a living. Between Lon and Lillie there was a little musical talent. Lon played the Jew's harp, and Lillie played the organ at the Mount Olive West Baptist Church and at the other churches they attended. She sang in her strong, resonant voice that some said made the skin on their necks tingle. She loved to tell how Hank always sat beside her and sang too, and Hank certainly seemed to view those Sundays at his mother's side as the beginning of it all. "My earliest memory," he told journalist Ralph J. Gleason, "is sittin' on that organ stool by her and hollerin'. I must have been five, six years old, and louder 'n anybody else."

One reason that Hank might have been drawn to music is that since he wasn't as physically strong as most kids, he knew from an early age that he would be unsuited to logging or farming. Lon told a couple of interviewers that there was a raised spot on the boy's spine, but neither he nor Lillie understood what it was. In all likelihood it was the first sign of spina bifida occulta, a condition in which the vetebral arches of the spine fail to unite, allowing the spinal cord to herniate or protrude through the spinal column. That birth defect would determine the outcome of Hank's life every bit as much as his love of music. From the beginning he was frail and spindly, and, much as he wanted to join in sports, he lacked the physical coordination and stamina. His was a society with strong shared values, chief among them pride in physical strength, and Hank's apartness sprang in great measure from his physical affliction.

Not long after Lon arrived back in McWilliams, his hometown as a child, he almost ceased working because his face was slowly becoming paralyzed. He quit W. T. Smith and got a lighter job with Ralph Lumber in Bolling. When he became unable to hold that job down, Lillie took him to the Veterans Administration hospital in Pensacola, Florida, in January 1930. From Pensacola, Lon was transferred to the V.A. hospital in Alexandria, Louisiana. He was later diagnosed with a brain aneurysm, probably a result of the beating he took in France, and he stayed in Alexandria until January 1937. Hank was six when Lon left, and while Lillie was more than up to the task of raising her children by herself, Lon's absence only heightened Hank's isolation.

After Lon left, Lillie's brother-in-law, Walter McNeil, moved her and the children to Garland to live with his family and Lillie's mother. Lillie then scrimped and saved enough to move her brood into Georgiana, the first town of any size Hank had ever lived in. It had been founded in 1855 by Pitts Milner, a preacher with a capitalistic streak who got into the sawmill business and named the town Pittsville in his honor. Later his daughter, Georgina, fell into a bog and suffocated, and he renamed the settlement in her memory. The Williamses joined fifteen hundred others in Georgiana, 30 percent of them black. The Louisville and Nashville Railroad bisected the town. All the stores, mills, and other businesses were on one side of the tracks or the other. The town is still much as it was when Hank lived there, just less thriving and less populous, and small enough that the major chain stores and fast-food outlets have passed it by.

The first house in which Lillie, Irene, and Hank lived was a dilapidated wooden shack on old Highway 31 (the major north-south route through Alabama) that burned down a few months after they moved in. Lillie and the children ran out wearing only their nightgowns. Lillie grabbed Lon's shotgun as she was leaving. They moved back in with the McNeils for a while, and then, as Irene wrote in the *Washington Post,* Lillie found a small house to rent near the railroad tracks: "She put Hank, me, and our few belongings on a wagon and started toward that little house. On the way she stopped to mail a letter. A man walked up to her in the post office and asked if she was the lady whose house had burned. 'I am Thaddeus B. Rose,' he told her. 'I have a house you are welcome to rent free until you can get on your feet.' "

It was an imposing house, by far the finest dwelling Lillie, Irene, or Hank had ever been inside. It was at 127 Rose Street, the street that Thaddeus B. Rose had named for himself. He had ordered that the house be built on stilts, raising it six feet off the ground. Rose was one of Georgiana's elite, a bachelor who lived away from the tracks and who later founded the library. Local wisdom has it that he got the idea for the house on stilts while traveling through the swampland around New Orleans. A long hallway ran through the center of the house, the toilet was in an outhouse, and there was one faucet. Lillie's possessions were few when she moved in. She stuffed feed sacks with corn shucks for beds, used apple boxes for her dresser, and cooked in the fireplace. Local families gave her what they could spare, but Lillie was determined that she would accept charity no longer than she had to.

Shortly after the Williamses moved into Rose's house, Lillie took on two more charges, her nieces Marie and Bernice McNeil, the daughters of her sister Annie Skipper and and Annie's husband, Grover McNeil. After Annie died of typhoid fever, Grover paid for Lillie to care for Marie and Bernice, and they all became part of Hank's extended family. From time to time, Lillie took on her mother too, all the while working as a practical nurse at what was called Tippins Hospital. The hospital, a large house that looked like a convalescent home, was run by Dr. H. K. Tippins and his brother. They offered overnight care, and Lillie was on night duty. Lillie prevailed upon Dr. Tippins to sign Hank's birth certificate and formally introduce him to the world. To supplement her income, she lobbied a local politician to collect Lon's full disability pension, and took in a couple of boarders, which gave her the idea of starting a rooming house business.

When the family was in Georgiana Hank got his first western outfit. The local movie house showed Westerns all day Saturday. Whites sat downstairs, blacks upstairs. The Old West, as Hank absorbed it on those Saturday mornings and from comic books, was something he never got over.

As I ride along just a-singing my song a happy roving cowboy,
Chasing the dark clouds out of the sky. . . .

The prairie romanticism attracted Hank because it contrasted so starkly with the reality that greeted him as he exited the theater. Who wouldn't want to be the happy roving cowboy, far from summer's suffocating heat and humidity and winter's cold, far from the vicelike grip of the Depression, and free of an ever less than healthy body? Out on the range it would all be different. For now, though, the neighbors just called him "Two-Gun Pete" when they saw him decked out in his cowboy hat, holster, and boots.

Lillie fostered Hank's interest in singing, but she was determined that if he was to sing, it would be in praise of the Lord. She scraped together a few dollars and sent him to a shape-note singing school in Avant near Georgiana. The hymns Hank learned there and in church every Sunday colored his approach to music as nothing else ever would. He later told a country music fan magazine that his favorite song was "Death Is Only a Dream"; its morbidity and superstition resonated within him in a way that the popular songs of the era never did:

Sadly we sing and with tremulous breath
As we stand by the mystical stream,
In the valley and by the dark river of death,
And yet 'tis no more than a dream.

He absorbed much else, but the essence of Hank Williams's music is there. From the holy songs, Hank learned how to express profound sentiments in words that an unlettered farmer could understand, and he came to appreciate intuitively the spiritual component of music. He also loved the warm glow of recognition that the simple melodies elicited, and their effect was so pervasive that his own melodies would rarely be more complicated than the hymns and folk songs he heard as a child.

Hank was a believer, but not, in later life, a churchgoer. Perhaps he felt unworthy, perhaps his schedule didn't permit it. Nevertheless, he included a hymn on almost every syndicated radio show, and even in beer joints he would sometimes throw everyone off guard with a hymn. Even when he knew himself to be a backslider and a fornicator, even when he knew he had been weighed in the balance and found wanting in so many ways, he seemed to find rare peace in singing the hymns and living their sentiments in that moment at least.

Another craft that Hank learned early in life was hawking. Lillie and Irene would roast peanuts and Hank would go out on the streets of Georgiana and sell them. "The first day," wrote Lillie in a booklet not always given to accuracy, "he made thirty cents, and I remember how proud he was when he brought home the thirty cents' worth of stew meat, tomatoes and rice he bought with it. 'Mama,' he shouted, 'fix us some gumbo stew. We're gonna eat tonight!' " A more believable coda to the story comes from Oscar Vickery, a neighbor of the Williamses in Greenville. He remembered Lillie counting the bags of peanuts before Hank left the house and then counting the nickels that came back in. Even then she didn't trust him, and even then Hank was outwitting her by taking a few peanuts from every bag, making up another bag, and keeping a nickel for himself. Low cunning to get the better of a grasping woman was a skill that Hank would rely on for the rest of his life.

For the beginning of the school year in September 1933, Hank moved in with his cousins, the McNeils, in Fountain, Alabama. At the same time, the McNeils' teenage daughter, Opal, lived with Lillie and attended high school in Georgiana since there was no high school in Fountain. For twenty-one years, Hank's uncle, Walter McNeil, was an engineer with W. T. Smith, and he moved his family from settlement to settlement. In Fountain, they lived in three boxcars, and Hank attended grammar school in a single-room schoolhouse. At the same time, his aunt Alice taught him some of the rudiments of music, and his cousin J.C. showed him what growing up out in the woods was all about. "We'd fish, hunt," says J.C. "Hell, there was nothin' else to do. Every dog we'd find, we'd try and make it into a hunting dog. We hunted squirrels, rabbits." In interviews and in songs, Hank would rhapsodize about rural life, but the year he spent with the McNeils was the last time he lived it. From the time he returned to Georgiana, he was a city boy.

The year with the McNeils also marked the beginning of Hank's drinking. He was eleven at the time, and he and J.C. would watch to see where the loggers hid their hooch when they went to a social, then sneak over, steal it, and make off into the woods. Then they'd drink, as the saying went around there, 'til they could have laid on the ground and fallen off it.

Hank returned to Georgiana in 1934. By now he was performing on the streets and at the railroad station, taking requests and learning how to hold an audience. He was also pestering the old-time fiddlers in town to show him what they knew. Cade Durham was a cobbler who walked with a stick, a stogie jammed into a cigar holder; Jim Warren owned a jewelry and instruments store. Both men showed Hank the rudiments of hoedown fiddling as well as the major chords on the guitar. Late in life, Hank would play the fiddle only when he was in his cups, but throughout his early career he was a half-proficient hoedown fiddler.

Where and when Hank got his first guitar has long been a matter of conjecture; he could have lined a wall with all the first guitars people claimed to have given him. In an interview with Ralph Gleason, though, Hank said the first one came from his mother when he was eight, which more or less supports what Lillie always said. Several people remember him practicing under the house on Rose Street. He would sit on an old car seat, pick out his chords, and sing. Lillie, trying to catch some sleep above, would lean out of the window and yell, "Harm, hush up that fuss."

It was probably in Georgiana that Hank met one of his acknowledged musical influences, a black street musician named Rufus Payne. His nickname was 'Tee-Tot,' a pun on teetotaler, which came from a home-brewed mix of alcohol and tea that he carried in a flask at all times. Details about Payne are sketchy. His death certificate states that he was approximately fifty-five years old when he died in 1939, which would place him in his early fifties when Hank first met him. He lived down by the tracks in Greenville and worked part-time at Peagler's Drug Store as a cleaner and delivery man. Some days, he and two other musicians went out into the surrounding towns to play on the sidewalks, and Hank almost certainly first met Payne on the streets of Georgiana. Some remember a steady crowd of kids following the group as they set up in front of one store after another.

Exactly what passed between Hank Williams and Rufe Payne will never be known for sure. If, as has often been said, Payne gave Hank lessons, it's hard to know what he imparted. Hank probably already knew all the chords Payne knew, so the lessons probably resolved themselves in broader strokes. J. C. McNeil, who insists he also took lessons from Payne, says that Payne always stressed the importance of keeping time and getting a good rhythm going. Later, one of the elements that would set Hank apart from the hillbilly mainstream was the irresistible drive of his music. He was never an accomplished guitarist but his forceful rhythm guitar playing acted as a cue for his band. He may not have remembered too many of the songs Payne taught him, but the lazy swing and sock rhythm on his up-tempo records were almost certainly Payne's legacy. The ever-present blues feel that permeates Hank's work is also something that Payne probably brought out.

Lillie says she fed Payne in exchange for Hank's lessons, but almost everyone's memories of him are vague. Most say that he had a humpback and long simian arms that stretched almost to his knees; no one remembers any of the songs he used to play. Irene told the story that Payne once came to Lillie's house and told her that Hank was going to get both of them into trouble by following him around, which seems to imply that Hank was fairly insistent in pursuing Payne.

As unfashionable as it was at the time to acknowledge the influence of black musicians, Hank later went out of his way to give Payne full credit. "All the music training I ever had was from him," he told the *Montgomery Advertiser* in 1951. Talking to Ralph J. Gleason in June the following year he said, "I learned to play the git-tar from an old colored man. . . . He . . . played in a colored street band. . . . I was shinin' shoes, sellin' newspapers and followin' this old Nigrah around to get him to teach me to play the guitar. I'd give him fifteen cents, or whatever I could get a hold of for the lesson." A few months later, Hank acknowledged Payne again in Greenville and searched for him there, but Payne had probably died by then. Records indicate he died in a charity hospital in Montgomery on March 17, 1939. He was on relief at the time, and his trade or profession was marked "unknown" on the death certificate.

Local musicians like Payne would have made a much bigger impression on Hank than the stars of the day. Lillie didn't have a radio or phonograph, although Hank did try to listen to the radio at other people's houses or in the stores where he worked. Even so, he was probably no more than fleetingly aware of the life and death of country music's first superstar, Jimmie Rodgers. When Rodgers succumbed to tuberculosis in May 1933, he was thirty-five years old, and Hank was nine. Many of Hank's contemporaries, particularly Hank Snow and Ernest Tubb, who were both nine years older, were in Rodgers's thrall, and they began their careers in emulation of him, but there's little evidence that he made an impression on Hank.

Rodgers was called the "Father of Country Music," but the core of his repertoire was an odd mixture of country blues and cloyingly sentimental pop songs. His trademark was the yodel. He never claimed to have introduced it to country music, but he certainly popularized it. With the fall in Rodgers's popularity in the years after his death, it's likely that Hank absorbed as much as he did of Rodgers's music secondhand through Jimmie Davis, Gene Autry, and Ernest Tubb.

Some say that Hank's yodeling came from Rodgers, but Rodgers's trademark was Alpen-style yodeling that consumed entire choruses. Hank would use only a flash of falsetto or a little trailing yodel at the end of a word or line, which was the trademark of the blues singer. Only once on a transcribed radio program do we hear him taking a stab at the Rodgers style. On a 1951 "Mother's Best" show he sang Jimmie Davis's "Where the Old Red River Flows" (". . . you can hear the darkies crooning soft and low"), and he yodeled his way assuredly through the breaks. Any similarity between Hank Williams and Jimmie Rodgers lay in the fact that they were both sickly men who probably started singing as a career because it seemed to carry fewer physical demands. They were also both entranced by the cowboy image, even though neither had much grasp of western music, and they both introduced elements of the blues into country music. Rodgers, though, put his own slant on prewar blues and occasionally used a Dixieland ensemble on records, while Hank brought the blues singer's passion and the lazy swing of black rural string bands to what was in every other respect hillbilly music.

It was probably after Lillie moved to Greenville that she acquired a radio, broadening Hank's horizons. Greenville was fifteen miles farther up the L&N tracks toward Montgomery, and it was four times bigger than Georgiana. As the seat of Butler County, the focal point of Greenville was the courthouse square rather than the railroad station. Lillie moved her family there in time for Hank and Irene to start school in September 1934. Several of Hank's contemporaries remember the eleven-year-old bringing his guitar to school. He would play it during lunch break and

tell people that to play and sing was his "highest ambition." The ditty
he sang repeatedly went as follows:

> *I had an old goat*
> *She ate tin cans*
> *When the little goats came*
> *They were Ford sedans.*

Lillie set up a boardinghouse by the cotton mills and worked in one
of the WPA self-help canneries, demonstrating canning methods for
around a dollar a day. It was the rooming house business that ideally
suited her "take no crap" temperament, though. "She'd just as soon
knock you in the head as look at you if you made her mad," said J. C.
McNeil. "She had to be tough. She'd bounce them suckers out of there if
they gave her any crap." One of Lillie's boardinghouse tenants in Montgomery later characterized her as mean and violent with a short fuse,
"looking as though she'd beat you up for two cents." Perhaps in emulation of Lillie, Hank never shied away from a fight, particularly when
drunk. He would pitch in with a wild-eyed fury even knowing he was
going to be thrashed.

For all her shortcomings, Lillie had a single-minded desire to better
the lot of herself and her family, and, with the help of Lon's disability
pension that she fought hard to get, the family wasn't as badly off as
many during the depth of the Depression. In Greenville, Lillie performed
charity work rather than being a recipient of it.

What happened to Lon during this period is the subject of some dispute. He later told his second family that his aneurysm burst and fluid
ran from his nose and mouth, but that far from being pronounced cured,
he was diagnosed with dementia praecox and kept in the hospital
against his will. He told Hank's first biographer that he was detained on
account of Lillie, who tried to get a commitment order against him.
Others have a different account, intimating that — for a while at least —
Lon was happy to be in the hospital. In January 1937, he was moved to
the V.A. hospital in Biloxi, Mississippi, and stayed there until August
1938.

The V.A. in Biloxi is situated on several acres of parkland within
walking distance of the beach. Three square meals a day would have
made it a very alluring proposition during the late years of the Depression. "He didn't particularly want to get out," said J. C. McNeil, who,

admittedly, would only have heard Lillie's side of the story. "He would pull all kinds of tricks. One time they came into his room and they looked everywhere — he had crawled up under the bed, pulled himself up to the springs and held himself there until they had left."

At some point, though, Lon decided that he wanted to leave, and found that he couldn't. He rarely spoke about it directly in later years, although he spat every time the word "psychiatrist" was mentioned, giving some idea of the problem he encountered. Lon's sister Bertha, who detested Lillie, insisted that Lillie kept Lon there against his will and told the administration that he had no relatives other than her and the kids. For his part, Lon always believed that Lillie put the word around that he had died, because when he returned to Georgiana and Mc-Williams he found people staring at him as if he had risen from the dead. He later went further and insisted that Lillie had tried to have him killed off.

Nobody remembers Lillie going to visit Lon very often, so it's unlikely that Hank saw his father more than once or twice during the '30s. Lon said that Hank came once when he was fourteen, which would have been in 1937 or '38. Perhaps Lon's disappearance meant that Hank, now a spindly kid with steel-rimmed glasses, was keeping more to himself while he perfected his public mask. Working the streets and having almost limitless access to Rufe Payne, Hank learned how to be conversational — even confidential — with people he hardly knew. This was a critical skill for someone in his proposed line of work, but it meant that from an early age the core of Hank Williams became a thing known only to himself, masked by the molassified haw-haw that led people to think that they were his closest friends.

By the time Lillie, Hank, and Irene left Greenville after school finished in 1937, thirteen-year-old Hank already had a pretty clear idea what he wanted to do in life. He told his cousin Clara Skipper, "I ain't goin' to school always. I'll sing my song and make more money than any of you."

*A Hill-Billie is a free and untrammeled
white citizen of Alabama who lives in the
hills, has no means to speak of, talks as he
pleases, drinks whiskey when he gets it, and
fires off his revolver as the fancy takes him.*
New York Journal, April 23, 1900

• •

"ROY ACUFF, THEN GOD!"

• •

*L*ILLIE, whose recollections after Hank died
were often studiedly vague, stated with un-
common authority that she, Hank, Irene, and Bernice and Marie McNeil
arrived in Montgomery on July 10, 1937. Walter McNeil, who had settled
in Montgomery a year earlier, moved Lillie and her extended family up
from Greenville on a logging truck. He laid planks across the joists, and
loaded her stove and all the family possessions onto the makeshift
trailer. Lillie was trying to improve her lot and the lot of her children.
The rooming house business was better, the schools were better, and
there were talent shows, more populous street corners, and a radio station for little Harm.

Montgomery was uptown about as far as you could get in Alabama. It
was the state capital, once capital of the Confederacy, and in 1937 some
seventy-two thousand people lived there. Lillie moved her brood into
114 South Perry Street, which she converted into a rooming house. Hank,
then thirteen, was sent out to shine shoes and sell peanuts on the street;
Irene was selling packed lunches at the fire hall, the police station, and
the Montgomery Curb Market. That September Hank was enrolled at the
Abraham Baldwin Junior High School. He arrived with the attitude that
learning interfered with the important things in life, chief among them
music. He took eighth and ninth grade at Baldwin, and then transferred
to Sidney Lanier High School in 1938, quitting in October 1939 shortly
after his sixteenth birthday.

Right away Hank set about getting noticed, although many of the specifics have been lost to time. In 1946 WSFA program director Caldwell Stewart wrote an introduction to one of Hank's songbooks in which he stated that Hank had been on the station since 1936 — the year before Lillie said she moved to Montgomery. When Hank came back to Montgomery for a show in July 1951, he said he had been on WSFA "eleven years, nine days, and six months," which, if we take him at his word, would place his radio debut in the late months of 1936, six months or more before Lillie says she moved to Montgomery. An article in the Greenville *Advocate* in 1951 also seems to imply that Hank went on radio in Montgomery while the family was still living in Greenville. To confuse the issue further, some around Montgomery swear that Hank was on WCOV before he was on WSFA, but WCOV didn't start operation until 1939.

WSFA was the only game in town when Hank moved to Montgomery. Launched in March 1930 by a partnership of two local businessmen, Howard Pill and Gordon Persons — later the governor of Alabama — it broadcast with one thousand watts from studios in the Jefferson Davis Hotel. In addition to its own programming, the station picked up feeds from NBC and one or two small southern networks. Several people who once worked for WSFA take credit for bringing Hank to the station. E. Caldwell Stewart was the one who persistently made the claim. He had been hired by WSFA as staff pianist in 1931, and, several years later, was made music director. His widow insists that Stewart discovered Hank singing on the street and selling peanuts, then put him on the air. Leaborne Eads, later a performer on WSFA, says that Stewart always told him that he found Hank outside WSFA and ran a remote down so that Hank could broadcast live from his patch on the sidewalk.

Certainly, Hank knew what he was doing when he set up shop outside the radio station. Bill Hunt, then the advertising manager at WSFA, remembered that Hank used to bug anyone he thought might work at the station. He would sing a song, then hawk the peanuts that Lillie had bagged: "Peanuts, Mister, only five cents, and believe me, Mister, I need the dough. One bag? Two bags?" Hunt claims that he put Hank on the air in a sustaining (that is, noncommercial) slot, adding that Lillie would arrange for people to phone the station demanding more of "The Singing Kid."

Dating Hank's debut on WSFA is made no easier by the fact that he was continually on and off the station, and the program schedules published in the local papers were often sketchy on local programming.

Hank isn't listed as the star of his own sponsored show until 1941. When he spoke of his eleven years on the station, he seemed to be implying that they were eleven blissfully uninterrupted years, but he was rarely on the air for more than three or four months at a stretch until 1947, his last full year in Montgomery. Between 1937 and 1941 he was off the air much more than he was on, and almost certainly didn't have a regular show under his own name or as "The Singing Kid."

If the details are blurred, Hank's ambition was clear, as was Lillie's intention to stoke it. For Christmas 1937, she bought him a new guitar, a Gibson with a sunburst finish. This was a major investment, perhaps the most expensive item in the Williams household. Lillie bought it from Art Freehling's Music Store around the time of Hank's first major public appearance at the Empire Theater talent show. Lillie always spoke of Hank's appearance at the Empire as if it was just one show, but others remember that he appeared so regularly, and won so regularly, on the Friday night talent shows that the management requested he not appear any more. Talent shows were the entry level of the entertainment business then, and Hank seems to have gone for them all. Members of Lon's family remember him entering talent shows at the Wilby Theater in Selma, fifty miles away.

At one or more of the Empire shows Hank sang a self-composed song, "WPA Blues," named for President Roosevelt's Work Projects Administration. It is generally reckoned to be Hank's first song. As Lillie remembered it, one verse went as follows:

> I got a home in Montgomery,
> A place I like to stay,
> But I have to work for the WPA
> And I'm dissatisfied — I'm dissatisfied.

There were a couple of tunes kicking around called "WPA Blues," one by Casey Bill Weldon, who later wrote the Louis Jordan hit "I'm Gonna Move to the Outskirts of Town," but if the words Lillie remembered were as Hank sang them, they had, for the greater part, been cloned from a record called "Dissatisfied" by string band veteran Riley Puckett. The one part of Lillie's account that is almost certainly true is that Hank partied away the first fifteen-dollar prize he won at the Empire. "When Hank was in the chips, so were his friends — as long as the money held out — always," wrote Lillie in a confused thought that barely disguised her lifelong contempt for the way money ran through Hank's fingers.

Early on in Montgomery Hank met fiddle player Freddy Beach. Born in Leakesville, Mississippi, in 1916, Beach was the closest thing to a seasoned musician Hank had met to that point. Beach had toured as a fiddler with Curly Fox and Texas Ruby and had worked as a traveling evangelist for a while. Freddy and another local musician, Dad Crysel, had organized a talent show at a hall on Commerce Street, and Hank appeared there in 1937 or '38 chaperoned by Lillie. He got up and sang a train song, and then started appearing every week. When Hank assembled his first band, Beach was the fiddle player.

It was also around this time, 1937 or '38, that Hank met Braxton Schuffert, who remains the most voluble source for Hank's early career. Born in Montgomery in 1916, Schuffert had an early morning radio show on WSFA when Hank was living in Greenville. Lillie later told Schuffert that she couldn't get Hank away from the radio when he was on, so he was a bona fide star in Hank's eyes when they met.

Schuffert worked in tandem with a harmonica player, Smith Adair, who called himself "Hezzy." Originally from Birmingham, Hezzy moved to Montgomery from Sylacauga when he was sixteen. Schuffert met him one morning when he was coming back from the station. Hezzy was walking down Bell Street playing his harmonica. "I said, 'Boy, can you play with a guitar?' " remembered Schuffert, "and he said, 'Hell, yes, I can play with a guitar,' so I said he should come up to the house and we'd play some. His mother was dead and his dad was a roving sign painter, rode a bicycle. Smith was on his own. We'd go down and play all the cafés. I'd sing, Smith would play the harp, pass the hat around." Schuffert and Adair figured out when the firefighters got paid, and they'd set up and busk outside the fire halls. They played small theaters, restaurants — anywhere they could draw a crowd and pick up a few nickels and dimes.

By the time Hank arrived in Montgomery and started introducing himself to Braxton Schuffert and others, he had decided to drop his given name, Hiram, and adopt Hank. He developed a little set piece about how he came to change his name, and, according to Boots Harris, one of his first steel guitar players, it went like this: "He used to say there was a fence outside his house and he'd sleep with the window open, and there was an old cat walking up and down that fence yowling, 'H-a-r-r-m-m, h-a-r-r-m-m.' He said he thought the cat was calling him so he changed his name to Hank." The truth, of course, was that Hank sounded much more like the name of a hillbilly and western music star than Hiram. That's why Clarence Eugene Snow became Hank Snow,

Herbert Penny became Hank Penny, and Lawrence Locklin became Hank Locklin. They all hoped the change of name would help them grow into the part.

In 1938, when Hank was starting to play with Braxton Schuffert, Freddy Beach, and Hezzy Adair, he heard the performer who would help him crystalize the nature of his music. Roy Acuff was twenty years older than Hank, and outlived him by almost forty years. He was from May-nardville, Tennessee, north of Knoxville, and originally he had his sights set on a career in baseball, only turning to music after he was felled by several bouts of sunstroke. Acuff led a band, the Crazy Tennesseans, and, beginning in February 1938 they had a regular spot on the *Grand Ole Opry* radio show, where Hank would inevitably have heard them. Acuff's calling card, "The Great Speckled Bird," was a haunting allegori-cal song drawn from the Book of Jeremiah in which the church, repre-sented by the Great Speckled Bird, triumphs over assaults from without and within. Set to an English folk melody, it was the cornerstone of Acuff's repertoire for almost sixty years.

Soon after Acuff appeared on the *Opry,* he put in place the last piece of his stage persona when he changed the name of his band from the Crazy Tennesseans to the Smoky Mountain Boys. Some of the smutty songs and novelties that the Tennesseans had incorporated into their act were now deemed never to have existed. Acuff assumed the mantle of the purist, the traditionalist, the man to whom country music meant just that: music for, by, and of the country people of the South and Southeast. It was Acuff's Appalachian music that resonated with Hank in a way that no sagebrush saga ever could. Spirituality coursed through Acuff's mu-sic. There were no electrified instruments, and no songs of liquor or sin that didn't end in death or perdition. His voice rang clear and true through the ethers; it was a perfect radio voice, full-throated and wracked with emotion. Hank Williams was riveted. Talking to Ralph Gleason in 1952, after his own star had eclipsed Acuff's, Hank was still clearly in the older singer's thrall: "Roy Acuff is the best example [of sincerity in singing]," he said. "He's the biggest singer this music ever knew. You booked him and you didn't worry about crowds. For drawing power in the South, it was Roy Acuff, then God. He'd stand up there singing, tears running down his cheeks." For Hank, Acuff became the benchmark both of success and of heart-on-the-sleeve sincerity.

According to Acuff, Hank would come by his dressing room when-ever he played Montgomery. The dates are hazy; he could have been talking about the late '30s or early '40s. "[Hank] would sit around, sing songs and play the guitar," Acuff told Roger Williams. "He was just a little fellow [Hank at age nine was already taller than Acuff, so what Acuff meant is unclear], and he just hunkered around in the corner waiting for a chance to sing." Later Acuff claimed to have gone out to see Hank in the honky-tonks, even going so far as to get up and sing with him. "I wasn't as big then as I am now," he said by way of explanation. "We both had a type of cry in our voice, and we sang with a lot of energy and feeling."

One of Hank's band members, Paul Dennis, remembers one encounter between Acuff and a half-tanked Hank Williams in the early '40s. " 'You got a million-dollar voice,' Acuff told Hank, 'and a ten-cent brain.' " For all the crocodile tears he shed over Hank's casket, Acuff's opinion never changed much. He later disinherited one of his grandsons who had been busted for drug possession, and his attitude toward Hank's transgressions was never marked by much compassion.

Hank, though, never lost his respect for Acuff, and from the late '30s until his death, he would pepper his shows with Acuff's songs. One of Hank's first recordings, an acetate (a recording made directly on a ten-inch aluminum disc coated with acetate) that ended up in his father's hands and probably dated to 1941 or 1942, featured the Acuff song "Lonely Mound of Clay." By the time Acuff entered his life, Hank was already determined to make a career in music, but Acuff was a beacon for him. On a commercial level, Acuff's success served notice that hillbilly music could sell nationwide, and that too paved the way for Hank Williams. Hank would have played music without Acuff's influence, but whether it would have sounded the way it did without Acuff, and whether he would have had a market as prepped to receive him is doubtful.

Hank's first taste of touring was probably in support of Juan Lobo, a.k.a. Jack Wolf, a cowboy performer who claimed to have been in Westerns with Ken Maynard. Somehow, he washed up in Montgomery around 1938, and he and Hank went out on a brief tour supported by Hezzy Adair, Braxton Schuffert, and Freddy Beach. Juan Lobo sold handmade bat-wing chaps and belts, and performed standard cowboy shtick, like whipping a cigarette out of someone's mouth with a bullwhip, or twirling lariats and dancing through them. Hank was in his element. School couldn't hold a candle to this, and Hank's teachers recognized as much. "Aw, don't wake him," they'd say when he fell asleep in class. "He isn't going to learn anything anyway."

Later, Hank, Hezzy, Braxton, and fiddler "Mexican" Charlie Mays went out and played the Ritz Theater chain in southern Alabama and northern Florida. Irene joined them as a duet partner, and at some point in the late '30s they took a steady date at a theater in Roanoke, Alabama, ten miles from the Georgia state line. Braxton remembers that they drove up in Lillie's Ford station wagon, and played three shows a day at 3:00 P.M., 6:00 P.M., and 9:00 P.M. for around one hundred dollars. Everyone came away with fifteen dollars, excellent money for that time.

The situation on South Perry Street was complicated when Lon arrived home in August 1938. Clearly feeling unwelcome and perhaps ill at ease after being so long out of circulation, he returned to the V.A. hospital that October. He insisted that he just came to spend Christmas with Lillie and the kids, although no one but Lon remembered this, so he might have been made to feel unwelcome before he even got his boots off. He went back to the hospital until April 1939. One of the apocryphal stories surrounding Lon's return is that he arrived home to find Lillie in bed with another man, but, even if that's stretching the truth, it's almost certain that Lillie had been keeping company with other men. Now built like a logger, and acid-tongued too, she still seemed to have no trouble attracting men. "She could be charming when she wanted," said Walter McNeil Jr., which seems to be the best explanation anyone can come up with. She also had a rotating cast of predominantly male boarders at the rooming house from whom to take her pick.

There have also been persistent rumors throughout the years that Lillie's boardinghouse business was a front for a whorehouse. Even Hank toward the end of his life told a fellow performer that he had started entertaining as a shill for Lillie's racket, but Hank was spinning stories wherever he went then, and the stories have never been reliably confirmed or denied.

Hank was fifteen when Lon was finally released from the hospital in April 1939. Lon went back to McWilliams and, after three years on his own, divorced Lillie and married Ola Till on September 12, 1942. They had a daughter, Hank's half-sister, Leila, on June 19, 1943. Lon never took regular employment again. He had a full disability check from the Veterans Administration, and he made his way doing odd jobs, occasionally running a country store with Ola.

From the time Lon went back to McWilliams, Hank saw him on a fairly regular basis. When he was appearing in the neighborhood, he and his band would arrive in the middle of the afternoon for dinner with Lon and Ola. Hank's relationship with Lon became more like that between uncle and nephew. Lon had been too gone for too long for there to be any intimacy, and Hank wasn't much given to intimacy anyway.

One of those who took Hank under his wing in Lon's absence was Pappy Neal McCormick, a Creek Indian who led a band variously called the Barn Dance Troubadours or the Hawaiian Troubadours. He was based 150 miles south of Montgomery in and around Pensacola in the Florida panhandle. Hank went down with Hezzy Adair to audition for him, but it was Hank alone who was hired. McCormick played steel guitar; in fact, he had invented a four-head steel guitar that had four guitars in different tunings mounted on a railroad tie which turned on a barbecue spit. McCormick's band played for dancing, and although nothing has survived of his music from that era, Hank almost certainly acquired elements of his presentation from McCormick, who is remembered mostly for his showmanship. Hank worked a few weeks at a time with McCormick for several years — well into the early '40s. Whenever the relationship between Hank and Lillie reached boiling point, he would take off for Pensacola, sometimes to work with McCormick, sometimes just to hole up in the San Carlos Hotel and drink. WCOA, where McCormick worked, was located in the San Carlos, so work and play were no more than an elevator ride apart for Hank.

Hank's very early career is largely available to us only as an accretion of fragments, and the picture doesn't begin to come together for several years. Those who knew him and worked with him say that Hank was serious-minded and career-minded. He had a stronger singing voice than anyone expected from such a scrawny fellow. He'd spend whatever money he made as soon as he got it, then borrow some more. He got loaded whenever he could. He started to write songs the way everyone else did — by setting his own words to an established melody. Lillie was seldom out of the picture; she drove the station wagon to dates, collected the money, paid the band members, often housed and fed them too, put up posters, encouraged Hank, chided him, and cussed him out when he screwed up. Not even extended family members got into the shows for free with Lillie at the door.

If Hank's early career in music is hazy, his life outside music as he desultorily finished school is even harder to piece together. Two sisters who lived near him remember that he would be out on the streets playing cowboys and Indians, and, when the time came for the other children to go in, Hank would stay outside by himself. Later he would call the early evening the "lonesomest time of the day," perhaps echoing back to those years when Lillie was serving and clearing up supper in the boardinghouse and no one had time for Harm.

One of the few artifacts to have survived from Hank's early years is a brief audition acetate that he cut at some point in the late '30s. It was clearly intended to land him a steady radio job because it was a demo for a show. Hank made up call letters for an imaginary station in Fort Deposit, Alabama, and, backed by an accordion, he sang "Happy Roving Cowboy," concluding with a brief pitch for himself. It is his earliest known recording, and already his voice sounded remarkably older than his tender years.

"Happy Roving Cowboy" was Hank's theme song from earliest times. It was a Sons of the Pioneers recording from 1935, and, like many of the Pioneers' early recordings, "Roving Cowboy" (as it was originally called) was written by a Canadian, Bob Nolan. Nolan's songs captured the outsider's wide-eyed wonder at the untamed vastness of the west, a wonder that filled Hank with ambivalence. The cowboy mystique was at its zenith, and life in the bunkhouse looked more appealing than life in the boardinghouse, but Hank got no further than renaming himself and calling his band The Drifting Cowboys.

Hank probably had the Sons of the Pioneers in mind when he brought an accordionist, Pee Wee Moultrie, into the band in 1939. Hezzy Adair was on bass, and Charlie Mays on fiddle. All of them except Hezzy shared a large bedroom on the top floor of the house on Perry Street. The couple next door would always keep the blinds open and the light on when they made love, and, when the Drifting Cowboys weren't working, that was the entertainment. Other times, they would go to the whorehouses on Pollard Street and flirt with the girls until the management found out that they had no money.

This new lineup of the Cowboys landed a regular date at the Dixie Graves Armory. They played on WCOV and WSFA and worked a few weeks at WBHP in Huntsville. Moultrie remembers only one extended road trip, and that was through Alabama, Georgia, and Florida. Lillie painted "Drifting Cowboys" on the side of her 1935 Ford, and they set off on a tour of movie theaters. Hank was sober for the first two weeks, but he fell off the wagon somewhere in south Alabama on the way home. The theater manager offered them some peach brandy, and after it was gone, Hank and Hezzy went hunting some more. Hank lost his pick during the show, played guitar with his knuckles, and made stupid jokes to the crowd. Hezzy threw up in full view of everyone.

Then, at some point in 1940, Hank took off for Texas with a rodeo troupe that was staying at the boardinghouse. The details are sketchy, and the only possible clarification was provided by Hank himself on his application for employment in Mobile during the war. At that time, he stated that he had played music as far away as Mexico in 1940. The western dream would resurface whenever Hank was in the middle of protracted arguments with Lillie. He would pack his suitcase, and tell everyone he was off to Texas. Then he'd usually sober up somewhere around the Alabama state line and wire for money.

Pee Wee quit for a while. Lillie had a way of figuring the accounts that usually left him and every other band member in the hole to her. Once she saw his mother give him five dollars and grabbed it from him in full view of her. "At times Hank and Lillie would seem to get along, but she would ride herd on him," said Pee Wee. "Then all Hell would break out. Lillie had a black house servant named Jabbo, and when Lillie beat up on Hank, Hank would beat up on Jabbo, kick him or pull his hair. Jabbo would go home crying and Lillie and I would go over and bring him back."

Pee Wee says that Charlie Mays told him about one particularly violent encounter between Hank and Lillie just after he had quit. Hank had persuaded a girl he had been eyeing during a show to go to a cabin with him afterward. Charlie drove the car home, and at three o'clock in the morning he was woken up by Lillie and the girl's parents. Lillie told Charlie that she would beat him to death if he didn't tell her where Hank was. Charlie took them back to the cabin, Lillie kicked the door in, and found Hank lying in bed wearing just his underwear and cowboy boots. Lillie picked him up and threw him in the car. Hank kicked out the back window and they fought all the way home.

Hank was barely getting by as a musician but seems to have had no other serious direction. Through high school, he had worked for a painter and contractor named Kenneth Hees who lived at the boardinghouse, and for seven months in 1941 he took a bookkeeping course at Draughron's Business College. For her part, Lillie saw how much the crowds liked Hank and sensed the opportunities if he would only straighten up. She, meanwhile, had married again, to a Mr. J. C. Bozard, and, in 1940, they had taken a lease on another boardinghouse at 236 Catoma Street. It had a small eating joint and a shoe repair shop in front, and would be Hank's permanent address for the next six years.

The first snapshot from 1941 is from the spring. Three guys fresh out of high school in Hayneville, Alabama (about 20 miles from Montgomery), had heard Hank on WSFA, and they got the idea to present him at the local courthouse. They wrote to him in care of WSFA at the end of March, and several days later Hank wrote back in pencil on lined paper saying he'd work for 60 percent of the gate. The promoters made up thirty signs and posted them around Hayneville. Hank and three pickers led by guitarist Zeke Crittenden arrived on the afternoon of Friday, April 4. Hank seemed shy and very unlike the outgoing performer the promoters had expected from listening to him on WSFA. He was shown the courthouse where he'd be playing, and he saw the jail cell. "Awright, boys," he said, "they're ready for us. Ever'body on their best behavior tonight." Hank went over well that night, and the following morning the three promoters went over to the courthouse to move back the benches and divide what was left of the thirty dollars they'd taken in.

Two weeks later, Hank was at Thigpen's Log Cabin, his bread-and-butter gig. Thigpen's had opened in 1931 just off old Highway 31 in Georgiana. Fred Thigpen, at six feet four inches and 230 pounds, made a formidable combination with Lillie for anyone who threatened trouble. Hank played for dancing in a walled-in skating pavilion behind the main dining room. The pavilion was roofed, but open to the air with canvas curtains that were lowered when it rained. Admission was a quarter, and Hank and The Drifting Cowboys would play from 8:00 P.M. until midnight or 1:00 A.M. Butler County was still dry, so Thigpen sold ice and setups, and the dancers would retire discreetly to fill their glasses with hooch.

Playing every second week, Hank quickly became Thigpen's major draw between 1940 and 1942. He alternated with a full dance band led by Cecil Mackey, and even outgrossed name dance bands like Wayne King's. He mixed up his set, and did a square dance interlude, when he would play fiddle tunes. He couldn't call a square dance, but he knew enough hoedowns to get the crowd on the floor. If Hank served any kind of apprenticeship, it was at Thigpen's, and he left there with all the skills he would need for the rest of his life.

With steady work at last, Hank assembled a fairly regular group in late 1941. Shorty Seals, who had worked with Hank in Neal McCormick's band, played the bass and did the comedy routines that bass players were expected to do; Charlie Mays was still on fiddle — the "swing fiddler" he was called in the band's announcements; "Indian" Joe Hatcher played guitar and fiddle — he was dubbed the "wrong shoulder fiddler"; and Clyde "Boots" Harris played the "singing steel guitar." Many other Montgomery area musicians, including Paul Dennis, who played bass and rhythm guitar, guitarist Paul Compton, and steel guitarist Millard

"M.C." Jarrett, came and went. No musician stayed long, and playing with Hank wasn't considered a plum job.

Few members of this group are still living. Shorty Seals died in Freddy Beach's arms. He was moving to Mobile and had a heart attack while carrying some furniture. Charlie Mays left Hank and word reached Montgomery that he had died in a car wreck in Texas. Joe Hatcher died shortly after an operation. It's from Boots Harris that we get most of our knowledge of what Hank was up to in 1941 and 1942.

Boots had led a band with his brothers, but decided to try for a job where he could play three or four nights a week, so he caught the bus to Montgomery in 1941. First, he went to WCOV, then to WSFA, where the program director told him that their only hillbilly act, Hank Williams, played solo. Boots went to see Hank after his show and they played a few songs together and then decided to get some refreshments.

> He said, "Let's go get a cup of coffee," so we went out the front door, and there was a little café right there and I started in it and he said, "Naw, their coffee ain't no good," so we went on down a ways to a little restaurant and they had whiskey lined up on the wall. I had just quit the mill in Opp and I had maybe a week's salary in my pocket. Hank said, "Have you got any money on you?" I said, "Yeah." He said, "Have you got enough for a half-pint?" I said, "I guess so." I didn't drink at all then, so I hadn't been knowing him but thirty minutes and I bought him a half-pint of whiskey.

Lillie put up Harris and other band members at the boardinghouse, docking their pay accordingly. When they were out on a job, Hank used to tell the audience that he paid his band $21.50 a week. "Twenty-one hamburgers and fifty cents." It got a lot of laughs, but it was too close to the truth for the band to find it really funny. They joined him on WSFA from time to time but their livelihood depended on joints like Thigpen's and the occasional schoolhouse date.

Like the courthouse date in Hayneville, schoolhouse dates worked on a split of the gate. Lillie would book a schoolhouse for an evening, and then she, sometimes in conjunction with Leaborne Eads, would put up posters all around the neighborhood. On the posters, Hank billed his act as "one-and-a-half hours of good clean comedy, songs and music," and he would announce the show on the radio every morning. After the show date, Lillie would share the door money with the school on a seventy-thirty or sixty-forty split.

Those who paid the twenty-five or thirty cents Lillie charged for admission heard a show comprised for the greater part of other people's songs and traditional favorites. Hank didn't make any commercial recordings during the early '40s, but he cut several acetates that have mostly disappeared. The discs can be played only a few times before the acetate begins to break up, which is what happened to the record Hank left with his father. It coupled Acuff's "Beneath That Lonely Mound of Clay" with the wholly appropriate "Mother, Guide Me." It was recorded on a Sears acetate, but after Lon had hauled it out and played it too many times, the grooves simply wore away.

One recording survives, though, and it illuminates an otherwise dark corner of Hank's career. Boots Harris insists that during this period, Hank had yet to find his own style; he would sing Ernest Tubb songs like Tubb and Acuff songs like Acuff. Hank himself said the same thing, but, on the scant evidence of this recording, the Hank Williams style was almost fully formed very early. "I'm Not Coming Home Any More" was an original composition recorded in April 1942, so it's possible that Hank sounds like his own man because it was his own song. Backed by just a steel guitarist and a bass player, he sings a little higher than we're used to, but his voice and his phrasing are remarkably similar to his first professional recordings five years later. The song too is identifiably a Hank Williams song, suggesting that his style was intact, and all that remained was for him to strip away the extraneous elements.

Shortly after "I'm Not Coming Home Any More" was recorded, Boots Harris left The Drifting Cowboys to join Curley Williams's Georgia Peach Pickers. The split came when Hank was on a short tour backing folk-and-western singer Tex Ritter. They reached Albany, Georgia, where they played a date with Curley Williams. Curley was hopeful of landing a spot on the *Opry*, which was still just a pipe dream for Hank, so Boots quit. He explained:

We'd hear records on the jukebox, and Hank'd say, "Someday, I'm gonna be doing that — they're gonna be playing my records." But I didn't see it coming any time soon the way he was going. He was pretty bad into the drink then. I was having to play guitar, emcee the show, do the jokes, and it was just more than I could put up with. I'd already quit him once because of the drinking. I told him if he'd quit the drinking and we'd get on with it, we'd get somewhere. I said, "If you keep drinkin' ain't nobody in the business gonna pay us no attention."

It was an admonition Hank would hear countless more times in the decade or so he had left.

The middle months of 1942 seem to mark one of Hank's periodic troughs. War had been declared in December 1941, but Hank was unfit for service because of his back. Even though he avoided the draft, the war took its toll on him. The pool of musicians in Montgomery was depleted, and then gas rationing was introduced. Hank was on WSFA consistently for a little more than a year, from July 1941 until August 1942, but then he was kicked off the station for habitual drunkenness. He was on WCOV until October, and then dropped out of music altogether.

That fall Hank went to Portland, Oregon, to work in the shipyards. Why he chose Portland is uncertain; there were shipyards 170 miles away in Mobile. It might have been to get as far as possible from Lillie, or perhaps simply for adventure. The incentive was provided by Kaiser Shipbuilding, which offered free tickets to Portland, free training, free accommodation, and good wages. Paul Dennis says that Hank was drunk on the day he left, so it might have been an impetuous decision made under the influence. The consensus is that Hank stayed in Portland no more than a few weeks before he came home.

On November 13, 1942, Hank applied for work at the Alabama Dry Dock and Shipbuilding Company. His application revealed that he had been jailed for "suspisition" in 1941. He insisted that his health was good, while noting that his complexion was, in his words, "sallow." He was hired as shipfitter's help, and worked on and off for the company until August 1944. He never stayed more than a few months at one stretch, and usually cited Lillie's health as his reason for leaving.

In her book, *Our Hank Williams,* Lillie insisted that she had come to Hank's rescue the first time. "I believed in [him]," she wrote. "I knew he had what it took, so I rented a car and went to every schoolhouse and nightclub in the Montgomery area. I booked Hank solid for sixty days. Then, the third week he had been out of the music business, I went to Mobile and got him and put him back in it. When Hank saw the datebook for those shows, he gave me the sweetest smile I've ever seen."

"Thank God, Mother," Hank is supposed to have said in one of the most uncharacteristic remarks ever attributed to him. "You've made me the happiest boy in the world."

Long Ike and sweet Betsy attended a dance
Where Ike wore a pair of his Pike County pants,
Sweet Betsy was covered in ribbons and rings,
Said Ike, "You're an angel, but where are your wings?"
(Trad.)

. . . .

SWEET AUDREY FROM PIKE

. . . .

AUDREY MAE WILLIAMS, née Sheppard, spoke often of her late husband. In the revisionist view of their life together, they were young star-crossed lovers, the bubba Rhett and Scarlett, such was their passion. Disturbingly quickly — within days of Hank's death, in fact — Audrey began finding it hard to distinguish between the Hank Williams who ruled her increasingly rich fantasy life and the one who had once walked this earth with her — and without her.

One afternoon late in her own life, during a deejay convention, Audrey was uncommonly candid with an interviewer she identifies as Lou. She had invited him out to the house, and, at one point, seems a little startled at her own frankness and makes a point of telling Lou that he's getting one hell of an interview. This is how she remembered her date with destiny:

> I met him on a medicine show. I had never seen a medicine show, did not know anything about medicine shows until I met him. My dad's only sister and myself was going down to Troy, Alabama, one evening to a club. Some friends owned the club. As we drove through Banks, my aunt said, "What's going on here?" and I said, "I don't know." There was a big crowd. She said, "Well, suppose we go over and see." [We were] in my own car at the time — a big four-door Oldsmobile. They had this like

a small mobile home with a stage on the back of it, and after the performance the performers would go around and sell all these herbs, you know. Hank came by my car and he said, "Ma'am, don't you think you need some of these herbs?" and then he took a quick look, and he said, "No, ma'am, I don't believe you do." Looking straight at me. The way he said it was so country. I'm from the country, but I thought Hank was talking so country — and he was from Montgomery. I was pretty shy back in those days. My aunt said, "Audrey and I are going down to this club in Troy. Would you like to go with us?" He said, "Yes, ma'am, I would if you'll just wait 'til I do the next show." She told him we'd wait. And that's how it started.

Audrey Mae fancied herself a member of southern Alabama aristocracy. She claimed that her family owned half of the county down around Banks, where she was born on February 28, 1923, some seven months before Hank. True or not, she was a prize: she was surely the loveliest woman in Pike County and not without guile. Life's finer fripperies would sit well upon Audrey, and, unlike Hank, she quickly acquired the demeanor of one who thought they were no less than her due.

From the beginning, Audrey characterized herself as independent — her father probably called her willful. As early as age eleven or twelve she had learned to drive and was taking herself off on trips. "I knew what I wanted and I went after it," she said, and her independent streak led her to run off one day with a neighbor's son, James Erskine Guy. She was seventeen years old. They lived in Gadsden for a while, but Audrey returned to Banks a year or so later unburdened of Erskine Guy but heavy with his child. Lycrecia Ann Guy was born August 13, 1941. Audrey was still married when she met Hank. She was back living with her parents, working in Brundidge as a drugstore clerk, and looking for a way out.

After their date, Hank asked Audrey to meet him the next day. It would be the first of his Bloody Mary mornings in store for her. He was unshaven, and he greeted her in the doorway of his trailer with no shirt on his back and the stench of last night's whiskey on his breath. They went for a drive that afternoon. Hank told Audrey a little about himself, confessed that his drinking had got him kicked off WSFA, and then, after the show that night, he asked her to marry him. "I told my aunt, 'This boy's crazy,' " said Audrey.

What did Audrey see in Hank? The only rung on the show business ladder lower than the hillbilly music business in southern Alabama was itinerant blues singing, but still it had a vestige of glamour that the Brundidge Drug Store didn't. Audrey also had a gift. She took abuse all her life for her pitiful singing, which obscured her true talent — seeing talent clearly in others. Later, after Hank's death, she gave an early break to good young songwriters like Mack Vickery and Sonny Throckmorton, and she got Johnny Rivers's career off the ground as well as Hank Jr.'s. Early on, she saw something in Hank Williams, something that Hank probably had trouble seeing in himself.

What did Hank see in Audrey? She was lovely, and that was enough to secure his interest, but she had other qualities he found attractive: she was feisty, sharp-tongued, and ambitious. Lillie, of course, was exactly that, and the pop-Freudian conclusion is obvious. No one remembers Hank having a serious girlfriend before Audrey. Women hung around the rooming house with him, and after a show he would often disappear into the woods with a woman, but Audrey reached a part of Hank Williams that was out-of-bounds to any woman before or after.

Hank and Audrey almost certainly met in the late summer of 1943 but didn't marry until December 1944. The year or more in between is hazy. It's unclear how often they met, or when they began living together. Audrey's father was bitterly opposed to the relationship, so Audrey might have been forced into Hank's arms with an ultimatum. No one even remembers if Hank quit the medicine show or if it was a victim of gas rationing.

One of the few snapshots we have of Hank Williams in 1943 comes from Hardrock Gunter, a Birmingham-based hillbilly musician who emceed a Labor Day show at the Montgomery municipal auditorium. The show's headliners were to be Pete Cassel, The Sunshine Boys, and Gunter himself. Gunter remembers Hank hanging around backstage drinking. Someone figured it would be a good idea if Hank introduced Gunter, so Hank grabbed Gunter's guitar, went out, and started singing. The crowd apparently recognized him and he went over well. When he got offstage, Gunter bawled him out, but Hank took no notice and sauntered out the door, still with Gunter's guitar slung around his neck. "The guitar's neck and body hit the doorway," remembered Gunter. "He tried twice more to get through the door before I pulled him round. He was belligerent and said, 'You just don't want me to play your guitar.' "

One snapshot doesn't tell us much, except that Hank was far from forgotten around Montgomery and that he was still drinking and messing up. Later that year he was booked as a local added attraction on a short tour of Alabama staged by Pee Wee King and his manager/father-in-law,

J. L. Frank. Born Frank Kuczynski in Wisconsin, Pee Wee was leading a polka band in Green Bay when Gene Autry came to town in the early '30s in need of replacements for a couple of men who had been injured in a car wreck. Kuczynski signed on, quickly changing his name to Pee Wee King ("Pee Wee" because he was short, and "King" in emulation of another Polish band leader, Wayne King). A few years later, Pee Wee lit out on his own, taking his western-and-polka band to the *Opry* in 1937, where he admits it was out of place.

While Hank was playing with Pee Wee King, he sold him one of his original songs, "(I'm Praying for the Day That) Peace Will Come." Pee Wee says that Hank first pitched the song to him in Montgomery because the band's female singer, Becky Barfield, had said she needed another patriotic number. Hank was hanging around the dressing room between shows and made his pitch. "Hey, King," he said, "listen to this." Hank ran it down, but Pee Wee was dubious, so Hank suggested that he try the song onstage. "He got a pretty good hand with a brand-new song, which is hard to do," said Pee Wee. "He said, 'Now, what do you think?' I said, 'Let's wait.' " According to Paul Dennis, the deal was closed in Montgomery at the municipal auditorium for fifty dollars, but according to Pee Wee, it was closed in Dothan, Alabama, for considerably less. "We were staying at this hotel," he said, "and the bellboy said, 'Mr. King, Mr. Williams, do you want something to drink?' and he said, 'See, Pee Wee, right there is ten dollars.' " Hank was prepared to sell half of his song for the price of a few days' drinks. The contract was written out by hand, and Pee Wee King became half-owner of "(I'm Praying for the Day That) Peace Will Come."

When King got back to Nashville, he placed the song with Acuff-Rose Publications, which registered it with the Library of Congress on December 20, 1943. As it turned out, the few dollars Hank got for the song were just about the most anyone made off it. By the time King landed his first recording contract with the Nashville-based Bullet label in 1945, peace had come, and the song languished until the Korean War, when Esco Hankins (recording as Roscoe Hankins) cut it with no success at all for Mercury.

At least once before he and Audrey married, Hank went back to work in the shipyards in Mobile, but, as on the other occasions, he doesn't appear to have made a significant contribution to the war effort. The McNeils moved to Mobile in 1943. Hank's aunt Alice and his cousins Opal and J.C. all worked in the shipyards on Liberty Ships, and Hank came down shortly after the McNeils arrived. Lillie's brother Bob Skipper was also renting a house there, and Hank lived with his uncle Bob for a while. "He would hit the joints at night," said J. C. McNeil. "He tried to get a band together when he was in the shipyards. It was in his blood. I would venture to say that he didn't work more than two or three months all told. He probably slept on the job more than anything else. It was encouraged by the foreman so that he could stretch the hours he could bill."

At some point, Audrey joined Hank in Mobile. It was an item of faith with her that they worked together in the shipyards:

> We worked side by side in these pit things [with a blowtorch]. I had never seen [them] before. We'd go back to the little old hotel room, which was terrible, in the evening. I'd wash out our clothes. We didn't do this too long — but we did do it. I knew he had something, and me or someone had to get it out of him. One day I said, "This is just not it, Hank. I want to go back to Montgomery, get a band together for you, and get you back on the radio station and start working shows." And that's exactly what I did.

If true, Audrey had come to Hank's rescue, just as Lillie had done a year earlier.

Hank quit the shipyards for good in August 1944, and returned to Montgomery. Audrey probably went back to Troy and drove to his gigs on weekends, although some remember her staying at the boardinghouse. Hank put together another group of Drifting Cowboys soon after he returned from Mobile, and the lineup included Don Helms and Sammy Pruett, two of the musicians who would later work with the most famous incarnation of the band.

Helms was eighteen years old when he joined Hank. He was from a farming family in New Brockton, Alabama. In 1943 he went to Panama City to work in the shipyards. He had an aunt in Montgomery who had studied music and had a Hawaiian guitar, and his father played fiddle, but even after his aunt had given him the steel guitar he still had no thought of a career in music. It was Pappy Neal McCormick who sold him on the idea of becoming a steel guitar player. He went to see Pappy Neal in a vocational building. "He was playing that thing," says Helms, "and I thought, 'Man, what a way to have to fun. What a way to make a living.'" The only steel guitarist who actually flogged Helms some licks was Boots Harris. When Harris would come back to Opp from Nashville where he was playing with Curley Williams, Helms would go see him and learn some of the steel guitar parts Boots was playing with Curley.

Very quickly, the steel guitar became the driving force in Helms's life. Every Sunday he tuned in a shortwave program called *Hawaii Calls,* and he listened to all the steel players on the *Opry,* like Bashful Brother Oswald with Roy Acuff and Little Roy Wiggins with Eddy Arnold. He bought his first electric steel guitar, a Silvertone, from Sears, but, because he had no electricity on the farm, he had to play it on an upended wash-tub, which resonated just enough for him to practice. Eventually, he took over the steel guitar chair in McCormick's band when McCormick felt like taking some time off.

Back in New Brockton, Helms put a band together with two cousins and two friends, one of whom was Sammy Pruett. Helms and Pruett had met in Panama City at a Neal McCormick gig, and they stayed in touch. Their band was called the Alabama Rhythm Boys, and they started playing the honky-tonks around southern Alabama Wednesday through Saturday. One of the guys in the band knew Hank and went to Montgomery to meet him on a day off. Helms recalled:

> He came back and said, "Hank Williams is putting a band together. Y'all wanna go work for him?" We said, "Aw, hell, it's probably better 'n this," so we gave three or four days notice and rode the bus up to Montgomery.
>
> We were supposed to meet Hank at Art Freehling's Music Store, but he wasn't there. We went outside and I saw this real long-legged guy coming. He walked up, and he said, "Y'all the group?" We said, "Yeah." He said, "Well, I'm Hank Williams. Follow me." We walked round the corner and down the block to a hock shop. He said, "Jake, you got any more of them blackjacks in there?" and there was a tray of 'em. He passed 'em out, he said, "Boys, if y'all gonna play with me, by God you're gonna need these." He wasn't kiddin' either.

Very soon after, Hank lined up Monday, Wednesday, and Saturday nights at the Riverside Club in Andalusia, and Tuesday and Thursday in nearby Opp. The Riverside was one of the biggest dance halls in Alabama, and there would often be six hundred people on the weekend. Hank bought or rented a trailer and moved to Andalusia. Helms and the band didn't live far away, so they drove in from New Brockton in Helms's fiancée's car and went home after the show.

Audrey was with Hank much of the time. It was understood that Helms and his fiancée, another group member and his fiancée, and Hank and Audrey would all get married at the same time, but Hank and Audrey jumped the gun. He pestered her constantly to marry him, but there were several hoops to jump first. One was that Audrey was still married to Erskine Guy, who by now was a serviceman. Divorcing a serviceman who was serving overseas was not easy, and both Hank and Audrey had grown attached to the eighty-dollar-a-month allotment check that Audrey received from the military while Guy was away. On a more frivolous level, Audrey insisted that she never liked the name Williams. "I told my aunt after I started dating Hank, 'I cannot imagine "Audrey Williams," ' " she said. As always, though, the biggest problem was Hank's drinking, but during those late months of 1944, he made a concerted effort to stay sober, and, as the year drew to a close, sobriety drew its reward.

Audrey always portrayed her decision to marry Hank as a spur-of-the-moment act, but she had to take the first step of divorcing Erskine Guy, a divorce that became final on December 5, 1944, on the grounds of voluntary abandonment. Hank then went to see a Dr. Parker, who declared him free of venereal disease, and then a notary public, who swore out the marriage license. The last stop was a justice of the peace, M. A. Boyett, who operated a filling station near Andalusia and pronounced them man and wife on December 15, 1944. Technically, it was an illegitimate marriage because they hadn't sat out the sixty-day waiting period necessary after a divorce.

Audrey said she cooked for the band in the trailer, but Paul Dennis, who came down to play with Hank, remembers only one meal — and that was inedible. The honeymoon soon ended. On the weekend that the Andalusia gig ended, Hank got drunk. Audrey pitched a fit, Hank threw her clothes into the mud in front of the trailer, and she called the police and had him put in jail. Don Helms had to go get him out. "I was embarrassed," says Helms, "but I went back in there. He was sitting on a bench in his cell, watching me. I didn't know what to say, but he was staring at me. He said, 'What d'ya want me to do? Stand on my darn head?' I paid the thirty dollars and got him out. As we were leaving, one of the policemen said, 'Come back 'n see us, Hank,' and he said, 'All of you can go to Hell.' "

By 1945 Hank was back in Montgomery, and he quickly re-established himself as the most popular hillbilly musician in town. He began selling a self-produced folio of songs called *Original Songs of Hank Williams,* which was printed by Leon Johnson, a local musician who ran a print shop. Johnson had been printing posters for Hank since the late '30s, although it was usually Lillie who came to pick up the order and take care of the account. Johnson didn't take much notice of Hank until he got a call for a second printing of the songbook. This time Hank arrived with a half-gallon jar of nickels, quarters, and dimes to pay the bill. He sold the books for thirty-five cents and told the audience that the money was for handling. "You send in the money," he'd say, "and I'll handle it." He had learned long ago that it was easier to wheedle money from folks who had none with a joke rather than a plea.

Only the words were published in the songbook — not the music. Hank told Johnson that if people wanted to learn the tune, they'd have to listen to his radio show, but the truth was that Hank didn't know musical notation and wasn't about to pay somebody to transcribe for him. The little folio included "I'm Not Coming Home Any More" as well as several songs that were recorded later and several more that never surfaced again. Among the latter was a saber-rattler called "Grandad's Musket," possibly born of Hank's guilt for having done so conspicuously little toward the war effort:

> The boys up in the mountains have closed down their stills
> They've moved to the city and are making leaded pills
> While me and Grandad's Musket, when we are off to War
> We'll join up with MacArthur and even up the score.

After the gig in Andalusia ended, the band moved to Montgomery, lived in Lillie's boardinghouse, and resumed the prewar routine of booking into schoolhouses and beer joints, or cracker-barrels, as they were called. Hank usually paid five dollars a night on top of room and board. Audrey would ride with them, sitting on his lap all the way down to the show and all the way back because Lillie's '37 Chevrolet was packed full. The bass sat on top. Lillie still went along to watch the door.

The lineup of The Drifting Cowboys was never stable for more than a few weeks. Helms quit the group shortly before he went into the service in 1945, but Pruett stayed on a little longer. Shortly after Helms was drafted, Hank hired Doyle and Bernice Turner, a husband-and-wife team from Panama City whom Helms had recommended. They had met Helms at a parade soon after he'd quit, and he had told them about Hank. When they got home they found Hank had called. "Doyle had made me practice and practice barre chords," said Bernice, "and when Hank heard me he had a fit. He had a good sock rhythm playing open chords, but he couldn't play barre chords. We auditioned at the boardinghouse, done two or three songs and he hired us. He knew we were exactly what he wanted."

Playing with Hank was still no plum job. Even the relatively unsophisticated musicians he hired looked down on his music. "I always thought Hank was too corny," said Sammy Pruett in conversation with Jim Owen, "because whenever he'd end a tune, instead of playing a chord up on the neck of the guitar, he'd do an [open] A or G or D, just as plain as you could get. We used to set around backstage, and he'd play a few tunes with a little pop taste, and he'd say, 'Awright, boys, get them pop licks outta ya before we get out onstage 'cause we're gonna keep it vanilla.' "

"Vanilla" to Hank was plain old hillbilly music. Occasionally, he would let his two guitar players cut loose on a Bob Wills–styled dance tune with unison passages, but the only music other than hillbilly and gospel for which he evinced a genuine love was cottonpatch blues. Band members remember him sitting around backstage and at home playing songs like "Matchbox Blues" and "Bottle Up and Go." He would even sit in with blues singers on the sidewalk, but, when it came time to go play for the people, the only items on the menu were Roy Acuff and Ernest Tubb songs and traditional or original hillbilly plaints.

Only on one occasion does Hank seem to have deviated from his course. In the summer of 1946, his band briefly consisted of E. B. Fulmer on piano, an instrument that Hank later asserted had no place in country music; Lefty Clark on saxophone, an instrument even more at odds with Hank's music; Lum York on bass; and a steel guitarist and a drummer. Together, they played dance music. The sharp double-breasted gabardine suit that Hank wore around this time seems to imply that he was giving some thought to shedding his old skin. As always, though, he had his ear cocked toward his audience, and he was probably hearing that they wanted the old Hank Williams back.

Hank was off WSFA from February 1945 until January 1946. He got back on between 6:35 and 7:00 A.M. starting January 26, and in September he got another sponsored show at 4:00 P.M. By the close of 1946, Hank was so popular that even the radio shows were an event. Fans would turn up to see him at the station, creating a disturbance in the hotel lobby. WSFA still cursed him for his unreliability, but tolerated him as a necessary evil. Hank started using his clout to wrest concessions from the station. One stipulation was that WSFA wouldn't hire a competing hillbilly band. WSFA acceded, although the agreement warped opinion against Hank among the other bands in town. The station's ownership couldn't comprehend his appeal; they simply knew they couldn't afford to lose him. In radio stores, the question from the country folk was often, "Will it pick up Hank Williams?"

"Hank was a big drawing card," said WSFA engineer Sebie Smith, "but the band didn't always dress up too well. They'd come straggling through the Jefferson Davis Hotel. Finally the manager of the hotel asked [WSFA owner] Howard Pill to have Hank's crew come in the back way." At the same time, Hank was attracting a lot of jealousy from the other local acts on WSFA, chief among them Camille Brown, the Oprah of Montgomery. She hosted a show called *Around the Town with Camille Brown*, and griped loud and often to the station's management about the amount of sponsorship Hank got.

Part of the chronic unreliability that dogged Hank can be attributed to the tensions at the boardinghouse. Lillie and Audrey were both strong-willed, belligerent, and grasping. In the name of loving Hank and help-ing his career, they tried to wrest control from each other. Lillie even hinted at the squabbles in her booklet: "I must admit I was a little jealous at times," she wrote, adding quickly and unconvincingly, "Not really. I'm joking. Hank's mother was always his first girl, and he never forgot it." She never let him forget it, either. "She would dictate to him," said Don Helms. "She'd say, 'You cain't do this. . . . I ain't puttin' up with that. . . .' I can't remember the times I heard Hank say, 'Goddamn, don't tell her.' " Hank and Lillie were one of those unknowable mother-son relationships like Elvis and Gladys or Jerry Lee Lewis and Mamie. They formed an eternal triangle: the strong mother, the ineffectual father, the talented, precocious son. Lon's absence not only meant that Hank didn't have a male role model, but also that he never matured from the depen-dent mother-child state; he simply transferred his dependency to Au-drey, a shift that Lillie felt acutely.

It's doubtful that Hank appreciated the full ramifications of the dan-gerous curve that Audrey had thrown into his relationship with Lillie. He tended to see it in simpler terms. "No wonder you and Audrey don't get along," Hank told Lillie on one occasion. "Because one of you's afraid the other one's gonna beat you to my pocket when I get drunk." Occasionally when Hank went on a bender, Audrey would take off, per-haps back to Banks — no one ever knew where. Then it was left to Lillie to organize a search of the local joints and hotels for Hank. Sometimes he would go to WCOV and pick a fight with Dad Crysel, and Crysel's band would take great pleasure in beating him senseless and tossing him out onto the street.

Occasionally, when the three-way strife mounted and he could bear it no longer, Hank would take off for the Florida panhandle. He would hole up in the San Carlos Hotel in Pensacola, order bottles to be brought to his room, and stay drunk for several days, often a week or more. Sometimes Lillie would send Hank to Lon's house when he was on a bender. Watching him sober up one morning, Lon's daughter, Leila, came to know why Hank would refer to himself as her "half a brother."

Everyone knew that Hank's drinking was abnormal. His cousin Walter McNeil Jr. (or O'Neil McNeil, as Lillie called him) had never — and would never — see anyone who drank with as much single-mindedness as Hank. Whether he was a happy drunk or a mean drunk depended on his mood when he started drinking. Lillie couldn't understand it at all. "She'd *demand* that he stop drinking," says McNeil, "but he needed to pitch his drunk and get it out of his system for a few weeks or a few months." As she always would, Lillie saw Hank's alcoholism in terms of weakness of will. She railed against it, cursed him, but never finally cast him out, perhaps because he was her only son or perhaps because of an intuition that he would one day amount to something despite himself.

A sense of how much of a problem Hank's drinking was at this early stage in his career can be gleaned from Bernice Turner. She remembers driving to a gig in southern Alabama. Hank couldn't drive because his license had been revoked, so he sat between Doyle and Bernice, asking them to stop every few miles so that he could get another beer. Doyle and Bernice decided to let him pass out, hoping that he would sleep it off and sober up in time for the show. "Hank mumbled something about wanting to lay his head in my lap," said Bernice, "and as he said it he was falling anyway. When we got there, I eased out from underneath him, went in and set up."

They'd almost played a complete set when Hank came weaving in. He picked up his guitar and started singing "There's a New Moon over My Shoulder." "He was singing in one key and playing in another," said Bernice. "Doyle looked at me and said, 'Blue Steel Blues,' and we started playing to try and drown him out. The place was packed, and Hank looked at us — a dirty look — then he looked at the fiddle player. He was gonna leave and take the musicians with him, but they didn't go." Later, there was a commotion outside when Hank picked a fight with a policeman. He was hauled off to jail, and the Turners went to get him out after the show, but found that the police had decided to keep him. They drove home, gave the takings to Lillie, and went to bed. The next day Lillie and Audrey drove down to get him out.

It seems that Hank was first treated for alcoholism early in 1945 at a sanatorium in Prattville, Alabama, although the treatment probably consisted of no more than rest and alcohol deprivation. As such, it was no more successful than any of the other treatments Hank was forced to take; going on a spree had become his way of dealing with life's stresses. It was also a means of relieving his back pain, which was already a factor in his life. When the band saw him gobbling aspirins, they knew that a bender was imminent. It probably never occurred to Audrey and Lillie that if Hank had a low tolerance for stress when the load was light, the success they craved might be a mixed blessing.

Everyone associated with Hank felt that he could be their passport to better times, and they all fell into a dispiriting cycle with him. For several weeks everything would be fine. Hank would be straight, on time and in tune for every gig. They'd go fishing down on the Alabama coastline. Hank and Audrey would be holding hands in the car, and the talk would be upbeat. Then something would snap, and Hank would be off on a drunk. The Turners eventually quit because he damned so many promising opportunities with his unreliability, which they — like everyone else — saw in terms of lack of willpower.

Toward the end of 1946, Hank tried to solve part of the problem by moving out of the boardinghouse and into a small rented house at 409 Washington Avenue. Lycrecia came up from Banks, and for the first time since he had lived with the McNeils, Hank was part of a mom-pop-and-the-kid relationship. He tried desperately hard to fill the part for which life had ill prepared him. No one denies the deep bond between Hank and Audrey, although few agree on what it was rooted in. When Hank was sober, it looked like true love. Lycrecia's presence prompted him to try to walk the path of righteousness, and now, with encouragement and not so subtle pressure from Audrey, he began to look beyond the limited horizons of south-central Alabama.

At some point in 1945 or 1946, Hank went to Nashville, intending to try out for the *Opry*. He went to see announcer Jud Collins at WSM, the home station of the *Opry*. "They said someone was outside to see me," said Collins, "and there was this guy with blue jeans and a white hat. He said, 'I'm Hank Williams. Charlie Holt from WSFA told me to come up here and see you. He said you'd tell me what I have to do to get on the *Opry*.'" Collins told Hank that there were no shortcuts and that he would have to audition for Jack Stapp like everyone else. "He wouldn't go see Jack," said Collins. "He said, 'You tell Jack Stapp I'm here.' I think he was disappointed that I couldn't take him by the hand and say, 'Hank, you're on the *Opry* tonight at eight.' "

Thousands of other hillbilly acts from small stations across the South came to WSM on a similar mission. Virtually all were turned away. If they got as far as "Judge" Hay, who had the last word on the *Opry* artist roster, he would listen politely and say, "Boys, come back and see me when you're hot 'nuff to draw flies."

Even though he returned home empty-handed, word about Hank was slowly seeping out of Montgomery. Ernest Tubb remembered him opening an *Opry* show as a local added attraction around the time the war ended. In exchange for a spot on the show, Hank would promote it on WSFA. "When I got there, Hank had already started the show," remembered Tubb. "He was supposed to do twenty minutes, and he was tearing the house down. He came off and they kept applauding. We like to never got him off the stage." Tubb suggested to his booker, J. L. Frank, that he take on Hank, but Frank knew Hank's reputation firsthand from working the Pee Wee King tour in 1943 and told Tubb to stay clear.

There have been persistent claims that Hank sold songs to visiting *Opry* stars, but there is no firm evidence that he ever sold anything other than half of "(I'm Praying for the Day That) Peace Will Come." One of the prime candidates for purchasing the kind of songs Hank wrote was his idol, Roy Acuff. In common with most of his contemporaries, Acuff bought songs outright when the opportunity presented itself. For a while in the early '40s, he had tried to administer his own music publishing, and it was probably a suspicion of the revenue he was losing that prompted Acuff to enter into a partnership with Fred Rose, the man who would secure his future — and Hank's too.

Fred Rose was born on the Kentucky-Indiana line in Evansville, Indiana, on August 24, 1897. He spent a miserable childhood in St. Louis, then set out for Chicago when he was in his teens. He later told an interviewer that he had been on his own since he was seven. He played piano and sang in the speakeasies, and was part of a twin piano feature on the Paul Whiteman show. Almost inevitably he turned to songwriting. Music came from every pore of Fred Rose, and he scored his first hit in 1921 with "Sweet Mama (Papa's Gettin' Mad)." In 1924 Sophie Tucker popularized "Red Hot Mamma," and Isham Jones cut the first of many versions of "Honest and Truly." Perhaps Rose's most enduring song, " 'Deed I Do," was published in 1926. He married for the first time when he was in Chicago, and had two sons, Wesley and Lester, whom he would later bring into Acuff-Rose.

Rose rode the blind optimism of the jazz age; he was a featured radio performer on WBBM and wrote songs prolifically. He remarried, and seemed set for life as a music mill, grinding out show tunes, frothy novelties, and topical songs to order, but the Depression and his own drinking problem combined to scupper his career. He was thrown off radio in Chicago, moved to New York, and then, in 1933, he went to work at WSM in Nashville. This was not the comedown that it might seem. Much of WSM's broadcast day was devoted to pop music despite the fact that it sponsored the *Grand Ole Opry*. The station's orchestra was among the most renowned in the NBC network. Rose had his own show, *Freddie Rose's Song Shop,* and he toured the mid-South with a trio. He also married for the third — and last — time during his first stint in Nashville.

One of the key events in Rose's career was his conversion to Christian Science in late 1935 or 1936. It came when Rose was back in New York, and his career was in a trough. His newfound faith enabled him to lick his alcoholism and screw up his courage for a new start in Hollywood. He went there at the invitation of Gene Autry, although he and his third wife, Lorene, kept their house in Nashville. Between 1938 and 1942, Rose and Autry wrote many songs, and all the while Rose commuted back and forth to Nashville. He also worked a stint at KVOO in Tulsa, where he met Bob Wills, whom he would later produce for Columbia.

Rose's conversion to country music was more gradual and less spectacular than his conversion to Christian Science. It probably started soon after he arrived in Nashville. "Fred Rose came to Nashville to laugh," Hank told Ralph Gleason in 1952, "and he heard Roy Acuff and said, 'By God he means it.'" Rose himself, in a 1954 interview, remembered seeing Acuff on the *Opry*. "Roy came out on stage," he said, "and sang 'Don't Make Me Go to Bed and I'll Be Good.' Real tears rolled down Roy's cheeks that night. Those tears stained his shirt. I felt I had discovered the real secret of country music. That secret is sincerity." In the summer of 1942, Acuff approached Rose, who was by now back on WSM, with the proposition that they form a joint music publishing venture. Acuff offered to bankroll the company with twenty-five thousand dollars, but Rose apparently never needed to draw on that capital. The partnership, technically between Rose and Acuff's wife, Mildred, was launched in October 1942, and the initial thrust was to produce and market Acuff's song folios, perhaps the artist's most profitable sideline.

Acuff was now at the pinnacle of his career. Meanwhile, Hank was just a local star in a small market. Unlike most hillbilly musicians, he wasn't even semi-itinerant. Usually, a hillbilly singer would move to a town, find a radio sponsor, and then play shows locally until everyone got sick of seeing him or he got a better offer elsewhere. No one was sick of Hank in Montgomery — quite the contrary — but he couldn't use his local success as a springboard to a bigger market because he was already damned as unreliable, and, in a business full of problem drinkers, his reputation was among the worst.

Chapter
4

• •

SONGS FOR HOME FOLKS

• •

*E*VERYONE has a celestial city. For Hank Williams and subsequent generations of wannabillies it's Nashville. It wasn't always that way, though. When Hank and Audrey got off the train in 1946, country music had a low profile in the city, but not low enough for a city establishment that wished it would disappear altogether. The hillbilly music business was poison to the city's view of itself as the self-proclaimed Athens of the South, a seat of government, learning, and commerce. Only gradually, over the last forty years, has the music industry become a city within a city and won the embrace of the city and state because of the vast and increasing revenue it generates.

Today Music Row, which is really more of a Music Rhombus, has parasitically claimed one old house after another in what was once a residential area south of the city core. At its apex sits part of the house that Hank and Audrey bought after they moved to town. Once on Franklin Road, it was moved to Music Row in September 1984, and, for a short time, it was a sparsely stocked Hank and Audrey museum run by Lycrecia; then, with grim irony that Hank might have appreciated, it became a bar and a comedy club.

Today, every record company, music publisher, public relations firm or booking agency looking to maintain a presence in country music is represented in Nashville, together with a sad peripheral cast of flimflam men with fistfuls of nebulous copyrights or nothing at all. Tour buses circle every few minutes from early in the morning until late at night. Hank Williams's name is invoked everywhere, but, if he were to heed the summons back, the only element he would recognize is the *Grand Ole Opry,* and even then he would recognize only the name — not the location. In 1974 the *Opry* moved from its home in the old Ryman Auditorium to an air-conditioned theme park northeast of the city that was little more than swampland when Hank came to town.

The country music business has not merely grown; it has centered itself in Nashville to the point where the two are now as closely associated as Mutual and Omaha. In 1946, though, Nashville was just one of several outposts of what was then a sidebar to the music industry, and one often treated with derision. According to a quick poll of record company artist and repertoire (A&R) men in 1946, Chicago was reckoned to be the city with the greatest concentration of country musicians. Country recordings were made there, in Dallas, Cincinnati, New York, and Los Angeles, as well as in field locations such as Nashville.

Country music — like the record business itself — was dominated by three companies headquartered in New York: Columbia, RCA Victor, and Decca. The quasi-major labels with volume large enough to earn a place on industry surveys were Capitol Records, which had been launched in Los Angeles in 1942, Mercury Records, founded in Chicago in 1945, and the now long-gone Majestic label, founded in 1945 as a subsidiary of Majestic Radio.

The majors usually assigned just one man to look after their country divisions (then known as the "hillbilly," "folk," or "western" division). At Columbia it was Arthur Satherley, an expatriate Englishman who looked and spoke as if he were an Oxford professor of some arcane discipline. Satherley did what prewar record men had done: he traveled more than seventy thousand miles a year making recordings in the field on acetate discs. Starting out from his home in Los Angeles with a portable recorder, half a dozen microphones, disc-cutting lathes, and a trailer full of blank discs, he cut records in hotel rooms, YMCAs, and small radio stations. Tape wasn't in common use until around 1950.

Today country musicians tend to have a homogeneity born of the fact that they have all been weaned on an identical diet, but, as Satherley explained in 1944, it wasn't always that way. "I would never think," he told the *Saturday Evening Post,* "of hiring a Mississippi boy to play in a Texas band. Any Texan would know right off it was wrong." In the midforties you could listen to a country record and stand a better than even chance of guessing where the performer was based. Anyone getting a demo of Hank Williams would have known at once he was a hillbilly performer from the South or Southeast. No one would have confused his music with country music from Pennsylvania and the eastern seaboard or with cowboy music, and Hank's music was so remote from Bob Wills's western swing and the country-pop blend that Eddy Arnold was forging that the three artists didn't really deserve to be lumped in the same category.

In the same category they were, though. In 1946 the music trade paper *Billboard* covered the entire spectrum under the blanket heading "American Folk Tunes." Hillbilly music was generally acknowledged as the lowest, least sophisticated rung of the Folk Tune ladder, and what respect it had was almost entirely due to Roy Acuff. "Hillbilly" itself was a pejorative term in 1946. Hank always called his music folk music when he was asked.

The industry put-downs gnawed at Fred Rose, and, with the zeal of the new convert, he made a spirited defense of hillbilly music in a letter to *Billboard* in August 1946:

> We pride ourselves in being a very intelligent people and good Americans, but are we? We put on our best bib and tucker and make quite an affair of spending an enjoyable evening being entertained with Russian, Italian, French, etc., folklore. . . . We read all kinds of books that will give us an understanding of foreign folklore, but what do we say and do about our own good ol' American folklore? We call it "hillbilly" music and sometimes we're ashamed to call it music.

Like Rose, Hank would become fiercely protective of his music and its populist base. "It makes me mad," he told an interviewer in 1951, "to hear these popular orchestras make a jammed-up comedy of a song like 'Wreck on the Highway.' It ain't a funny song. Folk songs express the dreams and prayers and hopes of the working people."

Billboard didn't abandon its "Folk Tunes" tag until June 1949, when it began using a new coinage, "Country & Western." By that time, Nashville had become the hub of country music. It happened surprisingly quickly in the mid- to late '40s, and the principal reason was WSM's *Grand Ole Opry.* Immediately after the war, the *Opry* was just one of many Saturday night radio jamborees — not the first, and not the only one broadcast on a maximum-wattage station — but the *Opry* had the right talent mix and thirty minutes of precious network airtime every Saturday night, when it blanketed the nation on NBC.

Anyone laying bets as late as 1945 or 1946 would have felt safer putting money on Cincinnati or Chicago to become the hub of the country music industry. Both had Saturday night jamborees on maximum-wattage stations, recording studios, a pool of sessionmen, even local record labels, and both were more centrally located than Nashville for touring purposes. Still, the *Midwestern Hayride* on WLW in Cincinnati and the WLS *Barn Dance* in Chicago didn't have the aggressive management, top performers, and the network airtime that the *Opry* did, and Nashville's pre-eminence resulted from that.

Quickly the other pieces fell into place. The first record company A&R rep to be located in Nashville was Mercury Records' Les Hutchens, who was appointed in August 1947.* In 1945 three WSM engineers started a recording studio as a separate enterprise within the WSM studio complex, and in 1947 they transferred their business to a self-contained studio in a remodeled dining room at the Tulane Hotel. Called the Castle Studio, it was where Hank would cut most of his sessions, and it was the first professional studio in Nashville.† After coalescing, the elements began to develop their own momentum. Everyone wanted to play on the winning team. Even though the *Opry* stars were constantly on the road, they were back in Nashville every weekend. The music publishers knew they could pitch to them then, the record companies knew that they could record them then, and the bookers knew they could line up dates then, so the industry started moving into town.

Country music was quickly earning industry respect, not, as official histories like to say, for its ability to express the hopes and feelings of the common man, but for its ability to generate good revenue with low overhead. *Billboard* offered a snapshot of the music industry's thought processes in a review of a Carnegie Hall concert in September 1947 that featured *Opry* acts: "A cornbilly troupe called the *Grand Ole Opry* ... took over the house and proved to the tune of $12,000 gross that the big city wants country music. The promoters, Sol Gold, Abe Lackman and Oscar Davis got more than a kick out of it because they garnered about $9,500 with a talent nut of about $5,000." The infrastructure of the music business — record labels, theater owners, bookers, agents, and profes-

---

* Hutchens didn't last long, and it wasn't until Dee Kilpatrick represented Capitol in Nashville in 1950 and 1951 that there was a permanent A&R office in town. Representatives of the three major labels flew in and out until the late '50s.

† Field recording sessions had been held in Nashville before the war, but the first modern country recording session held in Nashville is generally reckoned to have been by Eddy Arnold, who recorded at WSM studios on December 4, 1944.

sional managers — came to a quick and common realization: Hey! We can make money with this. Then the wheels began to turn.

Respect came quickly from the music industry, and then — belatedly and begrudgingly — from Nashville itself. The embrace that the state and municipal governments now extend to the music industry might lead one to think that it has always been that way, but Roy Acuff, who was photographed with politicians of every stripe, from local mayors to Richard Nixon, would have been the first to say that was not so. In 1943, in celebration of the fact that his radio show was being relayed to 129 stations nationwide, Acuff threw a party at the Ryman Auditorium. Prentice Cooper, the governor of Tennessee, was invited to attend, but declined, saying that he would have no part of a "circus," adding that Acuff was bringing disgrace to the state by making Nashville the hillbilly capital of the United States. Acuff responded by running for governor in 1948, unsuccessfully.

So by the time Hank, nudged as always by Audrey, started thinking seriously about a shot at the songwriting or recording end of the business, Nashville was the logical first stop. Early on Saturday, September 14, 1946, they took the train to Nashville, probably knowing that Saturday was very much a business day there.

Fred Rose's son Wesley always told the same story: One lunchtime he and his father were playing Ping-Pong in WSM's recreation room on the fifth floor of the National Life and Accident Company building when Hank and Audrey walked in and asked to audition some songs. After listening to his songs, Fred asked Hank to prove that he hadn't bought the songs by telling him to write one on the spot around a not particularly original theme — a woman leaves the one she truly loves to marry a man with money. Hank then took himself off into a side room and emerged with "Mansion on the Hill." Fred signed him; Wesley nodded in accordance.

The fine details of how Fred Rose came to sign Hank Williams aren't clear, but it's almost certain that Hank wasn't making a cold call, that Wesley wasn't there, and that "Mansion on the Hill" wasn't written until a year later. Despite what Wesley thought or said, Hank Williams almost certainly went to Nashville by invitation. What took him there was Fred Rose's need to find songs for Molly O'Day and the Cumberland Mountain Folks, an act he was about to produce for Arthur Satherley.

Molly O'Day's early career was very much a template for what Hank's would have been if he had been more reliable. Born Lois Laverne Williamson in Pike County, Kentucky, she was torn between sacred and secular music, a conflict she eventually resolved by shunning worldly music. A month or so older than Hank, Molly O'Day (as she began calling herself in 1942) had been entertaining for almost as long as Hank, shuttling around the mid-South, playing at radio stations and schoolhouses, and slowly building her career. She sang in Roy Acuff's emotional, full-throated jubilee style. Her husband and band leader, Lynn Davis, took care of the business aspect of her career. He had met Fred Rose when they both worked on KVOO in Tulsa, Oklahoma, in the mid-thirties, and Rose had kept abreast of Molly's movements.

During the war, Molly, Lynn Davis, and their group were playing a show sponsored by Black Draught laxative and tonic over a small network of stations in the South. One of the stations that picked up the feed was WSFA in Montgomery. "We'd go into the towns that picked up the show, and I'd bring in big acts and we'd play over the network," says Davis. "One time we were in Montgomery. Hank had announced the show on his program, and he was to be the local added attraction. He sang 'Tramp on the Street' and done four encores on it, and Molly said she had to have that song."

"Tramp on the Street" was first recorded by its writers, Grady and Hazel Cole, for RCA Victor in August 1939. Their version is like a parody of a hillbilly record; they harmonize weakly and fumble the low notes so badly that they should have been shooed back out onto the street. Still, the message of the song was so compelling that it survived the indignities the Coles inflicted upon it. Taken from the Book of Luke, in which Lazarus was a beggar driven from the doors of the rich, the song was a plea for compassion, written as the homeless victims of the Depression wandered the land. It was a theme that touched Hank Williams's heart as he refashioned it, changing the Coles' geeky waltz into a haunting piece that was an even more direct tug at the heartstrings. The song appeared in one of the songbooks he published while he was at WSFA, when the byline read "Author Unknown."

After Molly O'Day heard Hank perform "Tramp on the Street," she asked for a copy of the lyrics. Hank reached into his guitar case and gave them to her. This must have been no later than 1943, because "Tramp on the Street" was in a song folio that Molly published in January 1944. Hank's and Molly's paths crossed several times after that. Lynn Davis remembers that Molly was back in Montgomery for a show in 1946 and he was handling the box office. Hank appeared; he was very drunk and offered to sell a folder of songs for twenty-five dollars. Davis bought them and asked Hank to come to the hotel the following morning to complete the paperwork. The next day, Davis gave Hank his songs back and told him that he was sitting on a gold mine. Hank said he didn't have the twenty-five dollars to repay Davis; Davis said it didn't matter.

In the summer of 1946, Fred Rose was vacationing in Gatlinburg, Tennessee, and according to Lynn Davis, Art Satherley was with him. They heard Molly sing "Tramp on the Street" on the radio, and Satherley asked Rose if he knew the group. Rose said he did. At Rose's prompting, Satherley signed Molly O'Day and gave Rose the responsibility of scouting out some repertoire for the session. Rose asked Lynn Davis where "Tramp on the Street" came from, and Davis told them about Hank Williams and suggested to Rose that he contact Hank. No one else in Rose's little pool of writers was producing anything close to what Molly O'Day needed, so Rose wrote to Hank, and Hank sent back an acetate with a few songs on it. Rose then invited him to Nashville. At some point, Hank might have mentioned that "(I'm Praying for the Day That) Peace Will Come" had already been published by Acuff-Rose, but, if he did, it probably didn't curry too much favor with Rose because the song still hadn't been recorded — and wasn't likely to be without another war. Later Fred Rose realized that he had met Hank previously, around 1945 on one of his junkets through the South, but it was the need to find songs for Molly O'Day that brought them together in September 1946.

In 1946 and 1947 Molly O'Day recorded four of Hank's songs: "When God Comes and Gathers His Jewels," "Six More Miles," "I Don't Care If Tomorrow Never Comes," and "Singing Waterfall." All of them had appeared in the song folios that he had self-published in 1945 and 1946, so if Hank wrote anything especially for her in 1946 it must have been rejected. Perhaps the only song that he wrote with Molly in mind was "On the Evening Train," which was also the only song credited to both Hank and Audrey. Molly recorded it in April 1949.

Shortly before Molly O'Day's first session, Rose got a call from Al Middleman, the president of Sterling Records in New York. Sterling had started with grandiose plans. It was incorporated in July 1945, bankrolled by three investors, George H. Bell, Pearl Richards, and Eleanor Benedek of New York. It was to have wholly owned distributors in major markets and its own pressing plant in Los Angeles. Art Rupe was brought in as A&R manager, and his label, Juke Box, was made an affiliate of Sterling and was bankrolled by the same three partners. By the summer of 1946, though, Rupe had become disillusioned, and he took back his repertoire, which he used to start the hugely successful Specialty label. Shortly after Rupe quit, Middleman convinced himself that Sterling needed hillbilly and black gospel lines to complement its jazz, pop, and R&B series. He asked Fred Rose to find some acts for the hillbilly series, record them in Nashville, and ship the masters up to him.

According to Hank's bass player, Lum York, he and Hank had already made a trip to Nashville to demo some songs before Middleman's call. During the session, Fred had told Hank that he ought to be on a label himself, but, according to Murray Nash — then an A&R rep for RCA and later Rose's factotum at Acuff-Rose — it was Rose's secretary, Eleanor Shea, who actually remembered Hank Williams and suggested that Rose contact him. According to Wesley Rose, it was he who remembered Hank. According to Hank, Fred Rose's first thought had been to sign Johnnie and Jack, and he was brought into consideration only after Johnnie and Jack wouldn't or couldn't record for Sterling. Johnnie and Jack made their recording debut ten weeks after Hank for another New York indie, Apollo Records, so it's likely that they were already under contract when Rose approached them, which might, as Hank said, have prompted Rose to contact him. Whether he did so at his own initiative or that of Wesley or Eleanor Shea is unclear.

Rose also contacted a western group called the Willis Brothers, who traded as The Oklahoma Wranglers. Vic, Guy, and Skeeter Willis had grown up in rural Oklahoma, and had been making the rounds of five-hundred-watt stations before they ended up in Nashville in June 1946 after sending a demo to *Opry* manager Harry Stone. Rose offered them the same deal he offered Hank: a short-term, flat-fee, no-royalty contract with Sterling. Then Rose asked the Willis brothers to back Hank, who was to be arriving by himself from Montgomery, forewarning Vic Willis that Hank sang out of meter. Willis said that wouldn't be a problem because he and his brothers had backed a duo called Polly and Molly at the Kansas City Brushcreek Follies who were the world's worst at breaking meter.

The morning of December 11, 1946, arrived — and so did Hank Williams. He and the Willises rehearsed during the morning and then went to lunch at the Clarkston Hotel. The waitress asked Hank if he wanted a beer, and Hank replied, "No. You don't know ol' Hank. Hank don't just have *one* beer." Vic finished eating before the others and went back to the studio where Fred and Wesley were having a game of Ping-Pong. Fred asked Vic if Hank was drinking. Vic said, "No"; Fred said, "Good."

As their name suggests, the Wranglers played western music, and they were unimpressed by Hank Williams. "My brothers and I weren't used to anyone that *country,*" said Vic Willis. One episode in particular stuck in Willis's mind. Hank wouldn't pronounce "poor" properly on "Wealth Won't Save Your Soul." He sang the line as "[wealth] won't save your *purr* wicked soul." The Willises were supposed to join Hank on that line and sang "*poor* wicked soul," expecting Hank to wise up, but he didn't. Finally, in exasperation, Fred Rose said, "Dammit, Wranglers, sing it the way Hank does."

Just before the session, Rose gave Williams a prepared letter to sign in which Hank agreed to record for Rose in exchange for Union scale ($82.50) and to waive his right to future royalties. With his signature, Hank stepped onto what was, in every sense, the bottom rung of the ladder.

Hank cut four songs during his first session for Sterling. In addition to "Wealth Won't Save Your Soul," there were three other songs: "Calling You," (cribbed note-for-note from J. M. Henson's hymn "Watching You"), "Never Again," and "When God Comes and Gathers His Jewels." All four were traditional in form and execution, and only one, "Never Again," was secular. Sterling coupled "Calling You" and "Never Again," for the first record, and released it during the second week of January 1947. The recording quality was marginal, and the muddy overall sound was made worse by Sterling's pressing quality.

Billboard magazine reviewed Hank's debut in glowing terms: "With real spiritual qualities in his pipes, singing with the spirit of a camp . . . meeting, Hank Williams makes his bow an auspicious one." Whether the fulsom praise was related to a full-page advertisement that Sterling took out to promote their hillbilly and western debut is unclear, but it *is* clear that the *Billboard* reviewer understood more of what Hank was about than Sterling Records. Sterling's advertisement was a composite of everything that country music was trying to live down. Two hillbillies from the shallow end of the gene pool, holes in their britches and a bottle of hooch between them, are fiddling and, incongruously, playing a bull fiddle with a classical bow to greet Hank's debut. This was a reflection of the attitude that Fred Rose had railed against in his letter to *Billboard,* an attitude that still generally pervaded the media.

Sterling was almost as dismissive in its trade literature. "Hank Williams is the Acuff type of hillbilly," it said. "[He] sings a real country song, the kind folks buy." Then, in describing The Oklahoma Wranglers, it went on to say, "The Wranglers do a higher class song and can sell anywhere." It was not yet defiantly chic to be hillbilly.

Because of, or more likely despite, Sterling's efforts, Hank's first record sold well. Fred and Wesley Rose probably had a greater role in that success than Sterling. They were assiduous promoters of their copyrights. After one had been recorded, they would send the sheet music to every radio station that programmed country music to prompt the station's on-air performers to sing it. The Roses also had a full-time promo man, Mel Foree, who was sent on the road to hand out samples of the records to deejays and promote the copyrights at Saturday night radio jubilees. All this created what the industry calls a "buzz" around the songs and generated airplay royalties as well.

More than anything else, the success of Hank's first record showed that not every segment of the country music market was heading uptown as fast as some people thought. Hank's Sterling records were throwbacks to prewar hillbilly music. Without the electric guitar, they could as easily have been recorded ten or even twenty years earlier. The top-selling country record during the spring of '47 was Merle Travis's "So Round, So Firm, So Fully Packed." In that context, Hank's music was an anachronism. Travis's record had horn *obligati* and lyrical references to bobby-soxers, Frank Sinatra, and then-current ad slogans, like "The Pause That Refreshes." Hank sang of God, mother, and death.

Hank's second single, coupling "When God Comes and Gathers His Jewels" and "Wealth Won't Save Your Soul," was released three weeks later. Then, on February 13, 1947, Hank cut his second and last Sterling session. The Willis Brothers had signed with Mercury after their Sterling session, and Rose used a crew of WSM staff musicians. Murray Nash believes that one of the Sterling sessions was held at WLBJ in Bowling Green, Kentucky, an hour north of Nashville, and it's at least possible that the second session was held there, but more likely that it was held at WSM.

By now Rose had trawled through Hank's songbooks and demos and had selected four secular songs. On the second session, Hank came closer to defining his own sound. Two songs, "My Love for You (Has Turned to Hate)" and "Honky Tonkin'," were the clearest predictors of what he would deliver during the remaining five and a half years of his recording career. Hank had published "Honky Tonkin' " in his first song folio when it was called "Honkey-Tonkey" and contained the couplet "We are going to the city, to the city fair / We'll get a quart of whiskey and get up in the air." All of Hank's other Sterling songs were recorded much as he had written them before he met Rose, so it was almost certainly at Rose's behest that those lines were changed to: "We're going to the city, to the city fair / If you go to the city, baby, you will find me there." Even then, it's hard to know what Rose the skilled musician thought of a song that was delivered in one chord for fifteen and a half of its sixteen bars.

"Pan American" was about the Pan American Clipper, a train that ran on the Louisville and Nashville Railroad. As Hank related, the train ran daily from Cincinnati to New Orleans via Montgomery, highballing through Greenville, Georgiana, and other small southern towns without stopping. Since 1935, the Pan American Clipper's whistle had been broadcast every day over WSM in what was then a feat of remote engineering. Country folk would set their watches by it and could tell which engineer was at the throttle. Hank's melody came note-for-note from "The Wabash Cannonball," a Carter Family song that Roy Acuff performed regularly on the *Opry*.

The second Sterling session saw the birth of one of Hank's trademarks, the "crack" rhythm. It was the sound of the electric guitar keeping time on the deadened bass strings. Without drums in his lineup, Hank used the electric guitar to emphasize the pulse. It was the same sound that Johnny Cash later made into the centerpiece of his backing, often adding a rhythmic flourish to make "boom-chicka-boom."

By March 1947, Hank had two records on the market and two of his songs had been recorded by Molly O'Day, but he was still a virtual nonentity outside WSFA's listening area. He had a more or less permanent band for the first time, though. Don Helms had returned from the service and worked with Hank again for a while, but he quit and was replaced by R. D. Norred on steel guitar. Joe Penney, who took the stage name Little Joe Pennington, was on lead guitar, Lum York was on bass, and Winston "Red" Todd was on rhythm guitar. Hank sang, played occasional rhythm guitar and fiddle. Audrey joined them from time to time on bass and drums.

Norred was a fairly sophisticated musician, unhappy to find himself in a hillbilly band. He wanted to play western swing, not three-chord hillbilly music. Little Joe Pennington was from the Tampa Bay area. He replaced a guitarist called "Chris" Criswell in Hank's band. Criswell was also from Tampa, and Pennington had taken the job that Criswell had held down before he joined Hank. Then Criswell wanted his old job back because his wife wouldn't move to Montgomery. "He phoned me and said, 'Boy, you wanna get this job playing five or six nights a week,' " said Pennington. "He said he'd call Hank for me, and Hank says, 'Chris tells me you're a pretty good guitar man. Do ya want to come up and try it?' I said, 'Well, guess I could. Ain't there no good guitar players up around Montgomery there?' He said, 'None I'd want to hire.' Found out later he'd hired every one of them and run 'em off."

The promise of five or six nights' work a week was hollow too. The fact that he was now a recording artist made little difference to Hank's routine. He usually worked three or four schoolhouse dates a week. When the schools were closed up for the summer, he had to go back to working the joints. They were no place for a Sterling Recording Artist. Norred remembers one night in particular:

> We was playing a dance at a juke joint, and there was a poppin' sound and someone come up and said there was a fella out there shootin' with a gun. Directly, he come in. He was wearin' overalls — no shirt — and he had a big ol' loaded pistol and one of them bullets hit a heater and ricocheted 'round the room. Man, you talk about huntin' a table. Lum run into the girls' toilet — Hank had to go get him out. Another place down near Fort Deposit they had chicken wire out front of the bandstand so if they started throwing bottles they wouldn't hit the band.

Some of the band lived with Hank's mother, although Lum York lived with his own mother. Norred was paid fifty dollars a week whether they played or not because he had a family to support; the others were paid around seven dollars a gig. No one was getting rich, and no one in the band thought that Hank was on the brink of next-big-thingdom. "I couldn't stand Hank's music," says Norred. "I'd tell him so too. I'd make fun of it. He'd get on Audrey for not being able to sing, and I'd say, 'Hank, you ain't so hot y'self. I'm just puttin' up with you.' He wasn't nothin'. If you played with Hank, you was kinda looked down on."

For a few weeks toward the end of 1946 Hank headlined a Saturday afternoon jamboree with The Henley Harmony Boys featuring Leaborne Eads at the Capitol Stockyards in North Montgomery, a yard co-owned by the L. C. Henley Monument Company. The show was promoted by Marvin Reuben and Charlie Holt from WSFA, and Hank and the Harmony Boys performed off the auctioneers' stand, singing to around 250 people in the risers that had been erected for the cattle buyers. The show was starting to do decent business when Reuben and Holt decided that it would do as well without Hank and tore up his contract. Then they found out how big a draw he was when almost no one turned up the following week to listen to The Harmony Boys.

Those with no appreciation for Hank's music included most of the professional and technical staff at WSFA. They couldn't understand why he was so popular, and, as a consequence, never understood why another hillbilly singer who sounded as pitiful to their ears couldn't replicate Hank's popularity. The station management despised his unpredictability and occasional fits of arrogance, and would have dearly loved to rid themselves of him, but knew they couldn't. Hank knew it too.

During the early months of 1947, Hank probably sensed he was on the brink of getting out of Montgomery, and tried to stay straight, but something always happened to trigger a bender. Once, R. D. Norred remembers seeing a crowd gathered in the road and he went over to find his boss lying there with the cars going around him. The police came and hauled Hank home rather than to the drunk tank. Sterling Recording Artists were extended that small courtesy.

What success Hank found probably surprised even Fred Rose, who was watching Roy Acuff's sales slowly tail off and probably shared the view that hillbilly music was becoming an anachronism. The sales of the Sterling records made a believer out of Rose, but getting a true picture of his role in Hank's career at this juncture is made no easier by the fact that the Acuff-Rose story was later filtered through Wesley, who felt the need to cement himself to every critical moment in the company's history. Wesley never understood Hank, although he later asserted that they had been best buddies.

Born in Chicago on February 11, 1918, Wesley had stayed with his mother when Fred and his first wife divorced, and he hadn't seen his father since 1933. He became an accountant for Standard Oil in Chicago, and he never shed his accountant's skin. It wasn't until he made a trip to see an aunt in St. Louis in April 1945 that he was persuaded to visit Fred. When they met, Wesley didn't recognize Fred, and Fred, who was nearsighted, probably didn't recognize Wesley. Fred traveled to Chicago quite regularly because Acuff-Rose's first selling agent was there, and he began calling on Wesley. He offered him a job, but Wesley, who cared nothing for country music, and even less for the prospect of living in Nashville, stalled. He held out for the position of general manager with responsibility for all business decisions, and finally joined the family business in November or December 1945. His name quickly appeared on the letterhead just beneath the company slogan: "Songs for Home Folks."

Wesley's skills as an administrator were unquestionable. By common consensus he could be intransigent, but he was in a business in which intransigence and bloody-mindedness were minimum basic requirements. In hiring Wesley as the bad cop, Fred had freed himself to do what he did best: handle the music and the writers. After his father's death, Wesley began assuming credit for all manner of decisions and fancying himself a music man as well. His magnified view of his importance was reflected in sycophantic articles he commissioned, like "Wesley Rose Chooses Nashville — A Crucial Decision for the World of Music."

It was almost certainly Fred rather than Wesley who understood Hank's dilemma, though. Whatever promise there was in Hank was clearly being wasted at Sterling. The commitment to the label had now been worked off, but where was he to go? Fred took the Sterling recordings to New York and pitched them to Paul Cohen at Decca. Cohen told Rose that he was full up, but he found out that Hank was from Montgomery, and, as soon as Rose left the office, Cohen asked his secretary to call directory assistance in Montgomery. Hank didn't have a phone under his name, so Cohen called one of the cab companies to ask if they knew Hank. One of them did, and Cohen wired twenty dollars and instructions to find Hank and tell him to call Decca. When Hank called, Cohen gave him his spiel, offering him a recording and publishing contract. The way that Hank told it later, Cohen said, "What can Fred Rose do for you?" Hank said, "Well, he's doing pretty good. He's got you calling me," and hung up.

Rose had the best relationship with Art Satherley at Columbia, but Satherley clearly passed on Hank, although he hung on to an acetate of several songs that Rose sent him (which later surfaced on an Arhoolie Records EP and a Country Music Foundation album). RCA's head of folk and western music, Steve Sholes — the man who later signed Elvis Presley to the label — passed too, perhaps because he was tight with Hill and Range Music, Acuff-Rose's major competitor in the country market. Among the bigger labels, this only left Capitol, which was generally geared toward west coast country music, and Mercury, which had only just started recording country music, and wasn't a much better bet than Sterling.

A deal with a major or quasi-major label was crucial, though. Fred Rose knew that Hank couldn't follow the normal pattern for success, which involved working stations in ever bigger markets, then using the radio work as an entrée to recording. Hank was generally considered to be too much trouble and too hillbilly by half. He needed to reverse the paradigm by getting some hits that would convince a bigger station to take a chance on him, which would in turn increase his exposure. Records were the key.

*To travel hopefully is a better thing
than to arrive.*
Robert Louis Stevenson

Chapter

5

• •

THE YEAR OF THE LION

• • • • • • • • • • • • • • • • • • • •

*T*HERE was one more opportunity opening up for Fred Rose as he tried to place Hank Williams with a major record label in the spring of 1947. The giant Loews corporation, which owned MGM, was starting a record division. The same economic conditions that had prompted the formation of Sterling Records hadn't gone unnoticed farther up the corporate pecking order. MGM had seen songs from its fabled musicals go on to sell hundreds of thousands of records for other companies. The company had, for instance, stood by helpless while José Iturbi's "Polonaise in A-Flat" from *A Song to Remember* sold more than eight hundred thousand copies for RCA. This was income that Loews saw slipping through its fingers. Viewed from the outside, the record business in those immediate postwar years looked like a no-lose proposition, and Loews did what other corporations had done in similar circumstances: it tried to buy itself instant credibility in the marketplace.

The conduit to credibility was industry veteran Frank B. Walker, hired away from RCA in August 1945 to start MGM Records. Born in upstate New York in October 1889, Walker had, as he liked to tell Hank and Fred Rose, been cutting country records since before Hank was born. One of them had been the Coles' "Tramp on the Street." Walker had broken into the music business as a concert booker in Detroit after World War I. He joined Columbia Records in 1921, and, as the label's new head of "race" music, signed Bessie Smith in 1923. He recorded country music as well as blues on his field trips, and liked to recall how he rode horses back into the woods in search of a singer or musician whom someone had told him about. He sold records in the rural areas by renting a vacant storefront, setting up benches, playing the new releases, and taking in the cash himself. In 1933 Walker moved to RCA and started the Bluebird label. During the Second World War, he was seconded to the government's V-Disc production unit, resuming with RCA immediately afterward, before being seduced by MGM.

Walker had seen and done it all. He could talk as easily about injection molding in the plant as he could about the innards of music publishing or the respective merits of two cottonpatch blues singers. He was the sort of generalist who does not, or cannot, exist any more. Short and dapper, with steel-rimmed glasses and a patrician air, Walker wasn't entirely convincing in his attempt to make Hank feel like they were both ex-farm boys, but of all the record company CEOs in New York or Los Angeles, he was the only one with any understanding or firsthand knowledge of the traditions Hank Williams was drawing on.

MGM had made the commitment to launch a record division during the war, but it wasn't until Walker came on board that the company made plans to pay $3.5 million to convert a munitions plant in Bloomfield, New Jersey, into a pressing plant capable of churning out forty million discs a year. Walker also set up distribution through Zenith Radio stores, supplemented by a network of independent distributors. It was clear that he intended MGM Records to function as a major label from the outset. His first signings were in December 1946 for a scheduled launch in March 1947. Waving MGM's checkbook, Walker culled Jimmy Dorsey, Kate Smith, Ziggy Elman, and Billy Eckstine from the ranks of established artists whose contracts were up. His initial signings in what could loosely be termed country music were Sam Nichols, the Korn Kobblers, and a fifty-seven-year-old singing cowboy, Carson Robison, who had scored during the war with saber-rattlers like "We're Gonna Have to Slap the Dirty Little Jap (And Uncle Sam's the Guy Who Can Do It)."

To give MGM a little fillip at launch time, Walker lowballed the price of his records to sixty cents instead of the usual seventy-five cents, maintaining the lower price until May 1948. He had established the wisdom of lower introductory pricing when, in 1933, he had launched Bluebird Records at thirty-five cents. By the time Walker hiked the price of MGM product, the label had its first hits under its belt — one of them by Hank Williams.

Fred Rose offered Hank Williams to Frank Walker in a deal that saw him act as producer, or A&R Representative as the position was then known, in return for the music publishing, which at that time netted him 1.25 cents per song to be split fifty-fifty with the writer. This in itself was no bargain for Rose because the standard rate was two cents per song. When Hank's contract was renegotiated in April 1951, the publishing royalty (or "mechanical" as it was known) was increased to 1.5 cents. Rose himself was to receive no fee as producer; it was simply understood that he would use Acuff-Rose copyrights at every turn.

Most writing about Hank Williams has taken its cue from Wesley Rose who said that it was the success of "Honky Tonkin'" on Sterling that encouraged Fred to go seeking a better deal and pushed Walker over the threshold. This cannot have been the case, though. The MGM contract was dated March 6, 1947 — two months before "Honky Tonkin'" was released.

The contract became effective on April 1, 1947. It gave Hank an artist royalty for the first time. He was to receive two cents per record sold or roughly 3 percent of MGM's low list price of sixty cents. Three percent was, if anything, on the high side of what an untested act could expect. There is an apocryphal — but probably true — story that Hank didn't understand percentages and opted for the flat fee of one cent per side instead.

The first MGM session was aborted. Hank brought his WSFA band up to Nashville, but they clearly weren't up to the task. Lum York remembers that they cut "Move It on Over" and "On the Banks of the Old Pontchartrain" at the WSM studio. In an attempt to salvage the session, Rose brought in *Opry* star Red Foley's fiddle player, Tommy Jackson, to replace the man Hank had brought up, but they were still too ragged. Rose, who had his own credibility on the line as well as Hank's, threw one last ruined acetate disc into the trash can, then called a halt and scheduled another session for April 21, 1947, with Foley's complete band.

More than Hank, Rose knew how much was at stake with the first MGM single, and he knew that he had to make Walker feel good about his decision. Nashville had no career session men in April 1947, and the Foley band was the slickest in town. Rose probably figured that he needed a touch of class on the instrumental track to offset Hank's hillbilly edges. Guitarist Zeke Turner would play on several of Hank's sessions, and his brother Zeb would play several more. The yahoo aliases (Zeb and Zeke's real names were Edward and James Cecil Grishaw) disguised two of the more adroit pickers Hank ever used; they were perhaps too fancy for his taste. Brownie Reynolds played bass. Tommy Jackson, originally from Birmingham, Alabama, had played fiddle professionally since childhood. He was the only one of the group to go on to make a living in the studios as the scene opened up. Smokey Lohman was on steel guitar. This was a group capable of delivering exactly what Rose wanted, and more than what Hank wanted.

The first song Hank cut for MGM on April 21 was "Move It on Over." More than any other song he had recorded to that point, it betrayed his debt to black music. The melody was as old as the blues itself; a variant had done business as "Your Red Wagon" and another variant would become "Rock Around the Clock." Here was the first evidence that Hank, like Elvis Presley seven years later, never played black music in the tragically white way — over-souling and over-playing as if to compensate for some perceived lack. "Move It on Over" was a lazy record even at its brisk tempo. This may have been Tee-Tot's legacy to Hank, and if it was, it was worth all the nickels and dimes Hank had scrimped to pay him.

If its melody edged toward the public domain, the content of "Move It on Over" was pure Hank Williams. As Hank's future fiddle player, Jerry Rivers, once said, "[Hank's] novelty songs weren't novelty — they were serious, not silly, and that's why they were much better accepted and better selling. 'Move It on Over' hits right home, 'cause half of the people he was singing to were in the doghouse with the ol' lady."

The sound edged closer to Roy Acuff's preserve on "I Saw the Light," the second song they cut, and perhaps Hank's best-remembered hymn. If gospel composer Albert E. Brumley had been a litigious man, he would surely have sued over "I Saw the Light." Not only was the melody identical to his hymn "He Set Me Free," but the lyrics bore a passing resemblance too. The hugely prolific Brumley had published "He Set Me Free" in a 1939 songbook titled *The Gospel Tide.* It had been cut in March 1941 by The Chuck Wagon Gang, and had just been recorded by The Southern Joy Quartet.

Hank wrote as much as he wrote of "I Saw the Light" on the way back from a dance in Fort Deposit. If all the people who later claimed to be in the car with him that night had actually been there, Hank would have needed a twenty-passenger bus. One who claimed to be there was Leaborne Eads, who had handed out posters for the dance for Lillie. He remembers it this way:

Mizz Williams had given me money to hand out circulars at Fort Deposit. Hank was higher than a kite by the time the show was over. She drove home, and he was in the back seat sleepin' it off. There was a beacon light near Dannelly Field Airport, and Mizz Williams knew it always took time to get Hank awake when he was drunk like that, so she turned around and told him, "Hank, wake up, we're nearly home. I just saw the light." Between there and home he wrote the song.

Hank was the first to record "I Saw the Light," but he wasn't the first to release it. His version was held back until September 1948. On August 13, 1947, Clyde Grubbs recorded it for RCA, then, on November 18, the song's copublisher and spiritual mentor, Roy Acuff, recorded it. Both versions were released before Hank's.

The other two songs Hank recorded at his first MGM session, "(Last Night) I Heard You Crying in Your Sleep" and "Six More Miles (to the Graveyard)," were used as flip sides for "Move It on Over" and "I Saw the Light," respectively. An embryonic version of "(Last Night) I Heard You Crying in Your Sleep" exists as a lyric sheet in the Alabama Department of Archives and History. The words are almost completely different, but it's hard to know if this is early evidence of Fred Rose's rewriting Hank's lyrics, Hank's rewriting them at Rose's behest, or Hank's rethinking the song without prompting from any corner. Once again, his melody fell short on originality; it shaded toward a couple of old-timey songs like "I Loved You Better Than You Knew."

"Move It on Over" was released on June 6, 1947, and it became Hank's first *Billboard* chart entry two months later. On August 21, 1947, two and a half months after "Move It on Over" was released, Hank received his first extended write-up in the Montgomery *Examiner*. Calling him the "spur-jangling Sinatra of the western ballad," the writer stated that Hank had already sold over one hundred thousand copies of "Move It on Over." Then, inviting hoots and howls from those close to Hank, the article continued: "Where the inspiration for the song came from [Hank] couldn't say. . . . It's not his own married life. Mr. and Mrs. Hank Williams lead a model domestic life."

Around the same time, there was another write-up on Hank, this one by the Reverend A. S. Turnipseed in the Montgomery *News.* Turnipseed had evidently attended one of Hank's auditorium shows. He described the audience as young and "not dressed as to indicate any affluence." It was, he noted, a mostly restrained crowd. "Any preacher who has preached in the rural sections of the white counties of Alabama has observed the same restraint even when highly emotional preaching was going on," he said. Turnipseed noted that fully half of Hank's program was devoted to comedy routines and horseplay. There was one religious number, but the only time the crowd was whipped up was when Hank sang "Move It on Over" and "Pan American." Turnipseed concluded by trying to put Hank in a broader context. Changes were taking place in Montgomery as red-dirt farmers like Hank moved into town, he said, challenging the right to rule of the state's old-money families. "As Hank Williams plays," Turnipseed noted apocalyptically, "Rome is burning."

Beneath the bluster was a half-valid point. There *was* a migration into town from the rural communities, and if the new migrants weren't challenging the old money's right to rule, they were certainly bringing their music with them. That's why Hank had a ready-made audience when he eventually appeared not only in Montgomery, but in places like Cleveland, Washington, and even Oakland. He was like a letter from home.

On August 4, just as "Move It on Over" was breaking, Hank was brought back into the studio. Two of the four songs he recorded, "Fly Trouble" and "I'm Satisfied with You," were songs that Fred Rose had a hand in writing. During the '40s, it was common to release a new record just as a hit was peaking, which seems like commercial hara-kiri from this distance. So "Fly Trouble" was released in September 1947 just as "Move It on Over" reached its high-water mark — number four on *Billboard*. It was written by Rose and the blackface comedy team of Jam Up and Honey, and it was modeled on slick west coast country novelty songs, like "Smoke! Smoke! Smoke! (That Cigarette)." The record seemed to signal Rose's intention of easing Hank uptown. From the hokey lyrics to Zeke Turner's jazzy guitar breaks, the entire production was precisely what Hank's music was *not* about, and it was precisely what red-dirt farmers who had just moved to town did *not* want to hear.

Rose placed "On the Banks of the Old Pontchartrain" on the flip side of "Fly Trouble." It was a ballad in the traditional mold, written by Kathleen Ramona Vincent, a crippled woman who, the best anyone remembers, was from Louisiana. She had mailed it to Hank as a poem, and he had put a melody to it. One of the least typical entries in his canon, it told the saga of an escaped convict who, before his recapture, finds his hard heart melted by a woman he meets on the bank of Lake Pontchartrain. The folk-based melody that Hank used was one of his most affecting, but the single flopped miserably, and in later years Hank would use "Fly Trouble" and "On the Banks of the Old Pontchartrain" as a personal metaphor for a poor-selling record. More than anything, it proved how much Rose had yet to learn about Hank's music and his audience.

At this point, Hank was no more than a sidebar to Fred Rose's activities and he was still far from MGM's best-selling artist. In October 1947, Rose was in Chicago producing Bob Wills's last Columbia session on behalf of Art Satherley. As Satherley knew, Wills was leaving Columbia, and had been seduced by Frank Walker. The acquisition of Bob Wills seemed at the time to be the coup that Walker needed to reinforce his country division. By the end of that October, MGM's country roster consisted of Wills, Williams, Carson Robison, Denver Darling (a singing cowboy), Jerry Irby (writer of the beer-joint anthem "Driving Nails in My Coffin"), and another Rose protégé, Rome Johnson. Robison would give the country division its biggest hit in 1948 with "Life Gits Tee-Jus, Don't It." Bob Wills's career was in a slow, inexorable decline, and it would be another year and a half before Hank got his career back on track.

"Move It on Over" gave Hank the first serious money he had ever seen. When he talked to the Alabama *Journal* in 1947, he estimated that his songwriting alone would bring him between $15,000 and $20,000 that year. Hank put some of the money toward a down payment on a house — his first — at 10 Stuart Avenue in Montgomery, and some toward Audrey's first fur coat. Where the rest went isn't clear. Even if Hank overstated his income to the newspaper, as he would often do, he should have had enough for a full down payment. As it was, Citizens Realty (owned by Bill Perdue, who co-owned Radio Recording, where Hank cut his songwriting demos) had to give Hank the commission it made on the sale to help him with the $2,200 down payment he needed.

One possible destination of the "Move It on Over" money was 318 North McDonough Street, a large boardinghouse that Lillie appears to have purchased in 1948. Perhaps she had made it unambiguously clear that she had got Hank's career off the ground, supporting him from the first guitar to the first hit, and now the bill was due. Lillie had married yet again. J. C. Bozard was history, and on March 1, 1947, she had married one of her boarders, W. W. "Bill" Stone. Everyone liked Stone, who was a widower several years younger than Lillie, but he wasn't up to the task of helping Lillie manage Hank from the sidelines. He had been a taxi driver at one point and had apprenticed as a carpenter with Crump Craft. He was working at Pelham and Shell Antique Reproduction Furniture when he married Lillie, and later he got Hank's cousin Walter McNeil into the company as an apprentice.

Number 10 Stuart Avenue was small, boxy, and sparsely furnished, and Audrey spent money that should have gone into stocking the icebox on toney metal awnings over the windows. It might have been home, but what Hank found, now that he was away from the boardinghouse, was that he hated to be alone. If Audrey and Lycrecia were out of town, he would do anything to avoid being in his little house by himself. "He'd come over to where I lived," said Lum York. "He'd say, 'Come on, go with me.' I'd say, 'Where you goin'?' He said, 'I'm goin' to the house.' I'd say, 'Hank, I don't want to go out there. All you gonna do is git a funny book and sit there and read, and I'll be sittin' there with nobody to talk to.' " Like many entertainers, Hank always needed an audience. Nothing unsettled him more than his own company.

Lycrecia insists that times were good on Stuart Avenue. Others, particularly band members, tend to remember only the spats. Both Hank and Audrey had low boiling points, and, as ever, arguments would blow up out of inconsequentialities. Once, Hank called the Radio Hospital to come over to repair his wire recorder (the forerunner of the tape recorder) and the bill came to $17.50. Audrey started hissing at him for squandering all that money on his recorder, and Hank grabbed Audrey's fur coat and began trashing it. The repairman ran for the door. A couple of days later, Lillie appeared at the store with the $17.50. Peace had returned to Stuart Avenue.

On another occasion, Fred and Irella Beach were at Hank's house working up a new song. "Audrey was whining and whining," said Irella. "Then Hank said, 'Fred, let's us try another song,' and Audrey went storming off into the bedroom and sent her little girl into the living room. She said, "My momma says for you all to go home.' When we left, Hank was yelling at Audrey and screamin' at her like nothin' you ever heard. He hit her hard, too."

The Beaches had walked in on one of the problems that would plague Hank and Audrey's relationship for years. From the time they had married, Audrey had been a part of the show. She had played bass, even drums on occasion, and sang. Now she sensed Hank distancing himself from her professionally. She wanted to be more than a happy homemaker, which would be easier to applaud if she could have sung even passably well. It's hard to know if Hank was now trying to ease her out of the picture simply because she couldn't sing, or because he thought she should be at home baking. Clearly it was a source of tension between them. In a letter to Fred Rose dated August 19, 1947, Hank mentioned that he had mailed a demo of himself and Audrey singing "I Saw the Light," which still hadn't been released by Hank or recorded by Acuff.

"We didn't do much on [it]," he wrote, as if trying to discourage Rose from doing much about it either. "We never had tried it until we went to make the record." Rose certainly had no problem resisting the notion that Hank and Audrey should record together, but as Hank became more successful and Audrey more insistent, their pairing on record became inevitable.

If Rose didn't know it already, the demo would have told him that Audrey's voice sounded like fingernails scraping down a blackboard. She was shrill and tuneless, and her problems were compounded by a weak sense of time. "Audrey couldn't carry a tune in a bucket," said R. D. Norred, "and the more she practiced, the worse she got." Her duets with Hank were like an extension of their married life — she fought him for dominance on every note. For the present, she would be confined to occasional show dates and morning radio in Montgomery, but she would not be denied much longer.

In late 1947 music trade papers were consumed with talk of the upcoming recording ban. It was fairly clear that the American Federation of Musicians would call the ban effective December 31, 1947, when the agreements expired with all the record companies. The root of the problem was a dinosaur named James C. Petrillo, a failed trumpet player from Chicago who held the post of president of the AFM as a virtual fiefdom. Petrillo was bitterly opposed to records, the use of records on radio as well as the network broadcasting of live and prerecorded music, all of which he considered inimical to his members' best interests. The AFM's agreements with radio were good until 1949, but, with the recording agreements running out at the end of 1947, Petrillo wanted to send a message to the networks via the record companies. It was a more direct hit than it might seem because two of the three major labels, RCA and Columbia, were owned by NBC and CBS, respectively. As a long-term goal, Petrillo wanted to shut down the record business; one of his oft-repeated lines was, "These records are destroying us." In the short term, though, he wanted to test the union's strength against the Taft-Hartley bill, wrest a few financial concessions from the record companies, and fire a warning shot over the bows of the radio networks.

Petrillo's first attempt at strangling the record business had come a few years earlier. A recording ban had lasted from August 1942 until various points in late 1943 and early 1944, when the companies one by one agreed to the AFM's new rates. In 1947 the companies were ready for a long siege and were stockpiling masters as year-end approached. The majors viewed the ban as a blessing in disguise; they could work through their backlog of masters, press up catalog, squeeze out the independent labels and, as one unnamed executive said, there would be "no placating artists with expensive sessions."

Petrillo's quixotic crusades against records for home use and broadcasting as well as the networking of live broadcasts were all doomed. Fewer remotes of live broadcasts were being picked up every year, and, in a parallel move, more deejays were being hired. And, by 1947, the growth of the home record market was a tide that no one — least of all Petrillo — could stem.

Down in Montgomery, Hank Williams was unwittingly caught up in the dispute, the ramifications of which he almost certainly didn't understand. All he knew was that he was being called to Nashville for two sessions on November 6 and 7, 1947, with the aim of having eight usable sides that could be doled out over the length of the strike. MGM, in business for only nine months, had more reason to feel jittery than the other major labels because its overhead was already high and its back catalog was shallow.

"We had worked up some songs 'cause of the ban coming," says R. D. Norred:

Fred Rose had called Hank and told him to get his songs together, and we had maybe fifteen worked up. I knew you made forty dollars a session, so I went down to Art Freehling's [Music Store] and got me a real steel guitar and we was ready to go. We had it pretty well complete, then Fred come down to go over things, and he said he couldn't use the band. Hank said, "Why?" and Fred says, "You know how Lum was the last time he was up there. Fidget, fidget, it took all night cutting songs. This time, you ain't gonna get to try it twice." He said, "Them staff musicians up there, you're not gonna have to practice with them boys, you just do your part and they'll do theirs." Hank said, "Well, I'll take Norred with me, anyway," and Fred said, "No, you just can't put Norred with Zeke Turner and expect it to work." Hank didn't like it, but there wasn't too much he could say about it.

When Hank got to Nashville, he was paired with a group drawn from several *Opry* bands. Zeke Turner was there again. The steel guitarist was Jerry Byrd. Both were still with Red Foley. One of Bill Monroe's Blue Grass Boys, Chubby Wise, was on fiddle. The first song they cut, "Rootie Tootie," was a Fred Rose song that Rose also pitched to Pee Wee King and country bandleader Paul Howard. All three versions were released in January 1948. Rose later did very well from King's version when it got a free ride on the flip side of "Tennessee Waltz." Then they recut "Honky Tonkin' " despite the fact that the Sterling version was available.

The following day, Hank cut "Mansion on the Hill." For years the story circulated that Hank had written the song in a side room when he first met Fred Rose to prove that he was indeed writing his own material and not buying it. Twenty-five years later, Audrey put a different spin on the story:

> Fred said . . . , "To prove to me you *can* write, I'm gonna give you a title, and I want you to take it back to Montgomery and write a song around it." Hank worked with it and worked with it, but he never could do too much good with it, and the reason he couldn't was because it wasn't his idea. One night I had just finished with the dinner dishes, and I started singing "Tonight down here in the valley . . ." After I got through with it, I took it in to Hank and said, "Hank, what do you think of this?" He really liked it, and it was a mixture of my lyrics, Hank's lyrics, and Fred Rose's lyrics. Hank sent it in, and for a long time I wouldn't tell anybody that I had anything to do with that because I wanted it to be all Hank.

The reason Hank had a problem with "Mansion on the Hill" was that he was very weak at writing narrative ballads. All of his best songs were interior snapshots. The only shred of personal experience he could draw on for "Mansion on the Hill" was unrequited ardor he had once had for the daughter of the mayor of Montgomery. Boots Harris remembers driving him around in Lillie's station wagon looking for her night after night in theater lineups, knowing all the while that she was unattainable. Perhaps a little of that surfaced in the song.

Hank set "Mansion on the Hill" to a melody he had poached from Bob Wills's 1938 recording of "I Wonder If You Feel the Way I Do," a tune Wills himself might have found in the public domain. Released in December 1948, just as the ban was ending, "Mansion on the Hill" did little business until March 1949, when it was caught up in the tidal wave of Hank's career.

The two pre-record ban sessions were a template for the years ahead. Under Rose's guidance, Hank began to realize his strengths and weaknesses as a writer, and he brought along songs that showed a steady improvement. The sessionmen might have looked down their noses at Hank's music, but they were attuned to the essential challenge, that of bringing the Acuff sound into the honky-tonk. Rose's role was to hone Hank's songs before the session and work with the pickers during the session to keep a tight commercial focus. He seemed happier now to let Hank follow his instincts, although he was still bringing along frothy little novelties like "Rootie Tootie" for Hank to record. He may have force-fed them to Hank to double his money from a song, but it's likelier that Hank simply wasn't generating enough material that Rose considered worth releasing.

By the time the ban came into effect, Hank's band was still composed of R. D. Norred, Lum York, Little Joe Pennington, and Red Todd. The stability in the lineup was itself an indication of the growing confidence level around Hank. That November it looked as though Rose would land them a gig on WLAC in Nashville, which would be a step toward the *Opry*. Pennington recalled the group buying matching outfits in anticipation:

> We'd ordered in western outfits. Pea-green shirts, western-cut khaki pants, and western boots. Marie Harvell did appliqué embroidery on the shirts from a pattern that you ironed on. We were a real band when we had suits like that, but those outfits cost thirty dollars each, and thirty dollars was about what we made a week, and we had to pay our board out of that. Hank paid for all the outfits when the order come in. He said, "Boys, any y'all got the money you can pay me off, the rest that don't, come on down to the loan company and we'll sign you up." So Lum and Red and me went down and signed up with the Montgomery Loan and Finance Company to pay off these outfits.

The loan agreements were dated November 3, 1947.

Rose's approach to WLAC fell through, so it was still a rare day when the band got more than a day's drive out of Montgomery. One occasion that Norred remembers was when Hank was booked as a supporting act on a show in Birmingham. Pennington discovered that it was a union gig, checked with the union hall and found out that scale (the minimum that could be paid) was roughly twice what Hank was paying:

> Hank said, "I want y'all in the back room." We got in there and he said, "Who's the little bright boy been down to the union of-

fice?" Joe said, "I did." Hank said, "Did you find out what you
wanted to know down there?" Joe said, "Yeah, union scale is
fifteen dollars." So he paid us. Joe said, "I just wanted to make
sure I was gonna get what was coming to me," and Hank said —
sarcastic like — "Friend, you'll get what's comin' to you."

It was a pattern Hank would follow throughout his professional life;
later, he would leave a twenty-dollar tip for a thirty-five-cent breakfast,
or simply forget where he had stashed the night's takings, but he would
still chisel his band members out of five bucks if he could.

When the approach to WLAC fell through, Hank could do no more
than cement his already high standing around Montgomery. As he told
the Montgomery *News* that year, "I got the popularest daytime program
on this station" (the nighttime programming was drawn from the NBC
feed). "Fans?" he said. "There's a mob of them up here [at WSFA] every
mornin' and every afternoon. Some come from fifty miles. A lady from
Opelika wrote me just this mornin'. She says, 'Hank, How much do it
cost to come up and hear you sing? If it don't cost too much, we may
come up there.' " Hank read his audience well. "If anyone in my business knew as much about their business as the public did," he said ellip-
tically, "they'd be all right." Whether this was a covert knock at Rose for
trying to steer him uptown, or the radio station management, which still
couldn't penetrate his appeal, is unclear.

During the spring of 1948, the group landed a regular gig at the 31
Club, a juke joint in Montgomery with a big dance area. Then, on April 8,
a package show came to the Charles Theater. Cowboy Copas and Johnny
Bond were the stars, and Hank was to open for them while the group
kept his spot warm at the 31 Club. Perhaps he was drunk, but for some
reason he didn't go over too well at the Charles. Johnny Bond took it
upon himself to tell the people of Montgomery not to take Hank for
granted. "You people don't know 'bout this boy here," Bond told the
crowd. "He won't be 'round here very long. His records are going like
wildfire all over the west coast."

Hank had promised that he would bring the headliners back to the
31, so the band was surprised when Bond appeared without Hank.
"Johnny come in, sang a song," remembered Pennington, "and we said,
'Is Hank with y'all?' One of them said, 'Well, the last we saw him, him
and Copas was backstage with a couple of women and a bottle.' R.D.
said, 'Well, you needn't look for him for a while.' "

Two or three nights later, Hank showed up. He hadn't shaved since before the Charles show, and was still pitifully hungover. He went up to the bandstand and tried to play a few songs, but he'd known better nights. He tried to smooth things over with the bartender, who was also the owner, but it didn't work, and he staggered off into the night. The band was offered Hank's job and they took it. "Now, who's gonna tell Hank?" said Pennington.

They decided I was gonna do it, and me and Red went up there — a sanatorium somewhere. Audrey was up there and Hank was propped up in bed. They knew where to take him. Hank said, "How you fellas doing? What's happening down at the club?" I said, "Well the owner's fixin' to get another band." Hank said, "Oh?" I said, "Well, he's offered us the job, and we thought we'd go ahead and take it." He said, "Well, do what you want to," and he got kinda surly.

Hank probably never got another regular gig or a band while he was in Montgomery. His life was always a series of peaks and troughs; many times the trough seemed more like a downward spiral from which he would never recover, but he would pull himself back just in time. He did it so many times that he probably made the fatal mistake of thinking he could always do it. Hank was in one of his deepest troughs during the spring of 1948. The first indication that something was wrong had come in February, when Audrey took Lycrecia back to her parents' farm near Banks, and returned alone to Montgomery.

On March 18, Fred Rose composed the following letter to Hank. It clearly shows that Hank was straining the loyalty of everyone close to him.

I feel kinda let down today after receiving your call 'cause I knew you were drinking again, and Hank that is something I refuse to go for because I know it only proves a man's weakness.

If you love Audry [sic], why don't you try and straighten out and be man enough to tell her you love her and are willing to change and treat her like you love her. Both times I visited you folks I noticed you bossing her around for my benefit and I knew she would get filled up one of these days and get enough. If I talked to Lorene the way I heard you talk to Audry, she would walk out in nothing flat and I wouldn't blame her one bit . . .

If you really want Audry back, get a haircut and buy a new

suit, wash your face and throw that damn whiskey bottle out the window, and become a man that she would be proud to have back. A woman always wants a man, not the bum that whiskey makes out of a man.

I am trying to be your friend 'cause I know you need a friend. The guys that are drinking with you are not your friends, they just like the whiskey you buy and when you run out of money enough to buy them whiskey they will leave you all by yourself and tell everyone you are a drunk . . . I know what I'm talking about because I've gone through the same thing . . .

Don't get the idea I'm trying to bawl you out because I'm just trying to see you become what I know you can become when you act like the swell guy that I remember.

Please don't phone me when you are drinking as it only makes me feel like I'm being let down by a guy I felt would never let me down.

The following day, March 19, Rose wrote another letter to Hank, his patience now at the breaking point.

Wesley tells me you called this morning for more money, after me wiring you four hundred dollars just the day before yesterday. . . . We have gone as far as we can go at this time and cannot send you any more.

Hank, I have tried to be a friend of yours but you refuse to let me be one, and I feel that you are just using me for a good thing and this is where I quit. You have been very unfair, calling my house in the middle of the night and I hope that you will not let it happen again as it isn't fair to Lorene.

When you get ready to straighten out, let me know and maybe we can pick up where we left off, but for the present I am fed up with all your foolishness.

The letter was signed, "Your friend, Fred Rose."

On April 3, Hank sold his house at 10 Stuart Avenue. He got his $2,200 deposit back, and the new owner assumed the $10,000 mortgage. Then, on April 8, there was the fiasco at the Charles Theater, and the commitment in the sanatorium that followed. On April 28 Audrey filed for divorce. "Hank Williams my husband is twenty-four years of age," she said in her complaint. "He has a violent and ungovernable temper. He drinks a great deal, and during the last month, he has been drunk most of the time. My nervous system has been upset and I am afraid to live with him any longer." On May 26 Hank and Audrey were divorced.

Clearly, in March and April 1948 Hank was burning every bridge that connected him to his personal and professional lives. In Audrey's complaint and Rose's letter we can sense the frustrations involved in dealing with him on a regular basis. He was manipulative, selfish, violent and indiscriminately unfaithful when drunk, and now apparently drunk much of the time. If, as everyone says, Audrey was a shrew, then Hank was doing nothing to encourage her to be otherwise. She saw Hank's talent, saw him shooting himself in the foot, damning himself to the joints of south-central Alabama, and she railed against it. Like Lillie, she saw the alcoholism in terms of self-control, a view that was reinforced by the fact that there were times when Hank *could* control it.

After the separation, Hank moved back to Lillie's boardinghouse. His old band members would see him there sometimes sitting on the swing, wearing his hat and his suit. He had clearly bottomed out and it appeared that he was finding his equilibrium again. He and Audrey reconciled, although the divorce proceeded. The bridge to Acuff-Rose was mended, and later in April Hank formally signed with the company. Fred Rose put him on a fifty-dollar-a-month draw against future earnings, the first such arrangement he had made. Hank and Audrey used the money to vacation in Norfolk, Virginia, that June. By that point, Hank knew he was leaving town sooner or later. Fred Rose was on the case.

Rose knew that he had to get Hank out of Montgomery, and onto a station with more wattage, but Hank was still tainted with the twin curses of unreliability and drunkenness. The industry was small, and even though Hank hadn't been far outside south-central Alabama, his reputation had. The *Opry* was out of the question, but Saturday night jamborees were proliferating.

Down in Shreveport, Louisiana, a maximum-wattage station, KWKH, had started a Saturday night jamboree while Hank was on his springtime bender. It didn't have any big-name acts yet, but it was the best Fred Rose could get. On Thursday, July 29, 1948, Hank signed off WSFA. He and Audrey packed their belongings and headed for Louisiana. One way or another, Hank had to get out of Montgomery, and Shreveport seemed to be the place for him to take his stand.

I'll tune up my fiddle, rosin up my bow,
I'll make myself welcome where ever I go.
"Rye Whiskey" (Unknown)

Chapter

6

• •

THE HAYRIDE

• • • • • • • • • • • • • • • • • • •

*S*HREVEPORT, two hundred miles east of Dallas and hundreds of miles from anywhere else, had a brief, half-serious chance of preempting Nashville, itself a torpid, isolated southern city, as the general headquarters of country music. It might just have happened if, at a moment that, as always, is blindingly obvious with hindsight, those who controlled the purse strings had appreciated what they had and had been prepared to invest.

During a seven-year period between 1948 and 1954, Shreveport's *Louisiana Hayride* gave the first decent break to Webb Pierce, Faron Young, Johnnie and Jack, Kitty Wells, Johnny Horton, Slim Whitman, Jim Reeves, the Browns, Elvis Presley, Johnny Cash, Tommy Sands, Claude King, Billy Walker, and Hank Williams. One by one, they all left, together with a crew of backing musicians that included James Burton, Floyd Cramer, and Jerry Kennedy. If only some had been induced to stay, Shreveport might have taken a run at Nashville's preeminence, which had only recently been established and was that much more vulnerable. As it was, the *Hayride* simply became an *Opry* farm club, or, as it called itself after everyone had left, the Cradle of the Stars.

Just as WSM was the key to Nashville's preeminence, KWKH could have made Shreveport's hillbilly music industry achieve critical mass. The station had been launched in 1922, the creation of W. K. Henderson, whose initials it bore. Henderson used its megawattage to conduct quixotic crusades against chain stores and the like, and his abuse of clear-channel wattage (whereby the frequency was assigned exclusively to one station) made him one of the first targets of the Federal Communications Commission. Hillbilly music had been a staple of the station's programming as far back as the mid-thirties. Jimmie Davis, copyright holder of "You Are My Sunshine," and twice governor of Louisiana, was one of the first to launch a career from KWKH; Davis had even made his first recordings for Henderson's short-lived "Doggone" Station label.

In 1936, KWKH sponsored the Sunday afternoon *Hillbilly Amateur Show*, hosted by Bob and Joe Shelton (The Sunshine Boys), a show that was, in fact, anything but amateur. In 1940, the show switched time slots and became the *Saturday Night Roundup*, and the Sheltons were joined by the Rice Brothers and several others. The *Roundup* was discontinued during the war, when the draft claimed most of the performers and gas rationing grounded the rest.

At some point in the late '20s, KWKH had become the property of John Ewing, who owned a little media empire in what's known as the Ark-La-Tex, where Arkansas, Louisiana, and Texas converge. Ewing's daughter, Helen, married Henry B. Clay, a naval pilot originally from Atlanta. Before the war, Clay had managed a radio station in Florence, Alabama, and, as part of Helen's dowry, he was handed KWKH. It was Clay who provided the impetus to resume the jamboree, and he handed over responsibility for its programming to Horace Logan.

Logan had joined KWKH as an announcer in 1932 after winning a contest, and he stayed until he was drafted. After the war he opened a gun shop, but was asked to return to KWKH to take over the morning shift and act as program director. "They were toying with the idea of starting another show like the *Saturday Night Roundup* but hadn't reached a decision," he says. "Then after I came back, they decided that they would go with it because I had worked with the prior show."

Louisiana Hayride was a name that was associated with Huey P. Long, governor of Louisiana. One of the first books about Long was Harnett P. Kane's *Louisiana Hayride: The American Rehearsal for Dictatorship*, published in 1941. There had also been a pop hit in 1932 called "Louisiana Hayride" from the Broadway show *Flying Colors*, so it was a far from original name. Logan says he decided upon it because he wanted something that would "connote country music — and then localize it."

Logan also takes credit for the show's presentation. He went to the *Opry* for what he claims was his first and only visit, and came away with a rival vision.

With the *Opry,* they'd bring a guy on, and you'd have to suffer through him for a half-hour whether you liked him or not. He'd bring on some guests, but essentially you had the same guy, say, Roy Acuff, for a half-hour. If you liked him, it was great; if you didn't, it wasn't. My idea was to put the artists in extreme competition with each other. If they were going to be stars, they had to establish themselves and then reestablish themselves every Saturday night. When one of my artists came onstage, he did two numbers. If he encored, he came back later and did another two numbers, and that was all for the evening. It forced the artists to reestablish their eminence; it was a terribly difficult show to work.

The only venue for the *Hayride* was Shreveport's 3,800-seat Municipal Auditorium, a capacity marginally higher than the Ryman Auditorium where the *Opry* was staged. The first *Louisiana Hayride,* held on April 3, 1948, was headlined by the Bailes Brothers, Johnnie and Jack, with Johnnie's wife, Kitty Wells, and a supporting cast of also-rans that included Curley Kinsey, Harmie Smith, Tex Grimsley, and Pappy Covington's band.

When Hank arrived in Shreveport four months after the *Louisiana Hayride* started, the show had nowhere near the clout that it did when he left. Not one of the performers had yet had a hit, and it was just another Saturday night jamboree. The attraction for Hank lay in KWKH's clear channel; KWKH's fifty thousand watts (compared with WSFA's one thousand) meant that the *Hayride,* like the *Opry,* blanketed much of the eastern United States. The only stations with more power were the five-hundred-thousand-watt stations, like XER, which operated just across the border in Mexico, and they obliterated everything within fifty kilocycles of their frequency path. Fifty thousand watts was enough for Hank Williams and Fred Rose, though, and Hank became equally as good for KWKH and the *Hayride* as they became for him. Their stars rose in tandem.

Quite how Hank came to join the *Hayride* is still a matter of speculation. Most of the key players are long dead, and Horace Logan's account strains credibility:

When we started the *Hayride,* we publicized it through *Cashbox* and *Billboard* and the like, and we immediately started getting deluged with audition tapes to be on the show. Hank was one of

the fellows who phoned in, but [it was] Fred Rose [who] decided
to try and get Hank on the *Hayride*. He called KWKH and talked
to Henry Clay, and Henry talked to me about it. I'd heard of Hank
Williams, heard his records on some little ol' label. I'd also heard
that he was a drunk. I suggested that we tell Fred Rose if Hank
could stay sober for six months and prove it, we'd put him on the
Hayride. Hank called me every week, and almost invariably he
would have the manager of his radio station with him. "Mr.
Logan, Hank has been sober, he's been here every morning, he
hasn't missed a single morning. He's sober as a judge," and
Hank'd say, "That's right! I'm sober." And at the end of six
months, we told him to come on over.

It's entirely plausible that Hank tried to get on KWKH before Rose got
into the picture, but it was unlikely that the manager of WSFA would
have smiled benignly while his star attraction was trying to secure a job
elsewhere. And, of course, Hank was anything but sober during the six
months before he joined the *Hayride*.

The key factor that landed Hank the spot on the *Hayride* was probably Fred Rose's long-standing relationship with Dean Upson, commercial manager of KWKH since 1946. Upson had been one of the Vagabonds
who had been on WSM when Rose had first come to Nashville in the
'30s. The pair had written songs together, and it's likely that Rose prevailed upon Upson to give Hank a place on the *Hayride* and find him
some sponsored morning shows. To confuse the issue, though, Johnnie
Bailes, one of the Bailes Brothers, insisted that he had known Hank for
several years, and in interviews before his death, he said that he arrived
at KWKH one day to find Hank leaning disconsolately against a parking
meter. Hank told Bailes he had been turned down by KWKH, and Bailes,
who was the show's star attraction, says that he went to see Upson to
insist that Hank be hired.

It's at least possible that Hank's reputation was already so bad that it
took Bailes, Rose, and Upson to prevail upon Henry Clay and Horace
Logan. What *is* clear, though, is that KWKH wasn't mortgaging the farm
to acquire Hank. He wasn't offered a long-term contract, and, like the
Opry, the *Hayride* paid only American Federation of Musicians scale.
Financially, Hank was going to be in worse shape than if he had stayed in
Montgomery; only the exposure afforded by KWKH made the move at-
tractive.

Hank and Audrey went to Shreveport one Friday afternoon in July

1948 to discuss their prospects with Clay and Logan. The next day, Hank sat with the KWKH regulars at the Bantam Grill opposite the studio and chewed it all over. Homer, another of the Bailes Brothers, went to get Tillman Franks, who, he told Hank, held the key to foraging what little money there was to be had from Shreveport and the vicinity. Franks, at one time or another, has been a bass player, booking agent, songwriter, song plugger, producer, and manager. He made, lost, and — to some extent — remade his pile managing or booking acts like Johnny Horton, Claude King, David Houston, Faron Young, Webb Pierce, and Elvis Presley. On that day in July 1948, Tillman, like everyone else in the Bantam Grill, was broke.

Hank said Henry Clay had offered him fifty dollars a week. He said he couldn't live on that, but if I booked him into schools, he'd come over. I said I'd do my best, but people didn't really know him. I told him, "If you can get a program on the radio and announce a few times that you're open for bookings I'll take a crack at it." I was starvin', and me and my wife was living with my mom and daddy, and I invited Hank and Audrey out for Sunday dinner. We had a catfish supper and Hank and Audrey really put it away. After the meal, Hank sat down at this old upright piano and played "When the Roll Is Called up Yonder" and "Will the Circle Be Unbroken," chording the piano like a guitar and Audrey was singing with him. After he'd finished playing my daddy got me in a corner and he said, "Son, I hope you ain't thinking of making any money with him, 'cause he just cain't sing."

Then Hank launched into one of his set pieces:

He was talking about how he had to leave Montgomery 'cause he owed ever'body in town. He said, "I bought this stove and bed on credit at this furniture store, and ever' month they'd send me a nasty note, and ever' month they was getting nastier. I went down to see the owner of the place, and said, "I'm Hank Williams. I thought I'd come by and tell y'all how I pay my bills." The guy said, "Good," and Hank said, "Ever' month I take ever'one I owe, I write their names on a little bit of paper, put them all in a hat, shake 'em up real good, and I pull out one name and that's the one I pay. You write me one more nasty note and even if I pull your name out, it's going back in the hat."

This was one of the routines Hank had developed for shows around Montgomery. His songs, his stridently hillbilly accent, and his between-song patter made up Hank's complete package. The part of his appeal lost to time is the way that he made his audience feel that ol' Hank was truly one of them, always in the "dawghouse," always one step ahead of the bill collector. This was Lon's parting gift, an easygoing demeanor and fondness for tall tales that Hank used so that he could put a happy face on the naked ambition inherited from Lillie and stoked ceaselessly by Audrey.

Starting August 7, 1948, Hank began working the *Louisiana Hayride*. He was the fifth act on the opening 8:00–8:30 P.M. segment, and he sang "Move it on Over." Then, after a commercial from the Asco Loan Company, Johnnie and Jack launched the second half with a gospel song followed by a comedy sketch. Next came Curley Kinsey's band playing an instrumental, "Red Wing," and then Hank and Audrey came out to sing "I Want to Live and Love," a hokey Wiley Walker and Gene Sullivan song from 1941 that was one of Audrey's favorites. Then Hank was through for the night, and the show was rounded out by The Four Deacons, The Mercer Brothers, and Johnnie and Jack.

Merle Kilgore was hanging around the *Hayride* that night. Kilgore was a starstruck teenager then; later, he was a performer in his own right and composer of such songs as "Ring of Fire" and "Wolverton Mountain." Later still, he was an opening act for Hank Jr., and, more recently, vice president of Hank Williams Jr. Enterprises. In 1948, though, Kilgore carried the artists' instruments up to the studio for the morning shows because the elevators didn't operate until 7:00 A.M. On Saturday nights he went backstage at the *Hayride*. "Hank had the same look in his eye that Elvis had," said Kilgore. "That 'I know somethin' you don't know' look. Hank was cocky. That first night, the Bailes were on before him and he said, 'How did they do?' I said, 'Real good. I hate that you have to follow 'em.' He said, 'I'll eat 'em alive.' "

Johnnie and Jack actually separated Hank and the Bailes Brothers that first night, but, as with most of Kilgore's stories, the essentials are probably true even if the detail has been refined.

Three days earlier, Hank had started his regular fifteen-minute show that went out at 5:15 A.M. He arrived in Shreveport with a band he had recruited in Montgomery. Lum York dutifully rejoined, and Hank rehired guitarist Paul Dennis, recruited a fiddle player called George Brown, and picked up a steel guitarist somewhere along the way. He had tried to get Don Helms to join him, but Helms was earning more money working in a band with Boots Harris's brothers. Boots had briefly quit Curley Williams to play with his brothers at a skating rink in Andalusia, then moved back to California to rejoin Curley, and Helms was brought in to replace him. The skating rink gig paid well, so, when Hank called, Helms turned him down. "I'm gonna let you off this time," Hank told him, "but one of these days I'm goin' to the *Opry* and I ain't gonna take no for an answer." Helms wouldn't have bet much on the chance, but he told Hank he would go with him to the *Opry* when the day came.

Hank rented a garage apartment at 4802 Mansfield Road, and the band lived in a trailer. The arrangement didn't last long, no more than a few weeks. Hank meant nothing in Shreveport, he couldn't get show dates, and the group starved out. Most of them went back to Alabama. "He said he'd let me stay out at the house, and he'd feed me and buy me cigarettes," said Lum York, "and as soon as he got started again, we'd start playing, but I went back to Montgomery to work with Uncle Bob Helton."

By late September 1948, Hank was picking up some work in schoolhouses and honky-tonks around Shreveport on weeknights, pulling musicians from the *Hayride* staff band as he needed them, or booking out with other *Hayride* acts so that he could share their band. Tillman Franks's diary for September shows Hank working double-headers with Johnnie and Jack. They were in Plain Dealing, Louisiana, on the twenty-second, playing the high school auditorium in a show sponsored by the American Legion. Five days later, Tillman booked the same show into American Legion Post 304 in Jefferson, Texas. Tillman remembers that Hank preferred dates like these to honky-tonks. "I think he'd got beat up a few times," he says. "In schoolhouses and auditoriums he could really put on a show." Staying away from the joints was probably part of Hank's sobriety program too.

Tillman sold Hank a stage outfit. A year or so earlier, he had worked briefly in Houston with Claude King and Buddy Attaway. A car dealer named Elmer Laird had sponsored them on radio, bought them matching uniforms, and was working with them on a song called "Poison Love." Then a customer got angry with Laird over a car he'd been sold and stabbed him to death on the steps of the dealership. Tillman and the others returned to Shreveport, and their song eventually became the first hit for Johnnie and Jack, but Tillman had no use for his stage outfit now that he was booking acts, so he sold it to Hank. Tillman was fairly short and quite rotund; Hank was tall and almost emaciated, so the outfit was far from a perfect fit. "Mrs. Maxie Goldberg, who had a tailoring place across from KWKH, tailored it to fit Hank, but the britches never did fit," says Tillman. "I sold it to him for sixty dollars, but he never did pay me."

The fact that Tillman Franks was booking acts into schoolhouses in northern Louisiana and eastern Texas was symptomatic of the problem that plagued the *Hayride* from beginning to end: the Ewings had no faith in it. Franks remembers Henry Clay telling him that the family patriarch, John D. Ewing, viewed KWKH as a sausage factory; in other words, he didn't care what went into it — only about the profits coming out the other end. At the same time, WSM had the Artist Service Bureau to assemble and book out *Opry* package shows. "The KWKH management wasn't interested in the future," says Horace Logan, in rare agreement with Tillman Franks. "They were interested in this fiscal year. They wouldn't put up the money to let me start an Artist Service Bureau, which would have been self-supporting very quick."

In fact, the Ewings made a couple of half-hearted stabs at setting up a booking agency, first with Jim Bulleit in 1951, and again with Tillman Franks in 1957 after most of the chickens had flown the coop. When Hank was in Shreveport in 1948 and 1949, though, he couldn't unravel the paradox that hundreds of thousands, perhaps millions, heard his voice every Saturday night, but the following Monday he was driving all day to play a schoolhouse in east Texas for a hundred people. Then he would have to drive back in time to do his early morning show. All that for thirty or forty bucks.

It was a marginal existence, but several people close to Hank throughout his career regard the early months in Shreveport as among his happiest. It was a new start. Audrey was several hundred blessed miles from Lillie, which improved her disposition enormously. Hank was mingling on a regular basis with some of the hottest minor-league prospects in country music, and he and Audrey got along particularly well with Johnnie Wright and Kitty Wells. Johnnie and Hank would go fishing on Sundays and have a fish fry that night. All the while, Hank was making a determined effort to stay sober, which improved Audrey's disposition still more.

Starting in January 1949, Logan found a sponsor for Hank's morning show. The Johnnie Fair Syrup company was a local family business. Its owner had died shortly after Hank arrived, and Logan and KWKH's time salesman, Red Watkins, persuaded the new owners of the company to invest five thousand dollars in print ads and in sponsoring Hank Williams on KWKH. Hank dubbed himself "The Ol' Syrup Sopper" and performed alone with his guitar at an hour when he would ideally have been crawling into bed.

Later, as Hank's reputation grew, he was often out on the road midweek, so Logan told the engineer to record the shows Hank made on sixteen-inch acetates so that the station would have something to play when he wasn't there. Around 1955 those vocal-guitar acetates, which date from early to mid-1949, somehow ended up in the hands of Leonard Chess, boss of the R&B label Chess Records. Chess turned around and sold them to MGM, already running short of Hank Williams material, and they have been issued in various forms since.

The Johnnie Fair transcriptions rank alongside Hank's most affecting work. At that unsociably early hour, with just a bleary-eyed engineer behind the glass, Hank performed the old alchemist's trick of turning base metal into gold. On one show, he sang both sides of Jimmy Wakely's current hit, "I Wish I Had a Nickel" and "Someday You'll Call My Name." Trite and affectless in Wakely's hands, both songs were filled with unrequited longing and a thirst for vengeance by Hank. He made The Sons of the Pioneers' "Cool Water" into an eerie, haunting blues. He needed no more than his guitar, never appeared to strain, yet never let the tension falter. He once told Tillman Franks that he loved the sound of his own voice, something these acetates make clear. Parodists and critics have Hank singing in a high nasal whine, but he actually had a light baritone, and without a band behind him, he explored the natural warm contours of his voice. After every song, Hank would break the spell with a pitch for syrup in two delicious flavors, maple and cane. "Remember, friends," he would say in closing, "meals are easy to prepare when you set your table with Johnnie Fair."

As Hank left the KWKH microphone in the morning, his place was taken by Curley Williams and his Georgia Peach Pickers, featuring Boots Harris again on steel guitar. Curley Williams flitted in and out of Hank's life, from the time he poached Boots Harris in 1942 to the time he pitched Hank "Half As Much" a decade later. Born in southern Georgia, Curley had been christened Doc Williams because family legend held that the seventh child would be a doctor; instead he was a fiddle player. After he started booking out, he changed his name to avoid confusion with Doc Williams on the Wheeling, West Virginia, Jamboree. The Peach Pickers' music was at the opposite end of the country music spectrum from Hank's; it was light, jazzy, sophisticated western dance music. Curley, who talked so slowly it seemed like a put-on, rarely sang, and used a rotating cast of singers to share the spotlight with his daughter, Georgia Ann.

Curley's Peach Pickers had joined the *Opry's* parent station, WSM, in December 1942 — shortly after Boots Harris had quit Hank. They started working on the *Opry* the following September, and landed a Columbia Records contract in November, but because of the first recording ban couldn't record until 1945. Curley recorded for Columbia for seven years, and even backed Fred Rose — then recording for Columbia as "The Rambling Rogue," on one session. He lit out for the west coast to play dance halls late in 1945, returning east to join the *Louisiana Hayride* shortly before Hank arrived. Curley and Hank became friends then, and, in late 1948 when Hank was scuffling, he and Audrey lived with Curley and his wife, Louise, for a while.

The 1948 recording ban was in effect for the first five months that Hank was in Shreveport, and MGM worked through its backlog, releasing a new single by Hank every two months or so. Just before he arrived in Shreveport, MGM had issued the recut of "Honky Tonkin'." *Billboard* lauded its "deft ork beat," and it probably eased his passage onto the *Hayride* by briefly cracking the country chart in July 1948. There was some confusion immediately after release because the Sterling version was still available, but in June 1948 Rose bought back the Sterling masters and sold them to MGM, placing Hank on a royalty as he did so.

When Hank arrived in Shreveport he was promoting "I'm a Long Gone Daddy." It was in the charts the week he joined, and peaked at number six during its three-week stay. Unsure how long the ban would last, Fred Rose culled "Pan American" and "I Don't Care (If Tomorrow Never Comes)" from the Sterling masters for a single the following month. He followed it with two abandoned cuts from Hank's first session for MGM, "I Saw the Light" and "Six More Miles," which were released in September. After that, there were only three cuts left before MGM was staring at the bottom of the Hank Williams barrel.

MGM scheduled two of the remaining cuts, "Mansion on the Hill" and "I Can't Get You off of My Mind," for December 1948, but by then the ban was falling apart. Some companies were cutting instrumental tracks overseas, then overdubbing the vocalists (who were members of a different union) at home; others were simply violating the ban. MGM, RCA, and Columbia played closest to the rules because they had union-staffed affiliate companies and couldn't risk a strike. The ban was ended by an agreement reached on October 27, 1948, to become effective December 14. After all the upset, the union gained a very marginal increase in its royalties on record sales for the pension fund, and a couple of other minor concessions.

Hank's muse seemed to forsake him in Shreveport. In late 1948, Fred Rose sent his promotion man, Mel Foree, to check on him. Hank and Foree went on the road together to Jacksonville, Texas. Hank had just bought a new fishing rod, and threw a line into every creek along the way. Foree's presence seemed to spur him and they wrote four songs on the road. As soon as they got back, Hank went into the KWKH studio to cut acetates. Foree mailed them to Rose. "When I come back Fred had these acetates on his desk," Foree said. "Each song was written to a melody he had already written." Just one usable song came out of the four, " 'Neath a Cold Gray Tomb of Stone," which Bill Monroe's brother, Charlie, recorded in October 1950.

While Foree was in Shreveport, he and Hank wrote two more songs with Curley Williams. The best was a salty little novelty called "No, Not Now." In it, a fool is besotted with a woman, and, even after they're married, she's still telling him "no, not now — but maybe next week somehow." Curley recorded the song for Columbia in September 1949, but — like all of his records — it didn't chart. Hank also gave Foree some lyric sheets to take back to Rose, but Foree put them in a suitcase that was stolen before he got back to Nashville.

It's entirely possible that Hank's dry spell was connected with the change in his lifestyle. Not only had the umbilical cord to Lillie been severed, but Audrey had become pregnant just days after arriving in Shreveport. Pregnancy made her sick and irritable; clothes made her skin hurt, and she found little joy in bearing a child. The spats continued, but the relationship was as quiescent during the late months of 1948 as it ever was, probably because Hank was seriously trying to curb his drinking. Lycrecia was there to bring a little stability, and Hank, who took the rituals of procreation, gestation, and birthing very seriously, was trying to be the strong family head, a role for which Lon and life in general had done little to prepare him.

Until Audrey outgrew her outfits, she continued to insinuate herself into Hank's shows. "Audrey," said Horace Logan, never given to understatement, "was a pure, unmitigated, hard-boiled, blue-eyed bitch. She wanted to be a singer and she was horrible, unbelievably horrible. She not only tried to sing, she *insisted* on it, and she forced herself out on stage when Hank was out there. I'd never let her out, but Hank would say, 'Logan, I've got to let her sing, I've got to live with the woman.' I said, 'OK, Hank, here's what we do. We put two mikes out there. Don't let her sing on your mike. I'll bring down the volume on her mike, and keep yours up.' We let her sing some just so Hank would get along better with her."

By the end of 1948 it was still far from clear that the move from Montgomery had been a success. Hank hadn't recorded for a year because of the recording ban, and although the records MGM drew from the stockpile had done decent business, they weren't exploding over the charts. It must have seemed sometimes that he and Audrey hadn't much to show for the move.

Quite where and when Hank got the impetus to draw "Lovesick Blues" out of his reliquary of half-forgotten tunes is unclear. He had started playing it in Montgomery. The Montgomery pickers remember it clearly because they had to hit minor chords on the bridge, which was very unusual for a Hank Williams song. When R. D. Norred heard it on the radio he turned to his wife and said, "There's that blamed old song." It's likeliest that Hank remembered it, played it on a whim at some schoolhouse dates, got a good response, then played it on the *Hayride*.

Tillman Franks remembered the first time Hank did "Lovesick Blues" on the *Hayride*:

> He didn't have his own band. Dobber Johnson was on fiddle, Buddy Attaway was on guitar, Felton Pruett was on steel guitar, and I was on the bass. We were rehearsing up there and Hank was singing it in F. Then there was this part where it went from F to B-minor or something, and I said, "Hank, that one chord you got in there, I can't figure it out." He says, "Don't worry 'bout it, hoss, just stomp your foot and grin."

Hank's third eye was always attuned to his audience, and after he had played "Lovesick Blues" on the *Hayride* for three or four weeks he knew that he was onto something. He cut a demo at the KWKH studio with Boots Harris on steel guitar and Smokey Paul on electric guitar, and sent it to Fred Rose. Rose, according to Boots, wrote back and told Hank that he wanted nothing to do with it.

Then, on December 22, 1948, eight days after the ban ended, Fred Rose scheduled a session in Cincinnati. Around the twentieth, Hank and

Audrey, Johnnie and Jack, and Kitty Wells left Shreveport in a convoy. They dropped off Lycrecia at her grandparents' house in Alabama, then drove on to Nashville, where they left Johnnie and Jack and Kitty (all three were actually from Nashville, which — then, as now — was unusual for country musicians). Then Hank, Audrey, and Johnnie and Jack's mandolin player, Clyde Baum, drove on to Cincinnati, where Fred Rose was waiting for them at the E. T. Herzog studio.

After more than a year away from the studio, Hank had only one secular song that Rose liked well enough to schedule. It was "There'll Be No Teardrops Tonight," which had a half-share assigned surreptitiously to Cincinnati deejay Nelson King. King's *Hillbilly Jamboree* went out every night between 8:05 P.M. and midnight over fifty-thousand-watt WCKY, and was probably the highest-rated country disc jockey show on the air. Hank had been phoning King regularly since 1947 to plug his records, and, in tribute shows after Hank's death, King always told the story of how he and Hank had felt inspired to write "There'll Be No Teardrops Tonight" one night. In King's account, Hank stepped out onto the street and bought a guitar from a passerby who was glad to sell it to him because he was Hank Williams. The problem with that account is that in late 1948 a passerby was more likely to have said, "Hank who?"

A more plausible account of how King came to own half of the song came from Tillman Franks, who remembers a conversation with Hank in 1952 when he came up to the *Opry* with Webb Pierce. All three of them went fishing on Hickory Lake and started talking shop. By then, Tillman had more or less invented payola in the country record business. "I'd given Nelson King half of [Johnnie and Jack's hit] 'Three Ways of Knowing' to get him to play Webb's record of 'Wondering,' " said Tillman, "and Hank said, 'Franks, you and Pierce have done fucked up business giving these deejays songs.' I said, 'Hank, I didn't start it. Nelson told me you'd given him half of "There'll Be No Teardrops Tonight,' " and Hank said, 'I didn't mean to, I was drunk.' " Perhaps not drunk so much as grateful for the spins, and hopeful of more.

Hank had only two other original songs to record in Cincinnati; one was a hymn he had written, "Lost on the River"; the other was a hymn Audrey had written, "I Heard My Mother Praying for Me." For a fourth song, Hank was determined to record "Lovesick Blues" over Rose's objections.

After the session, Hank and Audrey and Clyde Baum drove back to Nashville, where they ate supper with Johnnie Wright's in-laws and dropped off Clyde Baum. Then they headed on to Montgomery for Christmas.

Shortly after Hank returned to Shreveport, he met Johnny Bond backstage at the *Hayride.* Bond, the writer of several big hits, including "I Wonder Where You Are Tonight," "Bartender's Blues," and "Drink Up and Go Home," had met Hank at the Charles Theater in Montgomery earlier that year. Now he found him almost despondent. "I'm tired of tryin' to get on the *Opry,*" Hank told Bond. "It's just too rough. I've recorded one song that's in the can now, a thing called 'Lovesick Blues'; if that don't make it, I'm thinkin' seriously of gittin' out of the business."

Chapter

7

A FEELING CALLED THE BLUES

*I*T wasn't a blues; it wasn't a country song; it wasn't even from Hank's pen. But "Lovesick Blues" *was* the spark that ignited his career. It was a phenomenon that no amount of punditry, conventional wisdom, or market research could have predicted. As with Davy Crockett hats and Banana Boat songs, it was one of those times when the public voted with its back pocket and damned the smart money.

When Hank, Audrey, and mandolinist Clyde Baum arrived in Cincinnati for the session, they met the core of the band that had backed Hank in Nashville before the ban: Zeke Turner was on lead guitar, Jerry Byrd on steel guitar, Louis Innis reinforced Hank's rhythm guitar, Tommy Jackson was on fiddle, and WLW announcer Willie Thall played bass. That group, with the exception of Thall, had worked with Red Foley in Nashville until WLW offered them twice as much money to relocate. They worked the *Mid-Western Hayride* and other local radio and television shows as The Pleasant Valley Boys, and then separately and together played sessions at the two studios in town.

Two of the songs Hank cut, "Lost on the River" and "I Heard My Mother Praying for Me," were duets with Audrey. Both featured the mandolin, an instrument that trilled along with old-time string bands. As much a lover of the old music as Hank was, he rarely used the mandolin on recordings or on the road; instead, he preferred the electric "take off" guitar that Ernest Tubb had done much to popularize in country music. Its sound could cut through a noisy barroom in a way that the mandolin never could.

By the time they had cut the duets and "There'll Be No Teardrops Tonight," there was less than half an hour left on the session. Hank pulled "Lovesick Blues" from his guitar case and ran it down for Rose and the band. "It was all out of meter," said Jerry Byrd, "and Fred said, 'That's the worst damn thing I ever heard.' He had eyes that went different ways — he couldn't look at you with both eyes — but he was starin' as hard as he could at Hank."

Clyde Baum remembered that Rose and Hank got into an argument. "I'll tell you one damn thing," Hank said to Rose. "You might not like the song but when it gets so hot that I walk off the stage and throw my hat back on the stage and the hat encores, that's pretty hot. And you said that 'Pan American' was no good, and that sold pretty good." Rose started to walk out to get a cup of coffee, telling Hank to cut it if he liked — but he was having nothing to do with it. As he got to the door, Rose turned to the musicians (whose fees were deducted from Hank's royalties) and said that he would give them time and a half if they finished before the three hours of studio time were up and MGM was into extra studio costs. "You're mighty damn free with my money!" yelled Hank, just as the musicians were kicking it off.

With so little time left on the session, the band was under the gun to come up with an arrangement. Byrd and Turner had worked on an Ernest Tubb session shortly before the recording ban, when Tubb, who was running short of material, had cut Jimmie Rodgers's "Waiting for a Train." Byrd and Turner had fashioned a unison yodeling figure for the song's intro, and, with no time to prepare anything else, they replicated it on "Lovesick Blues."

"We made two cuts," said Jerry Byrd. "I said to Hank, 'That's the sorriest thing I ever did hear.' " Faced with criticism from all sides, Hank started to become defensive. He said, "Well, maybe we'll put it on a flip side or something."

Wesley Rose always insisted that his father had set up the session in Cincinnati specifically to record "Lovesick Blues," but clearly no one who was there shares that view, and it doesn't jibe with the fact that it was the last song recorded. Wesley came to credit his father with papal infallibility, and in interviews given after Hank and Fred had died, Wesley always tried to ensure that there was room on the pin's head for two more angels: Fred Rose and Hank Williams — his daddy and his meal ticket. In truth, Fred Rose had reason to be upset. After a year away from the recording studio, the best that Hank could come up with was two mediocre hymns made almost unlistenable by Audrey, one undistinguished secular song, and "Lovesick Blues." It wasn't much to show for a new start and a year's creativity.

Hank told Fred Rose that "Lovesick Blues" was a song by Aulsie "Rex" Griffin that he had bought. This, as he probably knew, was not the case, but he also knew that Rose probably wouldn't release it at all if Acuff-Rose didn't have the publishing rights. By the time Hank recorded "Lovesick Blues," the song had been kicking around a year longer than he had. Irving Mills, later the gray eminence behind Duke Ellington's music, had written the words, and pianist Cliff Friend, who later wrote "When My Dreamboat Comes Home" and "Time Waits for No One," had written the melody. Friend was from Cincinnati, and he had been a test pilot and a vaudevillian before he and Mills wrote "Lovesick Blues" for an obscure musical about lovelorn airmen called *O-oo Ernest,* which appears never to have got as far as off-Broadway. The song was first recorded in 1922 by several artists. Later, at the depth of the Depression, when Friend had forty cents to his name, he is supposed to have sold his interest in the song to Irving Mills for five hundred dollars.

When Friend sold his share, the song was a dead issue. The artist who showed the most interest in it was vaudevillian Emmett Miller, who had recorded it in 1925 when he introduced the yodel, and again in 1928 when he kicked it off with a blackface routine. Miller was one of the first generation of recording artists whose work reached back into the void of prerecording history. He influenced not only Hank, but Jimmie Rodgers, and Bob Wills as well. The trailing yodel that Hank later used on "I'd Still Want You" is Emmett Miller note for note, as are many of Wills's little vocal trademarks.

The missing link between Emmett Miller and Hank Williams was Rex Griffin. In September 1939, Griffin cut "Lovesick Blues" for Decca Records with just his guitar, modeling his approach on Emmett Miller but shading closer to the arrangement that Hank would use. Hank had both Miller's and Griffin's records in his personal collection, and when he represented to Rose that he owned the song, he probably had a good idea that it wasn't his arrangement of a song he had bought from Rex Griffin. When Hank spoke to an interviewer from *National Hillbilly News* at the end of 1949, he mentioned Emmett Miller's record and confirmed that he had been performing the song for years, but still gave no clue where he had first heard it.

Griffin, from Gadsden, Alabama, was another drunk, chiefly remembered today for "The Last Letter," the suicide note of an older man besotted with a younger woman ("I cannot offer you diamonds and a mansion so fine / I cannot offer you clothes that your young body craves . . ."). Williams and Griffin played shows together, and although Hank assured Fred Rose that it was from Griffin he had purchased "Lovesick Blues," Griffin told Lum York that he wanted to sue Hank over what he thought was an infringement of *his* arrangement of a public domain song. Unfortunately, Griffin never gave a full account of his dealings with Hank to anyone before he died of tuberculosis in New Orleans in 1959.

Between 1922 and 1948, the melody of "Lovesick Blues" had become increasingly simplified, losing a few chords at every turn, but even so, it was the most harmonically complex song Hank ever recorded. And, at some point, Friend's first verse, starting with "I'm in love, I'm in love with a beautiful gal" became the chorus, and the original chorus ("I've got a feeling called the blues . . .") was doubled up and used as a verse. It was, as Fred Rose wasted no time telling Hank, a mess.

When Rose submitted writer and publisher information for "Lovesick Blues" to MGM in January 1949, it read "Composer: Rex Griffin; Arrangements by Hank Williams; Publisher: Acuff-Rose"; the composer credit on the original pressings was ominously blank. It was released on February 11, 1949. Rose coupled it with "Never Again," one of the Sterling cuts he'd acquired in June 1948. Clearly, he didn't want to waste "There'll Be No Teardrops Tonight," which he considered the only usable song from the Cincinnati session, on the flip side of a dog. Still, he took out advertisements in *Billboard* plugging what he thought was *probably* his song.

In March, Wesley Rose wrote to Hank saying that he had just got back from New York, and "had a hint" on who owned "Lovesick Blues." He asked Hank to send along the records by Griffin and "Emmett something or other" so that they could try to prove it was a public domain song. A few weeks later, Irving Mills got wise and sued. In a settlement arbitrated by Frank Walker effective November 1, 1949, Mills and Rose shared the publishing on Hank's recording only, each collecting five-eighths of a cent from MGM in recognition of the promotional work that Acuff-Rose had done on the song's behalf. Mills retained 100 percent of all other rights to the song.

Rose was not only proved wrong in his judgment of "Lovesick

Blues," but proved very wrong very quickly. For all its flaws, Hank's record was utterly compelling, and he already had prospective buyers who had heard it on the *Hayride* lined up across the eastern half of the country. By the end of MGM's royalty accounting period seventeen days after release, the record had already sold more than forty-eight thousand copies. On March 5 it showed up on the country charts. Rose was dumbfounded to the point of questioning his commercial instincts, and the Cincinnati session crew were dismayed that, as Jerry Byrd said, "anything as sorry as that could be a hit." A hit it was, though. On May 7, 1949, "Lovesick Blues" dislodged George Morgan's "Candy Kisses" from the number one slot.

"Hank was eating at the Bantam Grill," said Tillman Franks. "I'd bought a *Billboard* at the newsstand and 'Lovesick Blues' had just got to number one. I walked in and I showed it to him. It shook him up pretty good. He just sat there silent the longest time. He realized what that was." By the time Hank met his band later in the day, he had already turned it into a typically self-deprecating joke. When one of them said, "You got it made now, boy, you're number one in Nashville," Hank said, "I sure am glad it ain't another damn 'Pontchartrain.' "

"Lovesick Blues" stayed at number one for sixteen weeks, and lingered on the charts until the following January. Hank became "that Lovesick Blues boy," a sobriquet that would follow him for years. No hit from his own pen would ever eclipse "Lovesick Blues."

Hank was now a big noise around Shreveport. He had reassembled a band before "Lovesick Blues" took off, probably at some point between the recording and the release. On the way back from the session, Hank had stopped at Montgomery for Christmas, and, while there, he asked his mother to call down to the radio station where Lum York was working. Hank told Lum that he was thinking about putting another band together, and Lum rejoined him in Shreveport.

Then Hank recruited guitarist Clint Holmes and steel guitarist Felton Pruett from the *Louisiana Hayride* band. Holmes had first met Hank in Houston when he was working on KLEE with Hank Locklin. After falling out with Locklin, Holmes went back to Mobile, and he was on his way to join his brother in Abilene when he stopped by the *Hayride.* Hank cornered him and asked him to join the band. Holmes played the "sock" rhythm guitar that took the place of brushes on a snare drum and reinforced Hank's guitar. Steel guitarist Felton Pruett, from Sabine County, Louisiana, was only eighteen years old and had joined the *Hayride* staff band after a stint on KWKH morning radio with Harmie Smith.

The lead guitar was played by Bob McNett. The only northerner Hank ever hired, McNett was from rural upstate Pennsylvania, and he had arrived in Shreveport with the singing cowgirl Patsy Montana. Just as she was getting ready to break up her band, Hank walked up to McNett backstage at the *Hayride,* and, dispensing with formalities, got straight to the point. He said, "Can you make the introduction to 'Lovesick Blues'?" McNett said he could, and he was hired.

The band was rounded out by Tony Francini on fiddle. Originally a classical violin player who somehow got stranded in Shreveport, Francini was already fifty years old when he joined Hank. He learned his parts from listening to the records, copying out the fiddle part and sight-reading from his transcription. He hated the traveling, and, according to Pruett, hated country music. One day when they were playing a *Hayride* remote in Brownsville, Texas, they went across the border to meet a promoter from Mexico City, and on the way back, Francini surprised everyone by producing an Italian passport, which made him the only foreigner Hank ever hired.

Hank placed the band on salaries ranging between fifty and sixty dollars a week. On top of that, the band went out into the crowd during the intermission and sold songbooks and photographs on commission. Hank and Audrey were still taking care of the bookings themselves. Admission was fifty or sixty cents — double what they had charged in 1941. Often, Hank would come home with his pockets stuffed full of cash. "One night we worked a schoolhouse date, and I was wanting to talk to Hank about something," said Felton Pruett, "and I was standing there while he and the principal was countin' out the money, and they counted out eight hundred dollars. We'd played two shows that night, but eight hundred dollars. Man!"

Ever since Hank had ridden in Curley Williams's seven-seater '48 Packard sedan, he had coveted it. Originally, the car was owned by one of the Bailes Brothers, but, at some point in 1948, the note on it was assumed by guitarist Billy Byrd, who had come to Shreveport with Curley Kinsey and The Four Deacons. The Deacons split up, and Byrd had joined Curley Williams's Peach Pickers, bringing the Packard with him. Then, just after he joined The Peach Pickers, Curley broke up the band, leaving Byrd toting the note on the Packard. Hank took over the loan. He attached a trailer to the car for the instruments, but could never figure out how to reverse the car and trailer into his driveway, so someone from the band always had to drive home with him.

Soon after Hank bought the Packard, he drove it overnight to Montgomery so that he could show it off to WSFA-owner Howard Pill and advertising boss Bill Hunt as they sat having coffee at the Jefferson Davis Hotel. Then, briefly, he went on air to say howdy to all his old fans. Hardrock Gunter, who had last encountered Hank Williams drunk at the Labor Day show in 1943, was in town that day. He heard Hank and went to WSFA to reintroduce himself. Hank quickly proposed to Gunter that he come back to Shreveport with him to lead his band and act as his manager. Gunter thought about it for a while, then refused. "We'll make a lot of money," said Hank. "I know we will, but I couldn't spend it from prison," said Gunter. Hank said, "Whaddya mean?" and Gunter said, "In time, I'd want to kill you. If I booked you on a show with several hundred dollars at stake and you were drunk someplace, I'm liable to kill you."

Hank's career had turned around in the space of weeks. Now he had a band, a touring sedan, and a hit to pay for both. After an unpromising start, his gamble on the *Hayride* was paying off. The show's blanket coverage of the central United States offered a launching site that only three or four other shows could deliver. He may only have had six or seven minutes' exposure a week, but he needed only two minutes and forty-five seconds to sing "Lovesick Blues." "When Hank sang 'Lovesick Blues' on the *Hayride*," said Tillman Franks, "he would wobble his knees during the yodel. Ray Atkins, one of the guys who played with Johnnie and Jack, would stand underneath the stage on a platform and turn a flip right at that moment, and the roof would just come in. The auditorium had that natural echo, and, boy, it sounded great."

When Hank finally joined the Shreveport local of the American Federation of Musicians on February 4, 1949, he was living in an apartment across the Red River in Bossier City. Then in March 1949 he signed an agreement to purchase a small house on Charles Street in the Modica subdivision in Bossier. It was a typical postwar subdivision; the houses were small, boxy, and plentiful. Hank still had no inkling of the changes that "Lovesick Blues" would wreak on his career; all he knew was that he had a wife seven months pregnant and a chance at some decent income for a while.

As the heat and humidity kicked in that spring, Audrey became more and more irritable. One of her irritations was that what had once been *their* career was now evidently Hank's alone. "God, she was difficult to get along with then," said Horace Logan. "I saw her stand there, pregnant with Hank Jr. and Hank had given her a set of crystal ware and she threw it out, every bit of it, piece at a time into the carport and broke it."

One day, returning from a tour, Hank went upstairs with Clint Holmes and tripped over a vase. Probably thinking he was drunk, Audrey picked up some tea glasses and hurled them at him, sending him to the hospital. Even now in its most quiescent period, their relationship never lost its essential character, that of interdependence and incompatibility. Audrey, everyone agrees, acted as though she had a permanent chip on her shoulder, probably because of an uncomfortable and encumbering pregnancy that was thwarting her ambitions, while Hank, as always, had a deep-seated need for a strong woman to lean on, more so now that the pressures were mounting.

Hank started to resume the pattern he had once adopted with Lillie: drinking as soon as he left the house. In March, just as "Lovesick Blues" was breaking, he had to go to Lake Charles, Louisiana. He was half-drunk before he left town, and he bought another jug for the road. He and Lum York were tussling while Felton Pruett was strumming Hank's guitar. "Lum got sick of it," said Pruett, "and Hank made a swipe at me and I ducked down, and his ol' bony knee came upside my nose. We went on down the road, found a doctor and got my nose to stop bleeding. The doctor said, 'Was your nose crooked like that before?' and I said, 'No sir,' so he grabbed a hold of it and yanked it back into position."

They carried on to Lake Charles. "We poured Hank out," said Pruett.

He always wanted to play the fiddle when he was drunk. He got out and played "Sally Goodin' " for five minutes. We kept sayin', "That'll do, Hank, that'll do." He'd say, "Naw, naw, them people jes eatin' it up." They were, too. We sold ninety-seven dollars' worth of pictures that night at ten cents a piece. We give him the money two or three days later when he'd sobered up and he never did know where it come from. They loved him down there. Drunk or sober, it didn't matter. Funny thing was, his time was right on. If you could get him out there and prop him up, he'd do the show.

Right after Hank got back, the *Hayride* performers and their families went out for an Easter picnic northwest of Shreveport on Caddo Lake. There was an egg hunt and a wienie roast. There was also a big tub of beer, and Hank partook. While the others were hunting for eggs, Hank was quietly getting plastered. The party moved to Johnnie Bailes's house, and while the Baileses and Johnnie and Jack were working up some quartet pieces, Hank continued drinking. Audrey stormed off home with

Lycrecia, and when Hank straggled back later she took an ice pick to the tires of the car. Hank retaliated by breaking some of the furniture and threatening to attack Audrey. She called Johnnie Wright and Kitty Wells, and asked them to come over, but by the time they arrived Hank had passed out on the bed.

The Wrights agreed to stay that night. Johnnie climbed into bed with Hank, and Audrey went looking for her tranquilizers. She found just one or two pills left, then realized that Hank had gobbled almost the entire bottle. She panicked and called a doctor. He came, shook Hank, raising him up on the bed, asking him, "Hank, Hank, how many of those pills did you take?" Finally, Hank's eyes half-opened. He said, "You know too damn much," then slumped back.

The following week, Hank had to go out on tour with the Shreveport chamber of commerce. The city had hired a train to make a goodwill trip south through Louisiana and into Texas. It was a three- or four-day junket, and everywhere Hank went people remarked on his scarred appearance. Audrey had clearly wreaked her vengeance at some point.

It never took much stress to push Hank over the threshold. His first thought was always oblivion. For a few months, he had wrestled his addictions to the ground, but now they were returning. He was drinking again, and now that he was going farther afield and he needed to beat the torpor that overcame him on the long hauls, he began using a brand of nasal inhaler that had Benzedrine in it. He'd work his way through a sackful at a time, then tear them open and lick the lining. The band was disgusted.

In a gesture of appeasement toward Audrey as she performed the sacred task of perpetuating his line, he bought her jewelry and things for the home. All the while, Audrey was more interested in perpetuating her career. She pursued success like a medieval cleric pursued heresy, and she could truly see no reason why Hank's applause should not be hers as well. After four years as a singer, she still had little grasp of how she really sounded. When she screwed up onstage, she chewed out the musicians. The pregnancy only allowed Hank a respite from a problem that would shortly return. He was trying to run a professional show and get out of Shreveport. If his guitar player messed up, he would fire him, but, come June or July, Audrey would demand to be reinstated on the show. What would that do for his chances of ever getting out of Shreveport?

Audrey exacted one concession from the success of "Lovesick Blues" when she insisted that "Hank and Audrey" be promoted as a parallel recording act to Hank Williams. On March 1, 1949, she, Hank, and Clyde Baum drove to Nashville for a double session. There they met Fred Rose and a new crop of backing musicians. Zeke Turner's brother Zeb was on electric guitar, Dale Potter was on fiddle, and Don Davis, who had worked with Pee Wee King, was on steel guitar. Jack Shook, who had toured with Fred Rose when Rose had worked at WSM in the '30s, reinforced Hank's rhythm guitar. First they recorded two duets, "Jesus Remembered Me" and the maudlin "Dear Brother." Just over three weeks later, Johnnie and Jack with Clyde Baum also cut "Jesus Remembered Me" and had the first release with it; Hank and Audrey's version was held back until August 1950. "Dear Brother" was coupled with "Lost on the River" from the "Lovesick Blues" session, and shipped in MGM's all-hillbilly *After Planting* release in May, when its chances were thought to be the brightest.

Hank rounded out the first session with "Lost Highway" and "May You Never Be Alone." "Lost Highway," often assumed to have come from Hank's pen, was written by Leon Payne, who later wrote "I Love You Because." Payne was a blind musician who worked out of Jerry Irby's nightclub in Houston and guested on the *Hayride* and the *Opry*. His original version of "Lost Highway" had been released on the Nashville-based Bullet label in October 1948. Its theme of perdition laced with misogyny ("Just a deck of cards and a jug of wine / And a woman's lies make a life like mine . . .") would have made it standard Acuff fare, but for the fact that it was told in the first person rather than the third person as Acuff would have wanted. Hank made it sound like pages torn from his diary.

"May You Never Be Alone" trod the same ground. It was Hank's first terse, resonant poem of loneliness, taken at a surprisingly brisk tempo. Clyde Baum took a mandolin solo, the first and last Hank Williams record to have one. The song itself dated back to Hank's 1946 songbook, when it was called "I Loved No One but You." Surprisingly, it had taken three years for him to refashion and record it. Hank was starting to experiment with imagery, such as "Like a bird that's lost its mate in flight . . ." and "Like a piece of driftwood on the sea . . ."

After a half-hour break, Hank and the band resumed, working until two o'clock the following morning. They took a second stab at "Honky Tonk Blues," but Hank broke meter and Rose wouldn't touch it. This time around, it had a light, jazzy treatment. Zeb Turner took a solo that was probably a touch too florid for Hank's taste, and there was a bass solo that would have been inaudible on most car radios. The song had to be attempted a fourth time in December 1951 before Rose heard something he wanted to release.

Hank also took a first stab at the maudlin "My Son Calls Another Man Daddy." It too was put on hold, and the only usable cuts from the midnight session were "You're Gonna Change (Or I'm Gonna Leave)" and "Mind Your Own Business," both clearly born of the dissent on Charles Street. Hank had bought the genesis of "Mind Your Own Business" from a Montgomery musician, Smokey Metcalfe, but he refashioned it, adapting it to the melody of "Move it on Over." His delivery was measured, laconic, and dry. Introducing it in October 1949, Hank told his radio audience it was a "little prophecy in song," which it would indeed turn out to be.

Right after the session, Hank, Audrey, and Clyde Baum got back in the Packard and headed for Shreveport. It was a bright moonlit night. Hank told Baum to drive fast and not to stop suddenly for dogs because the jolt might make Audrey miscarry.

"May You Never Be Alone," "Mind Your Own Business," and "You're Gonna Change" seemed to indicate that Hank had rediscovered his muse, but Fred Rose held them back. Eighteen days later, Hank flew to Nashville (his first flight according to the Shreveport *Times*) to record a split session with Red Sovine. His sales of "Lovesick Blues" had been undermined to an extent by cover versions, and now he was to produce a pair of his own. "I've Just Told Mama Goodbye" was a dirge that had been written by two *Hayride* performers, "Sunshine" Slim Sweet and Curley Kinsey. Sweet had recorded a version for Mercury Records that was released in March 1949, and Hank wanted to get his own version on the market by Mother's Day. It was as close as he would ever come to the Acuff sound, a steel guitar imitating the tremulous Dobro that was Acuff's trademark. It would be tempting to impute some significance to the fact that in three weeks Hank had recorded two songs that had killed off his mother ("Dear Brother" was the other), but dying mothers were to hillbilly music what fair maidens walking out one morning were to English folk song.

The other side of the record was "Wedding Bells." It was an undistinguished song, and several artists had already passed it by. To that point, the only version to hit the market had been by Knoxville radio veteran Bill Carlisle, who had recorded it for King Records in 1947. The song was attributed to Claude Boone, longtime guitarist with Knoxville bluegrass musician Carl Story, but Boone had bought it from a local drunk, James Arthur Pritchett, who performed locally and sold songs under the pseudonym Arthur Q. Smith.

Pritchett was famous among industry insiders for selling songs; he is rumored to have written the wartime classic "Rainbow at Midnight," which Ernest Tubb made into the 1947 number one hit, "If Teardrops Were Pennies," which Rosemary Clooney made a hit in 1951, and "I Wouldn't Change You If I Could," later a hit for Ricky Skaggs. Several other songs that became big hits for other people were rumored to have come from him as well. Pritchett's usual asking price was fifteen or twenty-five dollars, but most of his songs were worth no more. Claude Boone bought "Wedding Bells" for twenty-five dollars, but he had the misfortune to live in the same city as Pritchett, which made him Pritchett's first call when he wanted a drink.

Hank loved the soap opera bathos of "Wedding Bells," although he knew nothing of its history when he cut it. "He told me it was the prettiest song he'd ever heard," said Boone. Surprisingly, for a songwriter who rarely lapsed into cheap Victorian sentimentality, Hank seemed to be a sucker for such lines as "a blossom from an orange tree in your hair." He had been unable to record the song throughout 1948 because of the recording ban, and may have been under some pressure from Fred Rose not to record it at all because it wasn't an Acuff-Rose copyright.

"Wedding Bells" backed with "I've Just Told Mama Goodbye" was released at the beginning of May 1949. Both were shipped a couple of weeks before "Lovesick Blues" began its stint at number one. "Wedding Bells" broke into the charts on May 14, peaking at number two, and spent the rest of the year on the *Billboard* listings. That alone would have stocked Boone's refrigerator for a while, but the song had an even bigger payday when the pop-western duo of Margaret Whiting and Jimmy Wakely placed it on the flip side of their number one pop and country hit, "Slippin' Around." By 1951 Boone had made more than forty thousand dollars from his twenty-five dollar investment.

In February 1950, MGM made out its royalty statements for the preceding six months. "Lovesick Blues" and "Wedding Bells" were just finishing their runs on the charts; during that period "Lovesick Blues" had sold 148,242 copies and "Wedding Bells" had sold 81,813 copies. "Dear Brother" had sold 739 copies. Altogether, Hank received a check for a shade over ten thousand dollars, his biggest payday to that point.

The success of "Wedding Bells" coming on top of "Lovesick Blues" compounded Hank's sense of isolation on the schoolhouse circuit in east Texas and Louisiana. Before he left Montgomery, he had met a promoter, Oscar Davis, who had booked Roy Acuff, Pee Wee King, and other *Opry* acts since the late '30s. Known as "The Baron," Davis was originally from Rhode Island, where he was born in 1902. He had drifted into country music promotion in 1936 after a spell in vaudeville and motion picture promotion. He was chiefly famous as the man who had promoted the 1947 Carnegie Hall concerts that brought country music to New York. The consensus about Davis was that he wasn't afraid to spend money promoting a show. In Nashville, the joke was that Oscar would still be promoting a concert two weeks after it had happened.

Hank had called Oscar Davis before he recorded "Lovesick Blues," and, according to Oscar, Hank told him, "Now I'm ready for you. Now you'll want me." Hank told him about "Lovesick Blues." "I do this number, Oscar, so help me God, I get fourteen, fifteen encores." "He played me 'Lovesick Blues,' " Oscar said, "and in my mind I said, 'This is the most horrible goddamn thing I heard in my life.' " Oscar told Hank to let him know when "Lovesick Blues" was on disc, and, like everyone else, was stupefied when it ruled the charts. According to Oscar, Hank promised him 25 percent of his booking fees for life if he could get him on the *Opry*.

In April 1949, Oscar signed Hank to a personal management contract and placed him on a tour with Ernest Tubb, Red Foley, Cowboy Copas, Minnie Pearl, and Rod Brasfield. This was Hank's first tour as a star, and probably the first tour to take him more than a day's drive from home. They started in Houston, swung out to Amarillo and Oklahoma City, then headed down to Dallas and on to New Orleans. In six days the unit grossed forty-one thousand dollars, although it's doubtful that Hank saw more than he would have from six packed schoolhouse dates that he had booked himself. Still, recognition counts for something, and it probably counted for a lot with Hank at this juncture in his career. He also found that he got along well with Tubb and Foley, whom he had never really got to know when he had been their local added attraction in Montgomery. Tubb in particular was constantly bemused by his own success and didn't seem to begrudge anyone else their applause. Hank was also gratified to find that his idols too had feet of clay; Foley, Tubb, and Brasfield could match anyone drink for drink.

Then, in the middle of all the uncertainty, Audrey gave birth to Randall Hank on May 26, 1949. She had been in the hospital several times with false labor pains, and when Hank Jr. was born, he weighed ten pounds two ounces, and, as Audrey later said, "practically killed the both of us." Hank and Clint Holmes's wife were at the hospital when Audrey finally gave birth. "It was really a bad scene for Hank," said Audrey. "They couldn't get him away from the door of the delivery room, 'cause he heard me inside screaming."

Hank refused to consider naming his son Hiram. Later, he nicknamed him "Bocephus." If it had been a biblical name, he might have stood a better than even chance of knowing its derivation, but it was a corruption of "Bucephalus," the favorite horse of Alexander the Great, which died in a battle around 300 B.C. Hank probably got the name from Rod Brasfield, who dubbed his dummy "Bocephus," rather than from his knowledge of Greek history.

The big paychecks from MGM and Acuff-Rose were still in the distance, so Hank had to borrow one hundred dollars from Murrell Stansell, owner of the Bantam Grill, to pay the hospital bill. "I can't tell you how happy he was," said Audrey. Frail and gauntly thin all his life, Hank was uncontrollably proud that his son was the biggest in the nursery. Technically, Hank Jr. was born out of wedlock because Audrey had been granted a divorce from Hank in Montgomery exactly one year to the day before Hank Jr. was born, but he was legitimized on August 9, 1949, when Hank and Audrey had their first divorce annulled.

With Oscar Davis's promises ringing in his ears, Hank disbanded his group in Shreveport just before he left for Texas to join the *Opry* stars on tour. "He said, 'I'm going to Texas tomorrow,' " remembered Bob McNett. " 'If I call you, you have a job. If I don't, you don't.' " He didn't, and the band was offered a job by Hank Snow, then trying for a spot on the *Hayride*. Snow, though, was still shuttling between the United States where he was starving, and his native Nova Scotia. He couldn't afford a regular band, so Hank's band went its separate ways.

Lum York hung around Shreveport for a while, then moved to Baton Rouge. Tony Francini went off to work in Paul Howard's Arkansas Cottonchoppers. Two years later, Bob McNett ran into him in a hotel in Hot Springs, Arkansas. Francini was destitute, trying to make his way back to New York. Clint Holmes stayed on the *Hayride*. McNett went back to Pennsylvania, and Felton Pruett was already primed to quit the business:

I wasn't really interested in moving up to Nashville. Hank couldn't guarantee the work up there that we were getting, and I thought, "I'm playing with the top man in the nation, and I'm making a whoppin' fifty dollars a week, and I'm gone from home all the time." You git in that doggone car and you drive and drive, gas up, git you a Coke, drink it halfway down, pour a packet of peanuts in it and you was gone again. You'd make it to the next gig, see if they had a dressing room — if they didn't you'd have to dress outside. We'd play, pack, get back in that durn car, and what sleep you got you got in that ol' car. I knew there had to be a better way of making a living.

The Texas and Pacific Railroad offered Pruett nine dollars for a regular eight-hour day, and he was pleased to accept.

At the time Hank broke up the group, Fred Rose and Oscar Davis were angling to get Hank on the *Opry.* Clint Holmes says that Rose didn't want Hank's band to accompany him to Nashville because he didn't think Hank would hold up under the stress, and the band would be unemployed far from home. After working his show dates with the *Opry* stars, Hank went back to Shreveport and played out his remaining commitments with Holmes, picking up a band at every place they played.

As he worked off his final *Hayride* dates, Hank told Holmes that he was "fadin' out" of Shreveport, and that is more or less what happened. His family stayed there until Lycrecia finished school and it was clear that there would be enough work to support them in Nashville. With a too vivid memory of the first few months in Shreveport, Hank and Audrey had no desire to move only to struggle like they'd struggled early in Shreveport.

"He was the first real star we had," said Horace Logan. "The last show he encored 'Lovesick Blues' seven times — he could have encored it ten times — and I never let anybody encore more than seven times to keep Hank's record. Hank left saying he was coming back, and there was never any indication that he was not coming back — it was just a question of when."

More tears are shed over answered prayers
than unanswered prayers.
St. Teresa of Avila

• •

THE MOTHER OF ALL JUBILEES

• • • • • • • • • • • • • • • • • • • •

WITH "Lovesick Blues" and "Wedding Bells"
delivering a one-two punch, the management of
the *Grand Ole Opry* simply could not afford to ignore Hank Williams any
longer. Fred Rose and Oscar Davis were keeping up the pressure on the
WSM and *Opry* management team of Harry Stone, Jack Stapp, and Jim
Denny. "I came to Jim Denny," said Oscar Davis, "and Jim said, 'No, we
won't [have him]. We talked about him with Harry Stone and he's got a
bad reputation with drinking and missing shows.' So I plead and plead
with him, and finally he agrees to square it away." Among other things,
Davis said that he guaranteed Hank would be sober for a year, and reports reaching Nashville from the *Opry* acts who were working with
Hank spoke of his newfound sobriety. Stone, Stapp, and Denny had been
around enough alcoholics to know that promises of sobriety were as
good as a trailing incumbent's election promises, but they also knew that
they couldn't afford to ignore Hank Williams if they wanted to remain
preeminent. The *Opry* was running scared of the *Louisiana Hayride*,
scared too that another jamboree would be set up in Nashville. To
sweeten the pot, it's almost certain that Fred Rose offered the composer
credit on "Chattanoogie Shoe Shine Boy," a song he had written that was
about to be recorded by Red Foley, to Stapp and Stone.

The radio jamboree is generally credited as having started on WBAP
in Fort Worth in 1923, and the first big-time jamboree, the WLS *Barn
Dance,* was launched in Chicago shortly before the *Opry*. By the mid-

forties, there were numberless others on stations great and small. The *Opry*'s inauspicious debut as the WSM *Barn Dance* came when an eighty-three-year-old fiddler, Uncle Jimmy Thompson, sawed away for an hour to the accompaniment of his niece. The date is usually given as November 28, 1925. The show was renamed *Grand Ole Opry* in 1926. It began to reach a much wider audience when WSM was boosted to fifty thousand watts in 1932, and it edged ahead of the pack after the 8:30–9:00 P.M. portion of the show was sponsored by R. J. Reynolds' Prince Albert Tobacco in January 1939 and picked up for networking by NBC in October that year. Initially, only twenty-six stations on NBC's Red Network took the *Opry* (with another five taking it on transcription), but by July 1940 it was networked coast to coast on more than 150 stations and it attracted around ten million listeners every Saturday night.

By 1949, when Hank joined the *Opry*, it had become WSM's principal money-spinner, accounting for two-thirds of the station's advertising revenue. The eighty cents scooped up at the door from the three thousand admissions per week more than covered the hall rental, talent, and backstage staff. Sponsors were lined up five deep, and WSM would soon start a Friday night jamboree (the *Friday Night Frolics*) and pre-*Opry* shows in WSM's auditorium to increase the sponsorship opportunities. The hokiness, in which the *Opry* took a great deal of inverted pride, disguised ruthlessly aggressive management and shrewd organization.

Since 1943, WSM had leased the Ryman Auditorium for the *Opry* show. The story goes that the Ryman was built in 1891 by riverboat tycoon Tom Ryman. He had come onshore to heckle an evangelist, Sam Jones, who was working at a tent meeting, but the Reverend Jones chose "mother" as his subject that night — the one topic certain to reduce Captain Ryman to tears. Ryman apparently rushed back to his riverboats, tore out the gambling fixtures, dumped them overboard, and declared that a great preacher like the Reverend Jones should not have to preach in a tent, so he built the Ryman Auditorium for him.

The networked portion of the *Opry* made stars of Roy Acuff, who joined in 1938, Eddy Arnold, who joined in 1942, and Ernest Tubb, who joined the following year. Those three mixed tradition, modernity, and "jus' folks" radio presence — the mix that Hank Williams was to master. When Acuff quit for a year in 1946, he was replaced on the Prince Albert portion by Red Foley, who had already established his presence on WLS in Chicago and WLW in Cincinnati. In hiring Foley away from WLS, Harry Stone and Jack Stapp served notice that they were determined to keep the *Opry* preeminent.

Hank was eased onto the *Opry* through a guest spot on the non-networked portion. It was the back door, but a door nonetheless. His first appearance was on June 11, 1949, during the 9:00–9:30 P.M. Warren Paint segment hosted by Ernest Tubb. Hank sang "Lovesick Blues" and made another appearance on the 11:00–11:15 Allen Manufacturing segment, when he sang "Mind Your Own Business." Still, with WSM's fifty-thousand-watt clear channel, the *Opry* didn't need the NBC feed to blanket much of the eastern United States and Canada. Hank's reception that night guaranteed that he would be offered a spot on the Prince Albert section the following week.

The structure of the thirty-minute Prince Albert *Opry* was much tighter than the nonnetworked portion. The cast held a rehearsal on Saturday morning to do a complete dry run, with commercials, jokes, and music timed out to the second. Every word, every wordless gooberism was scripted. For his debut, Hank was to work with the house band, which included Grady Martin on fiddle or guitar, Zeb Turner and Jimmy Selph on guitars, Billy Robinson on steel guitar, and Ernie Newton on bass. The Prince Albert host, Red Foley, introduced him: "Well, sir, tonight's big-name guest is making his first appearance on Prince Albert *Grand Ole Opry*. He's a Montgomery, Alabama, boy, been pickin' and singin' about twelve years, but it's been about the last year he's really come into his own . . . and we're proud to give a rousing Prince Albert welcome to the 'Lovesick Blues' boy, Hank Williams."

Hank walked out to fairly muted applause. Foley stepped back up to the microphone. "Well, sir, we hope you'll be here for a good long time, buddy."

"Well, Red," said Hank, coming in right on cue, "it looks like I'll be doing just that, and I'll be looking forward to it." The band kicked off "Lovesick Blues," and the audience buzz rose noticeably during the song; the crowd may not have known the name, but it certainly knew the song. Contrary to myth, there were no encores, but, as Hank indicated to Foley, he had now been accepted for membership in the most restricted club in country music. When they played acetates of the show at the usual postmortem in Jack Stapp's office on Monday morning, everyone was well pleased. Hank's quick acceptance was such that less than a year later, Easter 1950, when Foley was off the Prince Albert show for what was called some "much needed rest," Hank emceed the *Opry*'s flagship show.

After the June 18 show, Hank prepared to fly back to Shreveport to mop up some engagements and see his family. He was staying at the

Hermitage Hotel when Bob McKinnon, a deejay from Hank's part of the world, came to see him. McKinnon offered him a drink while he got dressed. "No, I quit," said Hank. "I can't handle it. I don't ever expect to take another drop." And he truly, truly meant it. With the world falling into his lap and a healthy boy child less than three weeks old, he must have felt that he would never again feel the need to take to the bottle.

Soon after he became a fixture on the *Opry,* Hank set about putting another band together. He called Bob McNett in Pennsylvania and asked him to rejoin. Then he tried to find Don Helms. When Helms had turned down Hank's offer of going to the *Hayride,* he had been making good money playing at a skating rink that he and Boots Harris's brothers leased in Andalusia, but one night someone was shot and a preacher got up a petition to close the rink. This left Helms and the Harrises with two thousand pairs of skates and nowhere to play. The Harrises went off to Mississippi, and Helms went up to Richmond, Virginia, where his wife's sister lived. He'd heard that Buddy Wheeler, the steel guitarist on the WRVA *Old Dominion Barn Dance* was moving to Phoenix, and hoped to take his place, but, by the time he got there, Wheeler had decided to stay. Four or five days later, Helms's wife called and told him that Hank Williams was trying to reach him. Helms called Hank. "You remember when I was going to Shreveport you told me that if I ever got to the *Grand Ole Opry* you'd go with me," said Hank. "Well, have your ass here next Friday night." Helms said, "You got it, chief."

Perhaps Helms didn't realize that for Hank, the steel guitar was the crucial instrument; its notes were the wordless cry that completed his vocal lines. The steel guitar sustained the mood and took most of the solos. Nearly all of the great country singers had a steel guitarist who functioned as their musical alter ego. Roy Acuff had Pete Kirby (a.k.a. Bashful Brother Oswald), Eddy Arnold had Roy Wiggins, and later Buck Owens had Tom Brumley. For Hank, it was Don Helms.

Technically, Jerry Byrd was probably a more accomplished player than Don Helms, but Byrd's tone was rooted in the cloying sweetness of Hawaiian music and his melodic invention was sometimes a little too florid for Hank's liking. Helms had precision, economy, and a bluesier tone that echoed his master's voice. He liked to use the high E6 tuning on one neck of his lap steel, and the notes he found there and juggled into Hank's rudimentary chord changes were simple, direct phrases that precisely complemented Hank's words and the emotionality of his singing.

Fiddle player Jerry Rivers was born in Miami in 1928, the son of a dentist, but he grew up in Nashville and started playing semiprofessionally in 1945. Three years later, he quit his job as an electronic parts salesman to become a road musician with The Short Brothers, a breakaway unit from Ernest Tubb's Texas Troubadours. When the Shorts decided to stay in Houston, Rivers returned to Nashville and began working with Big Jeff Bess, husband of Tootsie, owner of Tootsie's, the legendary drinking hole near the *Opry*. Rivers says that Hank phoned from Shreveport offering him a job at the time the Shreveport band was being put together, but he'd turned him down. Hank was offering fifty dollars a week then, and Rivers was making that much or more closer to home.

Rivers was still kicking himself for turning Hank down when he heard through Jack Boles, who worked with Little Jimmy Dickens, that Hank was looking for a fiddle player. Rivers headed straight for WSM, looked around and found Hank at the shoe-shine stand. Hank listened in silence while Rivers made his pitch, then beckoned him into unoccupied Studio C. Rivers opened his fiddle case and was surprised when Hank reached in, grabbed the fiddle and started sawing away at "Sally Goodin'." When he finished, he said, "Kin you play 'Sally Goodin',' boy?" Rivers lit into it, and Hank picked up his guitar. "He was stompin' that foot, flailin' on the guitar," says Rivers. "We must have played it for five minutes, then he set down his guitar and I set down the fiddle, and he said, 'Well, anyone [who] can play "Sally Goodin' " better 'n me is a darn good fiddle player. You're hired.' "

Rivers found out that Hank still needed a bass player, so he called his friend Hillous Butrum. From rural Tennessee, Butrum had also been raised in Nashville, and he had played with Rivers when they were growing up. He graduated from tent shows with the blackface duo Jam Up and Honey to the staff band on the *Opry*, and by 1949 he was working with Benny Martin and Big Jeff Bess on WLAC. Just after Hank arrived in town, Butrum headed out to North Carolina to work on a tent show, but he starved out a few weeks later and came back to Nashville. When Rivers called asking if he'd like a job with Hank, Butrum told him he'd like a job with *anyone*. Butrum, Helms, and Hank met at eleven o'clock the next morning at WSM. They ran through a few tunes, and Butrum was hired. He went straightaway to see Big Jeff and bought a western suit for twenty bucks to look the part of a Drifting Cowboy.

Hank rehearsed the band in an empty WSM studio, then brought in Jim Denny, who was in the position to let them play on the *Opry* or insist that Hank use staff musicians. Denny said, "They sound good to me," and Hank settled their wages at fifteen dollars a show, five dollars over union scale. They could make as much or more selling songbooks and photos during the intermission. Hank was making around $250 a show (from which the *Opry* deducted commissions) shortly after he went to Nashville, but his asking price soon increased.

Rivers reckons that they started playing together on Thursday, July 14, 1949. They worked the *Opry* that Saturday, then rolled out of town in Hank's Packard en route for Cincinnati. "In those few moments on the stage of the *Opry* watching Hank perform, and watching the audience respond," Rivers wrote later, "I regained a humility I had lost somewhere along the line." The really great musicians evince that kind of respect from other musicians; "God is in the house" a jazz player once said when Art Tatum stepped up to the piano stool. With the applause of the *Opry* crowd still echoing in his ears, Rivers knew he had met the man who would change his life. Helms and McNett were less in awe of Hank because they had known him earlier. Helms in particular was more overwhelmed by finally playing the *Opry* and meeting all the artists he had heard about all those years.

Hank had never been happier. The atmosphere in the Packard was warm and convivial. Very soon, Hank had given everyone in the band a nickname. Don Helms was "Shag" because, as Rivers says, "before the days of much hair, Don had much." Rivers had a G.I. crewcut, so Hank called him "Burrhead." "When I'd tip my hat, he'd say, 'Look at that, looks like stump full of dead granddaddies,'" said Rivers. Hank called Hillous Butrum "Bew" because he was intrigued by his middle name, "Buel," and he called Bob McNett "Rapid Robert" because he liked to hear him play the barn-burner "Fingers on Fire." Occasionally he'd call McNett "The Mayor of Roaring Branch, Pennsylvania," and tell the audience that he had to roll peanuts off the mountain to get McNett to come join the band. That was the sort of homespun humor the crowds liked; Hank knew it too. The Cowboys called Hank "Bones" or "Gimly" (short for "Gimly-Ass") because he was so skinny he had no ass to speak of.

Hank's early *Opry* tours were organized by Oscar Davis in conjunction with Jim Denny, the *Opry*'s Artist Service Bureau manager. Second only to his relationship with Fred Rose, Hank's relationship with Denny was the critical relationship of his professional career, one founded on a mixture of mutual respect and antagonism. With a steely sense of purpose, Denny had worked his way up from the mailroom at National Life and Accident, the parent company of WSM. He had persuaded National Life to give him the concession stand at the *Opry* as a side venture, and he sold souvenirs, food, and fans. It became the first of many operations he conducted in which the distinction between his own interest and that of his employer was blurred. One of Denny's moonlight ventures was a short-lived recording studio that he operated before Castle Recording opened.

Denny found his niche when he was made Artist Service Bureau manager in November 1946. Originally set up in 1934 to arrange charity appearances, the Bureau under Denny came to control how the *Opry* name was used on touring packages, and it acted as a coordination point for the various tours and shows that *Opry* stars were on. Quickly, Denny parlayed his position into one of the most powerful jobs in country music. He could have written the book on winning through intimidation. Although only five feet nine inches tall, he was built like a bear, and he had been a bouncer at the *Opry* stage door during the '30s. He had a habit of staring at people and saying nothing, which spooked the naturally garrulous country performers, who abhorred a vacuum.

Denny divided the country into regions, and assigned them to different promoters who would have the right to book *Opry* shows into those regions. He would then work with the artists' managers if they had one or directly with the artists if they didn't to assemble package shows, which he offered to these franchisees. For this service and the right to use the *Opry* name on shows, the Artist Service Bureau took a percentage of the artist's fee; in fact, the fee was required whenever the *Opry* trademark was used, regardless of whether the Service Bureau had booked the show. That is how Hank Williams, who for three years was one of the *Opry*'s biggest stars, was often in hock to it.

If Hank didn't have much leverage at the *Opry*, he had newfound clout at MGM. In June 1949 he signed a new contract with the company, and on August 30 went back to Cincinnati to cut another session, the first since his *Opry* debut, and his last in Cincinnati. Records were the key to everything now. Hank had to answer the question of whether he was a flash in the pan who had got lucky with a pair of tunes or an artist with staying power. Increasingly, he decided to stand or fall with his own songs, and on the evidence of this session and every other session until his last, he was now the most accomplished writer in country music. Everyone has one great song in them — a few have several — but from among his contemporaries, only Floyd Tillman and Lefty Frizzell could rival Hank in the critical test of bringing an apparently infinite variety to an essentially limited format.

Floyd Tillman, the least known of the three, was perhaps the most innovative writer. Originally from rural Oklahoma, he graduated from

Texas country swing bands to write standards like "Slippin' Around," "It Makes No Difference Now," "I Love You So Much It Hurts," and "This Cold War with You," as well as wryly observed non-hits like "Small Little Town." His problem was that around 1949 he adopted a new singing style in which the world seemed to be viewed through the bottom of a shot glass. Radio play quickly dried up. Lefty Frizzell was still playing beer halls in Texas when Hank first appeared on the *Opry*. He had yet to make his first record, and was wondering if he would ever get a decent break, but a little more than a year later, his records were all over the charts.

Hank Williams, Floyd Tillman, and Lefty Frizzell all brought a new confessionality to country music. "May You Never Be Alone" was clearly born of a night wrestling despair; "You're Gonna Change (Or I'm Gonna Leave)" has the immediacy of an overheard argument. Frizzell's "I Love You a Thousand Ways" started as the poem of a penitent, written while he was in jail; Tillman's "Slippin' Around" forthrightly addressed a subject usually considered unsuitable for Home Folks — and did so without the usual escape hatch of singing in the third person or a moralistic tone. Other songs that hit the high spots on the country charts as the '40s gave way to the '50s, such as "Candy Kisses," "I'm Throwing Rice (At the Girl I Love)," and "Don't Rob Another Man's Castle," wouldn't have caused a ripple at a Victorian parlor recital.

To talk, as many have talked, of the poetry in Hank's lyrics is to overstate the case. Frank Walker popularized the phrase "hillbilly Shakespeare," but it had first been applied to Hank as early as 1947 in a Montgomery *Advertiser* feature, suggesting that Hank may himself have had some role in perpetuating it. In truth, there was more pure poetry in songs the bog Irish sang on the way back from the pub, like "Rose of Tralee" and "Last Rose of Summer," or in half-forgotten Tin Pan Alley clunkers like "Violets for Your Furs." Hank's achievement lay in casting the highs and lows of everyday life in terms that were at once simple enough to register quickly over a car radio or jukebox, yet sufficiently pointed and succinct to invite empathy and bear repeated listening. At best, every art form has the one-on-oneness of physical intimacy, and that was what Hank and, to a lesser extent, Lefty Frizzell and Floyd Tillman were bringing to country music.

To talk about Hank's writing only in terms of its simplicity is to miss the point. Like most of the truly great songwriters, Hank flirted with the banality of the obvious, but nearly always managed to sidestep it, which is as fine a line to walk as any. After he'd been writing for a few years, he stopped rejuggling clichés and gave his songs the little flashes of detail that invited identification, never losing his audience with wordiness or obscure images. From Fred Rose he'd also learned the importance of starting with a commanding image, like "Mind Your Own Business."

One of the enduring tales about Hank Williams the songwriter is that he purchased, even stole, ideas, finished songs, or half-finished songs. He certainly did that occasionally, and even wrote new songs to titles he had found on MGM release schedules ("I'm So Lonesome I Could Cry" was one), but to what he bought or purloined he added a piece of himself. Many, perhaps most, Hank Williams songs were the pure product of Hank himself, and, with a few exceptions, the songs that bear his name have the imprimatur of sole authorship.

Hank's melodies were the least original element in his craft. They usually impinged to a greater or lesser extent upon public domain folk-based melodies or archetypes. One consequence of this was that they had the instant recognizability that psychologists call perseveration. It also meant that his melodies bobbed up quickly from the subconscious, bringing with them the warm glow of recognition after surprisingly few listens. This was especially important since music didn't tend to saturate peoples' lives as it does today.

Starting with the last Cincinnati session, Hank came closer to hitting a home run every time at bat than anyone in country music before or since. Some claim to see promise in the songs that he wrote before his Acuff-Rose contract — indeed, Fred Rose must have been one of them — but most of Hank's early efforts were jejune and littered with clichés. The dramatic improvement has led many to the conclusion that Rose was responsible, and some, such as songwriter Boudleaux Bryant, who heard some of Hank's first drafts, go so far as to give Rose the lion's share of the credit. From among the hundreds, perhaps thousands, of songs that Rose wrote, though, few sound anything like a Hank Williams song. Rose himself emphasized that point when he spoke after Hank's death: "Don't get the idea that I made the guy or wrote his songs for him," said Rose. "He made himself, don't forget that!"

Two final points worth emphasizing are that even though Hank's writing is littered with clichés by today's standards, they weren't clichés in 1949. It's a measure of his success that they're clichés now. Also, the overall impact of Hank's songs can easily be weakened through textual investigation. The mood Hank captured so effectively in simple words and the cumulative effect of those words strung together, particularly when sung by him, can easily be lost when parsed and analyzed too thoroughly.

Rose deliberately excluded everyone from his writing sessions with Hank, so we'll never know who did precisely what, but in all likelihood, Rose brought no more than a commercial gloss and organizational skills to Hank's work. He encouraged him to write bridges rather than simply string verses together, and provided a much needed element of quality control. Another lesson was probably that Hank should dispense with archaic folk forms like "ne'er" and "o'er," and assert the primacy of everyday speech.

Hank did most of his writing on the road. There wasn't even room to break out a guitar in the sedan, so he'd beat out a rhythm on the dashboard and someone would get something like a cardboard stiffener from a pressed shirt and take the words down. Hank would come back off the road with a billfold full of scraps of paper on which he had verses, half-completed songs, and abandoned ideas. The band would kid him because his billfold was so thick. They'd say, "Hoss, be careful, you'll fall off that billfold, break an arm and we'll have to get us a new lead singer." All the melodies were in Hank's head.

Whenever Hank was asked about his songwriting, he was careful to downplay the element of song craft, something he perhaps thought unbecoming a "folk" musician. "People don't write music," he told *Pathfinder* magazine in 1952. "It's given to you; you sit there and wait and it comes to you. If [a song] takes longer than thirty minutes or an hour, I usually throw it away." It was up to Fred Rose to separate the wheat from the chaff and to work with Hank to make integrated, complete songs taut with commercial logic. If Rose contributed over 50 percent, as he did on "Mansion on the Hill" and later "Kaw-Liga," he took half the credit; if he simply doctored a song up, he didn't. Rose knew that he would collect on the publisher's share of the royalty, and, according to general consensus, he was not a greedy man.

The only person to walk in on Hank and Fred Rose working together was Roy Acuff, and his description was studiedly trite, adding little to our understanding. "They worked as a good team of mules," Acuff said on an MGM Records documentary. "They pulled right together. Hank would come up with the ideas, and Fred would say, 'Well, write it down and let me look at it.' Hank'd bring it to Fred, and Fred would sit at the piano and complement Hank and say, 'Well, maybe you ought to express this a little differently. Let's change it a little bit,' but Fred never changed Hank's thinking."

For his part, Hank took Rose's lessons to heart, worked hard at his craft, and received the best positive reinforcement there was: glory. Quite simply, his music improved.

Even so, the songs were only half the story. It was Hank's delivery that etched them into memory. On tour with Tubb earlier in 1949, Hank told him, "I've found me a place right between you and ol' Roy Acuff," but in saying that, he was shortchanging himself. On the slow numbers, called "heart songs," Hank sang with Acuff's riveting conviction — they were literally cries from the heart. To the faster songs and the talking blues, he brought Tubb's measured irony. Never, though, did he sound as though he was alternating between two styles; rather, it seemed that in performing, Hank found a means of expressing all that seethed within him, and what emerged was identifiably Hank Williams, not a crude pastiche of two of the most popular styles in town.

Hank's ultimate triumph was that he learned to tell an audience of thousands what he couldn't tell someone sitting across the room. "If he'd had the personality offstage that he had onstage, he'd have been all right," said Lum York, so often the victim of Hank's interminable, impenetrable silences. Too often, Hank felt the need to mask his tenderheartedness with callousness and shitkicker bravado, but in his songs he let his weakness show, increasingly so once he discovered that everyone else was weak too.

By late 1949, Hank Williams was no longer in the process of becoming a songwriter. He was one and the session held between 2:00 and 5:30 P.M. on August 30, 1949, at the Herzog Studio in Cincinnati was proof. Although Hank now had the most accomplished band he had ever led, Rose still wanted him to record with The Pleasant Valley Boys — Zeke Turner, Jerry Byrd, and Louis Innis — and Rose was prepared to go to them in Cincinnati. Hank drove down to meet them from Milwaukee, where he had been working a weeklong stint at the Palace Theater with Ernest Tubb, Cowboy Copas, and Minnie Pearl. His road band stood in the studio and watched, but didn't play.

The first song they cut was "I'm So Lonesome I Could Cry." Here is the chill of the void that would become one of the hallmarks of Hank's writing. It is the most oft cited example of Hank Williams the hillbilly poet, but its poetic form comes from the fact that it was originally intended to be spoken, not sung. Acuff-Rose staff writer Vic McAlpin said that Hank had written it for his first session of recitations slated for January 1950, but at some point he changed his mind. "I think ol' Hank needs to record this," he told McAlpin. Hank was concerned that some of the lines might sound self-consciously artsy and alienate his audience, but, as he so often did, he tried out the song on friends, fellow performers, and Fred Rose, and let them convince him that he had excelled.

Zeke Turner underpinned "I'm So Lonesome I Could Cry" with recurring figures on the bass strings of his electric guitar. A few weeks earlier, he had led the backing on The Delmore Brothers' King recording of "Blues Stay Away from Me," using very similar licks, and they were clearly still echoing in his mind. Jerry Byrd played a solo of unusual simplicity, paraphrasing the melody to haunting effect, with subtle adjustments of tone and volume. Hank delivered his words with utter conviction that never once sunk to bathos.

"I'm So Lonesome I Could Cry" was a triumph — and the record Hank would often cite as his personal favorite. However, when it was released on November 8, 1949, it was on the flip side of "My Bucket's Got a Hole in It," another song that Fred Rose didn't want to touch. Quite how or when Hank got the notion to record it is unclear. The most commonly accepted theory is that Tee-Tot taught it to him, although Pappy Neal McCormick also took the credit. Whatever its provenance, it's hard to know why Hank chose that moment to revive it. Perhaps he was scouring his mind for other old songs because "Lovesick Blues" had been so successful, and his own songs less so.

"My Bucket's Got a Hole in It" had made the rounds as "*The* Bucket's Got a Hole in It" (and had been recorded as such by Tom Gates for Gennett in 1927) before it was copyrighted in 1933 as "*My* Bucket's Got a Hole in It" by Clarence Williams. Williams was a black New Orleans composer, pianist, and A&R man who wrote "Baby, Won't You Please Come Home" and "Royal Garden Blues" and had worked with Frank Walker back in the '20s. His own recordings bridged jazz and hokum, and "My Bucket's Got a Hole in It" was firmly in that tradition. By the time Hank got around to the song, it had been lying fallow since 1938, when blues singer Washboard Sam had cut it. Both Clarence Williams and Frank Walker were based in New York, so it's just possible that Williams pitched it to Walker, but more likely Hank retrieved it from his own storehouse of half-forgotten songs. He sang only a fraction of the eight couplets, leaving out this delightfully oblique verse about a frigid woman: "Wintertime is cold, dear, summertime is too / You know a doggone iceberg'll turn black to blue."

The unique feature of Hank's record was that it had an acoustic guitar break that Hank apparently played himself, making it his only recorded solo. Louis Innis played rhythm guitar on the session, choking up on the neck to get the percussive effect that Fred Rose wanted, and he can be heard keeping time under the solo, so he's clearly not the soloist. The song was delivered with the mellow, compelling swing that underscored Hank's feel for black music.

The other two songs Hank cut that day in Cincinnati were somber reflections on what his life had quickly become. "A House Without Love" resonates with emptiness and unfulfillment. The words "we slaved to gain a worthless treasure" and "the simple things have gone forever" were bleak commentaries on what success was doing to the Williamses' ever less-than-stable relationship. "I Just Don't Like This Kind of Living" was a tad faster and had flashes of Hank's dark humor ("You ain't never bin known to be wrong, and I ain't never bin right"). Audrey's thoughts can only be guessed at as she heard the substance of their domestic disputes on the radio, particularly as only one side ever got aired. Perhaps, like a game show contestant, she was willing to live with any amount of humiliation for the prize money.

Audrey, in fact, was spending the prize money, and more that Hank had yet to make. She and Hank had picked out a house at 4916 Franklin Road, and the deal closed four days after the session on September 3, 1949. They paid twenty-one thousand dollars for the three-bedroom, ranch-style house set back from the road on three acres. It was more or less in the country, but still conveniently close to the new Acuff-Rose building at 2510 Franklin, which Hank had also partly paid for. Audrey had big plans for the house, which, like Graceland, became a monument to what good money and bad taste can accomplish. A new bedroom, den, breezeway, and two-car garage were added almost immediately, and Audrey went out and bought the most expensive furnishings she could find. The prevailing motif was Oriental: shiny black lacquer and dragons — lots of dragons. To Audrey, kitsch was a step up. The furnishings looked and felt so unusual and cost so much that Hank told his band he was afraid to sit on them. He preferred to lounge on the floor instead. The simple things really had gone forever.

Just days after the house purchase, Hank and an *Opry* troupe including Ernest Tubb and Roy Acuff flew to the northwest, and while they were there Hank made his first public appearance in Canada when he appeared in Vancouver on September 13. On the same trip, Hank reoutfitted himself at Nudie's Rodeo Tailors in Los Angeles. When he arrived from Shreveport, his principal stage outfit was still the poorly fitting western suit that Tillman Franks had sold him, but now he had something more flamboyant in mind. Nudie Cohen later became famous for

Leila Griffin

Hank (left) with Irene.

Leila Griffin

Elonzo Huble Williams. Gentleman forester.

City of Georgiana

The Skipper clan, circa 1925. Lillie is on the far left next to her brother-in-law, Walter McNeil. Hank is in front of her. J.C. and Opal McNeil are fourth and fifth from the lower right. Irene Williams and her cousins, Bernice McNeil and Marie McNeil (Harvell), are third, second, and first from the lower right.

George Merritt

Walking the streets of Montgomery with the "WPA Blues."

Left to right: Hezzy Adair, Freddy Beach, Señor Juan Lobo, Hank, Braxton Schuffert.

HANK & HEZZY'S DRIFTIN COWBOYS FEATURING SEÑOR JUAN LOBO

Fred & Irella Beach/Escott/Merritt

Lum York/Escott/Merritt

Stars of WSFA. Left to right top: Winston "Red" Todd, Hank, Little Joe Pennington (Joe Penney), R. D. Norred; bottom: Lum York.

Audrey and Hank days before the happy day.

Richard Bennett

A photo call on the Lost Highway. Hank and Audrey with Lycrecia, circa 1948.

Richard Bennett

Leila Griffin

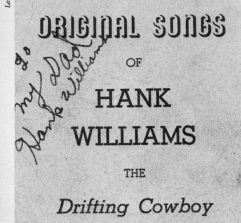

ORIGINAL SONGS

OF

HANK WILLIAMS

THE

Drifting Cowboy

BOOK 2

PRICE 50 CENTS

Colin Escott

A copy of the 1945 songbook. Hank has autographed it to his father.

Wesley (left) and Fred Rose selling Songs to Home Folks.

Sweet harmony— for now, at least.

George Merritt

Colin Escott

Frank Walker (left) and Hank.

Colin Escott

The Sterling Records advertisement. A composite of everything country music was trying to live down.

En route to Shreveport, Hank appears at Daily's record store, Houston, July 31, 1948. Left to right: Jerry Jericho, Hank, Biff Collie.

Don Daily

Don Daily

Ever so slightly stoned at the jukebox. Hank and Jerry Jericho at South Coast
Amusement Co., Houston, July 31, 1948.

making Elvis's gold lamé outfit and the suit with rhinestones inlaid as marijuana leaves, which he crafted for Gram Parsons of the Flying Burrito Brothers, but even as far back as the late '40s he was making sure that no one would walk onstage unnoticed. Audrey, who appears to have joined Hank on the trip, bought matching outfits for herself, clearly signaling that Hank *and* Audrey were back in business. When she hired a nurse/housekeeper, Audrey Ragland, in September 1949, she told her that she would be on the road with Hank.

Evidence of what a Hank and Audrey radio show was like comes from Hank's first syndicated radio series, the *Health and Happiness* show, in October 1949. It was an ironic title as Hank never had much of either. Eight fifteen-minute shows were recorded on two successive Sundays that October. They were the brainchild of Matt Hedrick, advertising manager at WSM. He pitched Dudley J. LeBlanc, a state senator from Louisiana and inventor of a foul-tasting patent medicine called Hadacol, on the notion of sponsoring Hank. LeBlanc had seen Hank in Lafayette, and was reaping the benefit of having Bill Nettles's "Hadacol Boogie" in the charts, so he leaped at Hedrick's idea.

LeBlanc had little direct involvement with the *Health and Happiness* shows except to underwrite them, and for once in his life, he was outscammed. Hedrick made sure that Hank never mentioned Hadacol; in that way, he had a set of generic shows he could resell to other sponsors. The transcriptions were duplicated onto banded sixteen-inch discs that ran at 33 rpm. After almost every song, Hank made an all-purpose pitch, like "Here's someone with some news that'll make you mighty glad you tuned in." At that point, the engineers on the local stations would stop the disc, a local announcer would read the pitch, and then the discs would be restarted.

Clearly, Hank was the new boy in town with something to prove. He sang every song with frightening conviction that was strangely at odds with his molassified patter between songs. Audrey was on the first four shows, joining Hank on the closing hymn and taking her own solo spots. She followed "I'm a Long Gone Daddy" with "I'm Telling You," a song that appears to be a self-composed attempt to vent her side of the story, but, as ever, she shoots herself in the foot by singing off-key and breaking meter. It was probably at LeBlanc's request that she was dropped when the last four shows were recorded.

Hank was, if anything, in even better form on the four shows without Audrey. He out-Acuffed Acuff on "The Prodigal Son," then stepped back, regrouped, and invested "Mind Your Own Business" with even more damning sarcasm than on the record, throwing in a fresh couplet after the break: "If I get my head beat black and blue / Brother, that's my wife and my stove wood too." The shows also included Hank's only surviving recording of "Tramp on the Street," the song that had earned him his break.

The *Health and Happiness* shows were the first recorded evidence of Hank's new Drifting Cowboys. In the three months they'd worked together, they had clearly been schooled in what he wanted. Hank hated pickers who were too busy. When he was singing he didn't want the impact of his vocals undermined by cute fills, and he wanted the solos as simple and direct as his singing. He would spin around and glare at any musician who got too close to jazz for his liking. "I know a lot of good guitar players," he once said, "who've educated themselves right out of a job." Later, when Hank Garland came to town and quickly proved himself the most technically adroit picker in country music, Hank was dismissive. "Aw," he said, "he's still searchin' for it. I've found it."

Hillous Butrum was one who occasionally got too fancy for Hank. "Mostly I'd play two-four time," said Hillous. "Hank come to me one night and he said, 'Hillous, you play as good a bass as anyone I ever heard — at times. Then all of a sudden you'll take off on that thing and I don't know where you're going.' When we'd do 'Move It on Over' I'd switch to four-four on the break and Hank never understood what I was doing. You wasn't supposed to hear a bass note except ever' other one."

Plain and simple — that had got Hank where he was, and he wasn't about to try for sophistication now. It was a philosophy that extended to his singing. If he sang "perhaps," he pronounced it "pre-haps"; if he sang "picture," he pronounced it "pitcher." Odder yet, when he sang "Armageddon" in "The Battle of Armageddon," he pronounced it "Am-be-gotten." It may have contributed to the social transmission of illiteracy, but Hank was there to entertain, not inform. "Vanilla, boys," he had said back in the mid-forties, and that was still his credo.

Right after the *Health and Happiness* shows, Hank and his band hit the road on a tour that took them up into Ontario, Canada, in late October 1949. Then, on November 13, Hank was sent over to Europe as part of the Prince Albert *Opry* revue. The *Opry* troupe was to play U.S. Air Force bases on a two-week tour sponsored by R. J. Reynolds. In Air Force–speak, it was to be a "non revenue mission," and, according to the protocol of the day, the Russians were informed. Hillbilly music was immensely popular among servicemen overseas. *Hillbilly Gasthaus* was the highest-rated show on Armed Forces Radio (AFN), and it was at the request of the enlisted men that the *Opry* was sent over.

Red Foley led the revue, backed by Roy Acuff, Jimmy Dickens, Minnie Pearl, and Rod Brasfield. Harry Stone, Jim Denny, and announcer Grant Turner also went along. Acuff took his daughter, Thelma, who did a tap-dance routine, and they all were allowed to bring their spouses because they would be away for Thanksgiving. Acuff and Foley brought their own bands, but Hank was to work with Foley's band.

The troupe left Nashville on what had been General Eisenhower's private plane. They landed in Newfoundland to refuel, then hunkered down for the night flight over the Atlantic. Hank, long habituated to sleeping in the sitting position, snuggled next to Audrey and put his coat over them. The next morning, they arrived in Paris, France, to refuel, then went on to Wiesbaden, Germany. A German oom-pah band played "Dixie" to welcome them. They visited all the base hospitals and put on shows in Berlin, Frankfurt, Munich, and Vienna. The Berlin and Frankfurt shows were recorded for transmission back home on the Prince Albert portion of the *Opry*. Hank only had three hits to draw on, but he was called back for encore after encore at every hall they played. A few surviving transcriptions prove emphatically how popular he now was.

Hank was straight as an arrow and so careful to avoid alcohol that he sniffed his glass at mealtimes to make sure that it contained water, not wine. That didn't stop him playing the part of the ugly American to the hilt, though. Faced with any dish he didn't recognize, he would holler, "Hey, Herman, bring me the ketchup!" Aside from brief forays into Canada and Mexico, this was Hank's first experience of a foreign country, and he wasn't going to let it broaden his mind if he could help it. On the way back, the plane touched down to refuel in Bermuda, and the troupe played at the U.S. Naval air base there.

Back home, Hank had a few days to shake off jet lag before heading out on the road again. In September, Oscar Davis had dropped all his other clients to handle Hank exclusively, and now Hank was beginning to understand what real pressure was like. In Montgomery or Shreveport he had usually played within driving distance of home, and if he missed a show date or two he could do a "make-good" later if he felt like it. Now he was working with structured itineraries that took him away from home all week. Too often, he would arrive home on Friday night and have to leave again on Saturday night or Sunday morning.

Hank arrived back to see "My Bucket's Got a Hole in It" climbing the charts. It had reached number two by the end of December. Among the records that kept it from the number one slot were The Delmore Brothers' "Blues Stay Away from Me" and Red Foley's "Chattanoogie Shoe Shine Boy," both creditable stabs at Rhythm 'n' Blues.

After successful tours out west, through the southwest, and up the Ohio valley into Canada, Oscar Davis had decided to promote Hank on the eastern seaboard during the period leading up to Christmas. On December 8, he was to star for a week at the Hippodrome Theater in Baltimore, and was scheduled to follow it with a Potomac River Cruise show and a headline appearance at the Roosevelt Hotel in Washington. But he started drinking in Dayton, Ohio, after losing some money in a crap game, and by the time he got to Baltimore he was well drunk. It was the first time the new Drifting Cowboys had seen Hank on a bender. The group checked in to the hotel behind the Hippodrome with everyone on edge because Hank, although drunk, still thought himself able to perform. The band was watching him closely, but Hank was more resourceful than anyone gave him credit for when he needed a drink. He bribed a bellhop to bring up whiskey miniatures hidden inside a pitcher of ice and arranged for one of the women in the square dance troupe to hide miniatures in her skirt for him.

The rule of thumb that people came to use with Hank was that it would take about three days for him to get good and drunk and then three days to get over it. As he had done in Louisiana, Hank would start by making the shows, swaying precariously but always somehow managing to remain upright. "Here I am in Baltimore," he told the audience. "I ain't never been in Baltimore. If I come back, it'll be twice I been here." He said that every show — four shows a day. Oscar Davis eventually took him off the bill and brought in old-time yodeler Elton Britt to fill in. Audrey was flown up from Nashville for her expertise, and Helms and McNett went to pick her up at the airport. Later, as she sat disconsolately in the hotel lobby, she turned to McNett and said, "I'm so upset and discouraged, I think I've lost the love I had for Hank." But, since she was there, she decided she would do some shows with him after he'd straightened out.

By December 16, Hank was clearly back on track. He and Cowboy Copas set an attendance record at the Victory Room in the Hotel Roosevelt in Washington. Nine hundred were admitted, with another five hundred turned away, but Audrey's insistence upon performing led to another rift. Finally, Hank refused to let her sing, and she stormed back home. Hank came into the room that McNett and Butrum were sharing, put his foot up on the window ledge and said, "Boys, it's heck to have a wife in the business that wants to sing, but it's worse'n that to have one that wants to sing and cain't."

Still, Hank was home for Christmas with Audrey, their first in Nashville, and their first with Hank Jr. The cracks were papered over, and when Hank went downtown, as he invariably did, to buy a copy of *Billboard*, he would have seen the year-end tallies that showed he had shot from nowhere to become the second-best–selling country singer of the year behind Eddy Arnold. He had placed eight songs on the country charts in 1949, but Arnold had placed thirteen and was still clearly the man to beat.

Among the unanswerable questions that Hank may have asked himself as he wriggled uncomfortably on his Oriental furniture that Christmas were these: Would he ever have made it without "Lovesick Blues," without that nothing song that, in terms of song craft at least, Fred Rose was right to disparage? Without its catalytic effect would Rose have lost interest in the undistinguished songs that Hank was sending up from Louisiana? Would MGM have dropped him when his contract was up that year? Would Hank himself have become so discouraged that he would have left the business, as he had told Johnny Bond he would do the preceding Christmas? What if Fred Rose had stuck to his guns and refused to let Hank record "Lovesick Blues"? Then, instead of soaring in 1949, Hank Williams's recording career might simply have petered out that year.

Chapter

9

The songs always seemed to drift out of a
cold dark room, which just a few hours
before had been brightly lit and filled with
the voices of friends.
Mark Moses, *New Yorker*, May 9, 1988

• •

HELL IN TEXAS

• •

*T*HE year 1950 opened with Hank preparing for
two recording sessions, scheduled for January
9 and 10. Frank Walker came to Nashville to work with Rose on the
ninth, the only time Hank worked with anyone behind the glass other
than Fred Rose. It was also the first time Hank was allowed to use his
road band. Still, he had a concern that ran far deeper than working with
Walker or prepping his band for studio work; Hank needed another
blockbuster. "Mind Your Own Business," "You're Gonna Change," and
"My Bucket's Got a Hole in It" had all sold well enough, but none of
them had come close to eclipsing "Lovesick Blues" or "Wedding Bells."
The midsize hits were fine — they kept the pot boiling — but Hank
needed a song that would rule the airwaves for months. As with a successful sports franchise, he needed to deliver the big prize every now
and again to keep the attendance up.

Hank and Fred Rose decided that their best shot rested with "Long
Gone Lonesome Blues," a song that had in almost every sense been sired
by "Lovesick Blues." Rose, of course, couldn't risk another lawsuit from
Mills Music, so the melody wasn't litigiously close, but Hank had con-
sciously crafted a song that had "blues" in the title, with windows for
the yodels and flashes of falsetto that had proved so effective on "Lovesick Blues." The tempo was almost identical, and the lyrics were as inconsequential. The song's architecture and arrangement were kissing

cousins too, right down to the unison yodeling figure from the lead guitar and the steel guitar at the intro.

Hank liked to tell interviewers that he just closed off his mind and let God write his songs, but "Long Gone Lonesome Blues" was squeezed out line by line from a title that Hank had been nursing for a while. The pieces came together on a fishing trip with songwriter Vic McAlpin. They had left early to drive out to the Tennessee River where it broadens into Kentucky Lake, but Hank had been unable to sleep on the trip, and was noodling around aimlessly with the title all the way. As McAlpin told it to Roger Williams, he and Hank were already out on the lake when McAlpin became frustrated with Hank's preoccupation. "You come here to fish or watch the fish swim by?" he asked, and that was the key that unlocked the song for Hank. "Hey!" he said. "That's the first line!" Then it fell into place. All the old blues clichés he had ever heard about going to the river, jumping in three times, and only coming up twice came flooding back to him. McAlpin contributed a few lines, but Hank later bought him out.

In case "Long Gone Lonesome Blues" didn't make it, Hank had written himself an insurance policy, "Why Don't You Love Me (Like You Used to Do)." It showed that he could still afford to be lighthearted about the persistent difficulties with Audrey. "I'm the same old trouble you've always been through," he told her. "Why Should We Try Anymore?" was a wintry variation on the same theme. It was based loosely on "I'm Not Coming Home Any More," and in its four verses, written without a bridge, Hank limned a bleak picture of a marriage gone stale. It was impossible not to draw the conclusion that it was his own.

The session was rounded out with another stab at "My Son Calls Another Man Daddy." Developed by Hank from an original idea by songwriter Jewell House, it was a contrived piece that lacked all the compelling immediacy of the songs Hank drew from his own experience. There were hundreds of similar songs in the history and prehistory of country music. The man in jail loses his son; "I'll ne'er know his name or his face," sang Hank, once again resorting to an archaic form as he often would when he was trying for something with a traditional flavor.

After admitting that he was wrong to steer Hank uptown with songs like "Fly Trouble" and "Rootie Tootie," Rose had come to appreciate that Hank was plugged in to a segment of the market that neither craved nor aspired to sophistication. He had come to share Hank's "vanilla" philosophy: plain and simple. Bob McNett remembered that during rehearsals he hit some licks and then looked up at the control room. "Is that too country?" he asked. "You can never get too country," Rose told him. Not on a Hank Williams session, anyway.

As they began working together, Rose helped the band refine and define what is still known as the Hank Williams sound. He gave Don Helms what he considered the golden rule for accompanying Hank. "Fred said it was useless for me and Hank to be in the same register," said Helms. "He said, 'When Hank is singing something low, why don't you play high, and if he's singing high, you play something low,' so the steel would always be in a different register." Once, when Helms wasn't playing high enough for Rose's liking, he came out of the control room and moved the steel guitar, gesturing with his hands, showing how much higher he wanted it. That was hands-on production circa 1950.

Rose also told Jerry Rivers to play in the traditional double-stop fiddle style, in which the melody and the harmony are carried on two strings. Hank always called it the "garden seed" fiddle. There was to be no more jazzy single-string western swing fiddle on a Hank Williams record.

When the Turner brothers had been in Hank's backing group, they had been allowed to take solos, but from this point on, the electric guitar was mostly limited to keeping time with the bass. Hank played acoustic rhythm guitar, although Rose tried to persuade him to drop it and concentrate on his singing. Hank probably knew that the guitar helped him keep time, so he hung on to it, but Rose wouldn't put a microphone on it. He brought along a rhythm guitarist, usually Jack Shook, to carry the load, and it's Shook's driving acoustic guitar that underpins most Hank Williams records.

Rose had very precise ideas about the pace of every song. If it was going too fast or dragging, he would come down from the control room, sit at the piano, and pound it out at the tempo he thought suited the piece. At first, the band was surprised at the way Hank and Fred Rose seemed to be at each other's throats in the studio, but the bickering was, they found out, just the dynamic of their working relationship. Hank took note of Rose's suggestions most of the time, and, for his part, Rose gave Hank a lot of latitude. "Hank needed Fred to say, 'That's a good un,'" said Don Helms, "but if Fred said, 'Naw, naw, it needs . . . such and such,' Hank would say, 'I don't see it,' and Fred would say, 'It does. Let me show you why,' and then Hank would usually say, 'Awright, okay.'"

Rose's true feelings about the second day's sessions are hard to guess at. On January 10, Hank returned to cut his first set of recitations as Luke the Drifter. The recitation was a tradition embedded deep in country music, and one that was still kicking as it went down; in fact, T. Texas Tyler's narration "Deck of Cards" had been one of the best-selling records of 1948. The recitation was a little homily, usually with a strong moral undertone, narrated to musical accompaniment. Hank would have heard Cowboy Slim Rinehart broadcast complete programs of recitations over the powerful unregulated Mexican border stations, and he performed them from time to time on his own radio shows.

Helms says that Hank pestered Rose long and hard to be able to cut the recitations, so they were clearly something close to Hank's heart; in fact, he says, Hank was more deeply committed to the Luke the Drifter recitations than to his regular songs. Rose's objection was one of commercial logic: the jukebox operators had huge standing orders for Hank Williams records, and, if the recitations were issued under Hank's name, the operators would complain they had been sold a worthless bill of goods. Virtually all of the operators serviced bars, and the last thing they needed was for someone to punch up a Hank Williams record and get a sermon. Credibility in the marketplace is hard to obtain and easy to lose, and Hank didn't have enough of a track record to take risks like that.

The *nom de disque* was a way of circumventing the problem, but from the beginning there was no attempt to disguise the identity of Luke the Drifter. An entry in *Billboard*'s "Folk Talent and Tunes" section made it obvious to the trade. It was one of those open secrets that deejays like to divulge on air to give the impression that they are somehow privy to a set of scrolls denied the ordinary man. In interviews, Hank never denied that he was Luke the Drifter, and he said that the records were primarily designed for the "take home" trade.

Just how valid Rose's concerns were is made clear by the numbers. The jukebox operators were a hugely powerful force in the industry. In 1950, there were 400,000 jukeboxes on location serviced by 5,500 jukebox operators. Even though the number of operators was dwarfed by the number of home phonograph owners (then estimated at between sixteen and seventeen million), the operators bought an average of 150 records a week, whereas the average record buyer bought fewer than ten a year. Wesley Rose estimated that if one of Hank's records sold 250,000 copies, the jukebox operators accounted for 150,000 of those sales. The ops, as they were known, were accommodated to the point that most songwriters, including Hank, kept their song titles to fewer than five words so that they would fit on the jukebox cards and made sure their records timed out at under three minutes and twelve seconds, the time at which a standard groove record would automatically eject from a jukebox turntable.

Every year the jukebox operators' organization, the Music Operators of America, held a convention that was celebrated with special issues of *Billboard* and *Cashbox*. Virtually all of the industry's grandees and wanna-bes took out advertisements to greet the ops and thank them for buying their product. The major record labels laid on entertainment at the MOA conventions, and Hank was sent to the March 1950 convention in Chicago. Rose wanted nothing less than to alienate the ops, but in refusing to let Hank cut the recitations he was alienating his prize asset, something else he could ill afford. "Luke the Drifter" was the best compromise he could hope for in the circumstances.

Hank was particularly keen to cut two recitations, "The Funeral" and "Beyond the Sunset." A matter of weeks before the Luke the Drifter session, Elton Britt had cut "Beyond the Sunset," and T. Texas Tyler had just cut both "Beyond the Sunset" and "The Funeral" (which he titled "Colored Child's Funeral"). Then, a few days after the Luke the Drifter session, east coast deejay Buddy Starcher also cut both. From this distance, it's hard to know why there was such a flurry of activity around these two commercially stillborn prospects. As poems, they had been kicking around in one form or another for decades.

"The Funeral" was, by contemporary standards, an almost hatefully patronizing account of a black child's funeral service. Originally it was a poem by Will Carleton, first published around 1909, and designed for recitation in black patois. This caricatured speech form was common in turn-of-the-century songs like "Carry Me Back to Ol' Virginny" ("Dat's where de darkie's heart am longed to roam . . ."). Unlike Starcher and Tyler, though, Hank delivered "The Funeral" in his regular voice, and was clearly extending every ounce of compassion within him. His sincerity is obvious, but the vernacular of the poem undermines it: "I pictured him while livin', curly hair, protrudin' lips. I'd seen perhaps a thousand in my hurried southern trips." Then the preacher arises: ". . . with a manner sorta awkward and countenance grotest [sic]. The simplicity and shrewdness in his Ethiopian face, showed the ignorance and wisdom of a crushed, undying race." In the background, an organ (played by Fred Rose or Owen Bradley) added the reedy chords of Rose's "A House Built on a Rock," with accenting from Don Helms's steel guitar. When Rose submitted artist and publisher information to MGM, he noted that there was to be no songwriter or publisher on the record label, but that he was to receive half the composer royalty for "A House Built on a Rock." Later, the Williams estate claimed "The Funeral" as one of Hank's compositions, and in a 1993 edition of his lyrics, it appeared absurdly in a new, politically correct version (the "protruding lips," for instance, were now "smiling lips").

Bob McNett didn't play on "The Funeral," but he was there when it was recorded. He remembers that when Hank and Helms finished, they both had tears running down their cheeks. "I've formed an opinion of Hank over late years that I had never thought of when I was working with him," he said. "Hank had a deep personal feeling for his fellow man. This didn't show on the outside. You had to get to know him, and then he'd give himself away every now and again about his deep concern for people who were less fortunate. 'The Funeral' touched him. When he did it, he lost himself in it." On his recitations Hank rarely gave in to mawkishness. He was simply, almost painfully, direct, letting his tenderness and compassion edge out the knucklehead swagger with which he often greeted the world.

The words that Hank spoke over "Beyond the Sunset" were pure Victoriana caught out of time. They came from "Should You Go First," a poem by Albert "Rosey" Rosewell that first appeared in a book called *Rosey Reflections*. Hank probably found it in a popular anthology called *Poems That Touch the Heart*. Tillman Franks claimed to have given Hank his copy of the book, but it was on almost as many shelves as the Bible in the late '40s, and tucked next to it as well. Even Elvis Presley on his way to serve in Germany said at a news conference that he had been reading *Poems That Touch the Heart* on the train and had been especially moved by "Should You Go First." The hymn "Beyond the Sunset" and the words to "Should You Go First" were first conjoined by Chickie Williams, a performer on WWVA, Wheeling, West Virginia. Elton Britt's version briefly cracked the charts in February 1950, three weeks before Hank's was released, but it didn't linger.

Two other recitations were cut that January day. The first was "Too Many Parties and Too Many Pals," a morality play in one mercifully short act by Tin Pan Alley veteran Billy Rose (no relation to Fred) and two other New Yorkers. It was first published in 1925, when Rose, the writer of songs like "I Found a Million Dollar Baby (In a Five and Ten Cent Store)," "Clap Hands, Here Comes Charley," and "I Got a Code id By Dose," was new to the business. The piece had become something of a hillbilly standard, and one of the earlier versions had been by Bill Haley, then leading his Saddlemen. Hank's version was released in June 1950 with his own sardonic "Everything's Okay," a

"What, Me Worry?" talking blues he had first sent to Fred Rose back in August 1947.

"Long Gone Lonesome Blues" did exactly what Hank calculated it would do. On March 25, 1950, it shot straight into the charts at number two, staying there until April 29, when it dislodged another Acuff-Rose copyright, "Chattanoogie Shoe Shine Boy," from the number one spot. It was the knockout punch Hank needed, and it ended up spending twenty-one weeks on the charts, eight of them at the top. None of the Luke the Drifter releases sold sufficiently well to attract chart action. By August 1950, "Too Many Parties" had sold 20,000 copies; "The Funeral" had sold only 6,600 copies. As a benchmark, "Long Gone Lonesome Blues" had sold 150,000 copies.

Hank's credibility was born anew, and "Long Gone Lonesome Blues" set the stage for the unprecedented success he would enjoy until his death, success that would create its own ceaseless pressure to keep delivering. For the present, Hank was desperately eager to rise to the challenge.

Nothing else was recorded until June 14, when, at a half-session, Hank cut Leon Payne's "They'll Never Take Her Love from Me" and a third version of "Honky Tonk Blues," which was abandoned. After "Long Gone Lonesome Blues" had spent eight weeks at number one, only to be replaced by "Why Don't You Love Me," Hank was probably disappointed when "They'll Never Take Her Love from Me" topped out at number five. The message was fairly clear: the public wanted brisk, up-tempo novelties from Hank. No matter that posterity might judge him the finest writer and singer of "heart" songs in the history of country music; his radio and jukebox audience wanted toe-tappers.

Even though he cut only two sessions between January and June 1950, Hank was in and out of Castle Studio with friends and relatives. Back in October 1949 Hank had played several days at the Michigan State Fair with Bill Monroe, the man who had to all intents and purposes invented bluegrass music. It was probably in Michigan that they wrote a song together, "I'm Blue, I'm Lonesome" (credited to "James B. Smith"). Monroe recorded it on February 3, 1950, during his first sessions for Decca. At the same time, he cut "Alabama Waltz," a song that Hank had written to stoke the ongoing craze for "state waltzes" (such as Bill Monroe's "Kentucky Waltz," Pee Wee King's "Tennessee Waltz," etc.). Monroe doesn't remember if Hank was at the session, but if he was in town, he usually liked to sit on the sidelines when his songs were being cut.

Hank was definitely at Castle for Braxton Schuffert's recording session five days later. It's hard to know if Hank felt a debt to Braxton that he wanted to repay, or if he truly thought Braxton stood a chance of making it. Since the war, Braxton had been working six days a week for Hormel Meats in Montgomery, still struggling to keep a hand in the music business by performing solo spots sponsored by Hormel on WCOV and WSFA. Whenever Hank went back to Montgomery, he dogged Braxton to take another stab at the music business, and in January 1950 he took matters into his own hands. He called Brack's wife and told her that he had train tickets ready, a backstage pass to the *Opry*, and reservations at the Hermitage Hotel. Braxton begged off work and took the Saturday morning train up to Nashville. He joined the melee backstage at the *Opry*, and the next morning Hank picked him up at the hotel and drove him out to his house. Then he brought over Fred Rose and ordered Braxton to sing Rose some songs.

Rose had been given more or less carte blanche by Frank Walker to sign country acts to MGM, and he either heard something he liked in Braxton's slightly antiquated style or he realized that this was a concession, like the Luke the Drifter sessions, that he needed to make to keep Hank sweet. In the business, they were known as "buy the rum to get the bourbon" deals.

"Fred said, 'What have you got for him to sing?' " said Braxton, "and Hank said he had a couple of songs, and Fred said he had a song by one of the Anglins called 'If Tears Would Bring You Back.' " Among the songs Hank pitched to Braxton was "Teardrop on a Rose," a sentimental parlor recital piece Hank had been toying with for years. He asked Braxton what he thought of it, and Braxton answered:

> I told him it was one of the most beautiful songs I ever heard, . . . and Hank said I could have it if I wanted. Then we needed one more. I was wanting to sing "I'll Still Write Your Name in the Sand," but Fred said, "No-o-o, we don't give other folks royalties. I'm going over to the house for a few minutes. You and Hank write something," so Hank and me wrote "Rockin' Chair Daddy" sittin' on the settee at his house. He'd write a line and I'd write a line. When Fred come back, I sang him "Rockin' Chair Daddy," and he signed me up that evening.

"Rockin' Chair Daddy" was the closest to a Jimmie Rodgers–styled song Hank would ever have a hand in writing.

The session was held at the Castle studio on February 8, 1950. Braxton played Hank's guitar, but Hank didn't participate except, as Braxton says, to "pop that heel — he wouldn't pat, he'd pop that thing." All four songs were released under the name Braxton Shooford. Like every record that Rose produced for MGM that wasn't by Hank, Braxton's failed to do much business. MGM's initial sell-in on "Rockin' Chair Daddy" accounted for just under thirty-five hundred copies.

At the end of March, Hank was back in the studio. This time he was sitting in on Audrey's first session for Decca. Having failed to woo Hank away from Fred Rose, Decca's country A&R chief, Paul Cohen, now had the worst consolation prize: Hank and The Drifting Cowboys were at a Decca session but Audrey was singing. Audrey cut seven songs, and six of them were released. First out of the box was a cover version of "Honky Tonkin'." Rose Maddox had revived the song in July 1949, and it had been picked up by Polly Bergen and Teresa Brewer for the pop market — the first pop cover versions of a Hank Williams song. Brewer was coming off her first big hit, "Music! Music! Music!" but "Honky Tonkin' " simply didn't adapt to the pop treatment. The song was attracting airplay, though, and Audrey decided that she would try to corner some of the action. Her version was released back-to-back with a Hadacol song called "What Put the Pep in Grandma" (the band yelled the refrain "Haddy-cole, Haddy-cole, Haddy-cole"). It was the kind of free advertising only Hadacol's competitors would have wished on it.

When *Billboard* got around to reviewing Audrey's second Decca single in October 1950, its review staff concluded that "Orking [is] much superior to thrush's singing," and gave it one of the lowest ratings of the week. Audrey now had an official recommendation, almost a request, that she stop singing, but she continued to insinuate herself onto Hank's radio shows and occasionally onto his live shows. If they were getting along, Hank would call her onstage at the *Opry* for a duet; if they were on the outs, she would stand backstage and pout while Hank did his portion alone. There, in a microcosm, was their relationship. Audrey felt excluded from a career she thought, with justification, she had done much to get off the ground, and having Hank's money to spend was not enough of a consolation prize.

Peace never broke out for long at the Williams household. Two weeks after the Decca session the troubles resurfaced. Hank returned from a tour, and Audrey, who had heard that he was drinking, locked him out. Hank checked in to the Tulane Hotel, where he was later arrested after he'd fallen asleep drunk with a lighted cigarette in his hand and set fire to his room.

Audrey always maintained that she had been signed to MGM with Hank, but Rose had evidently refused to produce her as a solo act. This had led to Hank's landing her the deal with Decca. Rose scheduled the two unissued Hank and Audrey duets, "Jesus Remembered Me" and "I Heard My Mother Praying for Me," for September 1950 — MGM's special "After Harvest" release — which was supposed to be the time when the market for hillbilly religious songs was particularly good. Even then, with Hank's credibility near its zenith, the record fell stillborn from the presses.

It was probably just as well Audrey was kept off MGM because the label had enough liabilities without her. The core problem was that MGM had been trying to function as a major label from its inception without having either the depth of catalog or the one megastar who could compensate for the flops. In 1949 the black crooner Billy Eckstine was the label's best-selling artist — his royalties that year totaled one hundred thousand dollars. Hank's 1949 royalties were reported by *Variety* magazine at sixty-five thousand dollars. If true, it means that "Lovesick Blues" had sold two million copies and "Wedding Bells" had sold around a million. Hank's royalties from MGM were on track for less than half that figure in 1950, although his total royalty income from records and music publishing combined would be much the same because he had written his hits that year.

Still, Billy Eckstine, Hank Williams, and MGM's other quasi-major names, like Blue Barron and Art Mooney, weren't generating enough sales to cover the giant overhead. When Loews, the parent corporation, was ordered to divide its business into independently operating studio and theater divisions, MGM Records devolved to the studio division. There were rumors in the trade that the theater division would shut down MGM Records when Frank Walker's initial five-year term was up in August 1950, but it was decided to keep MGM Records afloat, and Walker was re-signed.

One expense that MGM hadn't counted on when it broke ground at its plant in New Jersey was that it would soon need to retool the presses to accommodate 45 rpms and LPs. RCA had introduced the 45 in March 1949 in response to Columbia's introduction of the LP in June the previous year. To try and avoid the cost, MGM began pressing its 78s on a supposedly unbreakable compound in October 1949, but Walker had to face up to the inevitable, and he started pressing 45s in May 1950. For all companies, the LP and 45 "micro-platters," as they were called, represented additional overhead for a minimal return.* It wasn't until October 1950 that Seeburg introduced the first 45 rpm jukebox, and even though 45s quickly gained acceptance in the pop market, 78s would outsell 45s for years in the country and gospel markets. Jerry Rivers remembers seeing his first 45s in Cincinnati when Hank and the band went to Nelson King's house on one of their early tours together. Hank's first record to be released simultaneously as a 45 and a 78 was "They'll Never Take Her Love from Me" / "Why Should We Try Any More," in August 1950.

For Hank, records were no more than icing on the cake as far as his back pocket was concerned. His personal appearance fees made up the greater part of his income, which was estimated at $92,000 for 1950. A record that sold 150,000 copies, as "Long Gone Lonesome Blues" and "Why Don't You Love Me" had done, netted Hank all of $3,000 from MGM. If he had written both sides of the record, he would have received an additional $1,900 in publishing royalties. Airplay royalties would filter back from the performing rights society, BMI. The true value of a big hit, though, lay in the fact that Hank could hike his personal appearance fee or anticipate a higher turnout that would increase his share of the gate.

Even with a consistent flow of hits, Hank's personal appearance fee varied wildly. The rule of thumb was that you worked for what you could get. If Hank was playing a date as a headliner in a major center, he often settled for 50 or 60 percent of the gross after taxes, so if he filled a four-thousand-seat auditorium at ticket prices that ranged from a dollar for adults to fifty cents for children, he might expect to stuff two thousand dollars into his valise for the night's work. Hank never took checks after he'd been burned a few times. Then, if he had a free night and was expecting to pass through a small town where he knew a deejay or someone who promoted hillbilly shows, he might play a joint for a few hundred dollars.

Appearances on the *Opry* were even more of a loss-leader than records. Like the *Hayride,* the *Opry* paid American Federation of Musicians scale. For backing musicians, this was seven dollars a spot on the nonnetworked portion and twenty dollars on the Prince Albert portion. Hank's rate was roughly fifty dollars a show. Some claim that he later renegotiated his *Opry* fee, but it was still incommensurate with the lis-

---

* Of the 188 million records sold in 1950, 177.3 million were 78 rpms, 7.3 million were 45 rpms, and 3.4 million were LPs.

tenership. Soon after he arrived at the *Opry,* Hank was given some spon-sored fifteen-minute radio shows on WSM, like the *Duckhead Overalls* show, the *Pops-Rite Popcorn* show, and the *Mother's Best* show, but these brought him no more than one hundred dollars a week. The net result was that after Jim Denny's Artist Service Bureau deducted what Hank owed WSM for using the *Opry* name on his shows, he was usually in the hole to the station.

Hank had two additional sources of income, both almost unheard of today: sheet music and song folios. At the top end of the scale, Pee Wee King's "Tennessee Waltz" sold 1.1 million copies in sheet music form in 1951. Hank's sheet music sales were substantially less (between January and June 1950, for instance, "Honky Tonkin' " sold 4,769 copies as sheet music), but his ongoing sheet music sales still combined to provide a healthy adjunct to his income. Songbooks were a better business. Acuff-Rose reported to Hank that it had sold 7,300 copies of the *Hank Williams Country Folio* during the first six months of 1950. Hank would have dou-bled his money by selling many of those himself. The band went out into the crowd and sold song folios and photographs on commission during the intermission.

Hank grabbed wildly at every source of income. Having no inkling that his success would last, he saw opportunities suddenly opening up and lunged at them. It was a natural reaction for someone who had been trying for success for as long as he had. It's true that Audrey was spend-ing the money as fast as he was making it, but the reason he was making it was that it was there to be made.

By paying his band slightly more than scale, he was able to keep the steadiest lineup he had ever fronted. The only change during his first year in Nashville came when Bob McNett quit, in May 1950. He had messed up on the networked portion of the *Opry,* kicking off a song with the wrong intro. No amount of faking could cover it up that night, and they had had to stop and restart the song. Hank didn't dismiss him, but McNett came to believe that he wasn't cut out for the big time, and, as he says, "I wanted to do something on my own. I had the feeling I was traveling all over the country lookin' at someone else's back — and that's as far as I could see." He and his brother planned to open a country music park back in his native Pennsylvania, so he quit The Drifting Cow-boys.

Rather than recruit a guitarist from the growing pool of Nashville sessionmen, Hank replaced McNett with Sammy Pruett, who had played with the Cowboys in Montgomery. It wasn't a decision based entirely on musicianship, although Pruett was a fine guitarist generally reckoned to know as many chords and chord inversions as anyone then working in country music. Hank's decision was more an indication of his deep mistrust of the newfound success that Nashville both bestowed and symbolized. He needed to surround himself with familiar faces, and Pruett had stuck with him when they were lucky to walk away from a gig with five bucks each and their instruments intact.

Pruett was working with Happy Wilson's Golden River Boys on WAPI, Birmingham, when he got a call from Hank in Sioux City, Iowa. "I got to Nashville about nine o'clock one Saturday morning," he remembered. "Hank picked me up in front of the *Grand Ole Opry* and we left for somewhere out west and we were gone for three weeks." Like McNett, Pruett was confined to playing the tic-toc "crack rhythm," which was now one of the trademarks of a Hank Williams record. Hank called it the "cheap banjo sound" whenever he was interviewed, and Pruett soon grew bored playing it.

In June 1950 Hank and Oscar Davis came to a parting of the ways for reasons that Davis never specified. Hank tried to increase his share of the personal appearance pie by managing himself, but things quickly fell apart. On July 4 he was supposed to headline at the Watermelon Festival at DeLeon, Texas, a hundred miles southwest of Fort Worth. Despite the town's size, the festival drew some of the biggest names in country music in the late '40s and early '50s because it was a magnet for farming families for hundreds of miles around. The promoter, W. B. Nowlin, was also the mayor of DeLeon, and he had paid Hank a three-thousand-dollar guarantee for the July 4 date. Hank had committed to be there by ten o'clock in the morning. By two in the afternoon he hadn't shown and Nowlin had eleven thousand farmers and their families baking in the Texas sun, getting madder by the hour. Then, just after two o'clock, Hank's limo came racing into the field where the festival was being staged, and someone calling himself Hank's road manager got out and told Nowlin that Hank was "too sick" to perform.

Nowlin knew then that what had seemed like his biggest coup that morning was now an exercise in damage control that could threaten his career. He insisted that Hank at least get out of the limo and appear onstage, but the road manager refused, so Nowlin ordered the chief of police to handcuff the road manager to the steering wheel while two men dragged Hank up onstage. Nowlin got on the microphone and said, "Hank Williams's manager says Hank Williams is too sick to perform, but if you were standing as close to him as I am, you would know what he's sick from."

Then two men holding Hank let go for a moment and Hank fell almost to his knees before he regained his balance and staggered back to the limo. Word got back to Nashville that Hank was on a drunk, so Jim Denny flew Hank Snow to Dallas to do the evening show at the Northside Coliseum. Still in bad shape on July 5, Hank signed a curious document naming Jerry Rivers as his general manager while he was in Texas. He then registered himself at the Adolphus Hotel as Herman P. Willis, the band's pet name for anyone who couldn't win for losing. Later, Rivers saw Herman P. Willis walking around the hotel wearing dark glasses with a hat pulled low over his eyes. The reason, according to Rivers, was that Hank was trying to avoid a local booker, Jack Ruby, *the* Jack Ruby. If rumors of Ruby's mob connections were true, Hank probably had very valid reasons for wanting to lie low.

Rivers says Hank was hiding from Ruby because he didn't show at a party where he was supposed to have been the star attraction, but there were probably other reasons for his low profile — one might be that he had two bookers in search of their upfront guarantees. As he was bundled onto a plane back to Nashville, the conclusion that even Hank must have drawn from the debacle was that he was stretching himself too thin when he tried to handle his own business, so he was probably happy to have his bookings taken over by A. V. Bamford. Right away, Bamford placed him on a package tour with Ernest Tubb and Minnie Pearl.

Cuban by birth, Bamford had arrived in Nashville in 1949 from the west coast. He had been booking big bands into the Venice Pier when the orchestra business went sour. Then he took a chance on Bob Wills at the Pier, saw the huge turnout and experienced a conversion to country music that eventually brought him to Nashville. Bamford was a packager. He would figure out an itinerary, assemble a troupe of artists, book the halls, print up posters, arrange for advertising, and then ride with the artists.

The Bamford package took Hank out to Phoenix on July 17, and then to Albuquerque, El Paso, Odessa, and Lubbock on consecutive nights before heading back to Nashville. After a couple of weeks at home, Hank took off again on another Bamford tour with Lonzo and Oscar and Rod Brasfield that started in Ohio, then swung across to Richmond, Virginia. Working for Bamford netted Hank less than handling his own bookings as a single attraction, but it reduced the chance of messing up from a probability to a possibility.

After the swing through Ohio, Hank returned to Nashville to rest up and prepare for another recording session slated for August 31. He now believed that "blues" was the password to the top of the charts, and he was finishing up a song called "Moanin' the Blues" that he hoped would hold the spell. Once again, he fitted some inconsequential lyrics to what was virtually a public domain melody, leaving himself plenty of opportunities for the little yodels and flashes of trailing falsetto that he was now convinced sold records. The end result was greater than the sum of its parts. It rocked and rolled. The bridge was particularly compelling; Hank yodeled over the stops, setting up the smooth segue back to the verses. The rhythm was carried by Jack Shook's prominently miked acoustic guitar played up on the neck for a sound much like brushes on a snare drum, and it was accented by Sammy Pruett's electric guitar keeping time on the bass strings.

The second song they cut, "Nobody's Lonesome for Me," was clearly a designated B side. It had no bridge, and it lacked the radio-friendly and jukebox-friendly edge that "Moanin' the Blues" had. Then, for the last half of the session, Hank once again became Luke the Drifter. First up was a trite little homily, "Help Me Understand," a parable for the nag and the philanderer cast in almost cretinously simple terms with no detail to elevate it above the mundane. "One word led to another, and the last word led to divorce," said Hank tearfully, clearly cognizant of the threat of divorce hanging over his own head. Audrey had been the first to record the song back in March, and it was one that she and Hank often performed together as a two-part piece; Hank would narrate it and Audrey would sing the little girl's part, a rare occasion when her tuneless singing actually fit the bill.

The last song cut was Fred Rose's "No, No, Joe." The Cold War was heating up, the Korean War had started in June 1950, and the country's new *bête noir* was Joseph Stalin. Roy Acuff had already recorded "Advice to Joe" ("When Moscow lies in ashes, God have mercy on your soul"), Jimmy Osborne had chimed in with the slightly premature "Thank God for Victory in Korea," and Elton Britt among others had recorded "The Red We Want Is the Red We've Got in the Old Red, White and Blue." Red-baiting briefly became an issue in the music business, but the only casualty was black folk singer Josh White, who was forced to publicly confess that he had once held communist sympathies, then recant.

Set in the context of this near-hysteria, "No, No, Joe" was almost understated, leavening its message with intentional humor. *Billboard* noted as much in its review: "Tune and material are carefully wedded, not forced like so many of the recent patriotic tunes." Given the political climate of the day, it wouldn't have been stretching a point to issue "No, No, Joe" under Hank's name, but Rose held fast to his original intention and issued it under Luke the Drifter. MGM sensed that it had potential and took out full-page advertisements in trade magazines, but it failed to crack the charts. After Hank died and MGM was looking under every stone for Hank Williams recordings, they never once resorted to reissuing "No, No, Joe." Its first domestic LP appearance was on a Time-Life set in 1981.

When the year ended, "Moanin' the Blues" was number one — its only week in the top spot. The competition was now stronger than ever. The year 1950 saw the arrival of two major new players, Hank Snow and Lefty Frizzell. Snow's first big American hit, "I'm Moving On," had spent twenty-one weeks at number one, and Hank's "Moanin' the Blues" had to share the top spot with Frizzell's "If You've Got the Money, I've Got the Time." In the year-end tallies Hank was rated the third-best–selling artist of the year. Red Foley and Eddy Arnold were still ahead of him, and Hank Snow and Lefty Frizzell were snapping at his heels.

There's no darker place than the edge of
the spotlight.
Hal Cannon,
Elko Cowboy Poetry Gathering

● ●

THE PLEASURE OF THE
FLEETING YEAR

● ● ● ● ● ● ● ● ● ● ● ● ● ● ● ● ● ●

*H*ERE'S a little number we've been eatin' off of
fer a while," Hank would often say in his in-
troductions, and he had been depending on his music for income so long
that he probably saw it in those terms. If so, he had written and recorded
his meal ticket for all of 1951 even before he went out to play his New
Year's show. It was another little cameo of life with Audrey, and if, as
some said, the warmest she ever got was thawing, then "Cold, Cold
Heart" was one of the most awfully true songs ever written.

Stories vary. The way that Pappy Neal McCormick remembers it, Audrey was in the hospital, probably recovering from an infection that had
set in after she had had an abortion in September 1950. The abortion had
apparently been carried out at home without Hank's knowledge, and Audrey would have kept him in the dark if she hadn't developed the infection. The reasons for the abortion are unclear. It's likeliest that Audrey
didn't want the physical discomforts of another pregnancy, much less
the encumbrance of another child. According to McCormick, Hank went
to the hospital and bent down to kiss Audrey, but she wouldn't let him.
"You sorry son of a bitch," she is supposed to have said. "It was you that
caused me to suffer this." Hank went home and told the children's gov-
erness, Miss Ragland, that Audrey had a "cold, cold heart," then quickly
realized that the bitterness in his heart held commercial promise.

There are other stories surrounding "Cold, Cold Heart," and they
offer a few windows into the increasingly unhappy times on Franklin

Road. Audrey, like most musicians' wives, acquiesced to the fact that Hank had dalliances with other women out on the road. It was generally regarded as one of the few perks of the job. What irked her, though, was that Hank would often come back on Friday night or Saturday morning physically depleted and have nothing for her. Then he would be gone again on Sunday. She had more stamina than he did, and could have better coped with the rigors of the road, but she was left at home. So Audrey began taking lovers to fill the lonely hours, and it's at least possible that she suspected that the child she had conceived was not Hank's.

Years later, Audrey told one of her lovers that she had found out that Hank had been philandering while she was in the hospital, and that when he brought her some jewelry in atonement, she had flung it back at him. That, according to Audrey, was what had prompted Hank to go home and write "Cold, Cold Heart."

Talking to the *Wall Street Journal* in October 1951, Hank was economical with the truth. "Cold, Cold Heart," he told the interviewer, took about an hour to write; he just sat and waited, and pretty soon God had written it for him. If that was so, the most that God gave him was the words; the melody was copped note for note from T. Texas Tyler's 1945 recording of "You'll Still Be in My Heart." Lyrically the songs bore similarities, but melodically there was no difference at all. "You'll Still Be in My Heart" was originally copyrighted by Ted West in May 1943, then rewritten by Buddy Starcher and acquired in July 1943 by one of Starcher's affiliates, Clark Van Ness. Van Ness had cowritten "Filipino Baby," the World War II–era classic of interracial passion. He traded as Dixie Music, and, as was common, he waited until it was clear just how big a hit "Cold, Cold Heart" was before he filed suit on December 3, 1951.

Hank had recorded "Cold, Cold Heart" at an evening session at Castle on December 21, 1950. He sang it with almost palpable hurt that never once sank to a level of mawkishness. His restraint only heightened the record's impact and left the listener in no doubt that he was living every word. It was the first song recorded that night, but from the outset, Fred Rose saw it as a B side based on the now seemingly immutable law that Hank's faster numbers were the ones that sold. The A side — the fast side — was to be "Dear John," a song that Acuff-Rose didn't even publish. It was unthinkable that Rose would have wasted another company's song on a B side; B sides were known in the business as "free rides" because the publisher received as much for them from the record companies as for the hit side. From the paperwork he submitted to MGM, it seemed clear that Rose intended "Cold, Cold Heart" to get a free ride on the back of "Dear John."

"Dear John" was written by Aubrey Gass, a hard-luck Texas honky-tonk singer. It was his biggest song; in fact, it was the only hit he ever wrote. The first version was by Jim Boyd, younger brother of Dallas-based western swing artist Bill Boyd. Gass apparently knew Jim Boyd, offered him "Dear John," and Boyd recorded it on March 11, 1949. Soon after, Tex Ritter got his finger in the pie. Ritter probably promised to get the song cut by a big name, like himself, or to get Gass a contract with his label, Capitol, if he could get a piece of the song. The fact that Gass recorded "Dear John" for Capitol some six months after Boyd suggests that Ritter lived up to his half of their covenant. When MGM filed for a license for Hank's version in January 1951, it had to make an application to Tex Ritter Music in New York. For all his aw-shucksiness and his little homilies of life in the bunkhouse, Tex (or Maurice Woodward Ritter, to give him his full name) had a degree in political science and a year of law school under his belt, and he knew all the angles when it came to the business end of the music business.

How much of this Hank knew is unclear. If Tex hadn't beaten him to it, he could have bought out Aubrey Gass and no one would ever have known that "Dear John" wasn't a Hank Williams song. Clint Holmes, who had worked with Hank in Shreveport, remembers him singing it there, so Hank had probably picked up Jim Boyd's record and carried the song around in the back of his mind for a year and a half. Short a fast song for the session, Hank called up "Dear John." When the band hollered "dear John!" in the last line of every verse, it invited everyone in the bar, the auditorium, or even the car to holler right along. Once again, the upfront rhythm guitar carried the recording. Hank cruised at the brisk tempo, never once appearing to strain.

The last two sides recorded at the "Cold, Cold Heart" session were for another Luke the Drifter single, the fourth in the space of a year. "Just Waitin' " was a lusterless talking blues that Hank had adapted from an idea by another Acuff-Rose writer, Bob Gazzaway, but one that did little credit to either of them. Gazzaway had written or cowritten a few songs that got cut, including several by Little Jimmy Dickens, but none of his songs ever became a hit. "Just Waitin' " promised more than it delivered. Everyone is just waitin' for something. It was a good premise to hang a song on, but this wasn't it.

"Men with Broken Hearts" was Hank at his bleakest. Later, Montgomery journalist Allen Rankin recalled how Hank had played him the song. "Don't know why I happen to of wrote that thing," he told Rankin, "except somebody that fell, he's the same man as before he fell, ain't he? Got the same blood in his veins. How can he be such a nice guy when he's got it and such a bad guy when he ain't got nothin'? Can you tell me?" It was a theme that Hank harped upon often in his conversation, perhaps sensing that the people who crowded around him wanting to be his friend would one day disown him like johns fleeing a cathouse during a raid. If those were indeed his thoughts, they were a chillingly accurate premonition.

Rankin also remembered Hank saying of "Men with Broken Hearts," "Ain't that the awfulest, morbidest song you ever heard in your life?" and Rankin adds that Hank clearly regarded that as a self-compliment. Lines about "eyes staring in defeat" and "hearts pray[ing] for death" and "know[ing] pain with every breath" were from the darker side of life, which drew the poetry out of Hank. "Death Is Only a Dream" was his favorite song after all, and this was the man who, when asked by deejay Cottonseed Clark why he wrote so many sad songs, replied, "I guess I always have been a sadist." "Men with Broken Hearts" was too morbid by half to be released under Hank's name, but the hillbilly sermonettes were a side of his musical personality that would not be denied. MGM wasn't losing money on them, so Walker and Rose reconciled themselves to releasing them in the interest of keeping Hank sweet.

"Cold, Cold Heart" and "Dear John" were released on February 2, 1951. The year had begun with no inkling of the changes in store for Hank. He closed out a hugely successful New Year's weekend bash in Indianapolis when more than sixteen thousand people had paid to see him. Bass player Hillous Butrum had quit Hank's lineup by then, and was working in Indianapolis as a solo performer. On New Year's morning, Hank and the band went to Butrum's house for breakfast. As he looked forward into the new year, he could probably see no farther than the road stretching ahead of him forever. In the immediate future there was a swing out west followed by a swing through the southeast for A. V. Bamford.

"Dear John" began showing up in the charts a month later, but within two weeks "Cold, Cold Heart" followed it — and quickly overtook it. This left Rose gnashing his teeth because "Dear John" was now getting a free ride on the back of "Cold, Cold Heart." Still, it was useful to know for future reference that the right slow song would sell. "Cold, Cold Heart" eventually peaked at number one for a week in May, then hung around on the charts for the rest of the year. The reason for its longevity was that it acquired a new, and unexpected, lease on life in the pop market, which in turn kept Hank's version buoyed on the country charts.

It's part of Acuff-Rose mythology that, against all odds and against the deeply ingrained resistance of the pop music oligarchy, Wesley Rose went to New York and persuaded Mitch Miller to record "Cold, Cold Heart" with Tony Bennett. Wesley loved to tell the story about how he beat on every record company's door in New York with the song. "That's a hillbilly song," Wesley says he was told everywhere, "and there's no use kidding yourself otherwise." Then, finally, he got Miller, the goateed head of pop music A&R at Columbia Records, to take a listen, and the rest, Wesley was fond of saying emphatically, is history.

The line between pop and hillbilly had never been *that* hard and fast, but the notion of covering country records for the pop market had started to gather steam after Al Dexter's "Pistol Packin' Mama" was covered by Bing Crosby in 1943 and became one of the biggest records of the following year. By the time Wesley Rose went to New York early in 1951 hawking Hank's "Cold, Cold Heart," Leon Payne's "I Love You Because," and Pee Wee King's "Bonaparte's Retreat," the market for hillbilly songs in the pop market was so good that he should have had A&R men lining up outside his hotel room.

The first pop hit that Acuff-Rose had enjoyed was "Jealous Heart." It was written by Red Foley's sister-in-law, Jenny Lou Carson, and recorded by her for Decca in 1944. Tex Ritter picked it up and had a sizable hit with it the following year. Then it languished for four years, before — unexpectedly, and without any intercession on the part of Acuff-Rose — a Chicago pianist and singer, Al "Mr. Flying Fingers" Morgan, recorded it for a small local label. Morgan's record was picked up by London Records, and it became a top-five pop record in 1949.

It was also in 1949 that Acuff-Rose made a big splash with "Chattanoogie Shoe Shine Boy." Even though Fred Rose had almost certainly given the song to WSM executives Harry Stone and Jack Stapp in exchange for getting Hank on the *Opry,* he had at least kept the publishing rights. Red Foley's version went to number one on the pop and country charts, and it was covered by the likes of Frank Sinatra and Bing Crosby. And then came "Tennessee Waltz," which also hit by happenstance. Neither Wesley, Fred, nor their song plugger, Mel Foree, had any role in its success, which probably increased Wesley's need to cement himself to the success of "Cold, Cold Heart." His training as an accountant led him to downplay dumb luck, which has always counted for so much in the music business.

Pee Wee King had written and recorded "Tennessee Waltz" in 1947, and he released it in January 1948 back-to-back with his version of Fred Rose's "Rootie Tootie." It was a fair-sized country hit. King and Cowboy Copas, who covered it for King Records, sold roughly 380,000 copies combined, but the song was dead in the water by the time jazz bandleader Erskine Hawkins recorded it in 1950. Hawkins's record became what the trade calls a "sleeper": it sold well over a long period (typically breaking into one market after another) without showing up in the charts. *Billboard* columnist Jerry Wexler, who as vice president of Atlantic Records would later be the man responsible for signing Aretha Franklin among others, suggested to Patti Page's manager that she record "Tennessee Waltz." Page cut it in October 1950 and placed it on the back of her 1950 Christmas record. By early 1951 it had become one of those inexplicable, uncontainable smash hits. By May that year, Page's record had sold 4.8 million copies, cover versions had probably sold half as many again, sheet music sales had topped 1.1 million, and it was the highest-grossing song that BMI had represented to that point. So, when Wesley Rose went to New York in early 1951 with "Cold, Cold Heart" in his briefcase, he shouldn't have had to twist anybody's arm to record it.

Mitch Miller downplays Wesley's role in getting "Cold, Cold Heart" to him. He says it was Jerry Wexler who alerted him to "Cold, Cold Heart" as well. Miller confirms that Tony Bennett had to be coerced into recording it, though. "When I heard the song, I thought it was made to order for Tony," says Miller. "I thought the last four lines were particularly poetic, and so I played Hank Williams's record for Tony, with the scratchy fiddle and everything, and Tony said, 'Don't make me do cowboy songs!' I said, 'Tony, listen to the words. It's only a record. If it doesn't work out, I won't put it out. I'm not here to hurt you.' "

Bennett had not yet seen a chart entry when he recorded "Cold, Cold Heart" on May 31, 1951, so he wasn't the prize catch that Wesley might have been hoping for, but, three weeks after the May 31 session, his version of "Because of You" shot straight to number one. This gave "Cold, Cold Heart" a head start, and proved again how important dumb luck was. If "Because of You" had flopped, would "Cold, Cold Heart" have done as well? Would it even have shown up at all? As it was, "Cold, Cold Heart" jumped to the top of the pop charts, and every record label had to have at least one cover version; both the Fontane Sisters and Perry Como did it for RCA, Louis Armstrong and Eileen Wilson for Decca, Tony Fontane and Dinah Washington for Mercury . . . and so on. It wasn't half the phenomenon that "Tennessee Waltz" had been, but "Cold, Cold Heart" served notice that Hank Williams's songs now had a potential that was unthinkable when he sent up his acetate of God, Mother 'n' Death songs for Molly O'Day five years earlier.

Hank was tickled. He had always made it a policy to spin his own records on the jukebox in any restaurant where he ate; now he spun Tony Bennett's record as well. The first couple of times, he would slap the table, grin his shiteating grin and shout "Hot damn!" Now, when he looked in *Billboard* every week, he had a reason to check out the pop listings instead of heading straight for the country pages.

Miller's success with "Cold, Cold Heart" earned him a promise from Acuff-Rose that he would get prerelease demos of any songs that Wesley or Fred considered to have pop potential. "That way," says Miller, "I wouldn't have to scramble, but I agreed with Fred and Wesley that I wouldn't release my record until the original had got going on the country chart." It was an arrangement that would be mutually profitable for Acuff-Rose and Columbia over the next few years. When Rose spoke to the *Wall Street Journal* in late 1951, he stated that Acuff-Rose's gross for that year would be 40 or 50 percent up on 1950, which had in turn been 150 percent better than 1949. Mitch Miller made a substantial contribution to that.

In a broader context, the success of hillbilly songs refashioned for the pop market considered alongside the rush to record pop cover versions of rhythm 'n' blues songs a couple of years later meant that the music of the black and white underclasses was entering the pop mainstream through the back door. That in turn meant that the pop market was being prepped for rock 'n' roll. The "folk tunes boom" as it was termed at the time, not only caught the attention of the *Wall Street Journal,* but virtually every other periodical as well. *Collier's* approach was typical in its mixture of surprise and condescension; its headline was "There's Gold in Them Thar Hillbilly Tunes." Hank was often singled out in the press. Much of the comment focused upon his ability to write hits in half an hour, and Hank played the role of the intuitive folk artist to the hilt, never once mentioning the rigid application of commercial logic that took place in Rose's home studio before every session.

Not only were cover versions of hillbilly tunes selling well, but the original versions were doing unprecedentedly good business as well. Decca Records, which had Red Foley, Ernest Tubb, Webb Pierce, and Kitty Wells, estimated that 50 percent of its sales derived from country music, and even Columbia Records estimated that 40 percent of its gross came from country. The bottom line looked even rosier. A typical pop session of the day used as many as thirty or forty instrumentalists at $41.25 for three hours. Before the session, an army of copyists was required to write out the arrangements, and a contractor had to be engaged to call everyone in. Then, typically, only one or two songs would be recorded during a session. In Nashville, most sessions used no more than six or seven musicians, arrangements were cooked up on the spot, no contractor was needed, and three or four songs were cut in three hours.

Hank was happy to cash the checks that came when the palm court orchestras played his songs, but on another, far deeper, level he was suspicious of the trend, seeing it as a dilution of his music. "These pop bands," he told an interviewer in Charleston, South Carolina, "will play our hillbilly songs when they cain't eat any other way," and when he saw the trade advertisement for Bennett's "Cold, Cold Heart," it must have confirmed his darkest suspicions. The ad headline was "Popcorn! A Top Corn Tune Gone Pop." Tony Bennett was caricatured in a policeman's uniform holding up traffic while a witless hillbilly leads a pig and a mule across a busy city street. In terms of denigrating hillbilly music, this was no better than the Sterling ads four years earlier.

At first, the success of "Cold, Cold Heart" did nothing to change Hank's routine. After the Opry on Saturday night, he would head out of town on a four- or five-day junket. The crowds were getting bigger as his reputation grew, but otherwise it was all much as before. There was the backstage shake 'n' howdy, with no one more concerned than Hank to sign every autograph. There were deejays to be glad-handed, the phrases now tripping like a litany off his tongue. If there was time and if he had the energy, there might be a quick dive into a motel with some li'l ol' gal (some say a *very* little ol' gal).* Sometimes, the band would sit out in the car with the motor running while Hank took care of business. Then there was more wriggling inside that damned old car trying to find a position in which his back didn't hurt so bad, and more grief when he got home. It was a routine that was beginning to pall, but for the present it beat anything Hank had ever known, and he was still happy to be out there.

Hank had been without a manager since he and Oscar Davis parted

* Lurid allegations of Hank's dalliances with underage girls first surfaced in a magazine article, "The Strange Life and Death of Hank Williams," by Sanford Mabrie, which appeared in the September 1955 edition of *Behind the Scenes.* There are no arrest records or reliable eyewitness accounts to substantiate the stories, but equally no reason to doubt them. If the stories were true, Hank was not alone in fancying underage girls; Lefty Frizzell was jailed for statutory rape shortly before he became famous, and, of course, Jerry Lee Lewis married his thirteen-year-old cousin in 1957. Allegations about other singers keep the rumor mill abuzz.

company, and he tried to bring some order to his business affairs by appointing William R. "Bill" England. Again, rather than look around Nashville, Hank pulled someone from Montgomery. England had been a time salesman on WSFA, and he moved to Nashville in January 1951 and worked from his home at 1950 Richard Jones Road in the Green Hills district. England's first priority was to assemble a catalog of promotional items that could be sent out in advance of a show. The promoter could pick and choose from an array of predesigned one- or two-column advertisements for "The Sensational Radio-Recording Star Mr. Lovesick Blues Hank Williams with his Entire Grand Ole Opry Show." If Hank was paying to use the name *Grand Ole Opry*, he might as well get all the mileage he could out of it. England also wrote some prepackaged stories that could run in the newspapers on the days before the show, and he printed up huge stacks of 8" × 10" photos for store windows, giveaways, and intermission sales. It wasn't long, though, before England found that Hank's idea of a manager was really a gofer.

At roughly the same time that England came in to try to bring a semblance of order to Hank's affairs, a power play at WSM was resolving itself. In August 1950, Harry Stone quit as WSM manager to become a consultant, eventually ending up at KPHO in Phoenix, Arizona, where he discovered Marty Robbins. He was replaced by Jack DeWitt Jr., who was already president of WSM. DeWitt's background was in the technical end of radio. He had designed equipment that could bounce radar signals off the moon, and he had spent World War II working on radar technology, but, by all accounts, he had little or no feel for hillbilly music. Even so, he had the sense to place Jim Denny in the newly created post of manager of the *Grand Ole Opry*, despite the fact that he and Denny rarely got along. This left Denny the uneasy victor in a protracted campaign against Stone, a campaign waged on the personal and professional front. Although both men were married, they had been competing for the affections of a dancer in the *Opry* troupe named Dollie Dearman, and that too was a battle that Denny won. The bitter pill for Denny was that he had to surrender the lucrative concession businesses he had built up.

With Denny, who liked and had a grudging respect for Hank, in control at the *Opry*, and with Bill England as his manager, Hank had a team that could have done a lot for him. England was business-minded, but he was managing someone whose idea of calculating net worth was to empty his pockets and count up how much had fallen out. Frustration set in. "We never had a contract because to me a contract represents a lack of trust," says England. "But managing Hank was like a company asking a management consultant to come in and look at their business, make recommendations and so forth, then ignoring everything the management consultant says and going right back to operating the way they did before. I had the title of manager, but did not manage." England maintains that he was paid low and slow, and says that Hank, now at the height of his fame, couldn't cover a ten-dollar check.

Part of the problem endemic to Hank's finances was that Audrey was still buying everything that caught her eye, although England asserts that she and Hank were as bad as each other. "That went back to the early '30s," he says. "They'd never had anything, then the money came rolling in, and anything they saw, they wanted." Automobiles, of course, were the first call on the newfound money. Both Hank and Audrey owned Cadillacs; Audrey bought a four-thousand-dollar convertible against Hank's wishes — he thought a married woman had no business riding around in one. He bought a Cadillac Coupe for himself as well as a six-thousand-dollar seven-passenger Cadillac touring sedan.

Audrey may have found spending Hank's money a poor consolation prize for what she really wanted, but it was a consolation prize nonetheless. She bought at the most expensive couturiers, continued to buy overpriced furniture for the house, and treated herself to jewelry. As Hank sang "Dear John," the words must have rung truer than any from his own pen:

I went down to the bank this morning, the cashier said with a grin,
I feel so sorry for you, Hank, but your wife has done been in.

Hank later estimated that Audrey spent fifty thousand dollars during 1951 alone, much of it remodeling and refurbishing the Franklin Road house in what would become the Graceland school of interior decor. Soon after Hank joined the *Opry,* he had boasted to a band member that he was now making money faster than even Audrey could spend it, but she seems to have caught up.

Quite what Audrey would have said in her defense is hard to know. If the innards of Hank's finances could ever be laid bare, they would probably bear out England's assertion that *both* Hank and Audrey were spending too much because they'd been too poor too long to exercise self-control. Those who knew Hank say that he had simple tastes, but he was also prone to extravagance every bit as much as Audrey. He had partied away the fifteen dollars he won at the Empire Theater in 1937, and now he was buying guns, riding tackle, or anything else that caught his eye, and leaving huge tips on a whim. Sometimes he would simply lose money or send it to people who mailed him a hard-luck story. After he arrived in Nashville, he started banking with John Clay, the brother of KWKH manager Henry Clay, at the Third National Bank. He would often return from a trip with a suitcase full of money that he would simply dump on a cashier's desk. When he was asked how much was there, he would say that it was his business to make it and theirs to count it.

Hank's fascination with guns was particularly costly. Jerry Rivers remembers that Hank, curiously like Elvis, would befriend members of the police so that they would help him locate guns and even women. One night, a member of the vice squad in El Paso took Hank and The Drifting Cowboys on a late-night excursion into Juarez in search of exotic firearms. Members of the troupe that accompanied Hank to Oklahoma City in 1951 remember him buying a gross of expensive cufflinks with pistol motifs. He bought a Tennessee walking horse, figuring that its smooth gait would enhance his cowboy image with minimal damage to his back. Then, on September 1, 1951, he bought 507 acres of land with a derelict antebellum farmhouse south of Nashville in Williamson County. The purchase price was sixty thousand dollars, but Hank put up only fifteen thousand, and then proceeded to dig a deeper hole for himself by stocking the farm with whiteface cattle. So if Audrey was the thrusting arriviste, using Hank's money to buy social credibility, Hank was acting like a lottery winner with a month to live.

Hank had looked enviously at the success of Ernest Tubb's Record Shop, then located on Commerce Street close to the *Opry*. After the *Opry* went off the air on Saturday night, Tubb would host his *Midnight Jamboree* from the store, and the spin-off mail order operation was hugely profitable. Hank tried to replicate Tubb's formula by opening Hank and Audrey's Corral at 724 Commerce Street, next door to Tubb.

The Corral opened in June 1951, and Hank took out a five-year lease on the property at $160 a month, then stocked it with $7,000 of inventory, furbishing it like the western-wear stores he had seen out west. The walls were covered with barn board, wagon wheels, and hurricane lamps. In addition to the western gear, there were Hank and Audrey dolls and knickknacks for the Saturday night crowd. The gala opening was broadcast over WSM between 5:00 and 5:30 P.M. on June 16, and Hank planned to broadcast every week in that time slot, much as Ernest Tubb did after midnight, but the Corral show had to be relocated to the

WSM studios after three months because of the crowds blocking the sidewalk.

Hank placed the running of the store in the hands of Mac McGee, who later bought it, but, when Hank and Audrey ran it, it was too often a refuge for out-of-work musicians waiting for Hank to drop in and buy everyone Krystal burgers. He usually showed up on Saturday morning to sign the paychecks, and Audrey would come by most days to scoop the cash register.

Hank's success reached its zenith in 1951, the same year that the situation deteriorated rapidly at home. "Cold, Cold Heart" was turning into what Hank liked to call "a little prophecy in song." Audrey, now shut out from everything to do with Hank's career except the money it generated, closed off her heart to him. The Hank Williams she got was either dog tired or shipped home early from a tour because he was drinking. The good times hadn't all passed and gone, but they were fewer now. The two years of almost constant touring had taken their toll on Hank's health, while the career pressures in the wake of "Cold, Cold Heart" were placing an additional strain on his ever less than stable psyche. Audrey's well of sympathy was never deep.

Through it all, Hank never messed up in the recording studio. He was charmed like a man walking through a minefield. At 1:30 P.M. on Friday, March 16, 1951, just as "Cold, Cold Heart" and "Dear John" were breaking, he went back into the studio with four songs, four remarkably strong songs even by the standards he was setting for himself. They were "I Can't Help It (If I'm Still in Love with You)," "Howlin' at the Moon," "Hey, Good Lookin'," and "My Heart Would Know." It took half an hour of studio overtime on top of the three-hour session to get all four down, but Rose's glee must have been almost uncontained as he made his myopic way back home that afternoon.

Don Helms's opening notes on "I Can't Help It" held fast to Rose's credo that he must play high if Hank was to sing low. If Helms had played any higher, he would have been in the range that only dogs can hear. Jerry Rivers always told the story that Hank wrote the song in the touring sedan. He came up with the first line, "Today I passed you on the street," and then threw it open to the floor. "What's a good line?" he asked. Don Helms answered, "And I smelled your rotten feet." Everyone in the car broke up laughing, but Hank soldiered on. The hand of Fred Rose is clearly at work in some of the lines; the grammatical forms and scansion are unlike pure Hank, but the content and the prevailing mood are almost certainly from the Kingdom of Hiram.

In complete contrast, "Howlin' at the Moon" captures all the giddiness that a new love can bring. Much of its humor was rooted in Hank's passion for hunting. The performance rips along, punctuated by Jerry Rivers's hound dog yodels. "Hey, Good Lookin' " has lyrics that seem to demand the same insouciant treatment, peppered as they are with references to hot rods, dancing sprees, goin' steady, soda pop, and much else that prefigured the lyrical content of rock 'n' roll. Strangely, though, the rhythm plods along with a steppity-step piano, and Hank is almost dour in comparison with his performance on "Howlin' at the Moon." If Audrey was feeling a twinge of guilt over her affairs, she must have wondered if it was she or another who had inspired "Hey, Good Lookin' " and "Howlin' at the Moon."

Hank's *Opry* costar, Little Jimmy Dickens, says that Hank wrote both songs on a plane taking them to a date in Wichita Falls, Texas. Dickens also insists that Hank promised him "Hey, Good Lookin'." "He said he wanted me to record it," said Dickens, "and I was delighted. I thought it would be a good song for me. Then I met him in the hall of WSM, and he said, 'Tater [Hank called Dickens "Tater" after his first hit, "Take an Old Cold Tater (And Wait)"], I cut your song today. It's too good a song for you, anyway.' " Dickens says he laughed it off, but it wasn't the first time Hank had pulled a stunt like that.

Typically, Hank would offer a song around, and if enough artists seemed interested, he would record it himself. "Listen here what I wrote," he would say. "Ain't that a good un?" Chet Atkins remembers that Hank would "get right up close to you in your face," and he'd sing. "If you raved over it, he'd love that," Atkins says. "He was pitching songs to the hot acts of that time, and they'd say, 'That's a great song, Hank. I want to do that on my next session.' If he got enough people to say that, he'd say, 'No, it's too damn good for you. I'm gonna do it myself.' " The humility that all country performers were, and are, supposed to wear like a crown of thorns often drops in private, but Hank's hubris was alienating many of his peers.

Hank placed a surprising number of songs with other artists, but none of them ever amounted to anything. Many, like "There's Nothing As Sweet As My Baby," which he gave to a young and struggling Carl Smith, were inconsequential songs, and Hank probably knew he was doing no one a favor in bestowing them. All evidence points to his knowing exactly which ones to keep for himself.

The four songs recorded on March 16 were released in two couplings. "I Can't Help It" and "Howlin' at the Moon" were released on

April 27, 1951, and "Hey, Good Lookin' " backed with "My Heart Would Know" were released on June 22. Together those two singles kept "Cold, Cold Heart" company in the charts for the rest of the year. "Hey, Good Lookin' " spent most of August and September at number one.

Adhering to their agreement with Mitch Miller, the Roses offered him Hank's new songs, and Miller scored pop hits with Guy Mitchell's version of "I Can't Help It" and Frankie Laine's duet with Jo Stafford on "Hey, Good Lookin'." Laine and Stafford's record had much of the zest that Hank's lacked, thanks to six guitars comping in unison underpinned by a jazz bassist and drummer, all punctuated by Speedy West's eccentric steel guitar fills. The record peaked at number nine on the pop charts at the tail end of 1951.

Hank was back in the studio on March 23 for another session, a week after the "Hey, Good Lookin' " session. Decca Records had jettisoned Miss Audrey, and Hank had persuaded Fred Rose to record her for MGM as a solo act and to cut some more religious duets. The sacred songs they chose were "The Pale Horse and His Rider" and "A Home in Heaven." Hank had probably learned "The Pale Horse and His Rider" from its cowriter, Johnny Bailes, when he worked with the Bailes Brothers in Shreveport, but the song dates back to 1939, when Bailes was working with Molly O'Day and the song's other writer, Ervin Staggs, at WCHS in Charleston, West Virginia. It's chock full of images as vivid and haunting as any Hank ever wrote, and the band does a creditable job of capturing the feel of a brush arbor meeting. Still, the song and the band are undermined as ever by Audrey, who is strident and often woefully off-key.

"A Home in Heaven" was a song that Hank had kicked around in one guise or another for five years. A version of it was included on a set of demos sent to Columbia's Art Satherley in 1946, and it would later resurface as "Are You Building a Temple in Heaven?" Once again, Hank and Audrey's domestic disharmony seemed to find its extension on disc. Rose refused to okay the recordings for release, and it was not until almost four years after Hank's death, when MGM believed it was staring at the bottom of the barrel, that "Home in Heaven" and "The Pale Horse and His Rider" were shipped.

Part of the appeal of Hank's records was that they gave an inkling of the gulf that existed between the public mask and the inner disquiet. He was now one of the most successful artists in country music, perhaps *the* most successful, but the mood swing on every record between the bouncy up-tempo song and the slower one was more than a commercial formula; it was an echo of his life. He could josh around with the guys in the limo, bathe in the applause onstage, find a woman and head off to a motel, see his records plastered all over the charts, perform a gratuitous act of charity for someone who was as poor as he had once been . . . but still he seemed to find no peace or real contentment.

People who say they were close to Hank usually have to admit that — on some level — they really didn't know him at all. "I never knew anybody I liked better than Hank," Jim Denny said after Hank's death, "but I don't think I ever really got close to him. I don't know if anyone really could. He was so bitter. . . . He thought everybody had some sort of angle on him." The woods-animal mistrust and secretiveness wasn't a trait that developed in the wake of success. "This guy was afraid for anyone to get close to him, even to the point of being cold," said Doyle Turner, who had worked with Hank in 1945. "He was never the type of person to be close. Bernice and I were closer to him than any of the group, and it was as though we were a hundred miles away from him." Since working the street corners with Tee-Tot, Hank had acquired a cheery mask that led people to believe they were his confidants and to claim that Hank had befriended them and poured his heart out to them. In fact, all they had heard was one of his set pieces, every bit as well rehearsed and sincere as his songs. Audrey's betrayals probably hurt him all the more because she was one of the few to whom he had truly opened up.

Hank craved success until he found it, and then he wanted less tangible things, like a centered home life. Success alone didn't widen the gap between Hank and Audrey, but it did allow them to finance their aspirations, which in turn made it clear how different those aspirations were. Audrey wanted to integrate herself into the old-money Belle Meade country club set, while Hank's idea of recreation was to go fishing up on Kentucky Lake. He is generally reckoned to have been happiest out on the lake with a cane pole. He didn't even want to go hunting and fishing with the old-money crowd, who took their blinds, their servants, and all manner of expensive tackle and hardware. There are several stories of Hank's disgracing himself at dinners Audrey gave, and, even if they're exaggerated, they still show how divergent Hank and Audrey's paths had become.

Much as he liked to blame Audrey for his poor family life, Hank knew his own conduct, particularly his drinking bouts, drove a wedge between them. Guilt over his drinking, his inability to spend more time with his wife and son, and his little flings almost certainly ate away at him. Chiefly, it was the binges, now coming more frequently, that frustrated those who dealt with him. Everyone tried to make Hank feel guilty about his drinking — and he probably felt the guilt even as he was covering it up with truculence. "I tried to shame him," said Oscar Davis. "I said, 'Look, you got your son and your wife,' [but] you can't shake an alcoholic." Bob McNett says, "Some of the lonesomeness you found in Hank was guilt because he knew in his heart he wasn't living up to what he knew was morally right." The caricature of Hank Williams with the Bible in one hand and *Billboard* in the other has a grain of truth. He knew right from wrong, and knew he had been weighed in the balance and found wanting.

The year 1951 was the last good year, the last of only three. Hank spent the greater part of it on the road. Once in a while, one of his fellow performers told him his pace was killing him. He would shrug to hide the fact that he probably knew it, and say he had to strike while the iron was hot.

God guard me from the thoughts men think
In the mind alone
He that sings a lasting song
Thinks in the marrow bone.
W. B. Yeats, "A Prayer for Old Age"

FOLK AND WESTERN MUSIC
TO SELL

*T*HE year 1951 was a career year for Hank Williams. The bigger crowds, the sweet applause that greeted the beginning and end of all those songs he had written, the big city reporters taking an interest in ol' Hank, the admiration — sometimes grudging, sometimes freely given — of his peers. "Everywhere we were fixin' to go was a higher level," said Don Helms. Hank appeared to be cocky, treating it as no less than his due, but on another level it all made him deeply uneasy. Just a few years earlier, he had been refused jobs and turned away from radio stations as a damn drunk. He knew in his heart he was still the same person, and deeply mistrusted the embrace of the business. At some moments his mistrust extended toward everybody, because everybody seemed to want a piece of him; everybody, that is, except the one person to whom he wanted to give a piece of himself.

After eighteen months on the *Opry,* Hank had sufficient drawing power to tour as a single attraction. He no longer needed to be part of a package show. This gave him the opportunity to assemble his own show, and in February 1951 he hired "Big Bill" Lister as a warm-up act and rhythm guitarist. Lister stood out in just about any crowd except basketball players. He was gauntly thin, six feet seven inches tall, and he billed himself as the World's Tallest Singing Cowboy. He was versed in hunting and fishing, so he fit right in with The Drifting Cowboys, and he had a bluntness and directness that dovetailed with Hank's sense of what a person should be like.

Born Weldon E. Lister in Karnes County, south of San Antonio, on January 5, 1923, Big Bill grew up in the hill country around Brady and had been performing since 1938. By the late '40s, he had been a staple of San Antonio area radio for almost a decade. Like Roger Miller's "Kansas City Star," he was well known in and around his hometown. He got stopped in parking lots, his barber told him jokes, he had even made a few records for small labels, but he knew that the future held nothing for him unless he got out of town. Shortly after Christmas 1950, he and his wife, Lila, locked up the house, packed his Nudie suits and his Gibson into their car, and headed for Nashville.

During Lister's first week in Nashville he met Joe Allison, once a deejay in San Antonio, then a deejay in Nashville, and later the writer of "He'll Have to Go." Allison brought Lister backstage at the *Opry*, where he met Hank and Jim Denny. Hank was sitting quietly by himself on one of the pews reserved for performers. Lister chatted briefly with Hank, and they went out in the alley to smoke a cigarette. Later, Lister met Denny.

> Show how naive I was, I didn't know who Jim Denny was. He asked what I was doing, and I told him I'd come to Nashville to get on the *Opry*. I said, "I hear there are auditions over at WSM and some joker's supposed to listen to me over there." He kinda chuckled and said, "I wish you good luck." Joe had set up an audition for me the following week in Studio B at WSM, and I was sitting there with my guitar, and Jim come waltzing in. I said, "Jim, what're you doing here?" He said, "I'm the joker you gotta audition for."

Lister was caught in the hillbilly catch-22. The *Opry* wasn't interested because he didn't have a record contract; record companies weren't interested because he wasn't on the *Opry*. Tex Ritter, who'd worked shows with Lister in San Antonio, took care of the record contract. "Tex came to town," says Lister, "and he asked if I'd talked to Dee Kilpatrick [at Capitol], and I said he'd turned me down. Tex said, 'Meet me at the office in thirty minutes,' and he told Dee, 'Sign this guy.' As soon as I got that contract I went back to WSM and showed it to Jim Denny. I said, 'I come to find out if you're a man of your word. I've got a Capitol contract, now what you gonna do?' "

What Denny did was place Lister on a tour with Hank and give him a spot on Hank's early morning *Mother's Best* show on WSM. Lister didn't have any inkling of it at the time, but he came to believe that Denny was helping Hank ease Audrey out of his radio schedule by giving him a supporting act that needed to be featured. It was rare now for Audrey to join the group on a tour. Occasionally she would fly to do a show, then drive with the group for a few days before flying home, but as 1951 wore on, her appearances grew fewer and fewer. As much as this improved the shows, it did nothing for those moments when Hank would get into bed and try to pull Audrey close.

This was Lister's main chance; it was the reason he'd come to Nashville. He quickly found that life wasn't easy for an "XL" singing cowboy in the back of a touring sedan, though time has cast a rosy glow over it for him. He remembers the camaraderie, the hijinks, and the impromptu baseball games in the middle of nowhere. With a little prompting, he also remembers the rotten food and nights spent racing from somewhere like Omaha, Nebraska, to Corpus Christi, Texas.

Travel was usually at night because it was cooler and there was less traffic, but long jumps would often involve driving through the day, right up to show time the following night. In the days before interstates and orbital roads around cities, the highways went straight through the center of town. Driving through somewhere like Cincinnati at rush hour could mean a two-hour delay. "We'd stop to get gas," says Lister, "and at the same time, we'd get a gallon of milk and a dozen doughnuts or cupcakes. We didn't even have time to order hamburgers a lot of the time. There were many weeks that we'd maybe check into a hotel twice — the rest of the time you're driving."

When Lister joined, Hank bought a second touring sedan. The biggest item of baggage was the string bass that sat on top when it wasn't raining. The trunk was usually full of clothes, photos, and songbooks. There was only one amplifier, which Don Helms and Sammy Pruett shared. The summer months were hell in the cars, especially in heavy traffic. For a while, Hank had an air cooler fitted to his limo. The technology wasn't very complicated; a water tank was attached to the roof and a bat of gauze was fitted into the open window. Water was released from the tank by means of a cord, and leached into the gauze. The breeze then blew through the water-filled gauze and supposedly cooled the interior. Hank used the cooler for a while. It came at a time when Audrey was pressuring him to wear a toupee, which made him hotter still. He shaved off what hair he had on the crown of his head and the toupee was fixed in place. Somewhere in Louisiana, with the temperature inside the car around a hundred degrees, Hank pulled the cord to flush more water into the cooler, and the entire contents of the tank disgorged onto his head. He pulled the toupee off, threw it out the window and told everyone it was the last time he was going to wear it. Then he junked the air cooler.

The self-contained show that Hank put on would usually start at 8:00 P.M. Lister and The Drifting Cowboys warmed up the crowd. Howard Watts, the bass player who had replaced Hillous Butrum, did a little baggy-pants comedy as "Cedric Rainwater," and then the band played a few tunes before Hank did the first half of his show. There'd be a short intermission when The Drifting Cowboys would work the crowd, selling the photos and songbooks, and then Hank would play again until around 10:00 P.M.

Hank would usually work three- or four-day stands in major centers with other *Opry* acts, but his drawing power was so strong that he didn't need a supporting act on tour to fill a hall. Eddy Arnold may have sold more records nationwide, but Hank was king in the South and Southwest. His only serious challenger in the Southwest was Lefty Frizzell, so it was a surprise when A. V. Bamford placed the two on tour together in April 1951. Either of them could have filled the halls, so there seemed no reason to book them as a doubleheader.

The rivalry between Hank and Lefty simmered for a few months after Lefty first broke through at the end of 1950, and it was made more intense because Hank could see little good in Lefty's style. Once, when he was holed up on a drinking spree with Johnnie Wright and Jack and Jim Anglin, Hank's guard slipped and he took shots at Lefty's singing. It was whiny and no good, he said, ranting on until the others grew sick of it and told him to shut up.

Unlike Hank, Lefty wouldn't sustain a note or let it trail bluesily; instead, he worried words and vowels, glissing up or down on a syllable like a black gospel singer — a technique called melisma that almost certainly came naturally to him. Although he's not as well known today as Hank, Lefty's style more than Hank's prefigured modern country singing. Merle Haggard, Randy Travis, and Keith Whitley are just three of many who openly modeled their phrasing on Lefty's. His was an intimate style for which the microphone was a prerequisite, whereas Hank's full-throated delivery had been forged partly out of necessity from singing without amplification; in fact, Hank's pride in being able to sing unamplified over a band probably accounted in part for his disdain of Lefty.

Hank and Lefty met for the first time in Nashville shortly after Hank had done a radio interview with deejay Hugh Cherry. Hank and Cherry were sitting in Eddie DuBois's Key Club in Printer's Alley thinking about drinking. As Cherry recalled it to researcher Charles Wolfe,

Lefty came in by himself a little greased and sat down with us. Hank decided to feign displeasure and he started out by saying, "Here, boy, why don't you just stay down in Texas, this is my territory up here." Lefty got that great big smile on his face, and said, "Hank, the whole damn country is the back yard of both of us, can't you realize there's enough room for all of us?" Hank kinda smiled and said, "Well, I was just kidding. It's good to have a little competition. Makes me realize I gotta work harder than ever, and boy you're the best competition I ever had."

The tour they worked together started in Little Rock on April 1, 1951, and then swept along the gulf coast. It came while Lefty was dickering over an offer from the *Opry*. Talking about the tour in 1974, he said,

[Hank] had a way of influencing you. He could talk you into anything. We was on the road. I had "Always Late" and "Mom and Dad's Waltz" and "I Want to Be with You Always" on the charts. Hank said, "Lefty, what you need is the *Grand Ole Opry*." I said, "Hell, I just got a telegram from [music publisher] Hill & Range on having number one and number two, and I got maybe two more in there, and you say I need the *Grand Ole Opry?*" He said, "You got a hell of an argument."

Even so, Lefty briefly joined the *Opry* that July, although no one remembers if Hank influenced the decision.

Lefty insisted that Hank was stone cold sober throughout the tour:

I come in to Corpus Christi [April 5, 1951], and I brought in a bottle of bourbon and set it down in there. Hank and me was settin' around getting ready to do the show. I said, "Hey, I'm gonna have a shot. How about you?" He said, "If I was to have what you're fixin' to drink, I'd want another and first thing you know I'd be gone." I thought he was kidding, teasin' me. Found out later that he would have. When I saw that movie [*Your Cheatin' Heart*] it really made me feel bad, 'cause he was always late and always drunk, and I worked two weeks with him and he never sounded better. He was in good shape. But he didn't take a drink — and he put on a show.

We flipped coins to see who would go on first. Dad [Naamon Frizzell] was still driving for us, and there's enough stories to fill a book there. All Hank thought about was writing. He recorded a number he wrote because I was having trouble with my better half called "I'm Sorry for You, My Friend." We'd swap songs we'd written.

Between dates with Lefty in Baton Rouge, Louisiana, on April 3 and Corpus Christi two days later, Hank shot north by himself to play at the scene of his first triumphs, the Municipal Auditorium in Shreveport. It was the first time he had been back in almost two years. Then, after a short break, he was sent north on a tour of Canada. They played Ottawa on May 8, but a day or two later, the wheels started to come off. Hank started drinking somewhere in Ontario, and reportedly fell offstage, aggravating the already serious problem with his back. Jim Denny rushed Carl Smith up to complete the tour, and Bill Lister was given the unenviable task of hauling Hank and a suitcase full of money back to Nashville. It was the first time he'd seen his boss disabled like that:

Coming back we stopped one morning just after daylight, and I said, "Hank, you gotta have something to eat, son." He said, "Big un, I just cain't do this." I could understand. His eyes looked like watery fried eggs when he was in that shape, but I knew better than to let him wait in the car, so I just jumped up and paid the bill, and by the time I was outside, he was nowhere to be seen. In the middle of the next block, a big sign said "Cocktails" and I just broke into a dead run, and by the time I got there, he'd already had him one. I paid his bill and drug him back to the car. It just broke your heart, but I knew I had to get him home.

Lister carried on driving and got to the outskirts of Nashville around five in the morning. He stopped to call Audrey, to tell her to expect them shortly:

I said, "I'm at the edge of town, and I got Hank with me and he's in pretty bad shape. I just wanted you to be expecting us." She said, "I don't care what you do with the son of a bitch, just don't bring him out here," so I called Jim Denny, and Jim told me where to take him — the hospital out in Madison. Then I went by the studio and put the money in the safe, then around nine o'clock Audrey called me and wanted to know where her money was at. I said, "Lady, as far as I know you ain't got no damn money. I gave *Hank's* money to Jim."

From Madison, Hank probably went home but continued to mess up and was quickly transferred to the North Louisiana Sanatorium in Shreveport on May 21, 1951. When he was admitted he was complaining of acute back pain and mental worries, and he had apparently been drinking for several days. A complete physical examination under the direction of Dr. G. H. Cassity revealed the extent and nature of the degeneration of his spine, and arrangements were made to fit him with a lumbosacral brace. Hank was discharged three days later, sober but still in pain, a pain that would — from this point on — scarcely leave him. The brace was uncomfortable. It was made of stainless steel and leather, and it made road travel unbearable, so increasingly and whenever feasible, Hank would fly to the starting point of a tour in a private plane, often a Beechcraft Bonanza piloted by Minnie Pearl's husband, Henry Cannon.

After his discharge from the sanatorium in Shreveport, Hank appears to have rested up in Nashville for a few days and then prepared for a Luke the Drifter session on the evening of Friday, June 1. The lead-off cut, "Ramblin' Man," was one of Hank's few minor-key compositions. It was a taut, edgy performance, sung rather than spoken, which made it more like a Hank Williams record — a judgment MGM came to share immediately after Hank's death, when it was reissued under his name. Hank's keening falsetto was used to particularly good effect, and the prominently miked acoustic guitar punctuated by Don Helms's steel guitar gave the record a folky flavor that wasn't entirely accidental. The Weavers' hit version of Leadbelly's "Goodnight Irene" had sparked a shortlived vogue for traditional folk music, which Hank may have seen as an opportunity for Luke the Drifter.

The second Luke the Drifter cut, "Pictures from Life's Other Side," was a Victorian morality fable. The arrangement was credited to Hank, but, as researcher Bob Pinson discovered, the song was originally written around 1880 by John B. Vaughan, a composer and singing schoolteacher from Athens, Georgia. It had been recorded as a country song in 1926 by J. Frank Smith, then by Vernon Dalhart and Bradley Kincaid, so it was probably pulled from the arsenal of half-forgotten favorites that Hank dipped into when he was short a song for a Luke the Drifter session. His recitation showed that constant travel to nearly every state had done nothing to change his defiantly hillbilly pronunciation. "Poor" was still "purr" — just as it had been on his first session — and "picture" was still "pitcher."

"I've Been Down That Road Before" was another dose of the sage advice that Luke the Drifter seemed endlessly capable of dispensing — and Hank Williams seemed equally capable of ignoring. It was almost as if Luke the Drifter was the part of him that was censorious and wise at the expense of the willful and weak Hank Williams. The last cut, "I Dreamed About Mama Last Night" was a Fred Rose song rooted in the idyllic childhood that Rose had never even come close to knowing.

After the session, Hank eased himself back into his public appearance schedule. His July 4 date for 1951 was at a park in Huntingdon, West Virginia. Then, on Sunday July 15, he was the star of the Hank Williams Homecoming in Montgomery, sponsored by the Jaycees. There was an early afternoon show at the Veterans Hospital, a parade, then a 3:00 P.M. show at the Montgomery Agricultural Coliseum, known as the Cow Coliseum. It was the first music event to be staged there, so there were inevitably problems with the public address system. Hank headed a cast that included Hank Snow, Chet Atkins (billed that day as a "Teenage Tantalizer"), the Carter Family, and Braxton Schuffert.

For some reason, Hank didn't have a guitar with him, so just before the first show his cousin Walter McNeil drove him to French's Music store to borrow one for the afternoon. He came back out to the car, sat in the front seat quietly for a while, then said, "You know I tried to buy a guitar on credit there once when I was comin' up, and they wouldn't have nothin' to do with me. Now they want to give me one." It could have been a moment to savor, but Hank always saw the darker side. The city, which had once treated him as a worthless drunk, was now extending its embrace, but Hank knew well that it could be as quickly withdrawn.

At Hank's insistence, Lillie was presented with a gold watch by the Jaycees, and it was a chance for him to publicly acknowledge in front of nine thousand paying customers the role she had played in getting his career started. Hank could also celebrate a partial family truce held in his honor. Audrey didn't squabble with Lillie, and Lillie didn't squabble with Lon, who had come up from McWilliams for the occasion, but when Lon tried to hold his grandson, Hank Jr., Audrey snatched him back.

Braxton remembers sitting backstage at the Coliseum, when a kid with a guitar went up to Hank and asked to sing. At first Hank declined, but then, perhaps recognizing shades of himself fifteen years earlier, he agreed. "This guy said, 'All I do is sing your songs. Just let me sing one of your songs,' " said Braxton. "Hank said, 'Well, what d'you want to do?' This guy said, 'I want to do "Hey, Good Lookin'." ' Hank said, 'Well, that's my current song.' This guy said, 'Aw, Hank, let me sing it.' Hank said, 'Go 'head, I'll sing something else.' "

Hank's manager, Bill England, negotiated the show with the Jaycees, and he remembers it as a fiasco because of the poor public address system. His attitude, though, may have stemmed in part from the fact that he and Hank were headed for a parting of the ways. The Homecoming was one of his last acts on Hank's behalf, and they eventually parted backstage at the Ryman. He says that they had both seen it coming. WSM made England an offer to return to his old job, selling airtime, and he gratefully accepted.

Hank stayed overnight in Montgomery after the Homecoming. Back at the boardinghouse, he took off his shirt to show everyone his new brace. Swarms of people were around him pitching songs or trying to sell him something. The next day, Hank headed down the oh so familiar Highway 31 toward the gulf for a string of personal appearances that started in Biloxi, and he continued on through his old haunts in southern Louisiana and eastern Texas.

Ten days after the Homecoming, Hank was back in Nashville for another recording session, the first under a contract renewal dated July 5 that extended his MGM term by another two years. Only three songs from the July 25 session were deemed issuable by Fred Rose. Of these, the most unusual was "Lonesome Whistle," a title truncated in the interests of jukebox cards from "(I Heard That) Lonesome Whistle Blow." Credited to Hank and Jimmie Davis, it was a trite and cliché-ridden prison song. Davis was something of an elder statesman in Hank's eyes. He had started his recording career as a disciple of Jimmie Rodgers, and after cutting his first record for KWKH's label in 1928, he was signed to RCA Victor. He made some wonderfully libidinous blues for Victor, like "Tom Cat and Pussy Blues" and "Red Nightgown Blues," but, by the time he signed with Decca in 1934 he was trying to clean up his act and his image. His biggest hit on Decca was "You Are My Sunshine," which he claimed as his composition, although it was apparently written by a woman in South Carolina and sold to Davis by the Rice Brothers, whose recording predated his.

After a political career in Shreveport, Davis ran for governor in 1944, and won in the face of a viciously negative advertising campaign on the part of his opponent, which made political capital out of his old, smutty records and emphasized that he couldn't be in favor of segregation as he claimed because he owned an integrated honky-tonk in California. After his first term as governor (he ran again and was re-elected in 1960), Davis returned to Shreveport, and it was probably there that Hank met him. There's a grainy photo of them; Hank has the grin that he usually reserved for the times he was getting plastered, and Davis looks none too sober. It's unclear how or when they wrote the three songs that bear both their names; perhaps it was during Hank's return to Shreveport in April. Tillman Franks, who toured with Davis in the 1990s, when Davis himself was in his nineties, says that Davis told him that he supplied the title to "Lonesome Whistle" and Hank wrote the words after riding on a train with a convict under armed guard. But Hank didn't ride trains anymore.

Like "Ramblin' Man," "Lonesome Whistle" had the form and content of a folk song, and Hank's record gained what impact it had from the way he grafted the sound of a train whistle onto the word "lonesome." It was shipped on September 24, coupled with another song from the July 25 session, "Crazy Heart," the joint effort of Fred Rose and Maurice Murray — and a fairly undistinguished one at that. The single didn't do well. "Crazy Heart" got only as far as number four, and "Lonesome Whistle" pegged out at number eight, spending only two weeks on the charts. Both songs were covered for the pop market. Guy Lombardo made a dent in the Top 20 with "Crazy Heart," underscoring the judgment that it was better suited to a palm court orchestra than to Hank Williams.

There were two other songs recorded at the July 25 session. One was "I'd Still Want You"; the other was an aborted version of "Baby, We're Really in Love." Rose wanted to recut "Baby, We're Really in Love" and get some more songs in the can before Hank went off on the ten-week Hadacol Caravan, so he scheduled another Friday night session for August 10. Only two cuts from that session were released; the first was the rerecording of "Baby, We're Really in Love," and the other was "Half as Much." Rose used a piano (played by himself or Owen Bradley) to flesh out the rhythm section on this session, and — for the first and only time on a Hank Williams record — there was a flash of solo barroom piano at the very end of "Half as Much."

"Half as Much" was written by Curley Williams and it was recorded by him a month later, on September 13, for Columbia. Apparently Hank wasn't too interested in touching the song at all, but Rose insisted that he cut it. Like "Crazy Heart," it was a song that boiled down to nothing. Curley's version was released first, on November 2, probably because Rose wanted to give Curley a head start. If the two records had been released simultaneously, Hank's clout with the deejays and jukebox operators would have damned Curley's version. When Hank's version was finally released on March 28, 1952, it became a number two hit for him, and it gave both Curley Williams and Fred Rose an even bigger payday when it was covered by Rosemary Clooney, who took it to number seven on the pop charts. "Later," remembered Curley's steel guitarist, Boots Harris, "Mitch Miller said to Wesley, 'Ol' Hank's done it again, hasn't he?' and Wesley said, 'That was *Curley* Williams who wrote "Half As Much," ' and Mitch Miller said, 'Who's Curley Williams?' and Wesley said, 'A guy that's been on your label about seven years.' "

"Baby, We're Really in Love" was released on November 23, 1951. It was as good as any of the other bouncy mid- to fast-tempo songs that had become hits for Hank, such as "Hey, Good Lookin' " and "Why Don't You Love Me?" but it stalled at number four. The conclusion Hank probably drew from this was that repetition was beginning to set in, which probably explains why he was trying other peoples' songs like "Crazy Heart" and "Half as Much."

Hank was still writing as prolifically as ever, and still pitching songs to almost every artist he met. All of them flopped. Either Hank or Fred Rose placed "I Can't Escape from You" with Rusty Gabbard and Ray Price. "Countrified" and "The Little House We Built Just o'er the Hill" went to Big Bill Lister, and "Me and My Broken Heart" and "There's Nothing As Sweet As My Baby" went to Carl Smith. Hank and George Morgan's brother wrote "A Stranger in the Night" for Morgan, and Little Jimmy Dickens finally got a crack at a Hank Williams song, the bruisingly sarcastic "I Wish You Didn't Love Me So Much." Jimmie Davis recorded the other two songs that he and Hank had written together, "Bayou Pon-Pon" and "Forever is a Long, Long Time." None of them charted.

But Hank wasn't the only one using his name to get more business. The Drifting Cowboys were taking session work with anyone who wanted the Hank Williams sound, and Fred Rose was producing acts so prolifically for MGM that it's hard to see where he ever found time to work with Hank. Between March and June 1951, MGM released roughly one hundred records; Fred Rose produced nineteen of them. But, in the same way that Hank couldn't write a hit for anyone else, Fred Rose couldn't produce one for anyone else. The records he cut with the Louvin Brothers have acquired some cachet lately among collectors, but at the time they flopped — as did the records he produced on Al Rogers, Carl "Mr. Sunshine" Swanson, Hal White, Gene McGhee, and all the others.

Another of Hank's attempts to make a little capital out of his success was his booklet *Hank Williams Tells How to Write Folk and Western Music to Sell*. It was published in September 1951, and it would be good to be able to report that in it Hank divulged how he and Fred Rose set about their craft, but that was not the case. Probably Hank's major contributions were to put his name and face on the front, and to produce the radio spots that advertised the booklet. "I set down and started to writing," he said with his salesman's oily charm, "but pretty soon I decided I needed some he'p." That help probably extended to letting his cowriter, Jimmy Rule, author the entire booklet.

Rule was a fifty-year-old mathematics teacher at a local private school and a part-time songwriter who had yet to write any folk or western music that had sold. He'd had a hand in writing a number of pop songs, like Perry Como's first RCA recording, "Goodbye Sue," and a wartime saber-rattler, "Let's Sing a Hymn to G.I. Jim," but — sensibly — he had not given up his day job. *Hank Williams Tells How to Write Folk and Western Music to Sell* is rife with solid advice for the budding songwriter, but it offers little or no insight into Hank Williams.

Toward the end, the booklet lists the titles and publishers of two rhyming dictionaries, which, if Hank had indeed written the booklet, would open up the intriguing possibility of him sitting at home or in the touring sedan with *The New Rhyming Dictionary and Poet's Handbook* on his lap. Everything considered, the most interesting aspect of the booklet was Hank's lengthy and prolix radio spots. As he always did when he was selling something, he leavened his pitch with a little humor. WSM announcer Grant Turner, acting as straight man, mentioned that Hank's photo was on the front of the book, opening the door for Hank to say, "Yes, Grant. If any of the folks are bothered by crows gittin' in their corn, it might come in handy to scar' them critters away."

The twenty-page booklet sold for one dollar and was marketed through the border station XEDM, which broadcast out of Nogales, Mexico, but operated out of Nogales, Arizona. "It'll be a blessin' to you," said Hank in conclusion.

In October 1951, Hank pitched a third song to Big Bill Lister. The chart books have no entry for Lister, but his record of "Beer Drinking Blues" had sold well. "We didn't get no radio play on beer drinking songs," says Lister, "but they was killers on the jukebox, so every session

I had to do at least one beer drinking song." Capitol's west coast–based chief of country A&R, Ken Nelson, had scheduled a session for Lister on Friday, October 26. "I told Hank I needed a beer drinkin' song," says Lister, "and he said, 'Don't worry 'bout it, Big un, I got you covered. I got one that's hotter'n a pistol.' "

The song was "There's a Tear in My Beer." Hank had only written one other song, "I Can't Escape from You," that even hinted at his problem with alcohol (it contained the words "A jug of wine to numb my mind," which would have been innocuous enough from any other pen than his). "There's a Tear in My Beer," on the other hand, was an unambiguous celebration of getting blotto ("I'm gonna keep drinkin' until I'm petrified. . . . I'm gonna keep drinkin' 'til I can't even think"). Hank cut a demo on the night before the session right after he'd finished prerecording some radio shows. The song had the sing-along quality of the best drinking songs, and it was perhaps the strongest song that Hank farmed out, but he well knew that he couldn't risk cutting it himself. Ken Nelson recognized its potential and agreed to record it.

After the session, Lister threw the demo acetate, which had no markings on it, into a box of records at his house. At some point between Christmas and New Year's, he reconciled himself to the inevitable and moved back to San Antonio. Hank was more or less off the road by then, and his show had disbanded. The acetate went back to San Antonio with the Listers and sat out in their yard under a tarp for a few years and was then moved up to the loft where, as Lister says, it's hot enough to fry eggs in July. It was discovered during the mid-eighties when Lister was cleaning house. By then, Lister's son did occasional gun work for Hank Jr., and the next time Hank Jr. went to San Antonio, Lister presented him with the acetate. "Here's one they ain't never heard your daddy do," he told him.

Hank Jr. took the acetate back to Nashville, and, in September 1988, overdubbed himself onto it — a thirty-nine-year-old man duetting with his twenty-eight-year-old father. "There's a Tear in My Beer" finally became a hit, helped in no small measure by a video that defied any jaw not to drop. It merged footage of father and son in a dream sequence. Hank Jr. was shot against a neutral background and was superimposed onto the only reasonably high-grade performance video of Hank Sr. Video engineers slowed down the footage of Hank Sr. to match the tempo of "There's a Tear in My Beer," and then new lip movements were "pasted on" from an actor lip-synching the song. Hank Jr. was then superimposed over the four thousand frames that make up the forty-six seconds of "duet" footage. The result sent chills up Hank Jr.'s spine — and many others' besides.

Hank Jr. gave Bill Lister a percentage of the record's revenue, brought him to Nashville to appear on TNN, and awarded him a gold record. It was a sweet moment for Lister, who had exited the business in the mid-fifties, correctly concluding that no one cared about six-foot-seven-inch singing cowboys any more.

1951 was the last good year for the ol' Drifting Cowboy, too. It was capped that fall when he, Bill Lister, The Drifting Cowboys, and Minnie Pearl were scheduled to take part in the Hadacol Caravan. For the first time since 1943, Hank was to play in a medicine show, but he wasn't going to bump around the boondocks playing off the back of a flatbed truck this time; he was to travel first-class in a fleet of Pullman cars keeping company with the country's biggest stars and a troupe of dancing girls. He was to play to hundreds of thousands of people over the course of six weeks. It was to be the last and greatest medicine show.

On every pay day when my check is due
I hurry home to my momma on the p.d.q.
Professor Longhair,
"The Hadacol Bounce"

Chapter

12

THE HADDY-COLE BOUNCE

*H*ANK had been surrounded all his professional life by snake-oil salesmen who used more or less unregulated airtime to sell everything from absolution to job lots of live chicks shipped by mail. From them he acquired a little arsenal of salesman's come-ons and self-deprecating jokes that he would trot out when he was in the business of selling something. "Friends," he would often say, concluding his pitch, "I don't need the money, but the folks I owe it to need it awful bad." Still, the man who could make Hank and nearly every other salesman look like a rank amateur was Senator Dudley J. LeBlanc from Louisiana.

Dudley Joseph LeBlanc was born in Youngsville, Louisiana, on August 16, 1894, and claimed to be able to trace his ancestry back to René LeBlanc in Longfellow's *Evangeline.* He grew up speaking nothing but French, and never lost his Cajun accent. LeBlanc was fiercely proud of his heritage and eventually published a book on Acadian culture. After graduating from Southwestern Louisiana Institute, he became a salesman for a shoe company, working the same patch in northern Louisiana as Huey P. Long. LeBlanc and Long were both formidable salesmen, and they came to mistrust, then detest each other in the way that only rival salesmen can.

After World War I, LeBlanc got his introduction to selling patent medicines when he started representing Wine of Cardui, fetchingly called a "woman's tonic." His first brush with politics came in 1924, when he ran for the state legislature in Vermilion Parish — and won. This was at a time when the issues of the day included care of Confederate veterans. In 1932 he ran for governor but lost at the hands of the Huey Long forces. Then LeBlanc concentrated on his own patent medicines, starting with Happy Day Headache Powder, a concoction that, in common with most of his remedies, contained a stiff dose of laxative.

In 1942, after another unsuccessful run for the governorship and the Public Service Commission, LeBlanc fell ill with beriberi. He was cured with vitamin B_1 compounds, and, with the unquenchable enthusiasm of the autodidact, he set out to learn everything he could about vitamins. He then began distilling his own compound in the family barn. It was a mixture of vitamins, minerals, honey, and — not least — 12 percent alcohol. It was dubbed HADACOL, an acronym from HAppy DAy CO., topped off with an "L" for LeBlanc. Its alcohol content was roughly the same as wine, but at $3.50 it was four times as expensive and immeasurably more foul-tasting so that people would believe it was doing them some good. With many counties still dry in the South, Hadacol was the closest to a nip that many folks out on the rural routes could get — from a bottle with a label on it at least.

Hadacol went on the market in 1945 after LeBlanc had tested it on his cattle, himself, and his neighbors. Sales were static for a while as he rekindled his political ambitions, becoming a state senator in 1948. During this second stint in politics, he was instrumental in helping to pass the Old Age Pension bill, then used his newfound credibility among older citizens to sell them Hadacol.

LeBlanc more or less introduced saturation advertising to the South. His newspaper ads were rife with testimonials. Some claimed to be cured of cancer, epilepsy, heart trouble, strokes, or tuberculosis, and LeBlanc published their claims until the Federal Trade Commission stepped in. The advertisements concluded that the good senator "has served his people in public life faithfully and well. In private life, he brings you a service which is appreciated by suffering humanity — HADACOL." At first the advertising was designed to devour pretax profits, but it quickly began to assume a life of its own.

Early in 1949 LeBlanc hooked up with Murray Nash, then head of Mercury Records' southern division. "I asked LeBlanc what was in Hadacol," said Nash, "and he told me there was enough alcohol to make people feel good and enough laxative for a good movement." Nash's commercial antennae sensed an opportunity and he cut two paeans to Hadacol — one for the country market, Bill Nettles's "Hadacol Boogie," which charted in June 1949, and another for the rhythm and blues market, Professor Longhair's "Hadacol Bounce." The publicity generated by "Hadacol Boogie" convinced LeBlanc that country music was an effective medium for promoting his product, so he was primed when Matt Hedrick of WSM approached him with the idea of sponsoring Hank Williams's *Health and Happiness* shows in October 1949. Even then, Hank was just a bit player on LeBlanc's stage. In 1950 LeBlanc spent more than one million dollars a month on advertising, making him the nation's second-largest advertiser after Coca-Cola. His enterprise grew to the point where Hadacol was shipped by a wholly owned fleet of trucks from the plants in Lafayette, where the employees, dressed in white starched uniforms to simulate a lab environment, were a far cry from the barn where Hadacol got its start. Sales were as high as $1,500,000 a day at the peak of the operation in 1950 and 1951.

LeBlanc always said that the four S's of salesmanship were Saturation, Sincerity, Simplicity, and Showmanship, and with the last in mind, he mounted the Hadacol Caravan. Murray Nash says that he gave LeBlanc the idea based upon a hillbilly jamboree he had organized in Tampa; LeBlanc insisted that the idea came to him at 4:30 one morning in Abbeville, Louisiana. The first Hadacol Caravan ran in August 1950. Hank Williams didn't work it; the headliners were Roy Acuff, Connie Boswell, Burns and Allen, Chico Marx, and Mickey Rooney.

Researcher Floyd Martin Clay described how LeBlanc skillfully used the Caravan to promote Hadacol in areas where he hadn't secured distribution. He bought heavy advertising on radio in the form of a contest: a well-known song was played and the audience was invited to send in a card with the title. If they were correct, they got a voucher for a free bottle of Hadacol. Of course, Hadacol was nowhere to be found, but druggists were now getting a steady stream of requests for it and pestering the jobbers to carry it. Then the advertising for the Caravan kicked in, with admission restricted to those carrying Hadacol box tops. By this point, the Hadacol trucks were waiting outside the city limits, and the jobbers were begging for the product.

The 1951 Caravan was the largest show of its kind ever staged; it was the last and greatest medicine show. The mainstay of the bill was to be Hank Williams, backed by Minnie Pearl, comedian Candy Candido, emcee Emil Perra, juggler Lee Marks, a house band led by Tony Martin, a troupe of dancers, and twelve clowns. Other star attractions were to be added at various points along the route. Cesar Romero was on the first seven dates. Jack Benny and Rochester, Milton Berle, Bob Hope, Jimmy

Durante, Rudy Vallee, Carmen Miranda, Dick Haymes, and Jack Dempsey were all conscripted for one or two dates. Admission was one Hadacol box top for children, two for adults. There were prizes for the kids and "reserved seating for coloreds." Most shows were preceded by a parade.

By this point, LeBlanc had a weighty hidden agenda: he wanted to sell Hadacol, and he wanted to use the publicity generated by the Caravan as a base from which to launch another stab at the Louisiana governorship. His photo loomed larger than any other in his advertisements and he made an appearance on every show. He knew that demand had peaked, and he knew that the Food and Drug Administration, the American Medical Association, and the Liquor Control Board were sniffing around. More than that, LeBlanc's ruinous advertising budget meant that the corporation lost two million dollars during the second quarter of 1951 alone. With low cunning, he used the second Caravan as a smoke screen to disguise the true financial picture and to snare potential buyers.

Inevitably, the Caravan began in Lafayette. Hank and Bill Lister went into the senator's office before the tour started. They noted the shelf full of Old Forester whiskey with a subscript on the label that read, "Bottled Especially for Sen. Dudley J. LeBlanc, Lafayette, Louisiana." Hank and Bill Lister were impressed. A shelf full of premium whiskey with "Bottled Especially for Hank Williams" on the label was alternately Hank's darkest nightmare and his fondest dream.

The Caravan was scheduled to run from August 14 to October 2, although it had been agreed that Hank and Minnie Pearl would miss the Saturday night shows so that they could fly back to Nashville to meet their *Opry* commitments. LeBlanc had spared no expense in mounting the shows. He budgeted $500,000 for talent and another $750,000 for promotion. A fleet of fifteen Pullman cars was leased, and arrangements were made to transfer the fleet from one railroad company's engines to another as the show made its way across eighteen states. Fine food was laid on for the performers, laundry facilities had been prearranged, and the logistics of setting up and tearing down had been rehearsed with military precision.

For most of the performers, this was their first contact with Hank Williams and his audience. The dancers had been recruited from an agency in Los Angeles; they'd never heard of Hank, but by the end they were all standing in the wings every night while he performed. The reception surprised even Hank. Every night he had stadiums full of people eating out of his hand, and the legit entertainers were forced to work as his supporting acts. Even The Drifting Cowboys were surprised. They had always thought of themselves as working a lowly rung of the entertainment ladder; now they recognized the magnitude of Hank's stardom. The chorus girls, used to most stars' frosty hauteur, were also surprised at Hank's willingness to do the shake 'n' howdy routine. He would sign autographs for hours, turning no one away.

One week into the tour, the show touched down in Montgomery. Brack Schuffert remembers getting a call from Hank's mother asking him to meet Hank on the Hadacol train, which was parked down at the railroad yard:

> He was sittin' there and he had the seat in front of him pushed forward and he was sitting with his boots up on the other seat. I set down beside him. I said, "Hank, how you doin' boy?" He said, "I'm doing no good at all." I said, "What's the matter?" I seen them movie stars walking by outside the window. "All them pretty movie stars on this train, Hank." He said, "I don't have nothin' to do with them. They think they're better than I am."

Then Hank got to what was probably the true cause of his foul mood. "He pulled out a pink check about six inches long and three inches high," said Braxton. "It was for something like seventy-five-hundred dollars. He said, 'Ever'body on this train has got one of these.' " The paychecks had bounced.

Hank and Minnie Pearl eventually forced the issue of payment by threatening not to return from Nashville unless they were paid, and for a few weeks LeBlanc managed to juggle enough funds into the payroll account to keep everyone happy. From Montgomery, the show moved into Georgia. Walter McNeil drove Lillie to the show in Columbus so she could savor Hank's triumph one more time. Then the Caravan swung up through the Carolinas and into Virginia. After the show in Roanoke on Friday, August 31, Hank flew back to Nashville. It was then that he signed the papers to purchase his spread in Williamson County, but this new toy did little to mollify Audrey, who had spent her life trying to get off the farm. Band members recall that Hank often came back from his weekend furloughs distraught and angry, hinting broadly that all was not well on Franklin Road. There were rumors that Audrey was keeping company with other men while he was out on the road, and those rumors gnawed at him.

Hank, of course, was applying his usual double standard. He tried to start an affair with one of the dancing girls, and used his failing marriage as an excuse for coming on to her. He gave the impression that he wanted to get involved, took her shopping, bought her some cowboy boots, and squired her to clubs, but she wouldn't succumb.

"When we got to Louisville, Kentucky," said Big Bill Lister, "Dick Haymes said to his wife, 'Well, we're finally getting out of the sticks — the hillbillies won't be tearing them up now.' What he didn't know was that Louisville was a second home to a lot of *Opry* acts; somebody played there every Sunday afternoon on the way to somewhere." Bob Hope joined the show for two appearances in Louisville and Cincinnati. Hank had been closing the show up to that point, but LeBlanc asked him to take second billing and Hank agreed. To make things as difficult as possible for Hope, Hank reached back for something extra and took encore after encore. "That crowd wasn't gonna turn him loose," says Lister, "and LeBlanc was trying to introduce Bob Hope over all this hollerin' and clappin'. They got the crowd quieted down, and somewhere in his wardrobe Bob Hope had this old hat that he'd used in *Paleface,* and he wore that and just stood there, and when the place quieted down he said, 'Just call me Hank Hope.' " When he came off, Hope found Le-Blanc and told him that he wouldn't follow Hank Williams again. Hank could afford to smile inwardly, but — being Hank — he probably smiled outwardly as well because a triumph was for nothing if not to be savored.

Lister, in common with everyone in Hank's entourage, has less charitable memories of Milton Berle, who appeared on the show in St. Louis. Uncle Miltie, he recalls, had offered to emcee the entire show in addition to performing his usual shtick:

He had — and probably still has — an ego big as all outdoors, and when Dick Haymes was doing "Old Man River," Milton Berle had a red bandanna around his head and stood out behind Dick Haymes and just ruined the man's act. Nobody deserves that. Uncle Miltie had already been out and done his thing and now he was ruining everybody else's act. I told Hank, "If that joker comes out doing that when we're out there, he's really gonna mess things up. If he wants a good laugh, I'm gonna get this ol' guitar and crown him with it." Hank said, "If you do, I'll buy you any guitar you want," but the word circulated around and Milton's manager got him plumb offstage somewhere.

On Friday, September 14, the movable feast touched down in Wichita, Kansas, for a show designed to coincide with the Frontier Days Rodeo festival. A second show was laid on in the early hours to accommodate those who had just got off work at the aircraft plant. Hank and Minnie Pearl flew back to Nashville later that night and rejoined the troupe in Oklahoma City on Sunday. Over that weekend, though, LeBlanc had finalized a deal with the Tobey Maltz Co. in New York to sell Hadacol. He announced the sale in Dallas on Monday, September 17, just before the show scheduled for the Cotton Bowl. "The next morning we were having breakfast," remembered Bill Lister, "and Hank asked the senator, 'What did you sell Hadacol for?' He meant, 'Why did you sell it?' but the senator leaned across the table and said, 'Eight and a half million dollars,' and our jaws just dropped to the floor." Jaws dropped again when the performers were handed their final paychecks and tried to cash them, only to have the bank refuse to honor them because of insufficient funds.

The Caravan, so huge and unwieldy, was torn down in the space of hours. Everyone said their hurried good-byes. Some members of the chorus line who had been living for free on the train and sending their ninety-dollar paychecks back home ended up in Juarez and had to ride a cattle car back to Los Angeles. Hank flew back to Nashville, and he flew Don Helms and Sammy Pruett to Lafayette to pick up the limos. He gave Jerry Rivers and Howard Watts train tickets back to Nashville.

In fact, LeBlanc saw no more than $250,000 for Hadacol. Payments of half a million dollars a month from future profits were called for but not made because there were no future profits — only liens, overdue bills, returned shipments, and FTC and Liquor Control Board suits. LeBlanc exculpated himself neatly by saying, "If you sell a cow and the cow dies, you can't do anything to a man for that." Although he had sidestepped some potentially damaging fallout, he was nevertheless tagged as a loser, and he once again failed in his bid to become governor in 1952. Hadacol was officially declared bankrupt at the height of the gubernatorial campaign.

The tour was supposed to have ended back in Baton Rouge on October 2. On the way home, Hank had scheduled a date in Biloxi on October 3 and had committed to performing at the Mississippi-Louisiana Exposition in Vicksburg, Mississippi, on the same day. No one now remembers how he filled the two vacant weeks at the end of the tour, but when he played the *Opry* on October 6, he told the audience that he was "entertaining at home next week for the first time in nine weeks," suggesting that he had filled in the dates at short notice.

On the weekend after the wheels came off the Hadacol Caravan, Hank was photographed backstage at the *Opry* signing a motion-picture contract. His uneasy dance with the legitimate entertainment world that had started when Tony Bennett covered "Cold, Cold Heart" was now acquiring a momentum that would soon overtake him. The attention left Hank profoundly uneasy and carried with it pressures that contributed heavily to his precipitous decline in 1952.

Frank Walker had come down from New York for the MGM Pictures signing, and he, Wesley Rose, and Jim Denny circled predatorily around their meal ticket, cigars in hand, as Hank committed himself to a deal for what the local paper called "top quality motion pics." Hank, who had a keener sense of his limitations than his handlers, had never cared to capitalize on the link between MGM Records and MGM Pictures. He was happier telling people that the picture division was courting him, all the while keeping them at bay, but, inevitably and inexorably, the pressure grew. Hank read in *Billboard* that his fellow MGM Records act, Billy Eckstine, had been signed to *Skirts Away,* and all of his heroes, including Roy Acuff, Ernest Tubb, Jimmie Davis, and particularly Gene Autry, had made motion pictures. Still, Hank had reservations.

One consideration that weighed on Hank's mind when he rebuffed MGM was basic economics. He could make more money on the road than he could if he were tied up week after week in Hollywood. Soon after he arrived at the *Opry* he had put his band on salary rather than paying them a per-gig fee, which assured him of having his pickers on call but also meant that he was committed to paying them regardless of whether they worked. A deeper concern, though, was Hank's sure knowledge that he was getting out of his depth.

In holding out, Hank dug a deeper hole for himself. When the offer was made, MGM Pictures agreed to forgo screen tests and guaranteed to place him right away in costar billing roles. *Billboard* reported that the movies would "not [be] in the horse opera category," and that Joe Pasternak of MGM had already offered Hank a costarring role in an upcoming Esther Williams movie called *Peg o' My Heart.* He was offered a four-year deal, and no picture was to take more than four weeks of his time. The salary guarantee was between three thousand and five thousand dollars a week, with a ten-thousand-dollar guarantee per picture. Tellingly, at the signing ceremony, Hank wasn't smiling.

Hank still wasn't smiling when he went to meet Pasternak in California. Pasternak asked him to stand up and turn around, and the hair rose on the back of his neck. "He said it was like he was for sale," said Don

Helms afterward. The motion-picture deal also meant that Hank had to wear a toupee again. The remaining hair on the crown of his head was shaved off, and he went for several fittings. In Pasternak's office, Jim Denny, himself the owner of a lot of hair that nature hadn't given him, told Hank to take his hat off. Pasternak saw the toupee and asked Hank if he had any hair. "Hell, yes," he said, "I got a dresser drawer full of it." Hank left with some scripts for his consideration.

A few weeks later, the legit entertainment world beckoned again. On October 11, Hank appeared on *The Kate Smith Evening Hour.* Then CBS-TV offered Hank a spot on *The Perry Como Show* for Wednesday, November 14. Both carried with them an obligation to stay a week in New York, never Hank's favorite town. Even in his civvies, he felt out of place. He was always the first to feel condescension and to react to it with a mixture of truculence and boorishness ("If you don't like folk music," he once told an interviewer, "stay away from my shows. I can't stand classical music, but I don't tell the world about it"). No one found any condescension in Como, though. Like virtually everyone who worked the show, Hank responded warmly to Como's small-town charm. He and Perry smoked their Chesterfields, did a sketch, and then Hank sang "Hey, Good Lookin'." On the following show, Perry, billing himself as "Cactus Como," put on a cowboy hat, strapped on a guitar, and sang "Hey, Good Lookin'." Then he apologized to Hank.

While Hank was rehearsing for the Como show, he took time out to do an interview at *Billboard* in which he explained how careful he was to space his releases properly and to follow what he called a "jump tune" with a blues or ballad. The piece also mentioned that Hank was scheduled to do a spot on Ed Sullivan's *Toast of the Town,* although he never appeared. His rancor toward Milton Berle was still bubbling near the surface, though. He told the *Billboard* columnist that he had been offered a spot on Milton Berle's *Texaco Star Theater,* but had turned it down. "The last time I worked with him, there like to have been a killing," he said with a frankness that must have surprised the columnist, who, like most music columnists, had been weaned on show business platitudes.

On November 9, and perhaps in anticipation of a flood of orders from Como viewers who wouldn't ordinarily buy country music, MGM issued Hank's first album, unimaginatively called *Hank Williams Sings.* It was released in three formats: a ten-inch LP, or four 78s or four 45s packaged in an album. It was axiomatic then that country LPs didn't sell, and the notion of the single as a trailer for the hugely more profitable album was still more than ten years away. In fact, Rose seems to have used Hank's first album largely as a dump site for oddball songs that hadn't sold elsewhere. With the exception of "Wedding Bells," the tracks were the dogs of Hank's catalog, like "I've Just Told Mama Good-bye," "Wealth Won't Save Your Soul," and "Six More Miles." Rose's thinking in recycling the oldies and not-so-goodies was paraphrased by *Billboard:* "The release of an album [of eight new sides], they feel, would spread jockey and juke plays too thinly instead of getting the concentrated push on the single record."

For Hank, the contrast between the glitz and tawdry glamour of network television in New York and the mundane grind of personal appearances in the South was made all the more apparent by the fact that a week before the Como show he was appearing at the Wagon Wheel Club between Opelika and Auburn, Alabama. Hank almost certainly felt more at home at the Wagon Wheel than in New York or Hollywood, but if he found any incongruity playing the Wagon Wheel one week and Como's show the next, he didn't talk about it. But Hank didn't talk about anything substantive very much, anyway.

A month after the Como show, and just a few days before a scheduled operation on his back, Hank returned to the Castle studio to cut the last of the five hugely prolific recording sessions he held in 1951. It would also be the last session to feature all of the Drifting Cowboys. Nothing new was on the menu. The oldest song was "Let's Turn Back the Years," a plea for reconciliation that had first appeared in one of Hank's WSFA songbooks in 1946. Its words now held deeper meaning for him than they ever had. Several verses were omitted from the 1946 draft, including this one, which didn't ring true from either side of the fence any more:

> *You have been so faithful, darling*
> *Waiting for me all these years,*
> *And if you'll forget the vows I've broken,*
> *I'll try to pay you for all your tears.*

Finally, Hank got a releasable cut of "Honky Tonk Blues," a song that dated back almost as far as "Let's Turn Back the Years." He had first tried it in August 1947 at the session that had produced "On the Banks of the Old Pontchartrain." He'd taken another stab at it in March 1949, and yet another in June 1950. One reason that Rose held it back was that the title could have been confused with "Honky Tonkin'," but the flurry of activity around "Honky Tonkin' " in 1948 and again in 1950 had died away, and Rose now felt confident scheduling "Honky Tonk Blues" as Hank's first release for 1952. The version that hit the streets didn't contain all the lyrics on his original demo; the next-to-last verse, in which Maw and Paw are "really gonna lay down the law," was missing, emphasizing in a way that Hank himself never made it back from the honky-tonks to pappy's farm.

On release in February 1952, "Honky Tonk Blues" was coupled with another song from the December session, a second stab at "I'm Sorry for You, My Friend," the song Lefty Frizzell said Hank had written for him.

As 1951 was drawing to a close, Hank Williams needed repair. Two and a half years of almost constant travel, sleep deprivation, and unrelenting pressure had taken their toll on his body and mind. The drinking bouts were becoming more and more frequent. His back ached constantly, and now his career seemed to be controlling him rather than vice versa. If he felt guilty about his binges — as he almost certainly did because he had always been led to see them as a sign of weakness — he covered it up by simply refusing to acknowledge that there was a problem. When he was drunk or getting drunk, he was in no condition to discuss his alcoholism, and when he was sober, he pulled rank on his band and cut short any discussion. "I'd say to him, 'That's when you really showed your butt,' " said Don Helms, "and he'd say, 'I don't wanna talk 'bout it.' "

At some undetermined point in 1951 Hank was sent, or committed himself, to a sanatorium in Louisville, Kentucky, which was supposed to specialize in treatment for alcoholics. There he was told essentially what he wanted to hear: he wasn't an alcoholic because he went days, weeks, sometimes months without drinking. An alcoholic couldn't do that. Therefore, Hank was a spree drinker.

Hank almost certainly knew in his heart that he wasn't a spree drinker, and he knew how much strength it took on a daily basis to wrestle down his craving for alcohol. "He got so bitter about alcohol," said Ernest Tubb, one of the few to whom Hank opened up about his problem, which was one that Tubb shared:

He hated drinking, and he wanted to take this cure. You'd take this medicine, and you had to carry a letter in your pocket. If you're taking this medicine [and] you take a drink, if you don't get to a hospital quick enough it'll kill you. He asked me if he should do it, take this cure. I told him, "This you have to decide, 'cause if I advise you to do it and you get off some place late at night and you fall off the wagon, and start drinking, you could wind up dead and I'd feel responsible." He knew he was an alcoholic. Then it dawned on him.

Unlike Lefty Frizzell, characterized by his drinking buddies as a happy drunk, Hank was a miserable drunk. He became surly and contrary. "He was a pain, a real pain," said Don Helms. "If you wanted to leave, he wanted to wait; if you wanted to wait, he wanted to leave." Hank's problem was aggravated by a low tolerance for alcohol. Helms and Rivers agree that Hank probably drank less than just about anyone else on the *Opry*, but he drank in binges, and his low tolerance quickly put him out of commission. A few drinks and he was foaming-at-the-mouth, under-the-table drunk. When he was drunk, his natural bluntness turned into boorishness. According to Jerry Rivers, his band members knew all the little telltale signs, like the strange wave from the wings when they were warming up the crowd:

We'd all just wilt 'cause we knew then he was drinking. One time in St. Joseph, Missouri, we were onstage picking and he came to the wings and we knew right away he was drinking. He came on, swung into "Move It on Over," did the verse with "Remember pup before you whine," and then Don did a solo, then he sung the same verse and I took a solo. Then he did "I'm A Long Gone Daddy," which is basically the same tune, and he came out of the break singing "Remember pup before you whine." We'd rather he didn't show. It was just such a letdown to us.

Most of those who knew Hank have a pet theory about his drinking. He drank because of the pain in his back, because of Audrey, because of the pressures of his career, to gain attention . . . and so on. Wesley Rose had a complex theory that centered around blood-sugar levels, which was probably state-of-the-art thinking about alcoholism that month. Hank drank. It was a behavior he had acquired in his youth — before Audrey, before his back gave him much trouble, before his career took him over. It was a behavior to which he turned at sometimes predictable, sometimes unpredictable, junctures. It was a behavior that acquired its own momentum as his personal and professional problems mounted. More than anything else, it was a release from whatever ailed him at the time. "I'm gonna keep drinkin' 'til I can't even think," he had written with brutal honesty in "There's a Tear in My Beer."

Hank and Fred Rose would have inevitably discussed the problem, and it was one that Rose would have approached from the standpoint of a recovered alcoholic, but — if he tried — Rose was unsuccessful in getting Hank to tackle his alcoholism with a renewed spiritual awakening like his own. Joining an organization like Alcoholics Anonymous was also out of the question for Hank, partly because of his intensely private nature, but mostly because it would have been an acknowledgment that he had a problem. This left palliative professional help when he was on a binge, which was essentially limited to deprivation, a good meal when he stood a chance of keeping it down, a few vitamins, and a bill.

With most tours lasting just a few days between *Opry* commitments, Hank was usually brought home if he was drinking, and Audrey would, with good reason, refuse to let him into the house. Then Jim Denny would ask the band to take him to the Madison Sanatorium just north of Nashville. The sanatorium had some out-buildings with bars on the windows that it used for drying out alcoholics. To Hank, these were "the huts." Typically, the band would pull up in front of the sanatorium and Hank wouldn't have a clear idea of where he was. Someone would say, "Come on, Hank, let's get out," and he would see where they were and say, "Oh, no, oh, no, I ain't goin' in there. It's that damn hut." Then the attendants would have to come and get him, and he would stare daggers at the band as if he had been betrayed.

"Seems to me," said Helms, "that everyone would disappear round about that time," but Helms, who lived close by and had known Hank the longest, would come to visit after a couple of days, bringing candy bars and books. Usually, by the third day Hank would say, "Reckon they're gonna let us outta here?" Helms would think to himself, "Hoss, *we* ain't in here," but he would nod.

On another occasion in late 1951, Hank was committed to St. Margaret's hospital in Montgomery. His cousin Walter McNeil went to see him there and found a desperately unhappy man. As was often the case when he was coming off a drunk, Hank was paranoid and surly, and, some thought, occasionally suicidal. "O'Neil," he said, "I wish I was back at WSFA making twelve dollars a week. At least then if someone come to see me, I'd know they was coming to see *me*. Now I reckon they just want something from me."

Wondering what Audrey was doing while he was out on the road contributed to Hank's broodiness and generally upset mood. He saw the band members happy to get off the road and get home to their wives and families. He would go home and perhaps not find Audrey there at all. If she was there, they now stood as good a chance of having a fight as not. As early as 1950, coming in off the road, he had told the guys that he knew they were all looking forward to going back home. Meantime, he said, he was going to Acuff-Rose to pick up a check for two thousand dollars, go home, give Audrey half of it, then spend the rest of the night fighting with her over the other half. Now he couldn't even joke about it. It just wasn't funny any more.

Still, Hank was fixated on Audrey. He loved her, and he loved Randall Hank even more. A WSM engineer remembered that Hank had once left Nashville in a hurry and got halfway to Jackson before he realized that he hadn't said good-bye to Hank Jr., so he drove all the way back. Ernest Tubb remembers another time, when he and Hank and Minnie Pearl were playing the Tri-State Fair in Amarillo, Texas. "Hank had bought every stuffed bear and dog, and he had that Cadillac so loaded the boys said, 'Where we gonna sit?' I said, 'Hank, that kid ain't big enough to play with them,' 'cause Hank had a stuffed dog as big as a man, but he worshiped that boy. Never knew a man worshiped a child like that. He just couldn't buy enough things for Bocephus." In Hank's ideal world, little Hank was the centerpiece of the loving family that prayed together and stayed together. In that same dream, Audrey was baking a pie as he walked in the door.

The Hank Williams paradox was that he was easygoing on the outside, yet tense and querulous inside, and given to bouts of depression. He pretended to be as dumb as an old mule, yet he had a lively intelligence combined with what Minnie Pearl described as a "woods-animal distrust" of anyone who appeared to have more learning than he did. He wanted to be the drifting cowboy, herding the dark clouds out of the sky and keeping the heavens blue, yet he was naturally broody and introverted — and not much of a horseman. He still saw his own dalliances on the road as one of the perks of the job, yet was infuriated and aggrieved by Audrey's infidelities, perhaps because they were often conducted in full view of his peers.

Through his music even his fans probably sensed something of the chasm between Hank's onstage demeanor and his private disquiet, and that in turn accounted for part of his appeal. It didn't take much skill in reading between the lines to sense that when the spotlight was switched off, or the red recording light went off, and the people went home, that Hank was left with Hiram Williams, who was wretched company for him. "When he walked on the stage," said Audrey later, "it was the only time Hank was ever really sure of himself. It was shyness and lonesomeness."

Hank tried to get one aspect of his life under control when he finally surrendered his back to a team of surgeons led by Dr. Ben Fowler and Dr. George Carpenter at the Vanderbilt Medical Center. This was a major step for Hank, who had the country person's almost pathological fear of big-city doctors, so he put it off as long as he could. As early as March 31, 1951, *Billboard* had reported that he had a spine disorder and was expected to take six weeks off for surgery. At the time he signed the motion-picture deal, he was talking about working fewer shows to concentrate on songwriting (Bing Crosby was mentioned as a client waiting in the wings), but economic pressures and pure fear kept him on the road.

It took a hunting accident to finally force Hank into the hospital. Jerry Rivers had gone hunting with him, and Hank's dog had treed a large groundhog in a stump. The groundhog put up a fight, and Hank and Jerry began running to save the dog. Rivers jumped a gully, carrying a heavy double-barreled shotgun, and beat off the groundhog. Then he looked around for Hank.

Hank was on his back in the gully. His face was pale and he was wracked with pain. He had lost his balance jumping the ditch and had fallen four or five feet onto his back. His first step was to check in to St. Jude's in Montgomery, where he felt more at home, but the doctors there referred him to the Vanderbilt Medical Center. As he told the story later, Hank went to the doctors and said, "Cure me or kill me, doc. I can't go on like this."

Before the surgery, Hank had agreed to work Connie B. Gay's New Year's Eve bash. Gay had booked theaters in Washington, Baltimore, Toledo, Raleigh, Spartanburg, and Charleston, West Virginia. In conjunction with Jim Denny, he had arranged to bring in virtually every artist working on the *Opry* to fill those venues. Denny and Gay had worked together since 1947, and Gay held what amounted to the *Opry* franchise for the D.C. area. This was to be their biggest joint venture. It's likely too that Denny had a personal as well as professional stake in the financial outcome of the shows. Hank was to be the headliner, and the plan was to "bicycle" him (that is, have him play two locations) in Baltimore and Washington. Booking Hank was a calculated risk for Denny, who was in as close touch with Hank's condition as anyone. It was a risk that he was apparently willing to take, though, knowing that Hank had a history of showing up stone cold sober when he absolutely had to. Denny may also have planned to ensure his sobriety by assigning a minder.

Hank didn't make the shows, but not because he was drinking. The operation was less than a total success, and Hank aggravated his condition by insisting upon being moved home on Christmas Eve. Audrey got upset at him for ignoring the doctors' instructions and Hank threw a chair at her, which worsened his condition and necessitated another trip back to Vanderbilt. The house was thick with tension over Christmas, deeply at odds with the cheery family Christmas card Hank and Audrey had sent out. Guns were waved, vilenesses and insults traded.

Audrey's sister Lynette came up from Banks to spend the week between Christmas and New Year's, and she later said that Hank couldn't understand why he was in so much pain after the operation. Audrey would occasionally disappear in the evening, topping up Hank's jealousy, but he could do nothing but rail against it because he was in such pain it was all he could do to move from the bedroom to the bathroom.

Hank's mood became fouler when he realized that not only could he not make the shows in Washington and Baltimore, but he would have to prerecord apologies to the audiences. In effect, he was being asked to prove he wasn't drunk. Here in part is what he said:

> On December the thirteenth, I had to have an operation that I'd been putting off for about a year. I had to have it because it finally got to where I couldn't even walk on one leg hardly. . . . But when he started the operation, when the doctor got into my back he found a lot wrong that he hadn't anticipated before, so naturally he had to go ahead and fix it all. I had what you call a spine fusion. I had two ruptured disks in my back. The first and second vertebrae was no good, it was just deformed or broken when I was a child, or wore out or something. He said he thought I'd rode a few too many hundred thousand miles in these automobiles. So he went ahead and fixed it; so after I came to, after the anesthetic wore off he told me it'd be impossible for me to be out of here before the first of February.
>
> So then me and Mister Denny at the station here, we tried to talk him into letting me take an airplane with a stretcher in it, and fly up to Washington and take an ambulance from there to Baltimore, but he wouldn't go along with it, so he just finally said no.

Denny arranged for Jimmie Davis to take Hank's place, and for Audrey to sing with The Drifting Cowboys and play Hank's message for the fans. It wasn't an easy trip for her. On Saturday, December 29, Audrey alleged that Hank physically attacked her. She moved herself and the kids to the Garretts, a family that had sold Hank a pony for Lycrecia. Then on Sunday afternoon, Audrey said, she came back home to pack for the shows.

There were three elderly women who came back home with me so I could get some clothes and fly to Washington. I just wanted to slip in and out. We were just easin' around, and I knew he was there and very edgy, and as we were leaving the gun shot four times. I could hardly walk. I was scared to death. Thinking back, I don't know if he was shooting at me, or wanting me to think that he was shooting at himself. Anyway, I went on to Washington, and New Year's Eve night I called him and said, "Hank, I'll never live with you another day."

Johnnie and Jack and Kitty Wells were in town over Christmas. They came to see Hank to ask his help in getting them back on the *Opry,* and they arrived to find the screen door riddled with bullet holes and one of Hank's guitars smashed to pieces out on the patio. According to Johnnie Wright, Hank had just found out about Audrey's latest affair. He told Johnnie, "That busted my heart." The troubles, according to Wright, had started when Audrey had said she was going out to buy Hank Jr. a Christmas present and had come back with nothing. Hank suspected that she had been fooling around and exploded.

During the divorce proceedings, Audrey reiterated the story that Hank had shot at her, but Hank vigorously denied it. Wright's confirmation notwithstanding, the shotgun blasts were in keeping with Hank's frame of mind at the time. They were also in keeping with his wayward use of firearms when he was drunk, angry, or in acute pain. And that night he was drunk and angry and in acute pain. The year-end issue of *Billboard* showed that "Cold, Cold Heart" was the top country song of the year and was number thirteen in the year-end tally of the pop charts, but that was no comfort at all.

I've been a bad boy again.
John Prine, "Bad Boy"

Chapter

13

· ·

BOBBIE

· ·

*P*RESUMABLY it was at Audrey's request that Hank moved out of the family home on January 3, 1952. His first stop was the Andrew Jackson Hotel. Don Helms visited him there. He told Don that he didn't think he'd be going back this time — and how right he was. His next stop was Lillie's boardinghouse. While he was there, Hank sent word to Lon asking him to come pick him up. Lon drove into Montgomery from McWilliams, but just as he was parking he saw Hank being carried out of the boardinghouse on a stretcher, bound for St. Jude's Hospital. Lon followed the ambulance, and when he got to the hospital he was told that Hank was unconscious. One of the doctors took Lon aside and told him that Hank had overdosed and would have to stay in the hospital until what he called "the dope" had been flushed from his system. Lillie said she couldn't understand it; Hank had only had two beers and two aspirins all day.

The dope was probably a heavy-duty prescription painkiller that Hank had taken in nonprescription doses. If so, it was consistent with a pattern that he had established late the previous year as his back pain worsened. He would go to see several doctors, obtain multiple prescriptions, then take more than the prescribed dose. "It says, 'Take one every four hours,' " he would say. "Maybe I ought to take four every hour; that's four times as good, ain't it?" In point of fact, it would have been sixteen times as good if Hank's logic had held water, but instead, his self-medication had the effect of lowering his tolerance to heavy-duty painkillers so that he needed more and more to quiet his back, or his mind, all the while increasing the chance of an overdose.

When Hank got back to Nashville, he took a room in a house on the corner of Natchez Trace and Westwood Drive, about a mile from the Vanderbilt Medical Center. The house had been rented by Ray Price, newly arrived in town and hopeful of making his way in the country music business. Hank had been instrumental in bringing Price up from Dallas. He had introduced him on the Prince Albert portion of the *Grand Ole Opry*, given him a couple of his best minor-league songs, and now Price was pleased to return the favor.

Hank probably wasn't even back in Nashville when he received word that Audrey had initiated divorce proceedings. Her Bill of Complaint was filed on January 10, 1952, and its schedule of grudges went back to their days in Montgomery. She alleged that Hank's conduct toward her there had embarrassed and humiliated her to the extent that she insisted that they relocate, which constituted her explanation of how they came to move to Shreveport. They weren't completely happy in Shreveport, she said, because of what she termed Hank's "continued misconduct," but she conceded that they did enjoy "some degree of happiness" there. It wasn't until the spring of 1951, though, that Hank's conduct became what Audrey called "intolerable." "While he had been inconsiderate, and even cruel at times," she alleged, "he then became most abusive, cursing [me] without provocation, and striking [me] on numerous occasions."

Then Audrey gave her version of the events surrounding New Year's, concluded that "cohabitation was unsafe and improper," and she demanded that Hank disclose all of his income, then provide maintenance for her as well as child support for Hank Jr.

Gradually statements were forthcoming from Acuff-Rose and MGM concerning Hank's income, which provide the hardest data we have on his earnings. Even after payments to Hank on December 16, 1951, of over sixteen thousand dollars, Acuff-Rose still had more than twenty-two thousand dollars sitting in his account, due in August 1952. Ten thousand dollars of the advances Hank had been paid in December represented the amount held on "Cold, Cold Heart," which was frozen pending a judgment in the lawsuit from Dixie Music. Acuff-Rose had paid it on the understanding that they could reclaim it if judgment went against them. From that point, the "Cold, Cold Heart" funds remained frozen until 1955; by then another thirty-two thousand dollars (equaling two million records) had accumulated in escrow. The result of the suit wasn't made public, but the case was closed when Dixie Music was awarded its court costs of five thousand dollars on January 13, 1955.

For its part, MGM stated that between September 1, 1951, and December 31, 1951, Hank had earned $10,754 in domestic royalties and roughly $1,900 in overseas royalties, and that additional royalties covering the period from year-end to February 28, 1952, had yet to be calculated and would be paid on April 15. The MGM deposition also confirmed Hank's contractual obligation to make movies, something the company denied after his death.

Predictably, WSM stated that Hank was in the hole to the station to the tune of five hundred dollars, largely because of unpaid commissions on shows that had used the *Opry* name.

Hank told one of the New York reporters that he was playing to around fifteen thousand people a night in 1951, which seems more like a maximum attendance than an average attendance, but, even after expenses, there's no doubt that he was stuffing several thousand dollars into his valise every night. With money for radio appearances factored in, together with pocket money from selling songbooks and photos, Hank had clearly exceeded his declared 1950 income of $92,000, and he had almost certainly grossed well over $100,000 in 1951, perhaps as much as the $150,000 he told the *Wall Street Journal* he would earn that year.

After the depositions came Hank's cross-complaint against Audrey. He tried to hold himself up as a model of financial probity while contending that Audrey had indulged in "every extravagance she could possibly stretch his income to cover." He complained of her "insatiable hunger for clothes, jewelry, automobiles, and luxuries far beyond their economic status in life." His cross-complaint was, in essence, a Hank Williams song rendered in a voice that was an incongruous blend of his own and his lawyer's.

Hank's first shot across Audrey's bow was a predictable one:

> The first years of . . . married life were troublesome, because of the inattention of [Audrey] to her home and husband. . . . [She] refused to appreciate the obligations of married life, denying her attentions and affections to her home and husband, insisting that she too was an entertainer and singer of ability, continuously insisting that the defendant include her on his programs . . . despite the fact that she had neither voice nor musical ability.

Hank went on to say that he had lost many jobs during his early years in the business because Audrey had insisted upon being included in the act. She had, he said, been evicted from studios and other places of entertainment because of her fits of rage when her ambitions were thwarted.

Next Hank accused Audrey of "extravagant living and carousing . . . such as to keep [my] nose to the grindstone continuously to keep the bills paid." She had, he said, "no interest or disposition to [stay] at home . . . but has always insisted upon traveling about, acting independent and free of all marital restraint, seeking and having everything she wanted, and a good time all the time." Audrey hadn't spent one full day with Hank Jr. since his birth, contended Hank, unless she couldn't get someone to stay with him. "As a matter of fact," he added, "their only child refers to its nurse as 'Mama.' "

In return for all Hank's efforts to provide for Audrey, he said, she continuously referred to him as a "son of a bitch . . . and many other names too vile and vulgar to [mention here]." Then came the parting shots. First, Hank claimed to have evidence of Audrey's adultery with a highway patrolman while he was off on the Hadacol Caravan, and then he claimed she had had an affair with a car salesman. Next, Hank went into detail about Audrey's detestation of Lillie. She had "condemned and castigated him for showing any love or affection for her," he said, adding that Audrey had ordered Lillie out of Vanderbilt on the day after the operation. Finally, Hank confirmed that Audrey had become pregnant around September 1950 but had had an abortion performed at home that had led to an infection that in turn required treatment at St. Thomas's Hospital. In the cross-complaint Hank spoke of his humiliation and grief when he heard what Audrey had done.

Hank's cross-complaint was a document that was, by turns, sad and bitter. It was also a rather inept piece of legal maneuvering designed to place him in the least damaging position when judgment was rendered. Unrealistically, his cross-complaint concluded with a request for custody of Hank Jr.

Both sides of the action speak of a dead weight of hurt and recrimination that now occluded any love they had once shared, certainly any love Audrey had once had for Hank. The divorce proceedings now acquired a momentum that Audrey in particular would have found difficult to stop even if she had been inclined to do so this time. In accordance with the tradition of jurisprudence, both parties tried to off-load the full burden of blame onto the other, but in his heart Hank knew that he had failed and, according to those close to him, still hoped from time to time for a reconciliation.

When he signed his cross-complaint on March 5, Hank claimed not to have worked since the operation, which was almost true. He had taken The Drifting Cowboys off salary, and disbanded with the understanding that he would call them for dates in the hope that they were available. Sammy Pruett was the first to take full-time employment elsewhere when he joined Carl Smith's Tunesmiths. Almost since joining Hank, Pruett had felt stymied keeping the tic-toc rhythm going song after song with so few opportunities for soloing. Helms, Rivers, and Howard Watts tried to keep themselves available for Hank, but Pruett didn't work a day with him after his operation. The other Drifting Cowboys worked with Ray Price more than anyone else. They wanted to be on call for Hank but knew that it limited their chances of employment elsewhere because no one wanted to hire band members who were likely to disappear as soon as Hank Williams decided he was ready to put the Cowboys back together.

Hank's first engagement after his hospitalization was a disaster. He was booked into Richmond on January 29 and 30, 1952, and Charleston, South Carolina, the following day. Only Don Helms and Howard Watts were available, and local pickers were recruited to round out the band. Ray Price and Johnnie and Jack were also on the show. The troupe was booked into a hotel, and Hank had a minder assigned to him. With the low cunning that he summoned up when he was desperate, Hank called room service for tomato juice. When that was delivered, he told the waiter that his legs were hurting and he needed some rubbing alcohol. Room service brought it up. Hank mixed the rubbing alcohol with the tomato juice, drank it, then began puking violently. Just before show time he was allowed a beer to settle his stomach, but he was still in no shape to perform.

In a review for the *Richmond Times-Dispatch* the following day, Edith Lindeman's headline ran: "Hank Williams Hillbilly Show Is Different: Star Makes Impression of Unexpected Kind."* She went on to describe how Ray Price opened the show, then brought on a clearly inebriated Hank Williams. Hank had problems remembering his first song

---

* Lindeman was more than a local entertainment reporter. In addition to her stint at the *Richmond Times-Dispatch* (1933–1964), she wrote children's books, and, as Edith Lindeman Calisch, wrote with Carl Stutz "Little Things Mean a Lot" as well as "Red Headed Stranger," which Willie Nelson later recorded.

and staying in key, and after one song he quit. The emcee got up onstage and said that Hank was unable to make the show, but Ray Price would sing Hank's songs and anyone who wanted a refund would get one. Those who opted for a refund found no redress at the box office, though. The promoter was reported to be "ill at home," where the proceeds had been brought to him.

During the intermission, Hank's minder walked him around out in the frigid night air, forcing a sandwich and some coffee into him. Then Hank went back out to face the crowd. "I wish I was in as good a shape as you are," he said. "Hank Williams is a lot of things, but he ain't a liar. If they's a doctor in the house I'll show him I've been in the hospital for eight weeks . . . and if you ain't nice to me, I'll turn around and walk right off." Ray Price, acting the part of the cheerleader, said, "We all love you, Hank, don't we folks?" and tried to rally Hank with some applause. Hank muddled his way through a few of his greatest hits then headed for his limo. No autographs. No shake 'n' howdy. It was a typical Hank Williams off-night; the difference was that there was a newspaper reporter on hand to capture it.

The following night, Hank was hungover and vengeful. He dedicated a song to a "gracious lady writer" and swung right into "Mind Your Own Business." It was a quintessential Hank Williams moment: obloquy followed by swift redemption in song. If only all the large and small humiliations he had suffered could have been reversed so deftly.

By now word was spreading that getting to see Hank Williams was a hit-or-miss affair. Johnnie Wright reckons that Hank's average had slipped from its best — around .850 — to .500. Sober, no one had more respect for his fans than Hank, but when he was in his cups, still believing himself able to perform, he was obtuse and would respond rudely to hecklers. "Someone git a shovel and cover that up," he would say, or "Hey, pal, we got a surprise for you. After the show, we gonna git yore momma and yore poppa in here, and git 'em married." Mostly, though, if Hank was drinking, he was too drunk to stand much less play. Yet he attracted his own apologists, as George Jones later would. If someone said Hank was drunk, someone else would say, "Hell, he had a right to be."

On April 3, Hank and Audrey's lawyers arrived at a tentative property settlement and arrangements for the custody of Hank Jr. In the preamble to the settlement, buried among the "whereas's" and "hereto's," was a sentence noting that the parties couldn't agree upon a divorce, implying that Hank was still opposed to it and that Audrey would have to go to court to obtain it. Ray Price remembers that in one set of discussions with his lawyer, Hank more or less agreed to Audrey's terms, terms that his lawyer considered punitive. This, according to Price, was because Hank wanted to show his continued love for Audrey and his regret over what had happened, and he thought that acceding to her demands would achieve that.

Predictably, the care of Hank Jr. was entrusted to Audrey, with the provision that Hank could have Hank Jr. reside with him for three months during the summer of 1953. Audrey got the house on Franklin Road, including all the fixtures, as well as her 1951 Cadillac convertible, a thousand dollars in cash, and an agreement from Hank that he would pay her attorney's fees. More important, she got one-half of all Hank's future royalties with a binding obligation upon MGM and Acuff-Rose to remit them directly to her. If Audrey ever remarried, though, her claim upon the royalties would end and Hank's only obligation would be a maintenance payment of $300 a month for Hank Jr.'s upkeep, a payment to be made until Hank Jr. was twenty-one. Hank got Hank and Audrey's Corral, a marginal business at the best of times, and the farm in Williamson County with its derelict house and its forty-five-thousand-dollar mortgage.

In retrospect, it was a "She Got the Goldmine — He Got the Shaft" agreement, but at the time there was no means of knowing how rosy the future of Hank's royalties would be. Indeed, Audrey herself was so skeptical that she built in a provision for Hank to remit extra funds to her if her earnings from half of his royalties dropped below certain thresholds. Audrey would never remarry, not, as she was fond of saying, because no love could ever match what she and Hank had shared, but because her half of the oil well would gush in someone else's backyard. She didn't retire to a life of quiet contemplation, but she never did remarry, and all suitors knew that ground rule.

Whether Hank was still besotted with Audrey or not, his feelings didn't inhibit him from taking a new girlfriend. Bobbie Jett had lived a life every bit as troubled as Hank's when they came together in the early spring of 1952. Her family was from Nashville, but her mother had lit out for California shortly after Bobbie was born, leaving Bobbie in the care of her grandmother. Born on October 5, 1922, Bobbie was slightly less than a year older than Hank. After the war she too had gone to California, where, she later claimed, she had married a movie actor. Married or not, she returned to Nashville with a child in 1949, and she was working as a secretary when Hank met her. Hank was not alone in fancying Bobbie;

Decca Records' Paul Cohen was also beguiled by her, as were several others.

Quite when Hank and Bobbie met is uncertain. In her autobiography, Bobbie Jett's daughter (who had by then renamed herself Jett Williams), states that Bobbie went to see Hank in Montgomery in January or February 1952, suggesting that they had met before Hank and Audrey separated.

By the time the blossoms started to appear along Natchez Trace, Hank was venturing farther and farther afield. In March and again in early April he was in New York for television appearances. In mid-April he was in California. On April 16, he was feted by MGM Records distributors in Los Angeles, and then he went to renew negotiations with MGM Pictures. Wesley Rose went out to California to act on Hank's behalf, and, according to the account he gave to Roger Williams, things got off to a bad start when Hank wouldn't take off his hat as he entered Dore Schary's office. Schary was one of MGM Pictures' production chiefs, and he had what Rose later called a pompous and condescending manner. Hank had had a few belts, and he put his boots up on Schary's desk, pulled his hat down over his eyes, and answered all questions in monosyllables and grunts.

Wesley's accountant's soul couldn't comprehend this. When they got outside, he asked Hank for an explanation of his conduct. "You see this kid here," said Hank, gesturing to a black shoe-shine boy. "This kid is more of a man than that guy in the office will ever be." Hank, whose inferiority complex often manifested itself in truculence, developed lightning antipathy toward anyone who was even ever so slightly condescending toward him. It's possible that a chance remark from Schary brought all his simmering resentment of the business end of the entertainment business to a boil, but it's just as likely that Hank had already determined that he wasn't going to make movies for MGM or anyone, so he might as well put on an act for his own amusement.

Hank had been given the script to a Jane Powell and Farley Granger movie called *Small Town Girl*, which was to start shooting in late May or early June, but the bulk and complexity of the script had probably intimidated him to the point where he felt hopelessly out of his depth. He masked his lack of confidence with boorishness, because the ol' drifting cowboy couldn't appear to be intimidated. Hank wasn't the borderline illiterate that he has been made out to be — and sometimes made himself out to be — but bypassing minor roles and going straight to headliner was like going from high school ball to the major leagues. Few were suited to such a transition; Hank wasn't one of them.

A day or two later, Hank appeared in San Diego with Ernest Tubb and Minnie Pearl. On an MGM Records documentary Minnie told the following story, one she told with slight variations for years, usually referring to Hank as "ill" or "sick" rather than drunk.

> The boys were worried that Hank was ill and unable to perform. They kinda insisted that he perform, and it made me unhappy. Then I walked backstage, and they were bringing him up the steps, and the look he had on his face was of such implication that I never will forget it. He said, "Minnie, I can't work. I can't work, Minnie. Tell 'em." I had no authority. They went ahead, and he worked and it was bad. A. V. Bamford told me to stay with him between shows. He said, "He may listen to you. You may be able to keep him from getting any worse than he is." Maxine Bamford and Hank and me and someone else drove around with him. This was between shows, and we were trying to keep him from getting anything else that would make him get in worse shape than he was. We started singing. He was all hunkered down, looking out of the side of the car singing. He was singing, "I Saw the Light," then he stopped and he turned around, and his face broke up and he said, "Minnie, I don't see no light. There ain't no light."

Later on the same California junket, Hank was interviewed by jazz journalist Ralph J. Gleason, who was writing for the *San Francisco Chronicle*. He caught up with Hank at the Leamington Hotel in Oakland. Gleason was surprised by the number of pills Hank had about his person, and by the fact that the pills constituted most of his breakfast of champions. Hank talked about his background and about "folk" music in much the same terms as he had in Charleston the year before. He professed to like the petulant and melodramatic style of Johnnie Ray, and he told Gleason that he could never sing songs like "Mairzy Doats" or "Rag Mop" because he couldn't relate to the lyrics. Harping on one of his favorite themes, he said, "A song ain't nuthin' in the world but a story with music to it. . . . I've been offered some of the biggest songs to sing and turned 'em down. There ain't *nobody* can pick songs."

Gleason was sufficiently intrigued to catch Hank in person that night at Maple Hall, San Pablo. According to his account, the hall was a one-story white building. You parked in the mud, and inside the door there was a long room with a bandstand at one end and a bar in an annex at one side. Hank "had that *thing*," wrote Gleason. "He made them scream when he sang. . . . There were lots of those blondes you see at C&W affairs [with] the kind of hair that mother never had and nature never grew . . . guys looking barbershop neat but still with a touch of dust on them." Hank appeared a little stoned between sets, didn't remember Gleason from that morning, and was hanging out with a crowd of whiskey drinkers.

Here at least, in a northern California beer hall, Hank was on his home turf. He was playing to exiled southerners and Okies, most of whom had come out to work in the munitions factories during the war. He understood them, and they understood him when he sang about getting back to pappy's farm. His self-defeating conduct in the world outside the beer halls stemmed in great part from his perception that he was being marketed as a commodity, sent hither and thither to fly the flag for country music in general and the *Grand Ole Opry* in particular. His itinerary was dizzying. By April 26 he was back from California and off to Boston to headline the first *Opry* show at Symphony Hall. Then from April 29 until May 2 he was on another *Opry* package in southeastern Texas. He swung from there into Ontario for a short Canadian tour in early May, trying to expunge the memories of the 1951 tour. From there he was sent back to Texas, then off to Vegas.

A little snapshot of the risks involved in booking Hank was provided by Sergeant F. D. McMurry of the Beaumont, Texas, police department. The Beaumont Police Benefit Association was trying to raise funds, and they arranged for an *Opry* troupe led by Hank, Ernest Tubb, and Minnie Pearl to play there on April 29 as part of their swing along the gulf coast. They arrived in Henry Cannon's Beechcraft. Warning McMurry about Hank, Jim Denny had said, "If you take care of him, he's yours." Someone in the cast had advised McMurry to keep watch over Hank to ensure that he remained sober until after the show. McMurry took it upon himself to chaperon Hank, and, like Gleason, he was amazed at the number and variety of pills that he took. "He had pills in his hat band, his guitar, pills everyplace," said McMurry, to whom this was a new phenomenon.

The troupe arrived in the morning, and McMurry escorted them around to do some PR at the local stations, then took Hank out to his mother-in-law's house for a meal. "Ol' Hank sure did enjoy that," said McMurry. "He said he didn't get meals like that often. He stretched out on the couch, kicked his boots off. We took the pressure off of him." Hank made the show that night at the Municipal Auditorium, and everyone loved him. It was a good night. Hank was in fine form in Ontario a week later as well, showing off his operation scars and talking positively.

From May 16 for two weeks Hank was supposed to play Vegas. Roy Acuff, who had done *everything* first, had tried to introduce hillbilly music there without success. Hank was booked into the Ramona Room of the Last Frontier, where he played second fiddle to an old vaudevillian, Willie Shore, who sang and did comedy. Hank and a supporting *Opry* troupe were booked in connection with a western theme, Helldorado, that the Frontier and some other venues were running. No one had told the bookers that although Hank *dressed* like a western singing star and led a band called The Drifting Cowboys, he wasn't a western act, and wasn't likely to go over much better than Acuff.

Hank had managed to hire Don Helms and Jerry Rivers for the trip, and the three of them drove out together. "The closer we got to Vegas, the more nervous he became," said Helms. "We got there and checked in and the next day he was wiped out." Jim Denny told Don and Jerry to hire two minders to watch Hank in alternating twelve-hour shifts. He was sober by show time, but with more reason to drink than on any recent trip.

Hank felt ridiculed and out of place. For entertainers, Vegas had not yet become an elephants' graveyard where the elephants would come to sell their own tusks, but, then as ever, music was supposed to lull sensibilities and provide a backdrop for dining and gambling. There was and is an entire subset of performers, like Wayne Newton and Sammy Davis Jr., who were born to play Vegas. The unsettling emotionalism that was Hank Williams's preserve was precisely what Vegas did not want. His five-piece band sounded thin and his crowd wasn't there. When Hank peered through the curtain, it was at a sea of suits, ties, and dinner dresses. Those who had come especially to see him bought an overpriced fifty-cent Coke and nursed it until the end of the show, then left without staying to drink and gamble. Hank no more belonged there than Sammy Davis Jr. belonged at the Wagon Wheel in Opelika, Alabama.

On the morning of May 23, Hank was awakened with a phone call from the Last Frontier's booker. He was being canceled after one week, and comedian Ed Wynn was drafted in at short notice to take his place. "I could see a sigh of relief come over him," said Helms. On the way out of town, they checked out Rex Allen's show at the Thunderbird Lounge. Hank started drinking there, and he drank all the way back to Nashville. Don and Jerry drove in alternating shifts. Four years later, Vegas provided Elvis Presley with the first serious debacle of his career. It was a town without pity for anyone who didn't understand its very exacting requirements.

Hank now presented bookers with an acute dilemma. He was the biggest draw in country music, but the odds on his showing up sober were now no better than even. His chronic unpredictability was undermining his career to the point where he barely worked in July and August 1952. He didn't show up for work in Hollywood either, and MGM Pictures canceled his contract, later denying that he had even been signed.

There was only one reason that the Roses and everyone else connected with Hank's career hadn't given up on him and that he wasn't back at Lillie's playing the joints: he never struck out in the studio. "Baby, We're Really in Love" was in the charts for fifteen weeks starting in December 1951, and it was followed in March 1952 by "Honky Tonk Blues," which peaked at number two and stayed twelve weeks on the charts. "Honky Tonk Blues" was itself followed in May by "Half as Much," which also peaked at number two and stayed around for four months. "Cold, Cold Heart" was still on the charts as 1952 dawned, and "Hey, Good Lookin' " had yet to drop from heavy rotation. The streak continued as 1952 progressed.

On June 13 Hank went into the studio for a late morning session that produced four songs. It had been six months since his last session, and Hank apparently kept putting off recording, holding out for a cash payment. With Sammy Pruett gone, Fred Rose contracted Chet Atkins for the session. Howard Watts was also unavailable, so Charles "Indian" Wright of the Willis Brothers/Oklahoma Wranglers was drafted in to play bass. There were four songs on the menu; the first was "Window Shopping," written by Marcel Joseph. Murray Nash, who had joined Acuff-Rose in March 1951, remembers that Joseph was a New York journalist, and that "Window Shopping" was the only salable tune he ever wrote. Rose obviously coached Hank on his diction because "window" was pronounced faultlessly, not as "winn-der." Even so, it wasn't much of a song, and there wasn't much of it — just a verse and a chorus that were repeated after the break.

Next came "Jambalaya (On the Bayou)." Hank cowrote the song with Moon Mullican, one of the first singer-pianists in country music. Mullican had joined the *Opry* around June 1951, and he and Hank had worked some tours together; in fact, Hank cited Moon as one of his favorite musicians in an interview with *Country Song Roundup* that year. Mullican received 50 percent of the royalties on "Jambalaya" surreptitiously because he was under contract to King Records and its publishing division, Lois Music. He tried hard to get off King, even to the point of getting Jim

Denny to intercede with King on his behalf, but no one got out from under a King Records contract.

Most cajun songs are interbred, and the melody of "Jambalaya" came from Chuck Guillory's 1946 recording of "Gran' Texas." Mullican, who was from the part of east Texas that borders Louisiana, was familiar with cajun music. He had scored a hit in 1947 with an English version of another cajun classic "Jole Blon," and he is generally reckoned to have been responsible for what cajun content there was in "Jambalaya." Hank, though, had already shown a passing knowledge of cajun sayings in "Bayou Pon-Pon," so he may have contributed more to "Jambalaya" than has been thought. The cajun areas of Louisiana were among his favorite spots in his personal guidebook to the United States because the cajuns offered a view of life that Hank desperately wished for himself. "He loved the carefree life [down there]," said Jerry Rivers. "He longed for it because he was not ever a carefree person. He took everything seriously." He even seemed to take "Jambalaya" seriously; his performance is dour and completely lacking cajun esprit. On live shows, Hank would later deliver the song with the sparkle it required, but on record he sounds enervated.

"Jambalaya" proved to be the Hank Williams song that went on to cross all musical boundaries to the point where it is now no longer a country song. Fats Domino had a hit with it, John Fogerty had a hit with it, and every cajun and zydeco band is still obliged to play it whether they want to or not. Its success is probably due to the fact that it isn't really a cajun song. Ethnic music is usually unpalatable for a mass market unless it is diluted in some way, as Harry Belafonte proved with his calypso records a few years later and Paul Simon later proved with *Graceland*. The broader audience related to "Jambalaya" in a way that it could never relate to a true cajun two-step led by an asthmatic accordion and sung in patois.

The third item on the menu that morning was "Settin' the Woods on Fire," a song that, like "Hey, Good Lookin'," pointed unerringly toward rockabilly. It was the unlikely product of a collaboration between Fred Rose and a New Yorker, Ed G. Nelson Sr., the writer of "In a Shady Nook by a Babbling Brook" and "When a Yankee Doodle Learns to Parlez-Vous Francais." Nelson had written with Rose back in the mid-thirties and had been partly responsible for his conversion to Christian Science, but where the pair acquired the vocabulary of "Settin' the Woods on Fire" is anybody's guess.

Hank sounds curiously lifeless on "Settin' the Woods on Fire" as well, whether due to the early hour or general dissipation is unclear. His physical appearance certainly made an impression on Chet Atkins, who was playing the crack rhythm on the electric guitar that day. "We recorded 'I'll Never Get Out of This World Alive,' " he told Alanna Nash, "[and] after each take, he'd sit down in a chair. I remember thinking, 'Hoss, you're not just jivin',' because he was so weak that all he could do was just sing a few lines, and then just fall in the chair." Atkins may have been exaggerating a little. Hank probably sat down to ease his back, but he certainly doesn't appear to have been in peak form that day.

Much, perhaps too much, has been made of "I'll Never Get Out of This World Alive." It *wasn't* number one on the day he died, although it shot to number one in the wake of his death. Were it not for the coincidence that it was on the market when he died, it would have been seen for what it was, a novelty song tricked out from a W. C. Fields catchphrase. The addition of Fred Rose to the composer credit suggests that Rose had to contribute more than usual. In fact, this was the only Hank Williams session in which there were no songs that were solely his own work.

By now Frank Walker was sick of seeing Mitch Miller scoop Hank's songs and transform them into pop hits, so he gave "Window Shopping" to one of his hottest properties, band leader Art Mooney, who recorded it on July 21. Then Walker gave "Settin' the Woods on Fire" to Fran Warren, whose version was released the same day as Hank's, but he neglected "Jambalaya," which Mitch Miller eagerly picked up and recorded with Jo Stafford. Miller also covered "Settin' the Woods on Fire" with the duet of Jo Stafford and Frankie Laine. Once again, Miller got the hits; "Settin' the Woods on Fire" went to number twenty-one on the pop charts, and "Jambalaya" went all the way to number two. And if Hank's version of "Jambalaya" gave only a passing nod toward cajun music, Stafford's record didn't make the connection at all; it was sung incongruously to a mambo rhythm. They were *that* clueless.

The comfort and joy that Hank had once drawn from checking the charts diminished now that he came to see himself as a commodity to be sliced up and sold. Never an especially forthcoming person, he withdrew all the more now that Audrey was gone, but he still needed the constant distraction of people around him. On a night when he found himself home alone on Natchez Trace, he would phone all around the country trying to find Ray Price or someone else to talk to. Fame seems to carry with it an inability to be alone, or to be oneself without an audience, and the Hank Williams who encountered himself on Natchez Trace didn't like the company he found.

What infuriated those close to Hank was that he still appeared able to exercise considerable restraint over his drinking when he absolutely had to. The television appearances in late March and early April gave no indication that anything was awry in his life. On March 26 he was on *The Kate Smith Evening Hour* with Roy Acuff and a *Grand Ole Opry* troupe, and on April 9 he returned for another guest shot. *The Kate Smith Evening Hour* on NBC ran only from September 1951 to June 1952. It was placed head-to-head with *Arthur Godfrey and His Friends* — and lost.

For the March 26 show, Hank was backed by Billy Byrd, who had sold him the Packard back in Shreveport and was now playing for Ernest Tubb. Byrd brought along Tubb's bassist, Jack Drake, for the show. Grady Martin played fiddle and Don Helms was on steel guitar. The band drove to New York in Hank's seven-passenger Cadillac while Hank flew. They rehearsed every morning for several days, and the kinescope of the show would later provide the footage for the "Tear in My Beer" video.

Perhaps more than anything else, the television appearances show how Hank was being used as the *Opry*'s pawn on the board. The *Opry* management wanted to market the show nationwide via television and be first in the race to bring country music to network television. As a result, it was playing its aces, like Hank Williams, and calling in favors with NBC, which networked the *Opry* on radio. By the spring of 1952, there were fifteen country television shows in Los Angeles alone, and western-swing star Tex Williams was trying to find a network that would syndicate his *Roundup Time at the Riverside Rancho* show. The *Opry* didn't want to lose the initiative to Tex Williams or anyone else.

WSM, which owned the *Opry*, had done as NBC had urged. It had secured channel space and started picking up NBC's television shows. WSM-TV had started in September 1950, but, like almost every television station, it was losing money because few people had a television set, and, unlike WSM radio, WSM-TV's signal barely reached the Kentucky state line. WSM-TV had a hillbilly show, *Tennessee Jamboree*, but its viewership was pitifully small. The *Opry* needed a network show if it was to beat out the competition from California and elsewhere, and, with that in mind, Denny had not only arranged to showcase his acts on Kate Smith's show, but he also made an agreement to rotate the *Opry* cast through the rooftop ballroom of the Astor Hotel. With the prestige accruing from both, Denny thought, a network television offer was a foregone conclusion. The Roof was one of the top venues in New York, and the *Opry* was committed to providing a house band and a featured artist every week for sixteen weeks.

Country music, and the *Opry* in particular, was beginning its eternal quest for prime-time programming. The timing seemed right; the "folk boom" was on everybody's lips, Eddy Arnold was to be the summer replacement for Perry Como, Roy Acuff would be featured on the cover of *Newsweek* in August, and Hank Williams had songs dotted over two charts. Still, the plan failed. The Astor Roof engagement was canceled by mutual consent after four weeks, and Hank, who was the *Opry*'s ace and had been scheduled to close the series with a grand finale on September 13, didn't get to play.

As 1952 wore on, Hank was increasingly past caring what the *Opry*'s plans were and whether or not he figured in them. Most of those who worked with him in 1952 talk of his rapid disintegration, but the truth is a little more complex. He had been drinking and screwing up since the late '30s. His back had been troubling him for almost as long. His marriage and his other personal relationships had never been stable. The year 1952 saw the same patterns that had always been there; now they were magnified. The ever-present problems were exacerbated by his physical condition and the divorce, but perhaps even more by the fact that his career was entering uncharted territory, which spooked him.

Three years earlier, Hank had been playing schoolhouses in Louisiana and eastern Texas. Now he was expected to headline in Boston, New York, and Vegas, act in motion pictures, perform on network television, write songs that Bing Crosby could sing . . . and so on. Nothing had prepared him to handle this, and, unlike Elvis Presley, who left the hillbilly market for uncharted territory a few years later, Hank had no one like Presley's Colonel Parker to at least give the semblance of knowing what to do. His reaction was to withdraw. "You could see Hank's concern for his career decline," says Don Helms. "He'd often say, 'Aw to hell with it.' It reached a point where he didn't really care." A year or two earlier, he had been almost desperately eager to keep his hitting streak alive; as soon as one record was out and in the charts, he was itching to repeat, or do even better than he had done before. Now those around him sensed that he didn't care as much and sometimes seemed not to care at all.

Hank may have missed more show dates in 1952 than before, but he made a lot too. Sober, he was still as riveting a performer as there has been in country music, and that was the case to the very last show. The kinescope that survives from *The Kate Smith Evening Hour* is the only reasonably high resolution performance footage known to exist. Its images capture some of the magnetism that those who worked with Hank often spoke of. The focal point was his dark Indian eyes; they were burning and utterly alive in that moment. His legs moved, not with the burlesque contortions and pelvic thrusts that Elvis Presley would introduce to country music two years later, but with a sensual sway in time to the music.

On stage shows, Hank would often deliberately lower the microphone so that he would have to hunch over it, then he would swing his legs. All very innocuous today, but Hank has to be seen next to Eddy Arnold and Ernest Tubb, whose body movements were limited to changing chords, or next to Pee Wee King, a sawn-off Polish cowboy with a potbelly and an accordion. Beside his contemporaries, there was something vital, almost incendiary, in Hank Williams, so it was hardly surprising that he got a foretaste of the audience reaction that Elvis Presley would experience. Interviewed in Charleston, South Carolina, in March 1951, Hank spoke of how he was occasionally mobbed. "There's some folks who actually worship you," he said with a note of surprise in his voice. They tore at his outfits, he said, and even grabbed fistfuls of his thinning hair.

Hillbilly music was making its way blindly uptown, and as it did so, it inevitably changed its rural ways. Roy Acuff may have made the cover of *Newsweek*, but Columbia Records knew something that *Newsweek* didn't: Acuff's pure-bottled hillbilly music didn't sell any more, and he was dropped from the Columbia roster in November 1952. There is nothing as unsentimental as an A&R man with a sheaf of sales statistics in front of him. It would take another two or three years and the arrival of Elvis Presley to finish what Hank had started, but it was Hank who had the right mix for 1952. That's why he was forgiven his trespasses. For now.

Chapter

14

BILLIE JEAN

ON July 10, 1952, Hank and Audrey Williams, who had been married by the Bible, were divorced by the law. The following day, Hank cut "You Win Again." It was another quintessential Hank moment, one in which the seam between life and art appeared to be invisible. It might have been no more than pure coincidence, but, in the absence of hard evidence to the contrary, the songs that Hank cut the day after his divorce seem to be pages torn from his diary.

It only took two hours after lunch on July 11 for Hank to cut four songs; two to be issued under his name, and two as Luke the Drifter. The first, "You Win Again," is one of the most masterful recordings in country music. Its theme of betrayal had grown old years before Hank tackled it, but, drawing from his bottomless well of resentment, he gives it a freshness bordering on topicality. Apparently, Hank's first draft was titled "I Lose Again," but it was reversed at Rose's insistence. Having just signed the divorce papers, lines like "You have no heart, you have no shame / You take true love and give the blame" must have been viscerally real for him; he certainly sang them as if they were. Hank's use of common English, tightened and focused by Fred Rose, was now the standard for country song craft: terse, resonant, and exact.

The up-tempo song "I Won't Be Home No More" worked the same theme from a more defiant perspective. In it, Hank seems to have one finger raised at Audrey, rather than pointed accusingly at her. Even ough it's supposed to be a lighthearted song, Hank seems vindictive, even spiteful.

Then it was Luke the Drifter's turn. Fred Rose had found a song he ought suitable; it was Bonnie Dodd's "Be Careful of Stones That You hrow." Dodd was a steel-guitar player who had been recording on and f since 1937. She had written Tex Ritter's 1945 hit "You Will Have to y," and had worked a spell with him. Little Jimmy Dickens had recorded "Be Careful of Stones That You Throw" in October 1949, but it hadn't done much business and Rose clearly wanted to find a good home for the song. It was another cautionary tale: a hypocritical neighbor is saved by the "bad girl" down the street. Even cutting a song that wasn't his own, it's possible that Hank drew a parallel to his own life. The tide of criticism was mounting, but "unless you've made no mistakes in your life," he seems to be saying to his detractors, "be careful of stones that you throw." Rose saw the song as the top side of the next Luke the Drifter single, but with hindsight it paled in comparison with the other side.

"Please Make Up Your Mind," also known as "Why Don't You Make Up Your Mind," was the most rivetingly vengeful song Hank ever wrote or recorded. Over a slow blues backing and with bleak humor, Hank catalogs his grievances against Audrey: her tantrums, her attempts to belittle him, her ungovernable temper. "If a poor little rabbit had you on his side, every hound in the county would haul off and hide," he says. Audrey's feelings when she heard this can only be guessed at; it was as direct a hit at her as Hank ever took, almost too painful to be funny.

"Why Don't You Make Up Your Mind" had been written at least five or six months before the separation. As Hank recorded it, it was a laconic talking blues, but it had first been recorded by Little Jimmy Dickens in July 1951 as an up-tempo song. Dickens's version was called "I Wish You Didn't Love Me So Much," and was scheduled for release, then canceled at the last minute. It was issued in Canada, probably because someone forgot to tell the Canadian branch to pull the plug on it. Hank's version omits one of the couplets he gave Dickens: "The preacher man said 'For better or worse' / but lately I've been lookin' for that big black hearse." It's tempting to read Hank's intimation of his own mortality into his omission of those lines, but it could simply be that they didn't scan as well when they were spoken.

No one touched the song again until 1968 when Hank Jr., who then empathized almost as deeply with the lyrics as his father had once done, recorded it for his *Luke the Drifter Jr.* album.

One of the songs Hank had hoped to record in July was "Back Street Affair." During the presession discussions, Hank had pitched the idea to Rose, but Rose had balked at it, partly because he sincerely believed that type of song didn't belong on a country record, and partly because he didn't own the publishing rights. Hank had sung it on one of his early-morning radio shows, and Webb Pierce, who was in town to guest on the *Opry*, had heard it. Pierce collared Hank after the *Opry*. He said, "Hank, I sure like your new record, that 'Back Street Affair,' " and Hank said, "It ain't my new record. Fred Rose won't let me record it. Too risky. I think anyone's got guts enough to record it has got themselves a number one hit." Suggestive songs brought Rose's puritanical streak to the surface. He had immutable ideas about what was, and wasn't, a "Song for Home Folks." Writing to Tillman Franks a few years earlier, he had dismissed a song Tillman was pitching as a poor man's "Slipping Around." "The folks who buy real country records do not like 'Slipping Around,' " he wrote. Several million others did, though.

Billy Wallace, the writer of "Back Street Affair," already had it out, but Webb Pierce recorded it on July 9, two days before Hank's session. It gave Pierce, then the *Hayride*'s top act, his third number one hit in a row, a track record just long enough to ensure that, within a few weeks, he earned an invitation to join the *Opry*. His acquisition showed that the *Opry* was still making a policy of bringing in any artist who might act as a focal point for a rival jamboree.

MGM put the Luke the Drifter single into production immediately, and scheduled it for release on August 29. "You Win Again" was slotted onto the flip side of "Settin' the Woods on Fire" and was released two weeks later. Like most of Hank's flip sides, "You Win Again" got a little play, but only enough to get it into the charts for one week. The first hit with the song went to the black pop singer Tommy Edwards, best known for "It's All in the Game." Edwards cut it for MGM on August 12, a month before Hank's version was released. Frank Walker had Edwards's record rolling off the presses on the same day as Hank's. It climbed to number thirteen in the pop charts in the fall of 1952, but it didn't become a country hit until country deejays plucked it from the flip side of Jerry Lee Lewis's "Great Balls of Fire" in 1958. It didn't become a hit in its own right until Charlie Pride recorded it in 1980. By then it was already a standard.

Hank still seemed to be in good shape the day after the recording session. He introduced "Jambalaya" on the *Opry* on July 12. "I got a brand-new song ain't never been aired," he told Red Foley. "Ain't never been aired?" replied Foley, playing the straight man. "No, and it might need airin'," said Hank. Foley said he had the song title in front of him and couldn't pronounce it. "It's Jam-bal-eye-oo on the By-oo," said Hank, as the band kicked it off. A month later, it was on the charts, and by September 6 it was number one — where it remained until December.

Hank didn't hold up for long. Ray Price says that the divorce was a watershed in Hank's life, and it was the last straw for Price himself. After Hank had spent several days drinking relentlessly, Price and Don Helms arranged for him to be committed to the Madison Sanatorium. He was sedated and hauled off because Helms and Price thought that Hank seemed intent on drinking himself to death. Hank was furious and ordered Price to move out of the house, and Price did just that, probably with some relief. He found another place, and called Mac McGee, who ran Hank and Audrey's Corral, to verify that he was taking none of Hank's possessions. As he was loading the truck, Hank drove up still wearing his hospital robe, chauffered by someone from the hospital. He said, "You know I didn't mean it, Ray. You don't have to go," but Price went anyway. He told Hank he couldn't take it anymore.

After bottoming out, Hank turned himself around once again. Afraid of being alone, he brought a rotating cast of pickers and hangers-on into the house. The party continued, Hank often sitting in the middle of the floor scribbling away on his notepad. By the time the divorce was finalized, it seems as though Bobbie Jett was out of the picture, but Hank had met another woman who came to love him and wanted to help him.

Billie Jean Jones was born in 1933 on a farm twenty miles out of Shreveport. "I knew when I was five years old draggin' a cotton sack, if I ever got off that son of a bitch, I'd never be back," she says by way of explaining her motivation. She didn't have to worry; soon after the Second World War, her father became a policeman in Bossier City, Louisiana, and it was there that Billie Jean grew up with her two brothers, Alton and Sonny.

Hank Williams drove by the Jones's house on Modica Street every day in early 1949. Billie Jean says that she told her mother she was going to marry him, but when she married that year it was to Harrison Eshliman, a serviceman from Lubbock. She was sixteen and became pregnant during her first week of marriage without ever really understanding how. Her first daughter, Jeri Lynn, was born in March 1950. By then, Eshliman was history, and by 1951, Mrs. Jones was baby-sitting Jeri Lynn while

Billie Jean stepped out to dances at the Municipal Auditorium, attracting glances from the married and unmarried alike. She had long, flaming dark red hair and striking looks. "I thought I was something to behold," she says, and she was. She was no wallflower, either. The party crowd just seemed to gravitate to Billie Jean; she had that kind of personality.

Early in 1951, Billie Jean started dating Faron Young, who was then Webb Pierce's understudy. Young quit Pierce's band that year and very quickly got his own career off the ground. At some point in the summer of 1952, probably in June, he received a summons to Nashville to guest on the *Opry*. Billie Jean rode up with him. "He was wild as a bear cat," she says. "Oh, God! He knew he could sing and he was about half-way wise, but nothing could ever have worked out between us. I was dating him and about a hundred others, but my dad cosigned a note on a car to get us up there. I was just gonna go up and back."

The night before Faron Young arrived in Nashville, he was on a show date in Memphis with Hank Snow. Jerry Rivers worked the date with Snow, and he remembers Faron squiring Billie Jean around backstage. Early the following morning, Rivers and Helms were at WSM to work with Hank when Faron Young walked in. Rivers asked him where Billie Jean was, and Faron replied that she was asleep in the car outside. It's likely that Faron Young worked a short spell on WSM's early-morning radio schedule before he was offered a guest spot on the *Opry*. By then, Billie Jean had transferred from the Shreveport phone company to Nashville's.

For Young's first guest shot on the *Opry*, Billie Jean sat in the glassed-in visitors' box. She was wearing an off-the-shoulder dress, black and figure-hugging, with white lace at the top. It caught the wandering eye of the show's star, Hank Williams. He saw her and hunkered down, and looked at her through the glass, Billie Jean says.

He came in, sat down beside me. Just sat there and looked at me. I tried to ignore him. Finally, he said, "Girl, who you up here with?" I said, "Faron Young." He said, "Is that the kid that's guesting up here from Shreveport?" I said, "Yes, sir." About that time, Minnie Pearl came up to the glass, and he motioned to her. He said, "Minnie, find Faron Young, tell him ol' Hank wants to see him." So here comes Faron. Hank said, "Faron, you gonna marry this girl?" Faron said, "No-o-o, Hank. She's too mean and too fast. She's got too many boyfriends, I can't keep up with her." Hank said, "Well, if you ain't gonna marry her, ol' Hank's gonna marry her." He said, "Faron, go out there. You see that ol' black-haired gal in the front row with the red dress on. She flew down here from Pennsylvania to see me. After we get through working tonight, let's you and me go out 'n party. That gal, she's gonna be your gal, and Billie's gonna be my gal."

Sensitive new-age men may recoil, but Billie Jean was won over by Hank's brusque approach to courtship, and Faron Young, with the *Opry* in his sights, had no intention of crossing the show's star. Billie Jean continues:

When they got through that night, we went out to Faron's convertible. [Hank] said, "Boy, you drive." He told his girlfriend to sit in the front seat with Faron. We got out to some joint, I said I had a headache and I wasn't going in. He said, "Faron, you go in and have a good time. I'm gonna stay out here and talk with Billie." We moved up to the front seat. Me on the right-hand side with the door open, and him crouched down outside. We started shooting the bull about him living on the same street as me in Bossier. He was telling me about his problems with Audrey and so on. After a while, he said, "Why don't we go in, listen to the music and drink some coffee." I said, "Okay, if you'll drink coffee," 'cause I'd already heard about his clowning. . . . I didn't care if he was King Farouk — because I was Queen Farouk.

Faron Young later insisted any notions he might have had of another fling with Billie Jean were dispelled when Hank pulled a gun on him. Billie took a room in a girls' boardinghouse on Shelby Avenue. "It cost ten dollars a week," she says, "but I was sending money back to Louisiana to look after my kid and I needed the trolley fare. Hank looked so funny walking across my floor, 'cause it was on an angle, but I wouldn't let him pay my rent. He had hundred-dollar bills falling out of his pocket."

Within weeks, Billie and Hank agreed to marry. They hired a driver and went to Shreveport to visit her parents in mid-July; Hank dictated thirteen songs along the way. "He looked over to me in the car," she said, "and he told me, 'I can say one thing, baby. I could never be ashamed of you.' Like he had been of Audrey. He said, 'That'd be a good idea for a song. Write this down for ol' Hank, baby.' He'd call 'em off as fast as I could write." While they were in Shreveport, Hank paid ninety-five dollars to a lawyer to proceed with Billie Jean's divorce from Harrison Eshliman. They told her parents that they would marry as soon as the divorce became effective in mid-October.

As they neared Nashville on the return trip, Hank bought five pounds of fish and was planning to have the driver cook it up that night, but when they pulled up in front of the house on Natchez Trace, they found the plate glass in the front door smashed in. A woman's red shoes were on the doormat and luggage was in the hall. One of Hank's old flames had moved in. He ordered her out, then they started wrestling with each other. Billie Jean and the driver stood, mouths agape while Hank and his ex-girlfriend tussled. Billie told the driver to take her back to her apartment.

"We loaded up the car, got to my apartment," said Billie. "I got out, took off up the path and Hank came in with me. I was mad. He said he was gonna get rid of that broad but it was gonna take a club. I told him, 'That's it, I'm gone. I'm history. I ain't puttin' up with this crap no more.' It was like wolves chasing him. The rest of that week, I packed. He got rid of that sucker and came back over. I said, 'I'm going back to Louisiana. This is wrong and I don't want any part of it.' " A few days later, Billie Jean was gone.

Hank was now in a serious mess. According to Billie Jean, Audrey was refusing him access to Hank Jr., Bobbie Jett had reappeared, heavy with what she insisted was his child, and now his fiancée had quit him and gone back to Louisiana. His response was to plummet into another tailspin and miss show dates and radio commitments. It was a state of affairs that WSM wouldn't tolerate, and everything came to a head during the second week in August. At some point during that week, Jim Denny and Carl Smith visited Hank at his apartment, and Denny told Hank that WSM's management was demanding that he be dismissed. Denny had asked for Hank to be given one more chance, and told him that he absolutely had to be at the *Opry* on August 9 and at an *Opry*-sponsored show the following day.

August the ninth arrived. Hank didn't. He didn't appear for the show the following day either. Denny couldn't go back on his ultimatum. Jack Stapp, WSM program director, once took whatever credit was to be had for canning Hank, but it appears fairly certain that, on August 11, Jim Denny picked up the phone and fired him. "It was the toughest thing I ever had to do in my life," he said later. Ernest Tubb said he was hanging around WSM that day. In Tubb's recollection it was Friday that Hank was fired, although newspaper reports indicate that it was Monday. This was how Tubb remembered the events unfolding:

I heard Jim on the telephone. He said, "Hank that's it. You gotta prove to me. You call me in December, and I'll let you know about coming back to the *Opry* next year." When Jim hung up the telephone, he had tears in his eyes. He said, "I had to do it. I had to let Hank go." When I was in the parking lot, I ran into Mr. [Edwin] Craig [National Life Chairman]. He knew, and he said, "What do you think, Ernest?" I said, "Well, I hate it, but I saw tears in Jim's eyes, and I know it was the hardest thing he ever had to do. He told me he was going to try and get Hank to straighten up." Mr. Craig said, "I'm sure Jim means well, but it may work the other way. It may kill him." I was feeling the same way.

Johnnie Wright claims that he was sitting with Hank on Natchez Trace at the moment the phone call came through from Denny. According to Wright, the scene played out with far less sentimentality:

Jim Denny told him he was going to have to let him go. Hank said, "You cain't fire me 'cause I already quit." He had a check coming, about three hundred dollars. Jim asked Hank if anyone was there with him, and Hank said "Johnnie Wright's here." He said, "Tell Johnnie I want to talk to him." I got on the phone and Jim said, "Johnnie, he's got a check up here. You come by and pick it up." My brother-in-law had a Chrysler limousine, and Hank had his trailer with "Drifting Cowboys" written on the side. We put all his belongings in the trailer and his reclining chair in the back of the limousine, and put him in the reclining chair.

Don Helms had heard the news and, just as Hank was leaving with Johnnie Wright, he came over to Hank's house to return a few things, a shotgun and a watch, that he'd been holding. Helms's wife was with him; they had all been friends since 1944. "I told Hazel," says Helms, "Hank Williams won't live six months." Hank was drinking as he and Wright drove away.

According to Wright, the first call was at WSM:

Roy Acuff and Owen Bradley was in Jim Denny's office. Roy said, "Have you got Hank out there?" I said, "Yeah." Owen said, "Let's go out and see him, Roy." They went out and I picked up his check. Then we took off to Montgomery. We went out Broadway, and there was a liquor store out there at Sixteenth and Broad, and Hank said, "Johnnie, pull in there and get me some whiskey." So I pulled in and got him a fifth and cashed his three-hundred-dollar check. The guy that owned the liquor store said, "Is Hank out there?" I said, "Yeah," so the guy came out and spoke to him.

We took him to his mother's house. We pulled his clothes off, put him to bed, and talked to his mother 'til he woke up. Hank acted like he didn't care that he'd been canned.

Part of Hank's act was bravado, but he may have felt that he had outgrown the *Opry*, and that he was of greater value to the show than it was to him. Eddy Arnold had quit the *Opry* and was doing well, and Red Foley would soon quit. The *Opry* tied Hank up at a paltry wage on potentially the most lucrative night of the week. Instead of walking away from a Saturday night show date with several thousand dollars stuffed in his case, he was flying at his own expense back to Nashville to work for little more than exposure that he now thought he didn't really need. During their conversation, Hank had mouthed off to Denny about the number of records he had on the charts, but from Denny's perspective it didn't matter anymore. The *Opry* was a business that needed reliable suppliers and Hank may have had the best goods in town, but he was no longer reliable. In fact, his no-shows were damaging the *Opry*'s reputation.

Johnnie Wright always assumed that Hank was heading back to Montgomery to lick his wounds, but in fact he was heading back for another Homecoming, this one in Greenville arranged by the Rotary Club. It was scheduled for August 15, four days after the firing. Hank had to get himself straight and he had to get a car to squire himself through town because he had literally lost his tan Cadillac Coupe de Ville. He bought a 1952 powder blue Cadillac convertible, registered in Lillie's name for reasons that aren't entirely clear.

The Greenville Homecoming didn't pack quite the punch of the Montgomery Homecoming in July 1951. Greenville was a smaller city, and Hank had lived there only two years. Still, there were two shows at Greenville Stadium and a parade preceding the afternoon show. In the photographs, Hank has an ugly contusion above his lip, suggesting that he'd recently been in a fight. One strong possibility is that the welt came from a beating Lillie had administered after Hank returned home fired and drunk. Apart from that, Hank seemed to have bounced back yet again. In all, eighty-five hundred people turned out to honor him, including his father and his uncle Robert. Hank looked for Tee-Tot and acknowledged him publicly, but apparently no one knew that Tee-Tot had been in a pauper's grave since 1939.

After the Homecoming, Hank went back to Lillie's boardinghouse. The word in the local paper was that he was suffering from blood poisoning from an infected wound, and was lying low while he regrouped. On the *Opry* it was announced that Hank was sick, although his dismissal had been made public by the Nashville papers. Hank finally located his other car in Philadelphia, and arranged for it to be driven to Nashville. He and one of his band members from WSFA, Shorty Seals, drove up to collect it. Before he left Nashville, Hank went by Bobbie Jett's house on Acklen Avenue, picked her up, and brought her back with him. Now Hank had one girlfriend, two cars, no band, no show dates, and far too much time on his hands.

Lillie phoned Bob McKinnon, a deejay in Alexander City, Alabama, and asked him to take Hank out to the country for a few days. Hank was introducing Bobbie Jett around town as "Bobbie Blue," and telling people that she was his nurse. McKinnon had a cousin who was married to an automobile dealer named Darwin Dobbs, who owned a nicely appointed lodge out on a part of Lake Martin known as Kowaliga Bay. Originally, Kowaliga was the name of a creek that ran into the Tallapoosa River, and when the river was dammed up to make Lake Martin, the locals started calling the area where the creek had been Kowaliga Bay. Another legend goes that the Creek Indians had a settlement there called "Kia-leach-shi" (headdress) because they made headdresses there.

Hank, Bobbie, and Bob McKinnon got to Dobbs's lodge early on the afternoon of August 17. McKinnon left around 4:00 P.M. and went back to Alexander City. Hank was sober and looking forward to some rest. Around midnight, McKinnon was awakened by a call from the police department. Hank was no longer at the lodge nor sober. He was in the Alexander City jail.

"I believe he was more or less having DTs," said Chief Winfred Patterson. "He was running up and down the hall [of the Russell Hotel] yelling that someone was whupping old ladies and he was going to stop them." After he was arrested, the chief said that Hank was no trouble. He told the chief that he'd been in some worse jails, some better. Bob McKinnon went to get Bobbie at the Russell Hotel, came down to the jail, made Hank's bail, and got him released. No charges were laid. It has long been supposed that Hank was photographed shirtless and disheveled as he exited the jail that morning. He had the cornered-animal look that several people said he had when he was coming off a spree. It is a harrowing photo, but probably taken on an earlier occasion when he had been arrested in Alexander City. That time he had threatened to buy the town.

McKinnon took Hank and Bobbie to another motel, left Hank to sleep it off, then took Bobbie back up to the lake to get some of her things. McKinnon heard her vomiting in the bathroom and she told him that she was pregnant. Gradually, the story of that night unfolded. Hank had been playing with some kids on a bridge and he'd waded out into the lake. Some people from Red Hill had seen him, found out he was Hank Williams and produced a five-gallon jug of corn liquor. That was as much of a calling card as Hank needed to see.

The following afternoon, McKinnon went to get Hank and Bobbie. Hank was dreadfully hungover. He remembered only going to jail. "I got me in," he said to McKinnon. "Who got me out?" McKinnon told him the story, took him to Frank "Country" Duncan's house, then drove him back out to Kowaliga. Duncan and a black valet were to stay with Hank there for a few days, but Hank was restless. The following day, he appeared at the radio station where McKinnon worked and asked to go to the bank. Lillie had specifically told McKinnon, "No banks," but, as Hank had said for as long as he could remember, "What momma don't know won't hurt her."

McKinnon took Hank to the First National Bank in Alexander City, and Hank arranged to get some money wired in from somewhere. Bobbie asked him what he wanted the money for, and Hank said he wanted to get some clothes. Bobbie said, "Hank, what're you gonna do with clothes? We've got clothes scattered all the way from San Diego, California, to Portland, Maine." But Hank bought clothes anyway. He also bought some tires from Darwin Dobbs's dealership to repay him for the loan of the lodge. While the tires were being changed, Lillie drove up with Detective Louis King. She gave McKinnon some anti-alcoholic medication, had words with Hank, then drove back to Montgomery.

That night Hank, Bobbie, McKinnon, and a party of locals went back to Kowaliga. When it was time to send out for drinks someone suggested Whitley's near Montgomery. Hank said, "No, I might run into momma. I don't want to chance it." So they went to a bootlegger in Kellyton instead. On the way there and back Hank started pounding out a war-dance rhythm on the dashboard and chanting "Kowaliga, Kowaliga."

Hank worked on his song that night and told McKinnon to phone

© Menasco

© Menasco

Shreveport, April 6, 1949. Ranged around
Hank from left to right are Clint Holmes,
Lum York, Bob McNett, Tony Francini,
and Felton Pruett.

A piercing look. On the edge of
next-big-thingdom.

© Menasco

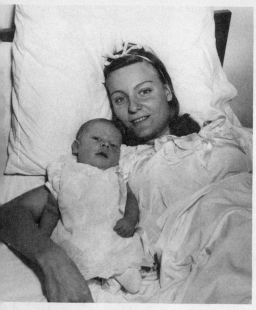

Shreveport, June 2, 1949.
Audrey with Randall Hank.

Surrounded by Oriental kitsch, Hank's
first Nashville band members and their
families gather for a photo op. Left to
right: Bob McNett, Hank, Audrey with
Hank Jr. and Lycrecia, Hazel Helms,
Frank Helms, June Rivers, Don Helms,
Betty Butrum, Hillous Butrum, Jerry
Rivers.

Colin Escott

Colin Escott

The 1950 Who's Who of Hillbilly Music. From the left: Hank, Milton Estes, Red Foley, Minnie Pearl, unknown (from *Cashbox* magazine), Wally Fowler (kneeling), Harry Stone, Eddy Arnold, Roy Acuff, Rod Brasfield, Lew Childre.

Colin Escott

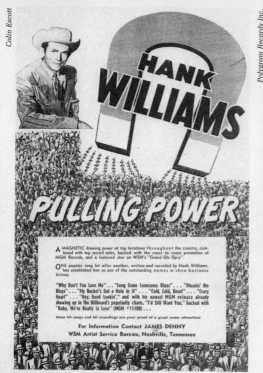

Polygram Records Inc.

Hey, good lookin'. On board the Hadacol Caravan.

Tom Sims

Exiting the place of employment, 1951.

Colin Escott

Blotto in Toronto, 1952.

George Merritt

The Greenville Homecoming, August 1952. Hank and Lillie are riding in the car. Lon is standing to the right.

Billie Jean Horton

Billie Jean Horton

Hank, a welt clearly visible on his left temple, marries Billie Jean in New Orleans, October 19, 1952.

Last stand at the Alamo. From left: Hank, Billie Jean, Clyde Perdue, unknown, Sonny Jones.

Colin Escott

Hank and Billie Jean at their wedding. Tommy and Goldie Hill are to the right.

Toby Marshall, 1953.

The last prescription.

© Daily Oklahoman

© Daily Oklahoman

CONNIE'S PRESCRIPTION SHOP

1209 N. Walker   Medical Center   2507 N. W. 23rd
Opposite Osler Bldg.   525 N. W. 11th   23rd and Villa
Phone 2-8133   Phone 2-4396   Phone 9-3311

For _Hank Williams_ Date _12-??-52_
Address _318 N. McDough_

R℞   Chloral Hydrate
Caps # 24
gr. VII.5

Sig: as directed

P.R.N.

U. S. Reg. No.   _Toby Marshall_ M.D.

Peter Trenholm/George Merritt

Buffeted by life, and by an
unknown assailant. Probably
the last photo.

Wesley Rose (second from left
holding casket) and Fred Rose
(third from left) accompany
Hank on his last ride.

A card so jarringly at odds with what the festive season held in store.

G. Merritt

How quickly we forget. Hank presides beatifically over country music while still providing for those left below.

G. Merritt

May Christmas bring such happiness
That long after it has gone,
Its joy remains like the sweet refrain
Of songs that echo on.

AUDREY, LYCRECIA, HANK JR., WILLIAMS

Fred Rose the following morning. He wanted Rose to get what he called an "arr-plane" down to Montgomery so that they could work on the song. Hank stayed at the lodge for several days and finished up several more songs, including "Your Cheatin' Heart" and one called "Lonesomest Time of the Day."

Rose didn't get an airplane to Montgomery; he drove down with Murray Nash. They set off early from Nashville and were in Montgomery by eight o'clock in the morning, just as Lillie was finishing up serving breakfast to her boarders. She went and roused Hank, and Hank produced the three songs he had written. Nash had brought along a little wire recorder, and Hank demo'd "Your Cheatin' Heart" and "Kowaliga" for Rose.

"I needed to get some things into the post office," said Nash, "and Fred said Hank should go with me to the post office and he'd work on the songs. By the time we came back, Fred had refashioned 'Kowaliga' into 'Kaw-Liga,' and made it into a song about a dime-store Indian." If nowhere else, the hand of Fred Rose was apparent in the way "Kaw-Liga" starts in a minor key and modulates to a major key on the bridge. Talking to the local paper a few weeks later, Lillie recalled that Hank and Fred Rose had sat in her front room, talked, and written songs until late into the night. "Sometimes," she said, "I woke up and heard the prettiest song I ever heard. They'd already put it on tape and recorded it and they were playing it back. It's so pretty, it made my hair stand on end." Coyly, she added, "It's called . . . well, I better not say."

One of the more important items on Hank and Fred Rose's agenda that night was to formulate a game plan to get Hank's career back on track. Rose had plenty of other irons in the fire, but Hank Williams was the ace of his staff. Aside from anything else, Hank was doing for Rose what Acuff had originally done — drawing other writers to the company. Then there was the income that Hank was singlehandedly generating for Acuff-Rose. Between January and June 1952 the company had a total of eighty-nine copyrights recorded; Hank's records and the cover versions they attracted made the biggest single contribution to that tally. To put those 89 copyrights into perspective, the top popular music publishing group, Robbins Music, which represented hundreds of standards, had 156 copyrights recorded during the same period.

After Rose got back to Nashville, he pulled some strings to get Hank back on the *Louisiana Hayride*. The deal was announced on August 30, 1952. Rose was able to play Hank's remaining trump: "Jambalaya." It had already sold two hundred thousand copies when Rose started talking to

KWKH, so many copies in fact that MGM had to lay on a Saturday shift at the pressing plant to accommodate the orders. The success of "Jambalaya" pushed the official tally of Hank's record sales over ten million in a shade over five years, and on September 12, MGM released Hank's second album. Once again, it was issued in three formats (10-inch LP, or four 45s or four 78s packaged in an album), and it was called *Moanin' the Blues*. Rose used the occasion as an excuse to off-load some more back catalog, in this case songs with "Blues" in the title.

For its part, KWKH needed Hank Williams or someone like him. Its sister station in Arkansas, KTHS, had just been alloted a fifty-thousand-watt clear channel; twenty other stations were picking up the *Hayride* on transcription, and CBS was talking about picking up part of the show for networking. The only cloud in the sky was that the *Hayride* had just lost two of its major stars, Webb Pierce and Faron Young, and only Slim Whitman remained. Sick, sober, or sorry, Hank Williams seemed just the ticket, and the negotiations started that would send him back to Shreveport.

On September 8, 1952, Hank cut one of his last remaining ties to Nashville when he sold his farm in Williamson County in what amounted to a fire sale. He got $28,500 — less than half what he had paid for it. A little earlier, he sold Hank and Audrey's Corral and the $50,000 or $60,000 worth of inventory and fixtures to the manager, Mac McGee, for $4,000. To compound the loss, he paid off the $12,000 in accounts payable to leave McGee with a clean slate. McGee ran it until April 1953, when it folded.

Clearly, Hank wanted to be out of Nashville at any price.

It's a great separation my friends
have caused me
By bearing the spite my favor has won,
It's a great separation, likewise a vexation
And they shall be sorry for what
they have done.
"Adieu to Bon County" (Unknown)

THE DEATH OF
LEAPY THE LEOPARD

BOY, thank you, Horace, thank you a lot. Boy,
sure feels good to be home, y'know."

"Been 'bout two years since you've been home, boy."

With that exchange, Hank Williams was back on the *Louisiana Hay-ride*. It had been a shade over three years since he had left with his heart full of hope. He was brought back on September 13 for a teaser — the date he was supposed to have closed out the *Opry*'s season at the Astor Roof. After Horace Logan's introduction, Hank sang "Jambalaya" as the crowd clapped and stomped in time. He promised to be back to play and sing every week.

Just before he left for Shreveport, Hank called Billie Jean from Montgomery. "Baby," he said, "this is ol' Hank." Billie Jean was taken off guard. "I do believe we've got a date October nineteenth," he said. It was the date they had planned to marry, after her divorce from Harrison Eshliman became final. "Well," she said, "we *had* a date."

"Listen," he said, "in a coupla days, ol' Hank's gonna be down. I'm movin' to Shreveport. I want you to find me a place." And a few days later, Hank turned up in a convoy of two cars, one of them driven by Clyde Perdue, who had staged the Greenville Homecoming and was now Hank's personal manager. Born in April 1914 in Farmersville, Alabama, some twenty-five miles out of Greenville, Perdue was an Air Corps veteran who had returned to Greenville after World War II, first as an express clerk and then as a theater manager. Neither occupation had groomed him to be Hank Williams's manager.

Everything Hank owned from his three and a half years at the top of his profession was in those two vehicles. Billie's brother, Sonny Jones, found him a room in an apartment hotel, and, as Hank drove around the streets he knew so well greeting a few old cronies from the first go-round, no one came away with the impression that he thought he'd been demoted to the minor leagues. He was upbeat, or, as he would put it, "spry," still insisting that he had quit the *Opry*.

"He called me from an Italian restaurant downtown, Tony Sansone's on Spring Street," said Horace Logan. "He said, 'Come on down, I want you to meet my French girl.' I went down, walked in, and there was Billie Jean. I said, 'Billie Jean, where in hell have you been?' Hank said, 'You know my French girl?' I said, 'She's not French — she's Irish as can be.' "

What had happened back in Montgomery isn't clear. Hank must have left Bobbie to wait out her confinement in the sweltering late summer heat in one of Lillie's boardinghouses. Then, after Fred Rose negotiated the return to Shreveport, Hank's thoughts turned again to Billie Jean.

Back in Shreveport, Hank tried to reassemble his old band. He called Felton Pruett, his steel-guitar player from the first time around, but Pruett had had enough Hank Williams for one lifetime. "He got real perturbed at me for not going back with him," said Pruett. "He was pretty strong with me. He had Billie Jean with him and he was treating her bad, cussin' at her and I thought, 'Hell, I don't need none of this.' "

Although he tried, Hank never succeeded in putting a band together for the three months he worked out of Shreveport. When he had a tour arranged, he sometimes used Red Sovine's band, which included pianist Floyd Cramer, steel guitarist Jimmy Day, and Tommy Bishop on guitar; sometimes he used the house band at the clubs. Like Chuck Berry, Hank figured that everyone knew his songs, so he wouldn't even bother to rehearse his pickup bands. At show time, he would kick off every song with a chord for the musicians to find the key (usually E or C), and then start singing. He'd telegraph the fact that it was the last verse by lifting his foot.

Hank managed to get Oscar Davis to rejoin him for a while. Perhaps with Oscar, he thought, it would be just like 1949 again. Hank found him in Vancouver, Canada, and persuaded him to come down to Shreveport. "He was living in a horrible, horrible motel," said Oscar. "Sparsely furnished. An old kitchen table and junk all around. He wanted me to meet Billie, so every night we had to go out and sit and drink."

Commercially, this would be life lived at a lower level than Hank had known it for several years. Oscar Davis notified *Billboard* that he expected Hank to tour every second week and spend the other week songwriting. It was a gauge of Hank's unreliability that although his recording of "Jambalaya" was number one in the country charts and Jo Stafford's recording was in the pop top ten, he and the song everyone wanted to hear were confined for the greater part to smaller halls and beer joints a day or two's drive from Shreveport.

Hank went out on a short tour right away. Billie and Clyde Perdue went with him. On September 17, they played the Barn in San Antonio. In the audience that night was Doug Sahm, then eleven years old. Already something of a child prodigy, he was brought up onstage to sit on Hank's lap and play "Steel Guitar Rag." "His breath stank of whiskey," says Doug, "and there wasn't nothin' left to him. His knees were sharp. Poked right into me." Hank was in a good mood that night, though. It was his twenty-ninth birthday, and during the day he and his entourage had visited the Alamo.

Three days later, Hank made his official return to the *Louisiana Hayride*. He had hassled with Henry Clay, insisting that he wasn't going to work for scale, and Clay had agreed to pay him around two hundred dollars a show instead of the usual eighteen. Horace Logan insists that Hank was tied to the show with a three-year contract, but, if he was, it has never surfaced.

On Tuesday, September 23, Hank went back to Nashville for a recording session. "Kaw-Liga" and "Your Cheatin' Heart," the two songs he had fashioned with Fred Rose in Montgomery, were due to be recorded, as was "I Could Never Be Ashamed of You," the song he had written for Billie Jean. To round out the session, Fred Rose contributed "Take These Chains from My Heart," perhaps the best song he presented to Hank. If Hank was in terminal decline, it wasn't obvious from this session. Most of those there remember him in better shape than the last couple of times he had recorded. The problems, such as they were, stemmed from the fact that Bobbie Jett had found out that Hank was recording and appeared at the studio. Billie Jean was there as well as Paul Cohen, who had been one of Bobbie Jett's suitors. Hank was denying everything to Billie Jean.

Under those circumstances, it's surprising that anything was cut, and even more surprising that the session was, in many ways, one of Hank's best and most productive. It was also his last. Most singers hope to cut one or two classics that they can hang a career on; Hank cut four

classics between 1:30 and 3:40 on the afternoon of September 23, including "Your Cheatin' Heart," the song that would become as much his anthem in death as "Lovesick Blues" had been in life. Cheatin' hearts are to
country music what the blues in B-flat is to jazz, and Hank Williams's
"Your Cheatin' Heart" is the song that to all intents and purposes defines
country music. The melody is folk-based and faintly redolent of everything that had come before.* The words are now part of the stock-in-
trade of the country tunesmith, but Hank's subtextual chisel and thirst
for vengeance still make the overfamiliar phrases spring to life. His performance of the song underscores its scalding bitterness.

Billie Jean insists that Hank began "Your Cheatin' Heart" on their
drive to Louisiana in August, and says it was aimed fair and square at
Miss Audrey. So, with an irony that Hank himself might have appreciated, Audrey was left collecting copiously off a song that was, in
virtually every respect, a character assassination. "You'll toss around
and call my name. . . . You'll walk the floor the way I do" were
prophecies truer than Hank could ever have hoped or imagined. Perhaps unable to come to terms with it, Audrey eventually tried to
believe that Hank had written the song about himself. "You or no one
else would ever believe this," she said late in life, setting up her
listeners for the required leap of faith. "Hank wrote ['Your Cheatin'
Heart'] immediately after he and I had just separated, and he wrote
[the] song about himself, hoping that I would think that he thought I
might have been cheating."

For "Kaw-Liga," Fred Rose brought in a drummer, Farris Coursey,
the first drummer to work a Hank Williams session. Drummers weren't
thick on the ground in Nashville because they were still prohibited on
the *Opry* stage, but Coursey was the drummer in WSM's dance band, and
he provided the Indian war-dance beat that Rose wanted. At the close,
"Kaw-Liga" was faded — the first and only Hank Williams recording to
end in what is now the industry norm of a fade. The lesson of "Jambalaya" had been that a novelty song with a faintly ethnic twist was a hot
prospect, and that's precisely what Hank and Fred Rose had crafted on
"Kaw-Liga." Hank carried an acetate of the song, and when he played it

---

* The same melody was used for a "Cold, Cold Heart" sequel called "My Cold, Cold
Heart Is Melted Now" that is credited to Hank and Johnnie Masters. It was copyrighted
before "Your Cheatin' Heart" was released, so it's at least possible that Hank set "Your
Cheatin' Heart" to Masters's melody.

for people he told them that it would be his biggest record yet. No one doubted him.

The first song from the September 23 session to hit the stores was "I Could Never Be Ashamed of You," which was slotted on the flip side of "I'll Never Get Out of This World Alive" for November 21 release. After Frank Walker got the session tapes, he set about covering the songs for the pop market. He gave "Your Cheatin' Heart" to Joni James, "Kaw-Liga" to Bill Farrell, and "Take These Chains from My Heart" to Tommy Edwards. After Mitch Miller got advance acetates from Fred Rose, he gave "Your Cheatin' Heart" to Frankie Laine. Both Laine's and Joni James's versions cracked the pop top ten in 1953. Dolores Gray's Decca recording of "Kaw-Liga" got up to number twenty-three on the pop charts in May 1953.

The week after the session, Hank went out on a tour of Georgia and South Carolina with Faron Young, but otherwise, the best that Oscar Davis could get was short tours with *Hayride* acts. The *Hayride* still didn't have anything comparable to the *Opry's* Artist Service Bureau, but that was just as well because the *Hayride* would have done exactly what the *Opry* had done: flung Hank from coast to coast, using him as a standard bearer for the show. Fred Rose was clearly hoping that the shock of being exiled from Nashville together with the less demanding schedule would be sufficient to make Hank shape up. The thought also probably occurred to him that if Hank screwed up, it would be in front of only a few hundred people somewhere in eastern Texas.

As it was, the biggest show that Hank played after he returned to the *Hayride* was his own wedding. Oscar Davis came up with the notion of a public pay-per-view marriage in New Orleans on Sunday, October 19. He presold tickets at prices ranging from $1 to $2.80. Around fourteen thousand people would see Hank married at the Municipal Auditorium at a three-o'clock "rehearsal" and again at seven o'clock. It appears as though no one from Nashville was invited — except Audrey. If Lillie was invited, she didn't attend.

The last unresolved item of business from Nashville was an ex-girlfriend now six months pregnant. On October 15, four days before the public weddings, Hank went back to Montgomery to sign a document that provided for Bobbie Jett and her child. In the first sentence of the agreement, it was stated that "Hank Williams may be the father of said child," and the document went on to note that Hank would provide for Bobbie Jett's room and board in Montgomery, that he would pay all doctor bills and hospital bills, and that, thirty days after the birth of the child, he would provide a one-way plane ticket from Montgomery to anywhere in California that Bobbie designated.

The child was to be placed in the care of Lillie and Bill Stone for two years, and during that time Hank was to pay for a nurse. The agreement then stated, "Both the father [and here Hank was referred to as the father, not the possible father], Hank Williams, and Bobbie Jett shall have the right to visit said child." Then, beginning on the child's third birthday, Hank was to assume custody of the child until his or her fifth birthday. At that point, custody was to be shared; Hank would have custody during school months and Bobbie Jett would have custody during the summer. On two other instances in the agreement, Hank was referred to as the father, although, contradictorily, the agreement concluded with the notation that the "paternity of said child is in doubt" and emphasized that paternity was not to be construed as admitted by the fact that Hank had entered into the agreement. It strains credibility, though, to believe that Hank would have entered into such complex custody arrangements for a child he did not believe to be his own.

For her part, Billie Jean contends that Hank signed the agreement partly at the urging of his mother and partly to get Bobbie Jett off their backs. "Every gig he played, she'd pop up," she said. "Here she is fixing to drop somebody's kid." Billie also contends that Hank was incapable of fathering a child in March or April, when Bobbie Jett's child was conceived, because when she met him in July he was still incapable of having sex as a result of his operation. "It was on his mind," she says, "but, as my momma always said, 'If it can't get up, it can't get out.' " If, as Billie says, Hank was impotent when she met him in July or August, it was probably because of alcohol, pills, and general dissipation rather than the operation. His ability to father a child in March or April might have been unimpaired.

On the trip back to Montgomery to sign the papers, Hank ran into his former bass player, Lum York. Lum was working with Lefty Frizzell and was resting up in town for a few days. Lillie tracked him down at the radio station and tried to get him to change Hank's mind about marrying Billie Jean. Lum told her he was having no part of it, but she said that since Hank was just around the corner in the barber shop, Lum should go look him up anyway. Lum recalled their conversation:

He was in the chair when I got there, so I went into the little coffee shop near the barber, and he come in and said, "Do you wanna go work for me?" I said, "Hank, how much you gonna pay me?" He said, "I'll pay you seventy-five a week." I said, "Hank, I'm making more than that." He said, "Aw, that's the way it is with Frizzell and them guys. They want to pay you all they make." I said, "Well, I'm satisfied where I'm working." He said, "How 'bout catchin' a plane with me and goin' to Shreveport?" I said, "Naw, I'm staying around here a coupla days." I never did talk to him 'bout marryin' Billie Jean. I figured he was a grown man.

In Nashville, the news of Hank's marriage was seen as evidence of his further disintegration. Billie Jean contends that Audrey flew into Shreveport a day or so before the very public marriage and tried to convince Hank to return to her by threatening that he would never see Hank Jr. again. According to Billie, they met in a hotel room, and Hank emerged with a welt on his forehead as a result of her hitting him. A welt is clearly visible in the wedding photos, although its provenance has never been established beyond doubt.

Audrey's visit threw a curve into Hank and Billie's plans. She had told him that she would disrupt the ceremony — in Billie's words, "throw a rigger." Part of the reason Hank had agreed to a public ceremony was to spite Audrey, and that now looked likely to backfire. So, after the first *Hayride* show on Saturday, October 18, Hank, Billie, and another *Hayride* act, Paul Howard, together with Howard's wife drove out to Minden, Louisiana, where Howard knew a justice of the peace, P. E. Burton, who was willing to marry them that late and that quickly. That way, if Audrey tried to disrupt the ceremony, Hank and Billie could wave a marriage certificate proving that they were already married. On the way back to Shreveport, the car ran out of gas and the wedding party had to hitch a ride back to town.

The late-night marriage in Minden created a problem when the minister in New Orleans found out about it and refused to marry a couple who were already married. Oscar Davis had to scout out another minister at short notice, and he found the Reverend L. R. Shelton of the First Baptist Church of Algiers. While Davis was finding a minister, a convoy of *Hayride* cast members arrived in New Orleans to perform at the pre-wedding shows. They had driven down overnight after the *Hayride*. Hank and Billie Jean left at 7:00 on Sunday morning from Bossier City airport in a private plane.

Oscar Davis had arranged for local merchants to donate Billie Jean's trousseau, as well as furniture and appliances for the new apartment.

According to Billie, Davis also arranged to take the lion's share of the proceeds for himself, and it became one of his last acts on Hank's behalf. Hank started drinking as soon as he got to New Orleans, and, just as *Hayride* newcomer Billy Walker started to sing his hit of the day, "Anything Your Heart Desires," Hank came onstage pulling Billie Jean. Walker stopped cold and looked at him in disbelief. Hank took the microphone and said, "When ol' Hank comes to git married, he wants to git married."

It was a three-ring circus — a fitting end to Hank's association with Oscar Davis, the old vaudevillian. Davis insisted that even on the morning of the ceremony Hank was hoping that Audrey would come and stop it, but the photos tell a different story. They capture a few moments of undeniable tenderness between Hank and his new bride. The marriage to Billie was more than simply an impetuous act to spite Audrey. Billie had the glow of health and beauty that attracted Hank; she also had the feistiness that simultaneously attracted and repelled him. For his part, Hank had a stray cat quality that made women want to take him in and nourish him with food and affection, but, like most alcoholics, he abused the love, frustrated it, and ultimately alienated it.

Billie Jean looked radiant that day, and Hank indeed looked younger than he had in years, despite his thinning hair. The old problems hadn't left him, though. His back hurt terribly, and he self-medicated himself from the crates of champagne that Davis had arranged for the guests backstage. After the wedding, Hank and Billie were supposed to fly to Cuba for their honeymoon, but the backache blues and the champagne got to him and he passed out in his room at the Jung Hotel after his third "I do" in two days.

Hank had put on thirty pounds, something that has usually been ascribed to edema common in sufferers of heart disease or drug abuse. Billie Jean, though, is adamant that Hank's weight gain was due to the fact that he was eating decently for the first time in years. They'd go on squirrel hunts, she says, then skin and eat the squirrels, and Billie's mother would fatten him up on syrup and biscuits. Shortly after he arrived in Shreveport, it's likely that Hank did indeed gain some weight, but in several photos from the last months of his life, he seems unnaturally bloated, and his fellow performers say that some weeks he would be gaunt and other weeks puffy. The systems were starting to break down.

Hank and Billie moved into a new development at 1346 Shamrock in Bossier City that Sonny Jones was managing for his father-in-law. It was sparsely furnished by the standards Hank had become used to on Franklin Road. There were no carpets, no Oriental furniture, no grotesque paintings, no chandeliers. Hank didn't appear to mind, though, and Billie Jean didn't miss what she'd never had. She made a concerted effort to give Hank much of the affection he had been sorely lacking on Franklin Road, and she and her brothers tried to get Hank to kick his self-destructive habits. Quickly and inevitably disillusion set in, but Hank and Billie Jean had their honeymoon. "He had never been held," she says. "I knew this. I was wise for my years. I knew I had to be a lover and a mother to him. We wrestled, had picnics. I gave him a childhood. I wouldn't wear shoes in a hotel lobby. He loved my simplicity. We held hands, and I'd sit on his lap. I wore short-shorts and T-shirts tied up in the front. I was a virgin in a lot of ways." It wasn't long, though, before Billie Jean began to realize that Hank's street called straight never ran for more than a few blocks, and that his problems couldn't be licked.

After his marriage, Hank spent two months working out of Shreveport. Sometimes Billie Jean would accompany him on the road, sometimes not. Her enthusiasm for the task she had undertaken almost certainly waned as she came to appreciate the nature of Hank's addictions and the extent of his physical problems. The back pain was always there, robbing him of sleep and peace of mind. If Hank understood the true nature of his illness — and it was very likely that the doctors at Vanderbilt had given him a bleak prognosis — then he wouldn't admit it or face up to it, at least not to his young wife. Whenever Billie Jean asked him about his back pain he would just say, "Damned ol' horse threw me, babe," and dismiss the issue.

It wasn't until Hank arrived in Shreveport that he began to exhibit the first signs of heart disease. Red Sovine was one to whom Hank complained of chest pains. Just as he was leaving the *Hayride* in 1949, Hank had installed Sovine as a replacement Syrup Sopper on KWKH, and Sovine was still there when Hank returned. Shortly before the marriage, Hank told him that the chest pains were so bad he sometimes couldn't sleep and couldn't get his breath at night. "We were going off to Oklahoma," says Sovine, "and he put both hands on his chest and he says, 'It feels like it's gonna bust, like it's gonna tear open. I couldn't hardly breathe last night.' "

The incontinence associated with spina bifida also began to manifest itself. Almost every night Hank would urinate on himself regardless of whether he had been drinking, and even when he was awake he had only marginal control of his bladder. "When he told you he had to go, if you were driving, you had better stop the car," says Billie Jean. "He'd say, 'Stop this thing or I'll flood the sucker.' " At the same time, the combination of pills, alcohol, and generally deteriorating physical condition had rendered Hank almost impotent. "He was doin' good if he could get it up," she says.

Nothing in Billie Jean's twenty years had prepared her for coping with this. Her brothers tried to act as Hank's minders, and they sometimes worked as his opening act as well, but, as Hank had proved throughout his life, he could outsmart anyone when he really needed a drink. He reacquired a taste for beer, perhaps because it enabled him to take in some alcohol without falling over drunk. Billie tried to keep Hank from drinking before a show, but she remembers one occasion when she came back to their hotel room after she'd been out shopping and found Hank on his hands and knees, digging under a chair. "He jumped up like I was an army sergeant and saluted. He said, 'Hot damn, baby, I was just lookin' for my shoes.' Sonny's eyes was this big, and I said, 'You've got your damn shoes on, Hank.' I looked under there, and there was two cases of beer. I took that beer and one by one I opened them and washed 'em down the drain. He said, 'Baby, just leave ol' Hank a couple. Just a couple.' "

Billie Jean and her brothers were out of their depth. They didn't understand the nature and complexity of Hank's physical disorders, and although they had been around spree drinkers all their lives they had never been around a confirmed alcoholic like Hank. Billie tried to bring compassion to the problem, but inevitably it defeated her. "Nobody ever trusted him and left him alone," she says. "That takes your manhood away. Sometimes you just had to let him do what he wanted to do. [Then] he'd say, 'Ol' Hank ain't never gonna drink no more, baby.' " It was the same promise he had made repeatedly to Audrey, but he was less capable of keeping it now than he ever had been.

Billie knew that Hank was going to drink, and she tried to keep him sober at least until show time. "Before a performance, I said, 'You go out there and put on a good show. You can't have no beer before the show, but I'll have two of the coldest ones you ever had waiting on the side of the stage.' He'd say, 'Hot damn, boys, let's pick.' That sucker, man, he'd put on a good show." Like every alcoholic, Hank would keep to his deals for a little while, holding out a glimmer of hope to those around him, then dash it. It was a pattern that had frustrated Audrey to the point where she had given up, it had frustrated Lillie for fifteen years, and it quickly frustrated Billie Jean.

Still, there were moments when everything was good. There is some grainy footage of Hank introducing Billie Jean onstage, which he did everywhere they went. Billie is winsomely shy, and the tenderness and affection apparent in the wedding photos is still there. They went on picnics and drove down to Lafayette to visit Dudley J. LeBlanc. Hank reckoned that LeBlanc still owed him the best part of ten thousand dollars from the Hadacol debacle so, when he and the senator were out drinking on the lake, Hank stripped LeBlanc's boat of everything he could take home with him.

Hank's problems in Shreveport were exacerbated by the one man he saw as his savior. Ten days before he was to fly to Montgomery to make the settlement with Bobbie Jett, Hank went to Oklahoma City for a show at the Trianon Ballroom with the *Hayride* cast. As he had told Red Sovine, his chest pains were bad before he left, and while he was there he started drinking. A member of the *Hayride* called someone who was supposed to be a doctor who specialized in treating alcoholics. His name was Horace Raphol "Toby" Marshall.

According to Billie Jean, Hank went off to Oklahoma City with three thousand dollars and returned with three hundred. He told her he had spent the rest of the money for "treatment," although he probably spent some to fly to Montgomery and back. It's likely that he didn't begrudge what he had paid Marshall though, because he thought he had finally found a medical person who had walked a mile in his shoes.

The treatment that Hank received from Marshall in Oklahoma City was chloral hydrate, a new drug in his pharmacopoeia, even though it had been introduced in 1860. It was a powerful sedative (classed at the time as a "hypnotic sedative") and anti-anxiety drug that had briefly become famous three years earlier when it had been used to sedate a leopard that had got loose from the Oklahoma City zoo. Leapy the Leopard had been sighted on the lam, and some meat laced with chloral hydrate was left for him. Leapy ate it and died soon afterward from a collapsed lung, still unable to shake off the effects of the drug. Further evidence of the effects of the drug came from Billie Jean, who later testified that she had taken Hank's usual dosage, four tablets, one night. "They made me groggy and crazy as a bat," she said in testimony in 1953. "I vomited for two hours and after that felt as if I was in a drunken stupor."

Chloral hydrate was a harmful, potentially lethal, drug when combined with any central nervous system depressant, such as alcohol. It was, in fact, the drug customarily used for making Mickey Finns. The combination of chloral hydrate and alcohol had been the means by which British poet Dante Gabriel Rossetti had offed himself in 1882. Chloral hydrate was not to be prescribed for anyone with heart disease, and patients were strictly advised not to exceed the stated dose. Various manufacturers produced the drug under different names and specified that a warning be placed on the bottle saying "Overdosage May Be Fatal." If the drug didn't produce a calming or sedative effect, patients were specifically warned not to do what Hank was habituated to doing — gobble more. If he was searching for something that would numb every part of his body — perhaps for good — chloral hydrate was just the ticket.

Marshall never told everything he knew, as he often threatened to do, but if he had, it's hard to know how much credibility he would have had. "I think you better list me for the record as a pathological, constitutional liar," he said at one of his trials. Even his date of birth has never been established. The date he gave to the prison system, March 20, 1910, has been questioned.

Marshall's first taste of life behind bars was in 1938 when he was jailed for a year in San Quentin on the charge of armed robbery. After release, he became by his own admission an alcoholic. He had drinks stashed in all corners of his house, and he would drink on the way home from work, he said. In what he called an "act of desperation," he offered himself up as a guinea pig in a Yale University study of alcoholism, and he claimed to be on his way there when he got into a card game in Miami, Oklahoma, lost all his money, and was arrested for passing a forged check for five hundred dollars. He entered McAlester Penitentiary in what he called "an alcoholic-barbiturate-Seconal-bromide haze interposed with flashes of hallucinations," a self-diagnosis that Hank could relate to even if he didn't understand it.

Marshall was jailed on October 15, 1950, and paroled on October 8, 1951. After his release, he later told an inquiry, he devoted himself "as unselfishly as possible to helping others as I could." Armed with a diploma from "The Chicago University of Applied Sciences and Arts," which he had bought from a traveling salesman at a filling station for a fee variously reported as twenty-five or thirty-five dollars, Marshall set himself up as an alcoholic therapist. At first, he prescribed drugs through a qualified physician, C. W. Lemon, and when Lemon was asked in March 1953 what had brought him together with Marshall, he replied simply, "I got drunk." Later, with a forged certificate from a board of medical examiners, Marshall had some prescription pads of his own printed up.

Even so, Marshall was not without insight into the needs of an alcoholic. "A drunk," he said in jail, "as anyone knows, is most disagreeable to live with. Most wives won't do it. I made myself available to families who needed me, and often spent twenty-four to thirty-six hours at a time giving the alcoholic the attention that his family wouldn't. I'd sit there beside his bed, in a hotel room or at home, for hours. I'd be there when he woke, and I'd talk with him. I'd show him he was wanted."

This was the best news Hank Williams had received from the medical profession. Most of the doctors he had seen couldn't approach his alcoholism with anything like the empathy that Marshall could. The only recovered alcoholic Hank knew well was Fred Rose, and Hank couldn't find the strength that Rose had drawn from religion. Marshall offered a sympathetic ear, compassion, and extended hope of a cure. Hank engaged him as his personal physician at three hundred dollars a week, yet another expense that necessitated constant touring.

The pattern that Hank had established in Nashville quickly repeated itself. When he was sober, he was riveting onstage; when he was drunk, he was boorish and occasionally lucky not to be lynched. Hank even turned up drunk for some of the Hayride shows. Horace Logan would announce him, and Hank would stand in the wings shaking his head, denying he was Hank Williams. On a bus ride to a *Hayride* remote show in Texas, he quickly wore out his welcome. "He decided he'd sing," said Logan. "Kitty Wells was there, my wife was there, the Rowley Trio and other women, and Hank was singing,

> *The dirty drawers that Maggie wore*
> *They was torn and they was split*
> *You could see where she had shit.*

I said, 'Hank, shut up!' He'd apologize later."

In November, Clyde Perdue put together a package show that consisted of Hank, Claude King, Tommy Hill and his sister Goldie, and Red Sovine and his band. "He'd start a trip," said Claude King, "and he'd say, 'I ain't gonna drink a drop.' Then his back would get worse and worse, and he'd get right back into the drinking." On one occasion King remembers hearing groaning from the back of the car and he turned around to see Hank supine on the car floor writhing in pain. "He and I were the same age exactly,"* said King, "yet to me he was an old man."

In Opelousas, Louisiana, everyone in the audience demanded their money back after Hank showed up drunk, and when light broke the following morning, there was a crowd around Hank's hotel. Claude King went and got Hank's Cadillac, and the plan was to sneak him out of a trade entrance and make a dash for the county line. Hank needed a cigarette, though, and walked blithely out of the hotel carrying his valise. He saw the crowd and sat down on the sidewalk in his white western suit. He opened the case and dollar bills started blowing in the wind. Everybody started laughing, picking up the money, and Hank left promising to come back and do a make-good.

On another night in Lafayette, Hank weaved up to the microphone and said, "You all paid to see ol' Hank, didn't ya?" The crowd roared. Hank set down his guitar, said, "Well, you've seen him," and walked off. At least part of his attitude probably stemmed from the fact that he was shaping up to be the best-selling country artist of the year, yet here he was playing the high school gym in Lafayette, the very gig he had worked so hard to escape. The interceding four years had ruined his health and wrecked his marriage, and now he was broke and back where he'd started. Money mattered most to Hank because it betokened success, and now, when he stuffed the takings into his valise at the close of a show, he knew it contained a fraction of what it had a year earlier.

In late November and early December Hank made a tour of Florida and the Southeast for A. V. Bamford. He was to fly to Florida, and then the tour was to wend its way back to Louisiana along the gulf coast. Bamford had assembled the backing group, and it included Ray Edenton, later the premier rhythm guitarist in Nashville. The supporting acts included *Grand Ole Opry* mainstays Radio Dot and Smokey (Swan). Hank was more or less sober for the entire trip, and talking positively. Bamford remembered later that Hank was complaining of chest pains, but he was sufficiently encouraged by his performance to offer him two prize engagements, New Year's Eve in Charleston, West Virginia, and New Year's Day in Canton, Ohio. Hank accepted.

The trip had a rough start. Hank and Billie had flown to Pensacola.

* Most reference books give Claude King's date of birth as February 5, 1933, but it was Tillman Franks, who managed King between 1960 and 1962, who made him ten years younger for publicity purposes.

They thought that she was pregnant, and Hank was overjoyed and vowing to remain sober. Often feeling weak and diminished as a man, Hank seemed to place inordinate emphasis on planting his seed and leaving behind something of himself. As he and Billie flew over the Gulf of Mexico, Hank took the controls for a while, but the plane began running low on fuel while they were still over water. It was touch and go whether they would make it to Pensacola, and Billie was panicking. The next morning in the hotel, she awoke in a pool of blood. She had either started her period or the shock had caused her to miscarry. Hank was sent to buy Kotex, but he stopped off in the hotel bar and it was several hours before he reappeared.

Hank took Billie Jean to see Pappy Neal McCormick in Pensacola. They went out to the Diamond Horseshoe; Pappy Neal played steel guitar, Hank sang a few songs — and got jealous as he saw Billie Jean with another man on the dance floor. That night, Hank and Billie stayed at the San Carlos Hotel, where Hank had holed up ten years earlier when he was drinking and trying to escape from Lillie. Memories were everywhere. He asked Pappy Neal to come to Shreveport to lead his band in January; it was an almost blanket invitation he extended to his old pals. McCormick said he would.

After a week or more of sobriety on the Bamford tour, Hank returned to Shreveport and went on a tear. Billie Jean and her brothers had him committed to the North Louisiana Sanatorium on December 11, but he got out early in the afternoon and found his way downtown to resume his binge. At 4:30 P.M. he was arrested after a complaint from a restaurant owner about a "drunk in front of my place." The arresting officer said that Hank had insisted that he shouldn't have to go to jail, but he was hauled off on charges of being drunk and disorderly. He was dressed that afternoon in a blue serge suit and a green hat with a big feather, and he was carrying a .38 revolver. Billie Jean and Sonny went to get him out of jail at 9:45 in the evening and took him back to the North Louisiana Sanatorium.

Two days later, December 13, Hank played the *Louisiana Hayride*. Right after the show, he and his personal retinue, together with Tommy and Goldie Hill and Billy Walker, lit out for Houston to start a one-week swing through eastern Texas. Hank had hired a cowboy singer, Al Rogers, to work the first few dates with him and 4-Star recording artist Charlie Adams to work the final dates. After the nonsense of the previous week, Billie Jean opted not to go. As Hank left town heading toward eastern Texas, it must have been with an overwhelming sense of *déjà vu*.

Hank was due to play Cook's Hoedown club on Sunday night. Tommy and Goldie were going on to San Antonio and arranged to drop Hank off at the Rice Hotel. On the way down, they heard a strange groan from the back, and saw Hank slumped forward, his head between his legs. He had stopped breathing. Tommy quickly pulled the car over and they got Hank out and walked him around until he got his breath back.

Later that week, Tommy saw the lethal combination of heavy-duty barbiturates and alcohol with which Hank was dosing himself. He also saw how Perdue and Marshall had worked out a procedure that would enable their meal ticket to make the show, but at a terrible cost. Hank was allowed a few beers after he woke up, then Marshall injected him with a drug that made him vomit up the beer. Then they would pour black coffee down him, hand him some Dexedrine tablets and point him toward the stage. After the show, he'd be allowed some more beers and put back to bed with some downers.

The Texas tour didn't start well. Cook's Hoedown was sold out, but Hank was nowhere to be seen. Around five in the afternoon, Cook phoned the booker, Warren Stark, in Austin and told him to "get his ass down to Houston" and find Hank. Stark told Cook that he couldn't get down to Houston in time to find Hank, but they should check the jail, then the hotels. They eventually found Hank at a hotel, got some of Toby Marshall's shots into him, and hauled him onstage.

Sergeant F. D. McMurry, who had booked Hank into the police benefit show in Beaumont at the end of September came to Cook's to see Hank. "They booed him off," said McMurry. "I met him backstage. He said, 'Man, they're killin' me, they're killin' me. They're workin' me to death.' He was all hopped up on those durn things. I said, 'Hank, they booed you offstage. Let's get you straight.' I put four cups of coffee in him, and he tried it again and they booed him off again. It just broke my heart." Some distant cousins of Hank's were also there that night. He was suffering ungodly back pain they said, and drinking heavily. They tried to get him to rest up at their house, but he insisted that he had to carry on. Hank called Billie Jean from Houston and told her that he had never been sicker. Marshall was giving him shots every hour, he said.

In Victoria, Texas, on Tuesday, Hank overdosed or had a heart attack. He couldn't make the show, and Clyde Perdue panicked. He phoned Montgomery to get Lillie down to take care of Hank. She flew in and rode with them the remainder of the tour. Hank began coming around. He was due to play the Sportatorium in Dallas on Wednesday, and he ran into Ray Price on the street. Price's version of "Don't Let the Stars Get in Your

Eyes" was starting to show up in several markets, and Hank started singing it as he went toward him. Price invited Hank to spend Christmas
with him and his mother, but Hank said he wasn't certain what he was
doing. They agreed to meet in Ohio right after their New Year's dates. As
ever when he met someone in the business, particularly someone from
Nashville, Hank tried to be upbeat. "I'll be back with you before you
know it," he told Price. After the show at the Sportatorium, Hank, Toby
Marshall, and Warren Stark went out to see Bob Wills play.

From Dallas Hank and Stark drove to Austin, and the following night
Stark drove Hank to a Thursday-night gig at a beer hall in Snook, Texas.
The last date on the tour was on Friday, December 19 at Stark's Skyline
Club in Austin. Lillie sat with Stark during the show and asked him to
take over Hank's bookings after Christmas. Stark said he would. On the
drive to Snook, Stark had been griping to Hank about his showing up
drunk, and Hank had told him what he told everyone else, knowing it
was false: People hadn't come to see him. The crowd had just showed up
for a night out, and if anyone wanted their money back they should get it
back and he'd make it good to the promoter. Stark told him he couldn't
do business like that.

Hank had first appeared at the Skyline as a young *Hayride* hopeful.
Horace Logan had called in a few favors to get him on the bill. Hank had
mesmerized the crowd that night, but four years later, he was a pitiful
sight. He was disheveled, his nose ran constantly from a cold he'd had
for weeks and couldn't shake, and he was sweating profusely. He'd lost
all pride in his appearance, and, from what was unsaid as much as what
was said, he gave the impression that he simply didn't care any more.
His show was no sad last hurrah, though.

Without much advertising, the Starks had sold out the date, then
oversold it. Usually, the Skyline's maximum capacity was around eight
hundred, but people were lining the walls, and the Starks were hoping
that the fire marshal wasn't one of them. Tommy Hill remembers the
show vividly:

> I went out and did a fiddle tune. Then I brought Charlie Adams
> on and Charlie did two tunes and Hank asked me to get him off. I
> didn't know why. He said, "It's time to get Goldie on." I put
> Goldie on, and he just wanted Goldie to sing two songs, and then
> I brought Billy Walker out, and Billy did four songs, and then
> Hank said he wanted him off. Then Hank wanted to go on. The
> show started at eight o'clock, so now it was about nine, and Hank

would usually do thirty or forty-five minutes, but that night he was still singing at one o'clock. He did not quit. He put on one of the best shows I ever saw. He didn't falter a bit. He done some songs over and over. Me and Goldie have talked about it since. He sung everything he knew, even a bunch of gospel songs.

Hank did two sets, backed by Tommy Hill, steel guitarist Jimmy Day, and the Skyline house band led by Leon Carter, a distant relative of the Carter family. After the first set, Hank went back into the office to get some shots, then did another set. He was running a high temperature, sweat was running off his fingers onto the floor. Right after the show, he refused to check in to a hotel, and began the long haul back to Shreveport.

On Saturday morning, Lillie went to see Horace Logan and told him that Hank would miss the *Hayride* that night because he was sick and she was taking him back to Montgomery. "I never gave him a release," insists Logan, "because he had a three-year contract, but I gave him a leave of absence on the proviso that he would only make [the] personal appearances that A. V. Bamford had booked for him. Hank also agreed to fly in for the *Hayride*, because I was paying him two hundred a week, and he could afford to fly in on that easy — and bring Billie Jean with him."

Once again, it's hard to know if Hank saw his departure from the *Hayride* in exactly the same terms as Logan. As he and Billie packed their belongings and got back in the car, he probably just knew that he needed to break out of the cycle he was in. He left contradictory messages behind him. He had told Billy Walker that he was going to the Caribbean to take a cure, and that he was going to divorce Billie Jean, go back to Nashville, and bring Billy with him. But if Hank had intended to split from Billie Jean, he had an ideal opportunity when he went to Montgomery; as it was, she went with him. On the other hand, Hank had left Austin telling Warren Stark that he would be back in Shreveport and that Stark would act as his booking agent.

In truth, Hank probably didn't have a concerted plan of action. He was running out of goals faster than he was running out of future.

My dear old mammy's waiting with arms
outstretched so wide,
Before the sun goes down again,
I'll be right by her side,
I can wait no longer for the sun to shine,
Til I get back to my mammy, and that
Alabama home of mine.
"That Alabama Home of Mine" (Unknown)

MIDNIGHT

*H*ANK WILLIAMS was back in his old room, the front downstairs bedroom of Lillie's boardinghouse, and he was sick. He told friends who came to call that he had the Asiatic flu, but he'd had it for several weeks now and couldn't seem to shake it. Toby Marshall had prescribed antibiotics but they hadn't worked, and now Hank's back hurt terribly from the long haul through eastern Texas and back to Alabama. On December 21 Lillie phoned Marshall, who wired a prescription for twenty-four capsules of chloral hydrate the following day. Billie Jean had it delivered by Walgreen's, and the prescription was refilled again within the week.

Clyde Perdue had been let go as Hank's two-car convoy swept through Greenville. "I told Hank all the time," said Billie, " 'You don't need him. He don't book you. The agents are calling you. If you decide to play, you can call the agents and they'll book you.' " So now Hank, who was in line to be the best-selling country artist of 1952, was without a manager, without a band, and, as far as is known, with few firm commitments other than the two dates for Bamford on New Year's Eve and New Year's Day. When Brack Schuffert came to visit, Hank told him that he was booked solid until May, but the only contract to surface was for a date in Oklahoma City on February 22 — and that had been agreed back in October. Hank seemed to be telling different things to different people, trying to maintain the impression that everything was rosy.

Braxton was still working at Hormel Meats, and Freddy Beach's wife,

Irella, worked there too in the baking room. Hank was invited to the Christmas party and was supposed to sing, but he was too sick. "I went up to get him," says Braxton. "He was laying in bed with his clothes on. He was sick in bed and Doctor Stokes had come out. He had a fever. Doctor Stokes tried to get him in the hospital, but he wouldn't go."

Hank's peace of mind could not have been improved much by the knowledge that Bobbie Jett was holed up in another of Lillie's boarding-houses just days away from giving birth. It's hard to know what Billie Jean knew of this. If she knew anything, it wouldn't have improved her disposition. Simply being confined with Lillie was close enough to pur-gatory for her. The two had fallen out when Lillie had demanded money for another boardinghouse from Hank, and Billie had vetoed the deal.

Then, as Christmas neared, Hank's thoughts kept drifting back to Nashville and his young son, now three and a half years old. Audrey may have brought Hank Jr. to Shreveport in October, but it's likelier that Hank hadn't seen his son since he left Nashville. He and Billie had had a fight after he bought Hank Jr. a toy and sent it to him. He must have wondered if his life could have been more of a mess.

Shortly before Christmas, Hank rallied a little and went down to Georgiana to show off Billie to his kin. Taft and Erleen Skipper owned a country store, and Hank sat outside with Taft in the wan December sun-light. Billie made a deep impression on the Skippers, not only because of her striking looks but also for her willingness to pitch in and help with the cooking and the washing-up. The Skippers held this up in stark con-trast with Audrey who, when Hank was visiting, wouldn't get out of the car unless it was to sit on the porch. Hank and Taft walked down to the pond. "We were going back to the house," said Taft, "and he got short-winded and he says, 'Taft, I believe I picked up asthma somewhere,' and he kinda felt toward his heart. We got up to the store and sat down and he said, 'That kinda makes me short-winded. I gotta get out and get a little more exercise.' " Hank showed Taft a cashier's check for four thou-sand dollars, and told him it was all the money he had in the world, although it was probably all the money he had on him.

On Christmas Eve, Hank and Billie went to church with the Skip-pers, but Hank wouldn't stand up front and sing. Later, though, he played the Skippers a song he said he'd just written called "The Log Train." Set in Chapman, it was in traditional ballad form, starting au-thentically with "If you will listen, a song I will sing . . ." It was a pre-dictably skimpy account of Lon's days as an engineer, and the fact that it survived on acetate meant that it had been kicking around longer than Hank let on, although just how long is unclear.

Hank and Billie stayed overnight with the Skippers, and on Christmas morning they drove on to McWilliams to see Lon, Ola, and Leila. Lon didn't have a phone, so Hank couldn't call ahead, and when he got there he found that Lon and his family had gone to Selma for Christmas. Hank scratched out a note and left a gift-wrapped five-pound box of candy on the back porch. This deeply affected Lon. He hung on to the wrapping paper for years, and refused to leave the house in case someone was coming to see him whom he would never see again. Hank drove on to see Lon's sister, his aunt Bertha, in Pine Apple and had Christmas supper with her and her family, and then he and Billie drove back to Montgomery.

On December 27, Hank and Billie went to see the Blue and Gray football game, but their seats were high in the stands and caught the wind. Hank felt chilled. Taft Skipper and his niece Mary were there too; they offered Hank their seats lower down out of the wind, but Hank refused, and he and Billie left before the end of the first half and went back to Lillie's.

It's almost certain that Hank made some contact, probably by phone, with Jim Denny at WSM over Christmas, although exactly what promises, if any, were exchanged is unclear. Billie said that she was supposed to meet Hank in Nashville on January 3, 1953, but, as she said much later, Hank was unpredictable. "He'd decide tonight, 'Hey, baby, let's us move to Nashville and buy one of them big houses.' " He claimed to have a piece of land picked out near Carl Smith's ranch in Williamson County, but it was probably another of the pipe dreams that were increasingly preferable to the reality of what life had become. It's likelier that he would have gone back to Montgomery. He had told his cousin Marie Harvell, who managed one of the boardinghouses, that he'd be back in four days. Lillie expected him back, and he almost certainly wanted to see Bobbie Jett's child as well.

Hank was spinning yarns everywhere he went. Horace Logan, Billy Walker, A. V. Bamford, Billie Jean, Audrey, Pappy McCormick, Wesley Rose, Warren Stark, and others all claim to have been told different things by Hank. He had even promised to do a tour in January for a new Spastic Children's wing of St. Jude's Hospital in Montgomery. The Bamford shows were a golden opportunity for him, though. Bamford was based in Nashville, and he was in more or less daily contact with Denny.

The bush telegraph was telling Denny that Hank was the same old trouble he'd always been through, but Denny knew that he couldn't risk having Hank spearhead a rival jamboree in Shreveport, especially with the television market still up for grabs, so he could very well have held out an olive branch. A lot hinged on how Hank performed for Bamford.

On Sunday, December 28, Hank gave a performance for 130 members and guests of American Federation of Musicians' local 470 in Montgomery at their eighth annual party. It was held that year to benefit a member who had been stricken with polio. Hank tucked into a steak, then got up to sing "Jambalaya," "Cold, Cold Heart," "You Win Again," and "Lovesick Blues." A newspaper report the following day described him as a "thin, tired looking ex-country boy with a guitar."

Over Christmas, the rumor started that Hank had sent Billie Jean back to Shreveport and that he was finished with her. The primary source of the rumor was Lillie. There's no doubt that Hank and Billie fought in Montgomery — they fought everywhere, just as Hank and Audrey had done. The tension went from simmer to boil several times as Hank continued his pattern of screwing up whenever he had a chance. Irella Beach says that she saw Hank and Billie at a bar. "Hank was up on the counter dancin' or something," she says, "and he hit Billie Jean in the face 'cause she was trying to get him to quit [it]. He was sloppy drunk, and she took off home. She said, 'Ain't no man gonna beat on me,' and she left."

Like almost everything to do with Hank Williams, his relationship with Billie has usually been viewed through the wrong end of the telescope. Hindsight tells us that Hank was the greatest star country music has ever known, a prize for any woman, but in December 1952, he was a falling star hanging on by a thread. Even if he kept his hit streak intact, he had a very uncertain future, physically and professionally, and he must have seemed sometimes more booby prize than prize. How close Billie was to the end of her tether during the ten days in Montgomery is unknown. "We wondered how Billie Jean could put up with him at all," said Horace Logan. "Falling down drunk, throwing up drunk, throwing up on himself." Billie had more reason to walk out on Hank than he had reason to put her on a plane back home. She was twenty years old; Hank was only twenty-nine but he sang like, and had the physical attributes of, a man twice that age. Was this what Billie Jean wanted from her life? In interviews later, she would have you think it was, but disillusion was probably setting in. When she married again in September 1953, it was to

Hayride star Johnny Horton, who didn't drink, and, as she says, "had no damn in-laws to bug the hell out of me."

Both Billie and Audrey later staked out their official positions from which they never wavered. Billie's position was that she had intended to go to Ohio on a charter flight with Hank, but the weather looked so unpromising farther north that Hank had to drive, so she went back to Shreveport to spend New Year's with her family. She was to meet Hank in Nashville on January 3. Audrey insisted that Hank called over Christmas and asked if he could come back, and she had said he could. Had she forgotten so quickly everything that she had spelled out in such petulant detail in her divorce petition? Had she received news from Shreveport telling her that Hank Williams was now straight and a joy to spend each day with?

On December 29, Hank started to make arrangements for the long haul to West Virginia and for the birth of Bobbie Jett's child. He prepaid Dr. Stokes to deliver the child, and left fifty dollars with Marie Harvell to take care of expenses. First he asked Braxton Schuffert to drive him, but Brack had to be back at work at Hormel. Then he asked several other friends, but they all had day jobs they couldn't walk out on, so he went down to the Lee Street Taxi company. The owner, Daniel Pitts Carr, had a son, Charles, a freshman at Auburn University who was home for the holiday season. He was eighteen years old and he'd driven Hank before. Hank had formed the opinion that he drove a bit recklessly, but he was starting to look like the only game in town.

Billie Jean's insistence that she was with Hank on his last night in Montgomery is borne out by Charles Carr, who remembers that on the morning they left, she wanted to go along, but Hank wouldn't let her. "He was shadowboxing all that last night," says Billie:

> He went down to the chapel [at St. Jude's Hospital], and he said, "Ol' Hank needs to straighten up some things with the Man." I'd say, "Hank, what in the world is the matter with you?" He'd say, "Every time I close my eyes, I see Jesus coming down the road." He couldn't even sleep in bed then, the pain was so bad. When he left he was looking at me kinda funny. I said, "Hank, are you sick?" He said, "No, babe, ol' Hank just wants to look at you one more time."

Hank almost certainly knew he was under sentence of death — and may have known it for a long time. Ten years earlier, the rumor had circulated that he was turning to stone, perhaps because of his stiff gait. Someone remembered confronting him with the rumor one night in 1943, and, as usual, he turned it into a self-deprecating joke. The only part of him turning to stone, he said, was his head, and it had always been that way. Public denial that anything was wrong was part of Hank's armor even then. He is supposed to have voiced his premonitions shortly before he left Nashville when he told *Tennessean* reporter H. B. Teeter, "I never will live long enough for you to write a story about me." He even addressed the issue in songs like "The Angel of Death"; in one haunting and unforgettable verse he wrote of the time when "the lights all grow dim and the dark shadows creep." When one hears those words, it is impossible not to sense that Hank knew he had little time to linger.

Charles Carr arrived at the boardinghouse around 11:30 on the morning of December 30. Hank loaded his guitars, stage outfits, songbooks, photos, and records into the trunk. This meant that he couldn't make use of the customizing job he'd had done to the rear seat. When the trunk was empty, the seat could be folded back to make a bed. First Hank and Carr stopped at one of the local radio stations, and then someone talked him into going to a highway contractors convention at a local hotel. Hank stayed a while and almost certainly had a few drinks. The next stop was Dr. Stokes's office. Hank wanted a shot of morphine to quiet his back on the long haul, but Stokes smelled liquor on Hank's breath and wouldn't give him one. Hank then went down to see another doctor, who injected him and sent him on his way. At some point in the early afternoon, Hank and Charles Carr left Montgomery heading north on Highway 31 toward Birmingham. Hank was wearing his white cowboy boots, a white felt hat, a blue serge suit, and navy blue overcoat. It was raining and unseasonably cold.

At around 4:30 that afternoon, Lillie phoned Toby Marshall. She told Marshall that Hank had recently undergone a "highly upsetting emotional incident that had caused him to resume his drinking." She asked Marshall to go to Charleston, West Virginia, to minister to him, and then to go on to Canton and return with him to Montgomery. "I accepted the assignment without reservation," said Marshall in a memo he wrote a year later from his prison cell in Oklahoma.

Hank and Charles Carr didn't get very far on December 30. Contradicting what Lillie told Toby Marshall, Carr remembers Hank in good spirits, singing a few songs along the way. They stopped in Birmingham and tried to get a room at the Tutwiler, the premier hotel in the city, but Carr, who had pulled a U-turn and parked illegally near the hotel, was pulled over by the police. Hank told Carr to remind the officer whom he was driving for, but that didn't seem to carry as much clout in Birmingham as it did in Montgomery, and Carr was told to move along. They drove to the Redmont and took a room there instead.

Within thirty minutes of Hank's checking in to the Redmont, three women had invited themselves into his room. Hank asked one of them where she was from, and she said, "Heaven." "Well," Hank said, "in that case, you're the very reason I'm goin' to Hell." The women eventually left, and Carr ordered two meals from room service.

They started early the following morning, heading northeast, and had breakfast and a shave at Fort Payne. Hank was sitting in the front seat with Carr, and he asked his young driver what he thought of "Jambalaya." Carr said he didn't much care for it because it seemed a little nonsensical. "That's 'cause you don't understand French," said Hank. Carr told him he had studied French in school. Hank just said, "Awww." Then he started singing a few songs; the last that Carr remembers was Red Foley's hit "Midnight." "Red would like that," said Hank.

By this point, Hank probably realized that he was running late and was going to be lucky to walk in the door at show time in Charleston. By the time they got to Chattanooga, it was snowing, and when they got to Knoxville Hank knew that the only way he could get to Charleston was by plane. They arrived late in the morning and found that there was a flight out at 3:30 P.M. Around 11:00 A.M. Hank told Carr to phone Cas Walker at WNOX and tell him that he would make an appearance on the *Mid-Day Merry-Go-Round*, but he never showed.

They left the car at the airport and caught the flight out at 3:30, but it was turned around because of bad weather, and they landed back in Knoxville a few minutes before 6:00 P.M. The Charleston show was now a write-off, so Carr booked Hank and himself into the Andrew Johnson Hotel in Knoxville at 7:08 P.M. The assistant manager, Dan McCrary, didn't see Hank and noted later that Carr appeared nervous. Hank had apparently bought himself some liquor somewhere along the way, and had probably been sipping, although Carr insists that Hank didn't drink on the plane. Two porters carried him up to his room. Carr ordered two steaks, and Hank ate a little. He lay on the bed fully clothed, and later fell onto the floor.

Later, in testimony, Toby Marshall implied that he had been contacted from Knoxville, and that he had instructed the hotel clerk to have a doctor examine Hank. Carr had called down to the front desk for a doctor because Hank had chronic hiccups that were sending his body

into mild convulsions. A Dr. P. H. Cardwell went to see him. He administered two shots of morphine mixed with vitamin B_{12} for the hiccups.
Cardwell apparently declared Hank fit for travel and told Charles Carr he
could proceed. The rumor persists, though, that Hank actually received
shots on two occasions that day. Murray Nash says that a nurse at St.
Mary's Hospital remembered Hank going in to get a shot from his
"usual" doctor in Knoxville, who was at the hospital to deliver a baby.

Carr also phoned A. V. Bamford to notify him that Hank couldn't
make the Charleston show, so Bamford told him to make sure that Hank
got to Canton. It would have made sense to leave early in the morning
rather than drive overnight in bad weather, and it's still unclear why they
left that night. One possibility is that Bamford wanted to give Toby Marshall some time to sober up Hank. Marshall had arrived in Charleston
and later drove on to Canton with Bamford. The matinee was at 2:00 P.M.
on January 1, and Marshall might have thought that he needed several
hours to get Hank in shape to perform. Hank was to be the headliner with
Homer and Jethro, Hawkshaw Hawkins, and Autry Inman in support.
More than four thousand tickets had been sold at $2.50 each, and Bam-
ford knew he would have a lawsuit on his desk from the local promoter,
LCL Productions, if Hank showed up drunk.

Porters carried Hank downstairs, bundled him into the back seat of
his car and laid his overcoat and a blanket on him. They noted that he
seemed to be lifeless, although he twice made a coughing sound. It was
10:45 P.M. when Carr set off from Knoxville. He had been traveling since
early that morning, and now the man whose care had been entrusted to
him was pallid and turning to stone. An hour after leaving Knoxville, he
was stopped near Blaine, Tennessee, by patrolman Swan H. Kitts, who
was from Roy Acuff's and Carl Smith's hometown, Maynardville. Carr
had pulled out to pass and had almost hit Kitts's patrol car head-on.

It is from Kitts's account that we have much of our knowledge of
Hank's last hours, and it was Kitts's opinion that it was already midnight
for Hank when he stopped Carr for speeding and dangerous driving. "I
seen him back there and I asked the driver about him — if anything was
wrong," said Kitts. "The driver said, 'No, he's been drinking a beer and
the doctor gave him a sedative.' I remember I said, 'He's not dead, is
he?' " Carr replied that he wasn't, but Kitts had his doubts. He had seen a
few dead men and Hank looked like one of them, but he didn't press the
matter when Carr asked him not to wake Hank.

Carr followed Kitts into Rutledge, Tennessee, where he was ar-
raigned before Justice of the Peace O. H. Marshall, tried, convicted, and

fined twenty-five dollars with costs. Hank's condition was mentioned to Marshall and Sheriff J. N. Antrican, but once again they bought Carr's story that Hank had been given a sedative and shouldn't be disturbed. Carr denies that he went outside and reached into Hank's back pocket to pay the fine, but says that he paid the fine out of his own pocket, intending to get the money back from Hank.

Hank was pale blue and immobile at 11:45 P.M. Life had probably slipped from him somewhere between Knoxville and Blaine, perhaps in Knoxville. He had died from the combined effects of alcohol, an undetermined number of morphine shots, and chloral hydrate, a combination that was destined to kill him from the time he first started mixing them two months earlier. His heart was ailing, his general condition was poor, and the effect of chloral hydrate on the central nervous system combined with other central nervous system depressants, like alcohol and morphine, almost certainly induced a respiratory depression much like the one he had suffered on the way to Houston two weeks earlier, and much like the one brought on by Elvis Presley's polypharmacy twenty-five years later.

Kitts was the first to voice the conclusion that Hank had possibly died in Knoxville. A dead man, he said, will often make a coughing sound if he is moved right after he has died, and that would be consistent with the coughs that Hank gave when he was moved to the car in Knoxville. Whether out of confusion or some other motive, Carr has always vigorously denied that.

It was 1:00 A.M. when Carr left Rutledge and carried on with his eerie journey. He was now a very apprehensive and nervous young man, tired to the point where his mind was reeling. What had seemed like a dream job that would pay most of the next semester's tuition had turned sickeningly wrong and was now a nightmare. By the time they reached Bristol, Tennessee, Carr had been traveling for almost twenty-four hours. He stopped to take on a relief driver, Donald Surface, from a local taxi company, and the two carried on toward Canton.

Before his death, Surface apparently told the story of how Hank Williams came into the diner where the cabbies hung out and asked if anyone could share the drive to Canton. It was almost certainly Carr whom Surface saw, though. Carr later claimed that he spoke to Hank in Bristol, but that doesn't seem consistent with his condition earlier that night or with the fact that rigor mortis had set in a hundred miles farther on.

The investigating officer in Oak Hill said later that Carr and Surface told him that they had pulled over at the Skyline drive-in movie theater just outside Oak Hill, checked on Hank, found him cold and lifeless, and drove into Oak Hill in search of a hospital, stopping at a Pure Oil station on the edge of town.

This account was challenged by Carr, who maintains that he paid off Donald Surface somewhere in West Virginia, perhaps at Bluefield or Princeton, where he stopped for coffee, and that he drove on to a gas station a few miles outside Oak Hill. Then Carr noticed that the blanket and coat had slipped from Hank. He was lying on his back, his arms crossed in a V on his chest. Carr pulled the blanket over Hank's hand, then noticed that the hand was stiff and sprang back.

Carr's account of how he discovered Hank dead outside Oak Hill is also challenged by Dr. Leo Killorn, a Canadian intern at Beckley hospital, West Virginia, fifteen miles down the road from Oak Hill, who claims that Carr drove up to the hospital and asked him to come take a look at a man in the back seat. Killorn said that the fact that Carr told him it was Hank Williams caused him to remember the incident. Killorn told Carr that Hank was most assuredly dead but that there was no coroner on duty, so he should drive on to Oak Hill. It was around 5:30 A.M. when Carr arrived in Oak Hill, the town where Hank Williams is usually assumed to have died.

According to the police account from Oak Hill, Carr and Surface pulled into the Burdette's Pure Oil station and told Burdette that there was a problem. Burdette called the police, and the duty officer, Howard Jamey, came down to the service station and was directed to Hank's limo across the road. Jamey told Carr that Hank was dead, and ordered him to follow the cruiser to the hospital. Carr denies all this, insisting that he drove straight to the hospital from the filling station six miles outside town.

At Oak Hill Hospital, two orderlies picked Hank up by his armpits and his feet and carried him into Emergency. An Italian intern, Dr. Diego Nunnari, pronounced Hank dead around 7:00 A.M. on January 1, 1953. Nunnari said that he couldn't tell how long Hank had been dead, but it could have been around six hours. Carr says that he went into the hospital lobby and phoned his father. Then he said he phoned Lillie, who didn't seem overly surprised. "Don't let anything happen to the car," she told him. She knew the vultures would be out. She was right — and she was one of them.

Carr was now reeling from exhaustion, and, according to the police reports, nervous enough to invite suspicion that foul play had been involved in Hank's death. A welt on Hank's head convinced local magistrate Virgil F. Lyons that an inquest should be convened. Hank was taken to the Tyree Funeral Home, where an autopsy was done. Tyree's assistant Jim Alexander took blood from him. They noted the needle marks on his arms. A corked bottle of blood together with a package of some internal organs was handed to a state trooper, Ted Anderson, with the instruction that they be taken to Charleston for analysis. Anderson looked at the bottle, turned green, and walked into the broom closet. The autopsy was performed by a Russian physician, Dr. Ivan Malinin, who arrived from Beckley. Malinin, who spoke almost no English, found hemorrhages in the heart and neck and pronounced that the cause of death was insufficiency of the right ventricle of the heart, an unusual conclusion. He also found that Hank had been severely beaten and kicked in the groin recently, something that no one remembered doing in the tributes that were about to flood out.

The coroner's jury was brought into the funeral home to look at the body. They awaited the findings from both the state police laboratory in Charleston and Malinin's autopsy. Later, the jury confirmed that Hank Williams "died of a severe heart condition and hemorrhage." Traces of alcohol but no drugs were found in Hank's blood, probably because no one looked for them. The jury entered its verdict on January 10, 1953.

By then, Hank had been in the ground six days.

*Darkling I listen; and for many a time
I have been half in love with easeful death
Called him soft names in many a mused rhyme
To take into the air my quiet breath;
Now more than ever it seems rich to die
To cease upon the midnight with no pain.*
John Keats, "Song"

WUTHERING DEPTHS

"*T*HERE'S no way to describe how it feels when they tell you," says Billie Jean. "There was a person-to-person call to my dad from [West] Virginia. I thought Hank was in some kind of trouble. My daddy said, 'Oh, Lord,' and asked the driver some questions, then hung up. I was sitting up by that point. He held me and said that Hank was dead, and I was screaming and crying. I said, 'Don't let them touch him. He often pretends he's asleep.' I thought they were going to bury him alive."

Now there was a race to Hank's remains. Lillie and Daniel Carr caught a plane out of Montgomery and tried to land in Charleston, West Virginia, but the airport was still fogged in, so they went on to Roanoke, Virginia, and hired a taxi. They arrived late on the morning of January 2, 1953. By the time Billie Jean and her father arrived from Shreveport, Lillie had already stripped the body of jewelry, including Hank's wedding ring. Toby Marshall drove down from Canton bearing a bill for $736.39, which he presented to Billie Jean, then Lillie. Both refused to pay it.

Joe Tyree says that he put up Charles Carr in the employees' quarters of his funeral home, but Carr maintains that he stayed at magistrate Virgil Lyons's house. He watched the New Year's Day football games on television while his father and Lillie took care of the details surrounding Hank's return. If Donald Surface was still in the car when it got to Oak Hill, the police must have let him go, and he must have caught a bus back to Bristol. The car itself was impounded in a bay at Burdette's Pure Oil station, then moved to N&W Motors, the local Ford dealership, where it was cleaned out by one of Burdette's employees. He remembered Pabst Blue Ribbon cans littering the floor, but little else of significance.

Pete Burdette apparently stole Hank's felt hat. Burdette was an alcoholic, and he had contracted jungle rot, a fungal disease that attacks skin tissue, while he was serving in Asia during the war. When his hair fell out after he started wearing Hank's hat, it was assumed locally to be a curse, and Burdette later killed himself around the back of his filling station. The hat continued to change hands. A pearl-handled gun was also taken. Lillie, who had fought hard for each and every one of her own possessions, developed an obsession with the car and its contents, and, according to Carr, she phoned him every few weeks until she died inquiring about this or that item that she had convinced herself Hank had taken with him.

Audrey had spent New Year's Eve with A. V. Bamford's wife, Maxine, at the toney Plantation Club in Nashville. Maxine remembered that Audrey said nothing about Hank's coming back to Nashville or to her. After Bamford had canceled the show in Charleston, West Virginia, he had driven on to Canton late on New Year's Eve. He checked in to the hotel where he had arranged to meet Hank and then went to bed. Hank had hired Don Helms to work the Bamford shows with him, and Helms had driven up from Nashville with Autry Inman. The bad weather had delayed them and they arrived late in Charleston. The theater was closed by the time they got there, so they drove on to Canton a few hours behind Bamford, checking in to the hotel around 5:00 A.M. "Bam got up early," said Helms, "and Autry and I got up and went down to the auditorium. Bam met me at the dressing room door. He said, 'Brace yourself: Hank died on the way here.'"

The Bamford shows had been staged by Harry Lashinsky's LCL Presentations, and after taking a bath on the Charleston show, Lashinsky and one of his partners, Lew Platt (who later managed rock 'n' roll deejay Alan Freed), decided that the Canton show would go on. That was the way Hank would have wanted it, they decided. One of Platt's associates found Eddie Wayne, a singing deejay on WCUE, Akron, to fill out the program, and the rest of the cast was already assembled.

Everyone on the show was grouped backstage before the matinee started. Akron deejay Cliff Rodgers from WHKK went out and took the microphone to make the announcement: "Ladies and gentlemen," he said, "I've been in show business almost twenty years, and I've been called upon to do many difficult things in front of an audience, but today I'm about to perform the most difficult task I have ever done." Rodgers heard some laughter from somewhere in the crowd. "This morning on his way to Canton to do this show, Hank Williams died in his car." There were a few more laughs from people who thought it was a joke. "Ladies and gentlemen," continued Rodgers, "this is no joke. Hank Williams is dead."

Now backstage the cast could hear some weeping. Some of the cast members were crying too. A single spotlight was directed at the empty stage as the band, still behind the curtain, played "I Saw the Light." A few people in the audience sang along. Then the curtain was opened and the show began. Homer and Jethro quickly broke the solemnity. Hawkshaw Hawkins gave the performance of his life, they said, perhaps sensing that there was now an opening at the top. Ten years later, Hawkins died in the plane crash that also took the lives of Patsy Cline and Cowboy Copas.

There were a couple of strange little codas to the Canton show. At some point in the 1960s, Jim Denny's family acquired control of the Hatch Show Print company, and faked up a poster for the show. Originally Denny's poster contained the titles of several songs by Hank that hadn't even been released in January 1953, and on both old and new versions, Hank was finally a *Grand Ole Opry* artist again. The poster is still on sale, typifying the culture of misinformation that Hank has attracted since death.

Then, in 1964, when Audrey was managing Hank Jr., she scheduled a promotional tour to coincide with his first record. The first show was on January 1, 1964; the location, of course, was Canton. Eleven years later, the story was to be continued. That same year, the execrable bio-pic *Your Cheatin' Heart* premiered. In it, Audrey placed herself backstage in Canton for the fateful New Year's Day 1953 show. She was leading the weeping section. Who had once said, "You have no heart, you have no shame . . ."?

Hank's funeral was held in Montgomery on January 4, 1953, and on January 3 the locus of activity moved back there. Before she left Oak Hill, Lillie elected to have Hank's body dressed in his white stage uniform after the embalming. Then, at 4:00 P.M. on Friday, January 2, Joe Tyree and his assistant Alex Childers began the drive back to Montgomery with Hank's remains, taking turns driving nonstop. "It was raining all the way down," said Tyree, "and when we got into Alabama and we'd pull into a filling station and they'd see the West Virginia plates they'd want to know if we was carrying Hank back. They'd start peeping in the windows." Lillie, Daniel Carr, Charles Carr, and Toby Marshall drove back in Hank's limo.

Before she had left Montgomery, Lillie had called Leaborne Eads, who had helped her promote some of Hank's shows back in the late '30s and early '40s. Eads worked for the Henley Monument company and sang with The Henley Harmony Boys in one of Hank's old spots on WSFA. Lillie was very calm, Eads remembered, and gave the impression that she'd half-expected the call. While Lillie was away, Eads made arrangements for Dr. Henry Lyon to preach the funeral service assisted by the Reverend Talmadge Smith, and he secured a burial plot in Oakwood Cemetery Annex, next to the grave of Irene's first child. On Lillie's instructions, Eads ordered a top-of-the-line Wilbert Continental copper-lined hermetically sealable casket from Atlanta.

The body arrived back on Saturday, January 3. A. V. Bamford had flown from Canton to Nashville, then driven down to Montgomery with Audrey. He took over the logistics of the funeral, renting the Municipal Auditorium, making arrangements with the police and fire department to escort the cortege as it made its way to Oakwood Annex. Then he chartered a plane to bring the *Grand Ole Opry* cast down for the funeral program. No one seemed to question why *Opry* rather than *Louisiana Hayride* artists were to be used.

Billie Jean and her father had flown back to Shreveport, then on to Montgomery on Saturday night. Already there was an unseemly grab for Hank's possessions. Lillie and Audrey were looking for a sheaf of Hank's lyrics as if they were maps to buried treasure. The sheets were found in the bedroom that Billie had been using at the boardinghouse. Lillie grabbed them while Billie was in the bathroom. She handed them quickly to Bamford, who put them in the trunk of his car and gave them to Fred Rose when he appeared the following day. Nobody realized that without Hank singing them, the scribblings were fool's gold.

The tension in the boardinghouse spilled over into violence at least once on Saturday night. Billie Jean and Lillie had been assigned separate viewing times, but they met accidentally in the bathroom and started arguing and then wrestling with each other. Billie remembers climbing onto the toilet to get a better swing at Lillie. While Hank was alive, Lillie had detested Audrey with all her heart, but now they quickly made an uneasy peace as they allied to oust Billie from the picture.

Hank hadn't left a will, so, in the normal course of events, the administrator of his estate would have been Lon. With that possibility very much in her mind, Lillie had listed Lon as "Deceased" when she gave information for the death certificate in Oak Hill. However, Hank's lawyer, Robert B. Stewart, who had prepared the agreement with Bobbie Jett, knew of Lon, and, when Lon came to Montgomery for the funeral, Stewart notified him that he would be the executor of the estate. Lon agreed, but Lillie confronted him and said that she would fight a lawsuit in Hell before she would see him have it. He said he'd fought her on earth all these years and when he died he hoped to be rid of her, and she could take it. At Lillie's prompting, he called Stewart to relinquish the executorship, although when he saw the sordid squabbling that followed he came to believe he should have kept it.

Lon had hitched a ride to Montgomery on the night before the funeral, and he had five dollars in his pocket when he arrived at the boardinghouse. Hank was lying in state by then, and Braxton Schuffert was on the door screening entrants. Lon told Braxton that he wanted some flowers, so Braxton took him to Rosemont Gardens, where everyone was working late preparing floral arrangements for the funeral. "I told them, 'I got Hank Williams's daddy out here with me, and he wants y'all to make him a bouquet of flowers for his son,' " said Braxton. "They let us in. The old man said, 'I'm a poor man. I just want a five-dollar bouquet of flowers for my son.' They made him a big bouquet. His voice right then was just like Hank's."

On Sunday, Hank was buried. Crowds estimated at between 15,000 and 20,000 were outside the Municipal Auditorium; 2,750 were inside. The balcony was set aside for black mourners, of whom there were around 200. The casket was brought in at 1:00 P.M. and opened at 1:15. Hundreds filed past. The Drifting Cowboys, now reunited, stood by in a guard of honor. The casket was framed by two guitar-shaped floral arrangements, one with silver strings. Two purple lamps were in the background. A tiny, white Bible was placed in Hank's frozen hand.

At 2:30 the doors were closed. "My friends," said Dr. Lyon, "as we begin this service this afternoon, Ernest Tubb will bring us closer to the Lord as he sings 'Beyond the Sunset.' " Then a black gospel quartet, The Southwind Singers, sang "My Record Will Be There" before Dr. Lyon read from the Bible. He had told Bamford that he needed half an hour, but Bamford had told him that he had only ten minutes. Then Roy Acuff made a confused announcement before leading the singing on "I Saw the Light." Other *Opry* performers there that day included Jimmy Dickens, Carl Smith, Lew Childre, Webb Pierce, Bill Monroe, Ray Price, June Carter, and Johnnie and Jack, as well as Eddie Hill from WSM's on-air staff.

Tears were on their faces, but the task was harder yet for Don Helms, who led The Drifting Cowboys. "It was the eeriest thing I ever had to do in my life," he says. "I had to stand up there and play with Hank's coffin right below me. I can never explain how I felt playing his songs for somebody else the way I played for him with him laying in his coffin."

Billie Jean had been moved up to the front row, where she sat uncomfortably close to Audrey. "Everybody wanted to sing. And did," she wrote. "For us who was hurtin', it just kept us lingering on for hours, having to sit silently looking at Hank. Cold. Still. Dreading the inevitable. . . . Dreading the coffin lid to shut because you knew you'd never see his face again." After Talmadge Smith led the congregation in prayer, Dr. Lyon introduced Red Foley and The Southwind Singers, who came forward to sing "Peace in the Valley." Foley said later that Hank had made him promise he would sing it at his funeral should he go first and Red remain. Foley's normally rich and measured baritone was cracking by the time he finished. Then Lyon gave a final, lengthy eulogy, saying that Hank's true eulogy was in his music. The Statesmen Quartet sang "Precious Memories" before the final benediction, and then the cortege moved slowly toward Oakwood Cemetery.

At the grave site, Lyon gave a rosebud to every survivor as they threw handfuls of earth on Hank's coffin. Fred Rose was one of the honorary pallbearers. Later, he sounded a more realistic note. "Whatever people say about Hank, he never hurt anybody but himself," he said. "He was his own worst enemy . . . but one thing he had — and all his friends recognized it — was loyalty. I don't give a hang whether he drank or not, I appreciate the fact he was loyal. . . . [If someone tried to bribe him away], he'd say, 'I started with Rose and I'll stay with Rose.' " Rose also threatened to sue anyone who duplicated recordings of the funeral. With so much litigation to follow, it was altogether fitting that the first threat of legal action over Hank's music was made even as he was being buried.

Horace Logan flew to Montgomery with Felton Pruett, *Hayride* guitarist Dobber Johnson, and a few others. "Acuff was talking about 'Hank's friends from the *Grand Ole Opry* . . .' " says Logan. "Jim Denny sat in front of me. He turned around and said to me, 'Logan, if Hank could raise up in his coffin, he'd look up toward the stage and say, "I told you dumb sons of bitches I could draw more dead than you could alive." ' "

It typified the ambiguity of Hank's life that his last journey wasn't quite his last. On January 17, 1953, his casket was dug up and moved. The Oakwood Annex housed Free French airmen who had been killed during training, and their remains were now disinterred and sent back to France. It was a gruesome job because they hadn't been buried in caskets, and not always in one piece. The remains of those who had no relatives to claim them in France were consolidated in one place, and this left a large plot that the cemetery owner, John Hart, sold to Lillie. On the afternoon of January 16, 1953, Leaborne Eads and a crew dug a new grave for Hank in what would become the family plot, and then, in the middle of the night, they moved Hank to the new site. Some passersby after midnight saw the lamps flickering and the coffin being moved, and the rumor quickly started that Hank had been taken from his casket, his boots taken, and his body pickled. Eads, though, insists that the casket wasn't opened.

A monument in Vermont granite, inscribed with a mawkish poem by Audrey that scans about as well as she sang, now sits atop several tons of poured concrete. Beneath that impregnable tomb lies the ol' Drifting Cowboy, almost certainly looking, according to Eads, exactly as he did on January 4, 1953, when the lid was closed on him. Perhaps the skin would have pinched a little around his nose, says Eads, adding with the undertaker's ghoulish detachment that the eyes might have popped open as well. One or both of the black, riveting Indian eyes that had burned so intensely for twenty-nine years now stare lifelessly into eternity.

Audrey began the task of rewriting history within a week of Hank's burial. It, together with her adventures in the music business, would consume the remainder of her days. "I knew he would never hurt me or anyone else," she said, all evidence — including her own — to the contrary. "The dream was good, it was true. . . . The heights of joy could not be told or even imagined of the happiness I [knew] as his wife. . . . Everything I ever wanted or could desire I found in Hank Williams." Hank might have wished for those flowers while he was living, but he might have stomped on them too. Audrey was only the first of many who found Hank so much more lovable dead.

In Nashville, Hank Williams was welcomed back in death to preside beatifically over country music. The story quickly circulated that he had gone to Nashville during the ten days he was in Montgomery to negotiate his return to the *Opry.* The *Opry* organization was as anxious to reclaim Hank in death as it had been to cast him out in life. Wesley Rose always insisted that Hank would have been brought back into the fold had he lived only another few weeks. Audrey was even more specific. He was to start back February 3, she said. Just after he remarried her.

The news of Hank's death was hardly unexpected in Nashville, and as Jerry Byrd, who had played steel guitar on "Lovesick Blues," remembers, his canonization didn't go unchallenged in private:

There was a bunch of us in the hallway at WSM on January 1. George Morgan, Ken Marvin, Jim Denny, and me. Jim Denny said, "We'll never see his likes again." I said, "I hope not." Everybody looked at me like I'd blasphemed, and I said, "You're trying to put a halo on him that won't fit." He had a great chance and he blew it. He did as much to hurt country music as he did to help it — doing shows drunk as hell and insulting the audience. Everyone forgets that. They have short memories.

George Morgan, who had been the butt of some of Hank's arrogance, broke the awkward silence. "I'm with Byrd," he said.

Out on Long Island, Frank Walker composed a letter to Hank addressed "c/o Songwriter's Paradise." Unctuous and oily, Walker started by saying that he always enjoyed writing to Hank on New Year's Day, although the only letter anyone ever found was a curt reply to Audrey, who had called inquiring where the year-end royalty statements were. "An hour or so ago," Walker wrote, "I received a phone call from Nashville. It was a rather sad call too, for it told me that you had died early this morning. . . . I think HE wanted to have you just a bit closer to HIM. Nashville's pretty far away, so HE just sent word this morning, Hank, that HE wanted you with HIM. . . . You'll be writing for the greatest singers too, the Angels, they're so wonderful — I know they'll want you to join them."

Then a voice borne on a sepulchral breeze spoke to Walker: "When the plant reopens tomorrow," it said, "take records by all other artists off the presses, lay on an extra shift, and press only Hank Williams records; this is the opportunity of your lifetime." Walker heeded the voice and reaped the rewards. "Honestly," Walker had said in his letter, "I'm not too unhappy, for I must rejoice with you at the tremendous opportunity you will have to do good for others." How true, how true. His old man's folly was that to the end of his presidency at MGM, he would sign average, occasionally above-average, country singers, believing them to be the next Hank Williams.

Shortly after Toby Marshall got back to Oklahoma City, he was unmasked. His wife, Fay, died in mysterious circumstances on March 8, 1953, and an investigation was launched. Lots of damaging innuendoes were heard, but in the end Marshall could be indicted for nothing more serious than parole violation. Before he was arrested, he contacted Billie Jean once again for payment, intimating that he knew things that could prove very valuable to her in the legal battles ahead. Then, while he was serving out his time, he claimed to have written a 272-page book detailing all that Hank Williams told him during their sessions.

Marshall's manuscript has never surfaced, but its thesis was almost certainly that Hank committed suicide. "It occurs to me," he said during testimony in March 1953,

> that perhaps Hank got to mulling things over in his mind, and having a very persuasive personality, he might have just talked the doctor in Knoxville out of enough stuff [barbiturates] to kick himself off. . . . He had been on a rapid decline. Most of his bookings were of the honky-tonk beer joint variety, which he simply hated. If he came to this conclusion [suicide], he still had enough prestige as a star to make a first-class production out of it. Six months from now, he might have been playing for nickels and dimes on skid row.

Marshall is the only person to have raised the specter of suicide. Many around Hank would have ruled it out, saying he had everything to live for — which, in a sense, he did. Even so, the world must have looked very different to Hank Williams when he was coming off a drunk, reeling from ceaseless back pain, soaked in his own urine, the taste of vomit still in his mouth, facing the prospect of a three-hundred-mile haul to the next beer joint, always knowing that midnight was approaching.

"He wanted to destroy the Hank Williams that was making the money that fair-weather friends and relatives were getting," said Marshall. "Although he had a multiplicity of personal problems, basically he was a very lonely person, and couldn't stand being alone. . . . He had a host of fair-weather friends, most of whom were parasites, who fawned on him, played up to him, and kept him supplied with liquor." Several of those who worked with Hank during his last year lend credence to Marshall's theory. Don Helms says that he sometimes dreaded coming into Hank's hotel room for fear that the window would be open and Hank would be gone. Whether he jumped on that final trip will forever be conjecture, though.

Suicide was almost certainly an option that occurred to Hank, but it probably wasn't a consistent idea, because he had few consistent ideas toward the end. By the time of his death, Hank had lost the focus that had driven him in 1949. One moment he felt suicidal, the next he wanted to reclaim his position at the top of the heap in Nashville. One moment he wanted to jettison Billie Jean and return to Audrey, the next he wanted to stay with Billie. He left so many contradictory messages behind him. He had lost the centeredness that had helped him achieve his success. So few years separated the intently focused Hank Williams of late 1949 and the bruised, buffeted, and directionless Hank Williams of late 1952.

Hank was buried with a haste that suggested a secret was being buried with him, and a conspiracy theory could still take root were it not for the fact that Hank would almost certainly have been dead within weeks or months anyway.

Bobbie Jett was a name on nobody's lips during the lying-in-state, the funeral, or its immediate aftermath. She was in Montgomery all that time, but whether she viewed the body or attended the funeral is unknown. Two days after Hank was buried, she gave birth to a daughter who, by the terms of the prebirth agreement, was offered up for adoption to Lillie. Bobbie gave the child the name Antha (her mother's name) Belle (her grandmother's name) Jett. After adoption, she became Cathy (a name Lillie picked from her favorite book, *Wuthering Heights*) Yvonne (from "Jambalaya") Stone.

On January 28, Lillie attended a hearing at the Montgomery County Department of Public Welfare. Lillie stated that the child was left at her house when she had gone back to Butler County, presumably to see friends and family. She told the Public Welfare officers that the child was Hank's and that she would be willing to adopt her because "this was what her son would want her to do, and he once commented that he did feel that Miss Jett was not a suitable person to take care of the child." Lillie seemed quite devoted to the child, according to the report, and wanted to keep her because she would help her feel closer to Hank. Already, though, Lillie had been diagnosed as suffering from heart disease, and her fitness to adopt was questioned.

The possibility that Hank's sister, Irene, might adopt the child was raised, but in a letter to Robert Stewart dated April 6, 1953, Irene's attitude was clear: "Tee [Irene's husband] says that if she [Lillie] adopts it and then can't take care of it, he is not going to let me take it. Keep this under your hat, mabey [sic] it will never be necessary for me to have the child at all. I feel that the poor child would have a better chance in life if it were adopted by someone that would never know its origin at all."

Irene expressed the hope that the child would help Lillie live to be a hundred, but in fact Lillie died in her sleep less than two years later on February 26, 1955. Marie Harvell found her the following morning. Cathy was placed up for adoption later in 1955. In a meeting with the Department of Public Welfare, Robert Stewart gave an indication of Irene's thinking on the matter. Irene would be in Montgomery for Hank Williams Day parades and the like, said Stewart, and "she could just hear the tongues wagging now when Cathy would ride down the street." Lillie had divorced Bill Stone in April 1954, but he was still the adoptive father and he was called upon to sign the papers necessary to put Cathy up for readoption. The matter remained on a back burner for many years, always an unresolved loose end at legal junctures. Still, it was the dogged persistence of Cathy herself as an adult, aided by her husband, Keith Adkinson, that brought her lineage into the open, paving the way for her to challenge the estate for a share. On April 17, 1974, before Cathy began her quest, Bobbie Jett died in California, leaving only the vaguest intimations that she had once been involved with Hank Williams.

Audrey's share of the estate was never contested, but the other half was up for grabs. The thought that Billie Jean would collect it prompted Audrey and Lillie to become strange bedfellows and act with a commonality of interest for the first time. On one level, they had a case; they had suffered Hank for nine and twenty-nine years, respectively, whereas Billie Jean had been in the picture only three months. Very quickly, Audrey and Lillie played their trump: somehow they discovered that Billie's divorce wasn't final when she married Hank; Audrey conveniently forgot that hers hadn't been either.

Billie's divorce from Harrison Eshliman hadn't been finalized as planned at a hearing on October 17, 1952, and the final annulment didn't take place until October 28, ten days after the wedding. Apparently, Billie's father was notified on several occasions that the divorce hadn't been finalized and that Billie would have to marry Hank a fourth time if it was to be a legal marriage, but it was a loose end that Hank and Billie never got around to tying up.

"If it was left to Audrey and me, we could work this thing out on friendly terms," said Billie Jean, striking an unusually conciliatory note a week after Hank died. "I don't want to fight over Hank's estate. He wouldn't have wanted it that way." Very soon, what Hank would or would not have wanted was irrelevant. Money was involved. Big, big money.

"Kaw-Liga" was the best-selling country record of 1953. The flip side, "Your Cheatin' Heart," also became a top-seller. Ironically, because the single wasn't released until January 30, 1953 — a month after Hank died, he almost certainly never performed onstage "Your Cheatin' Heart," the very song that came to define him as the singer of his own patently real songs.

It wasn't just "Kaw-Liga" and "Your Cheatin' Heart" that were selling, though. Hank's entire catalog was moving in unprecedented quantities. Two albums were on the shelves by March, the *Memorial Album* and *Hank Williams as Luke the Drifter* (the secret not a secret anymore). Within ten weeks of his death, Hank had as many albums on the market as he did all the years he had lived; hundreds more would follow. The oil well that Hank Williams became in death was starting to gush.

"I had youth, but no knowledge," Billie concludes today. She was trying to stay busy by volunteering at the V.A. Hospital, when two weeks after Hank's death Paul Howard called her. Howard was the bandleader who had arranged for Hank and Billie's Minden marriage. "He asked me if I could sing, and I said I'd been singing all my life in churches and at the officers' club. Paul said, 'G-o-o-o-d, because I'm fixing to make us a lot of money.' He rented a costume and took a picture of me with a hat on. We were making two thousand dollars or more a night not counting pictures. We could have sold as many pictures as we had. I was sending money home every day." At the same time, Audrey had put together an all-girl band, The Drifting Cowgirls, and Bamford began booking her out on show dates.

For several months there were two "Mrs. Hank Williams" on the road invoking Hank's memory and singing his songs. Sometimes they played at competing parks in Pennsylvania and Ohio. It was a situation that couldn't last, and in August 1953 Lillie's and Audrey's lawyers reached an agreement with Billie's lawyers on a buyout. For thirty thousand dollars, Billie signed away her rights. It was a sum that barely paid off the debt load of her next husband, Johnny Horton, whom she married a month later. Horton was a man who made Hank look like a model of fiscal probity.

It wasn't until the early '70s, when Hank's copyrights started coming up for their twenty-eight-year renewal, that a friend of Billie's put the word in her ear that she hadn't signed away the rights to the renewals because she couldn't have signed away what she didn't have. She found a music publisher willing to act on her behalf, and, in a complex and seemingly endless series of legal battles in which the legality of her marriage and the manner of her portrayal in *Your Cheatin' Heart* were also raised, Billie won 50 percent of the renewals. Judgment in her favor was rendered on October 22, 1975; on November 4, Audrey died, ostensibly of heart failure. She had lived her last years in a pharmaceutical and alcoholic daze as if in fulfillment of the prophecy Hank had made: "You'll walk the floor the way I do . . ."

The only person to remain above the squabbles with a modicum of dignity intact was Lon. He continued to live in McWilliams. He and Ola ran a store for a while; he fixed fences and spliced cable. After Lillie died, he didn't challenge Irene's right to become the administrator. He died at age seventy-eight, on October 22, 1970, and wasn't buried in the family plot that bore his name.

Anyone who dies as young as Hank invites endless "What if . . . ?" speculation. It has been an item of faith in country music circles that Hank would have had a rosy future if only he had lived. The reality might have been a little different. It's doubtful that he could have saved himself even if he had rested up in Shreveport or Montgomery, concentrated on songwriting, and made just short tours as he had once intended. Too many of his self-destructive behaviors were hard-wired. The spinal pain was irremediable, and the physical damage already done to his heart and perhaps his liver and other organs was irreversible. "He didn't have a chance," concluded Oscar Davis, who had seen the contrast between the Hank Williams of early 1949 and the Hank Williams of late 1952, "[but] I think he died happy [because] he proved to the world he was somebody." Whether that was as much a consolation to Hank at the last as Davis thought is far from certain.

Before two years were up, Hank would have encountered at least one major hurdle — the loss of his quality-control department. Fred Rose died on December 1, 1954. He had clearly been suffering from heart disease for several months, and had once suffered a heart attack in the recording studio, but his Christian Science beliefs prevented him from seeing a doctor. After Fred's death, Wesley Rose assumed total control and began to fancy himself a music man, but he could never have sat with Hank, as Fred had done, helping him polish those diamonds in the rough.

Even less could Wesley have helped Hank weather the upset triggered by rock 'n' roll. Seven months after Fred Rose died, an Elvis Presley record nudged its way into the country charts, signaling a wind of change in which the hard and fast borders between pop, country, and rhythm 'n' blues began to dissolve a little, and a new music aimed specifically at teenagers sprouted. In perhaps the most ludicrous statement he ever made, Wesley Rose said, "[If Hank had lived], I don't think we would have had a rock era." His contention was that rock 'n' roll filled the void left by Hank's death.

No one person could have arrested the social, economic, and musical elements that made rock 'n' roll. If a hypothetical question is to be asked, it is: How would Hank Williams have fared? If the fate of his contemporaries is any guide, the answer is: poorly. Webb Pierce, Hank Snow, Carl Smith, Faron Young, Red Foley, and Eddy Arnold all saw their careers take a precipitous downturn in the mid- to late '50s. One listen to Webb Pierce's *vocal* version of "Raunchy" is enough to appreciate the desperation that afflicted them. Hank's music, like that of his contemporaries, was adult in content; rock 'n' roll was teenage music. The exaggeration and overstatement of rock 'n' roll were alien to the fundamental values of Hank's music, and the sledgehammer beat was the opposite of The Drifting Cowboys' sweet, mellow swing.

It's doubtful that there would have been a place for Hank Williams, with his thinning hair, his incorrigibly rural ways, and his "Pitchers from Life's Other Side," in the era of the Nashville Sound. He didn't have the ability to cross over that those who followed him, such as Marty Robbins and Johnny Cash, had. Hank's music had always needed to be carefully combed through and then reinterpreted for the mass audience. The market would not have changed to accommodate him. If he had tried to change to accommodate it, he would have lost the essence of his music in the process.

Some of Hank's records, like "Hey, Good Lookin' " and "Settin' the Woods on Fire," prefigured rock 'n' roll to some extent, but that was no guarantee that he could have weathered the storm any better than his contemporaries. Rhythm 'n' Blues singer Wynonie Harris had much of what became the rock 'n' roll swagger on his late '40s and early '50s hits, like "Good Rockin' Tonight," but that didn't help him score one hit after rock 'n' roll broke. He was too old and too black. Hank was probably too old and too hillbilly, but by dying prematurely, he avoided the indignity of trying to answer the question of what he would have done. He also left the tantalizing promise of what might have been as well as a blank screen upon which vested interests could project all manner of fantasies. For its part, MGM tried to imagine the sound by grafting drums, electric guitar, and piano solos onto his records and bathing the results in echo, beginning a long, sorry history of reinventing Hank's music according to the season.

Hank would have had an even tougher time in today's Nashville, the city founded upon reverence for him. In April 1972, the German record company Polydor, which later amalgamated with the record division of the Dutch electrical giant Philips to form Polygram, bought the repertoire of MGM Records. In March 1985, Acuff-Rose was sold to Gaylord Broadcasting of Oklahoma City, the company that later bought *The Grand Ole Opry* and resituated it in Opryland, and later still launched the Nashville Network. Today, Polygram's corporate monolith and the Acuff-Rose/Opryland Music monolith face off across Music Row, symbolizing the new, business-minded face of country music. Would the ol' Drifting Cowboy have made easy conversation with the MBAs who now walk the corridors of power?

What Hank Williams would have thought of the cookie-cutter country stars who now invoke his name is even harder to determine. The only certainty is this: the circumstances that combined to make him the most powerfully iconic figure in country music will never come again. No one will cut three or four classics in an afternoon session again; no one will redefine the vocabulary of the music in the way that he did. No one will be allowed to mess up in the way that he did, either. The stakes are too high, and professional help would have been foisted upon him. The specialness in Hank Williams would then have ebbed away, because the compelling nature of his records stemmed in great measure from the fact that he was a pressure cooker, holding altogether too much inside.

It was a unique combination of circumstances that brought Hank Williams to the fore and allowed him to accomplish what he did when he did. If he had started his career a few years earlier, he would have lived and died in almost total obscurity because the social and market conditions that brought about the wider acceptance of hillbilly music weren't in place, and the country was mired deep in the Depression. If he had lived a few years longer, he would have become an embarrassment to the changing face of country music — too hillbilly by half. But in arriving when he did and dying when and how he did he became a prophet with honor.

The final paradox is this: Hank Williams left no journals, almost no letters, and no extended interviews, and the people who knew him best have to admit that on some level they didn't know him at all; yet, for all the ambiguity and unknowableness, Hank Williams appears almost desperately real through his music. He escaped the obloquy of seeing his drunks and his dalliances splashed over the tabloids, but he left a life diarized in verses sung with such riveting conviction that we feel as though we know him well. At his best, he froze a moment or a feeling in terms simple enough to understand quickly, yet meaningful enough to listen to forever. That's still the essential challenge of the popular song.

It's impossible not to feel that Hank Williams's "heart" songs with their sense of unshakable solitariness define his music and, in all likelihood, the man himself. He had his triumphs — many, many of them. He could grin his shiteating grin, slap the table, shout "Hot damn!" when someone who once hadn't given him the time of day or had once called him a damn drunk to his face was almost coerced into recording one of his songs or booking him, but the moment of victory inevitably passed and sooner or later he was left with Hiram Williams. Sometimes Hiram was good company, but too often he was not. There's the notion that the writer or poet calms his troublous soul by reducing it to rhyme. For Hank Williams, though, as he pulled off his boots and eased himself gingerly onto his bed, the little verses scratched out in his untutored spidery handwriting almost certainly offered him no relief at all.

SOURCES

GENERAL

DOCUMENTS AND RECORDS

Billboard magazine. Files 1945–1953 and selected other dates.

Birth Certificate. Williams, Hank. Montgomery, Ala.: Alabama Department of Vital Statistics.

Divorce Certificate. Guy, Erskine, and Sheppard, Audrey Mae. Troy, Ala.: Pike Co. Courthouse.

Divorce Certificate I. Williams, Hank, and Sheppard, Audrey Mae. Montgomery, Ala.: Montgomery Co. Courthouse.

Divorce Certificate II. Williams, Hank, and Sheppard, Audrey Mae. Nashville: Davidson Co. Courthouse.

Hatch Show Print Co. Business Records. Nashville. Courtesy of the Country Music Foundation.

Library of Congress Music Copyright Division.

Marriage Certificate. Williams, Elonzo, and Skipper, Lilly. Greenville, Ala.: Butler Co. Courthouse.

Marriage Certificate. Williams, Hank, and Sheppard, Audrey Mae. Andalusia, Ala.: Covington Co. Courthouse.

Marriage License and Certificate. Williams, Hank, and Eshliman, Billie Jean Jones. Benton, La.: Bossier Parish Courthouse.

MGM Records. Recording sheets 1947–1954, label copy sheets 1947–1974, and contract files. Unpublished. Cited courtesy of Polygram Records Inc.

BOOKS, ARTICLES, AND RADIO PROGRAMS

ASCAP. *Biographical Dictionary.* New York: Bowker Co., 1980.

Caress, Jay. *Hank Williams: Country Music's Tragic King.* New York: Stein & Day, 1979.

Fowler, Gene, and Bill Crawford. *Border Radio*. New York: Limelight Editions, 1990.

Gentry, Linnell. *History and Encyclopaedia of Country, Western and Gospel Music*. Nashville: Clairmont Corp., 1969.

Hank Williams and His Drifting Cowboys Stars of WSFA Deluxe Song Book. Montgomery, Ala., circa 1946.

Koon, George William. *Hank Williams: A Bio-Bibliography*. Westport, Conn.: Greenwood Press, 1983.

Malone, Bill C. *Country Music U.S.A.: A Fifty-Year History*. Austin, Tex.: University of Texas Press, 1968.

———. *Singing Cowboys and Musical Mountaineers*. Athens, Ga.: University of Georgia Press, 1993.

Odom, Mr. and Mrs. Burton. *The Hank Williams Story*. Greenville, Ala.: Butler Co. Historical Society, 1974.

Owen, Jim. "Hank Williams: The Man, the Legend." *Star Stories* (radio documentary). Nashville, 1977.

Pinson, Bob, and Charles Wolfe. Song Notes to *Hank Williams — Country and Western Classics*. Washington, D.C.: Time-Life Music Inc., 1981.

Radio Annual. New York: Radio Daily, 1938–1948.

Rivers, Jerry. *From Life to Legend*. Denver, Colo.: Heather Enterprises, 1967.

Rogers, Arnold, and Bruce Gidoll. *The Life and Times of Hank Williams*. Nashville: Haney-Jones Books, 1993.

Rockwell, Harry E. *Beneath the Applause*. 1973.

Rumble, John W. "Fred Rose and the Development of the Nashville Music Industry." Ph.D. diss., Vanderbilt University, 1980.

Sanjek, Russell, and David Sanjek. *American Popular Music Business in the 20th Century*. New York: Oxford University Press, 1991.

Shapiro, Nat. *Popular Music: An Annotated History of American Popular Songs*. 6 vols. New York: Adrian Press, 1964–1973.

Stone, W. W., and Allen Rankin. *Life Story of Our Hank Williams "The Drifting Cowboy."* Montgomery, Ala.: Philbert Publications, 1953.

Sutton, Juanealya McCormick. *The Man Behind the Scenes (Pappy Neal McCormick and Hank Williams)*. DeFuniak Springs, Fla., 1987.

Various Contributors. *Hank Williams: The Legend*. Nashville: Heather Enterprises, 1972.

———. *Hank Williams As We Knew Him*. Georgiana and Chapman, Ala.: Three Arts Club of Georgiana and Chapman, 1982.

Whitburn, Joel. *Top Country Singles 1944–1988*. Menomonee Falls, Wis.: Record Research, 1988.

Williams, Hank, and Jimmy Rule. *How to Write Folk and Western Music to Sell*. Nashville: Harpeth Publishing, 1951.

Williams, Lycrecia, and Dale Vinicur. *Still in Love with You*. Nashville: Rutledge Hill Press, 1989.

Williams, Jett, and Pamela Thomas. *Ain't Nothin' As Sweet As My Baby*. New York: Harcourt Brace Jovanovich, 1990.

Williams, Roger M. *Sing a Sad Song: The Life of Hank Williams*. New York: Doubleday, 1970.

CHAPTER 1: THE DRIFTING COWBOY'S DREAM

Gleason, Ralph J. "Hank Williams, Roy Acuff and Then God!!" *Rolling Stone*. June 28, 1969.

"Hank Williams Buried Sunday." *Advocate*. Greenville, Ala. January 8, 1953.

Hendrix, Vernon. "Father of Famed Singer Lives by Side of the Road." *Advertiser*. Montgomery, Ala. December 24, 1967.

MacGuire, Colin. "Only People Left Here Are Old Folks." *Advertiser.* Montgomery, Ala. March 16, 1969.
Mason, Red. "From Peanuts to Fame." *Tri-Co. News.* Millbrook, Ala. August 14, 1969.
McKee, Charles B. (Mac). "Hank Williams — The Musician." unpublished.
Smith, Irene Williams. "The Day Hank Williams Lived." *Washington Post.* January 1, 1993.
Williams, Elonzo H. Letter to *The Progressive Era.* Camden, Ala. n.d.

AUTHOR INTERVIEWS:

Leila Griffin, Mrs. M. C. Jarrett, J. C. McNeil, Walter McNeil Jr., Henderson Payne, Robert Williams

CHAPTER 2: "ROY ACUFF, THEN GOD!"

Coleman, Jim. Letter to the authors. Huntsville, Ala. May 11, 1993
Compton, Thomas H. Letter to Butler Co. Historical Society. April 7, 1980.
Linn, Ed. "The Short Life of Hank Williams." *Saga.* New York. January 1957.
" 'Hezzy,' Hank Williams Partner Dies." *Advertiser.* Montgomery, Ala. September 13, 1970.
"Homecoming for Hank Sunday." *Advocate.* Greenville, Ala. July 12, 1951.
Littleton, George. "Long Lost Hank Williams Song to Hit Airwaves." *Observer.* Eclectic, Ala. January 10, 1991.
"Red Mason Sez: 'From Peanuts to Fame.' " *Tri-County News.* Millbrook, Ala. August 14, 1969.
Rollings, Lynn. "New Found Recording Debated." *Advertiser.* Montgomery, Ala. April 14, 1990.
Smith, Irene Williams. "The Day Hank Williams Lived." *Washington Post.* January 1, 1993.
———. "My Life with a Treasured Brother." Draft in the Thurston Moore Collection, Country Music Foundation, 1971.
Williams, Elonzo H. Letter to *The Progressive Era.* Camden, Ala. n.d.

AUTHOR INTERVIEWS:

Jimmy Adams (principal, Sidney Lanier High School), Freddy Beach, Irella Beach, Paul Dennis, Leaborne Eads, Boots Harris, Walter McNeil, Pee Wee Moultrie, Mrs. Caldwell Stewart, Robert Williams

CHAPTER 3: SWEET AUDREY FROM PIKE

"Fred Rose: Writer of World's Most Powerful Folk Song Music." *National Hillbilly News.* December 1946.
Gunter, Hardrock. "A Guitarist's Lighthearted Memoir of Hank Williams." In *Hank Williams, the Legend.* Denver: Heather Enterprises, 1972.
Honicker, Bunny. "Rose Applauds Famed Protege." Montgomery, circa 1954.
King, Pee Wee. Interview on *Hank Williams: Reflections by Those Who Loved Him.* MGM PRO-912, 1975.

AUTHOR INTERVIEWS:

Paul Dennis, Don Helms, J. C. McNeil, Walter McNeil, Sebie Smith, Bernice Turner.

CHAPTER 4: SONGS FOR HOME FOLKS

"Acuff-Rose: Looking Back, Looking Ahead." *Cumberland.* Nashville. November 1980.
Foree, Mel. Interviews with Doug Green, Country Music Foundation Oral History Project. April 30 and July 29, 1974.

Harris, Jack. "Radio Broadcast Revels in Romance of the Rails." *Rural Radio.* Nashville. March 1939.
"A Providential Meeting: Fred and Wesley Rose Find Hank Williams." *Billboard* (Acuff-Rose suppl.). February 3, 1968.
Rose, Fred. Foreword to *Hank Williams' Country Hit Parade.* Nashville: Acuff-Rose Sales, 1950.
Rumble, John W. "The Emergence of Nashville as a Recording Center." *Journal of Country Music.* December 1978.
State of New York, Department of State certificates of incorporation for Sterling Records (July 27, 1945), Sterling Records Distribution (October 24, 1945), and Juke Box Record Company (October 24, 1945).
Sterling Records Release Flyer No. 111. January 1947.
Tribe, Ivan. Liner notes to *Molly O'Day.* Vollersode, Germany: Bear Family Records, 1992.
"Wesley Rose Chooses Nashville — A Crucial Decision for the World of Music." *Billboard* (Acuff-Rose suppl.). February 3, 1968.
Williams, Hank. Interview with *National Hillbilly News.* November–December 1949.
Zolotow, Maurice. "Hillbilly Boom." *Saturday Evening Post.* February 12, 1944.

AUTHOR INTERVIEWS:

Lynn Davis, Don Helms, Murray Nash, R. D. Norred, Joe Pennington, Vic Willis, Lum York

CHAPTER 5: THE YEAR OF THE LION

Cleghorn, William E. "Hank Williams Rides on Down Trail of National Popularity on Air Records." *Examiner.* Montgomery, Ala. August 21, 1947.
"Frank Walker." Obituary in *Billboard.* October 26, 1963.
"Frank Walker, Former MGM Exec, Disk Pioneer Dies." *The Music Reporter.* Nashville. October 26, 1963.
"A Platter for the Lion." *Time.* February 24, 1947.
Rankin, Allen. "Rankin File." *Advertiser.* Montgomery, Ala. April 4, 1948.
Walker, Frank. "Music Which is Distinctively Our Own." New York: Billboard Publications (*World of Country Music*). November 1963.

AUTHOR INTERVIEWS:

Leaborne Eads, Walter McNeil, R. D. Norred, Joe Pennington, Lum York

CHAPTER 6: THE HAYRIDE

Clay, John W. Letter to the authors. June 8, 1993.
Columbia Records. Contract File: Curley Williams.
Foree, Mel. Interviews with Doug Green. Country Music Foundation Oral History Project. April 30 and July 29, 1974.
Franks, Tillman. Diaries courtesy of Tillman Franks.
Hill, Dick. "Doc 'Curley' Williams." *Old Time Country.* Winter 1990.
Jones-Hall, Lillian. "A Historical Study of Programming Techniques and Practices of KWKH 1922–1950." Diss. Louisiana State University at Shreveport, 1982.
Rhodes, Don. "Bailes Goes to Hillbilly Heaven." *Herald.* Augusta, Ga. January 12, 1990.

AUTHOR INTERVIEWS:

Paul Dennis, Tillman Franks, Boots Harris, Don Helms, Merle Kilgore, Horace Logan, R. D. Norred, Johnnie Wright, Lum York

CHAPTER 7: A FEELING CALLED THE BLUES

Bledsoe, Wayne. "Knoxville's Great Lost Songwriter Arthur Q. Smith." *News Sentinel.* Knoxville, Tenn. May 12, 1991.

"Clyde Baum: He Picked Bluegrass Tunes with Hank." *The Times.* Shreveport, La. July 10, 1980.

Davis, Oscar. Interview with Doug Green. Country Music Foundation Oral History Project. July 24, 1974.

Gunter, Hardrock. "A Guitarist's Lighthearted Memoir of Hank Williams." In *Hank Williams, the Legend.* Denver: Heather Publications, 1972.

Roe, Gene L. "Got 'Lovesick Blues'? No, Sir, Not Hank Williams." *National Hillbilly News.* January–February 1950.

Tour data. *Sabine Index.* Many, La. April 22–23, 1949.

Vincent, Bert. "Strolling with . . ." *News Sentinel.* Knoxville, Tenn. July 24, 1951

AUTHOR INTERVIEWS:

Claude Boone, Billy Byrd, Jerry Byrd, Tillman Franks, Clint Holmes, Billie Jean Horton, Horace Logan, Murray Nash, Bob McNett, Felton Pruett, Zeke Turner, Audrey Williams, Johnnie Wright, Lum York

CHAPTER 8: THE MOTHER OF ALL JUBILEES

Chilton, John. *Who's Who of Jazz.* Philadelphia: Chilton Books, 1972.

Cunniff, Albert. "Muscle Behind the Music: The Life and Times of Jim Denny." *Journal of Country Music* 11 (1–2), 1986.

Davis, Oscar. Interview with Doug Green. Country Music Foundation Oral History Project. July 24, 1974.

Davidson, Bill. "There's Gold in Them Thar Hillbilly Tunes." *Collier's.* New York. July 28, 1951.

"Grand Ole Opry Competes with Europe's Own Hillbilly Gasthaus." *Variety.* November 30, 1949.

"Hank Williams Europe Bound." *Advertiser.* Montgomery, Ala. November 9, 1949.

Harris, Jack. "Hushpuckana: Judge Hay Is Back at WSM's Opry." *Rural Radio.* Nashville. April 1938

———. "True Story of the Famous WSM Grand Ole Opry." *Rural Radio.* Nashville. November 1938.

Honicker, Bunny. "Rose Applauds Famed Protege." Montgomery, circa 1954.

House, Jack. "Blues over Blues? Not Hank." *News.* Birmingham, Ala. November 13, 1949.

McDaniel, R., and Harold Seligman. *The Grand Ole Opry.* New York: Greenberg, 1952.

Rumble, John. Liner notes to *Red Foley: Country Music Hall of Fame.* Nashville: MCA Records, 1991.

Rust, Brian. *Jazz Records 1897–1942.* New Rochelle, N.Y.: Arlington House, 1975.

Shriver, Jerry. "Hank Williams' Buddy Remembers When." *Journal.* Pensacola, Fla. January 1, 1982.

Tubb, Ernest, and Roy Acuff. Interview on *Hank Williams: Reflections by Those Who Loved Him.* MGM PRO-912, 1975.

USAF orders for Grand Ole Opry overseas tour. Courtesy of Billy Robinson.

Walker, Frank. "Music Which Is Distinctively Our Own." New York: Billboard Publications (*World of Country Music*). November 1963.

AUTHOR INTERVIEWS:

Don Helms, Bob McNett, Billy Robinson, Grant Turner

CHAPTER 9: HELL IN TEXAS

Grand Ole Opry feature in *Variety.* October 26, 1949.
"Hillbilly Singing Star Forfeits Fire Bond." *Nashville Banner.* April 16, 1950.
Pruett, Sammy. Interview with Jim Owen, n.d.
Vinicur, Dale. Liner notes to *Audrey Williams: Ramblin' Gal.* Vollersode, Germany: Bear Family Records, 1989.
Williams, Hank. Letter. *Country Song Roundup.* April 1951.
Wolfe, Charles, and Neil Rosenberg. Liner notes to *Bill Monroe: Bluegrass 1950–1958.* Vollersode, Germany: Bear Family Records, 1991.

AUTHOR INTERVIEWS:

A. V. Bamford, Tillman Franks, Don Helms, Bob McNett, Bill Monroe, W. B. Nowlin, Braxton Schuffert

CHAPTER 10: THE PLEASURE OF THE FLEETING YEAR

Atkins, Chet. Interview in Nash, Alanna. *Behind Closed Doors.* New York: Knopf, 1987.
Clay, John W. Letter to the authors. June 8, 1993.
Cunniff, Albert. "The Muscle Behind the Music: The Life and Times of Jim Denny." *Journal of Country Music* 11 (1–2), 1986.
Davidson, Bill. "There's Gold in Them Thar Hillbilly Tunes." *Collier's.* New York. July 28, 1951.
Davis, Oscar. Interview with Doug Green. Country Music Foundation Oral History Project. July 24, 1974.
Donahue, Michael. "Memphians Recall Days with Famed Singer." *Press Scimitar.* Memphis, Tenn. May 19, 1979.
McWethy, John A. "Hillbilly Tunes Boom." *Wall Street Journal.* October 2, 1951.
Rankin, Allen. "Rankin File: The Hank Williams Tidal Wave." *Alabama Journal.* February 4, 1953.
Shriver, Jerry. "Hank Williams' Buddy Remembers When." *Journal.* Pensacola, Fla. January 1, 1982.
Van Ness, C., d/b/a Dixie Music v Hank Williams, Acuff-Rose et al. New York (S. dist.). December 3, 1951.
Williams, Hank. Interviewed in Charleston, S.C. March 2, 1951.

AUTHOR INTERVIEWS:

Jim Boyd, Jimmy Dickens, Bill England, Don Helms, Clint Holmes, Mac McGee, Bob McNett, Mitch Miller, Grant Turner

CHAPTER 11: FOLK AND WESTERN MUSIC TO SELL

Bocephus News. Data on "Tear in My Beer" video. Paris, Tenn. Spring/summer 1989.
Frizzell, Lefty. Interview on *Hank Williams: Reflections by Those Who Loved Him.* MGM PRO-912, 1975.
"Hank Williams Stars in Homecoming Event." *Examiner.* Montgomery, Ala. July 15, 1951.
Hospitalization Records in Louisiana in the possession of Billie Jean Horton. Cited in Flippo, Chet. *Your Cheatin' Heart.* New York: Simon & Schuster, 1981.

Russell, Tony. Liner notes to Jimmie Davis *Rockin' Blues* and *Barnyard Stomp*. Vollersode,
    Germany: Bear Family Records, 1983 and 1988.
Williams, Curley. Recording data from Don Law notebooks.
Wolfe, Charles. Liner notes to Lefty Frizzell *Life's Like Poetry*. Vollersode, Germany: Bear
    Family Records, 1992.
Wright, Johnnie. Interview with Eddie Stubbs in *Johnnie and Jack: The Tennessee Moun-
    tain Boys*. Vollersode, Germany: Bear Family Records, 1992.

AUTHOR INTERVIEWS:

Bill England, Tillman Franks, Don Helms, Billie Jean Horton, Bill Lister, J. C. McNeil,
Walter McNeil, Braxton Schuffert

CHAPTER 12: THE HADDY-COLE BOUNCE

Angers, Trent. "The Three Faces of Dudley J. LeBlanc." *Acadiana Profile* 6 (1) 1977.
Clay, Floyd Martin. *Coozan Dudley LeBlanc: From Huey Long to Hadacol*. Gretna, La.:
    Pelican Publishing Co., 1987.
Grand Ole Opry transcription. October 6, 1951.
Hadacol advertisements in *Sabine Index*. Many, La. Various dates, 1949–1951.
Movie contract. Announced in *Nashville Banner*. September 24, 1951.
Program (Connie B. Gay). *1952 New Year's Eve Folk Music Celebration*. Washington, D.C.
Tubb, Ernest. Interview on *Hank Williams: Reflections by Those Who Loved Him*. MGM
    PRO-912, 1975.
Williams, Hank. Interview in Charleston, S.C. March 3, 1951.

AUTHOR INTERVIEWS:

Art Celsie, Bill Lister, Frank D. McMurry, J. C. McNeil, Walter McNeil, Murray Nash, Braxton Schuffert, Johnnie Wright

CHAPTER 13: BOBBIE

Atkins, Chet. Interview in Nash, Alanna. *Behind Closed Doors*. New York: Knopf, 1987.
"Cold, Cold Heart Changeover into Cold, Cold Cash." *Advertiser*. Montgomery, Ala. Janu-
    ary 5, 1955.
"Country Music Is Big Business, and Nashville Is Its Detroit." *Newsweek*. August 11, 1952.
"Country Music Comes to Town." *Pathfinder*. June 1952.
Davidson, Bill. "There's Gold in Them Thar Hillbilly Tunes." *Collier's*. New York. July 28,
    1951.
Davis, Oscar. Interview with Doug Green. Country Music Foundation Oral History Project.
    September 25, 1974.
Gleason, Ralph J. "Hank Williams, Roy Acuff and Then God!!" *Rolling Stone*. June 28, 1969.
Lucas, Mike. "Hank Williams: The Original Country-Western Superstar Flopped in His
    Only Las Vegas Strip Appearance." *Sun*, Las Vegas. January 2, 1983.
McWethy, John A. "Hillbilly Tunes Boom." *Wall Street Journal*. October 2, 1951.
Pearl, Minnie. Interview on suppl. disc to *Insights into Hank Williams in Story and Song*.
    MGM M3HB-4975, 1974.
Price, Ray. Interview with Lee Arnold. n.d.
Stark, Mrs. Warren, and Leon Carter. Interview (interviewer unknown). April 1986.
Williams, Audrey. "Hank's First Wife Tells of Ups and Downs of Marriage." *Advertiser*.
    Montgomery, Ala. January 13, 1953.

Williams, Audrey Mae, complainant v Hank Williams et al. defendants. Action no. 71124, Part II of the Chancery Court of Davidson Co., Tenn.

Williams, Hank. Interview in *Country Song Roundup.*" Charlton Publications. June 1953.

AUTHOR INTERVIEW:

Don Helms

CHAPTER 14: BILLIE JEAN

Clayton, Frank. "Remembering Hank." *Alabama Journal.* February 20, 1971.

"Friday is Hank Williams Day for Greenville, Butler County." *Advertiser.* Greenville, Ala. August 14, 1952.

"Hank Williams Is Booked Here." *Advertiser.* Greenville, Ala. July 17, 1952.

"Hank Williams Is Rated No. 1 Goodwill Ambassador: Butler County Native to Appear Here." *Advertiser.* Greenville, Ala. July 31, 1952.

McKinnon, Bob. "Hank Williams' First Week After the Opry." unpublished. n.d. Used courtesy of the McKinnon estate.

Pierce, Webb. Interview on *Hank Williams: Reflections by Those Who Knew Him.* MGM PRO-912, 1975.

Rankin, Allen. "Rankin File." *Advertiser.* Montgomery, Ala. September 28, 1952.

Rose, Fred. Letter to Tillman Franks. November 11, 1949.

"WSM Drops Contract for Hank." *Tennessean.* Nashville. August 15, 1952.

Young, Faron. Interview with Biff Collie. TNNR. February 26, 1990.

AUTHOR INTERVIEWS:

Billie Jean Horton, Ed Harvell, Don Helms, Mac McGee, Murray Nash, Johnny Wright

CHAPTER 15: THE DEATH OF LEAPY THE LEOPARD

"Clyde Perdue Dies." *Advertiser.* Greenville, Ala. November 26, 1963.

Cromley, Allan. "Secret of Quack's License Baffles Narcotics Probers." *Times.* Oklahoma City. March 25, 1953.

Davis, Oscar. Interview with Doug Green. Country Music Foundation Oral History Project. September 25, 1974.

"Dope Witness Parole Revoked." *Daily Oklahoman.* March 13, 1953.

"Famous Song Composer Is Arrested Here." *Journal.* Shreveport, La. December 12, 1952.

"Hank Williams and Wife Said Married Illegally." *Register.* Mobile, Ala. January 15, 1953.

Mackey, Wayne. "Singer Given Leopard Drug." *Times.* Oklahoma City. March 11, 1953.

McKee, Don. "Legality May Be Questioned in Williams' Second Marriage." *Advertiser.* Montgomery, Ala. January 9, 1953.

Medley, Robert. "The Manuscript in a Black Bag." unpublished, circa 1992.

"Pretty Witness Tells Hillbilly's Bizarre Story." *Daily Oklahoman.* March 18, 1953.

Price, Ray. Interview with Lee Arnold. n.d.

Stark, Mrs. Warren, and Leon Carter. Interview (interviewer unknown). April 1986.

State of Oklahoma Department of Corrections. Letter to authors. Re: inmate #58545 and 51646. November 12, 1992.

Stone, Catherine Yvonne v Gulf American Fire and Casualty Co., et al. Supreme Ct. of Alabama, docket no. 87-269. Cited in *554 Southern Reporter,* 2d series. July 5, 1989.

U.S. Army. Honorable Discharge Certificate: Walter Clyde Perdue. January 4, 1946.

Van Dyke, Bill. "Forged License Cost Him $25, Quack Declares." *Daily Oklahoman.* March 25, 1953.

Ward, Ed. Liner notes to *Sir Doug's Recording Trip.* London. Edsel Records DED 255, 1989.
"Was Singer a Suicide?" *Times.* Oklahoma City. March 15, 1953.

AUTHOR INTERVIEWS:

Ray Edenton, Tommy Hill, Billie Jean Horton, Claude King, Horace Logan, Felton Pruett, Billy Walker, Lum York

CHAPTER 16: MIDNIGHT

Brown, Ricardo, and Martha Garrett. "Hank Planned to Remarry Her in February, Former Wife Says." *Alabama Journal.* January 9, 1953.
"Country Boy Returns." *Alabama Journal.* December 29 and 30, 1952.
"ET Officer Suspected Williams Wasn't Alive." *News Sentinel.* Knoxville, Tenn. January 2, 1953.
McKee, Don. "First Wife Out of Hank's Plans, Widow Declares." *Advertiser.* Montgomery, Ala. January 10, 1953.
Morris, Doug. "Hank Williams' Death Still Issue." *Journal.* Knoxville, Tenn. December 15, 1982.
"Mystery Shrouds Death of Singer Hank Williams." *Journal.* Knoxville, Tenn. January 2, 1953.
"Six Man Jury Awaits Autopsy Report in Hank Williams' Death." *Fayette Tribune.* Oak Hill, W.Va. January 5, 1953.
Taylor, J. Nelson. "Pretty Witness Tells Hillbilly's Bizarre Story." *Daily Oklahoman.* March 18, 1953.
Teeter, H. B. "Hank Williams Had Premonitions of Death." *Tennessean.* Nashville. January 2, 1953.
Tyree, Joe, et al. Interviews with Vic Gabany. Oak Hill, W.Va.
"Williams' Death Laid to Heart Condition." *Tennessean.* Nashville. January 11, 1953.
Williams, Susan. "Did Hank Williams Die in Oak Hill?" *Fayette Tribune.* Oak Hill, W.Va. December 22, 1982.

AUTHOR INTERVIEWS:

A.V. Bamford, Charles Carr, Marie Harvell, Billie Jean Horton, Dr. Leo Killorn, Murray Nash, Erleen Skipper, Taft Skipper

CHAPTER 17: WUTHERING DEPTHS

Azbell, Joe. "Hank's Funeral Is Far Largest in Montgomery's History." *Advertiser.* Montgomery, Ala. January 5, 1953.
"Clyde Perdue Is with Hawkins." *Advocate.* Greenville, Ala. January 1953.
Davis, Oscar. Interview with Doug Green. Country Music Foundation Oral History Project. July 24, 1974.
"Hank Williams, 29, Dies en Route to Show Here." *Repository.* Canton, Ohio. January 2, 1953.
Honicker, Bunny. "Rose Applauds Famed Protege." Montgomery, circa 1954.
Horton, Billie Jean. "Fear and Loathing at Hank's Funeral." *Texas Music.* June 1976.
Jones, Eddie. "Thousands at Rites for Hank Williams." *Nashville Banner.* January 5, 1953.
Rose, Wesley. Interview in "Remembering Hank." *Country Music.* March 1975.
Stone, Catherine Yvonne *v* Gulf American Fire & Casualty Co. et al. Supreme Ct. of Alabama, docket no. 87-269. Cited in *554 Southern Reporter,* 2d series. July 5, 1953.
Sullivan, Phil. "Williams Estate Left in 3-Way Tangle." *Tennessean.* Nashville. January 9, 1953.

Swietnicki, Ed. "Hank Williams Legend Grows." *Advertiser.* Montgomery, Ala. June 23, 1957.

"Was Singer a Suicide?" *Times.* Oklahoma City. March 18, 1953.

"Williams' Body in New Grave." *Advertiser.* Montgomery, Ala. January 18, 1953.

"Williams Failed to Leave Will." *Alabama Journal.* January 6, 1953.

AUTHOR INTERVIEWS:

A. V. Bamford, Charles Carr, Leaborne Eads, Leila Griffin, Billie Jean Horton, Horace Logan, Braxton Schuffert

DISCOGRAPHY

For the MGM sessions, only the "on location" master numbers ("S" following the year of recording) are given. The master numbers assigned by MGM in New York (XY following the year of recording or overdub) have not been given.

Only session recordings and issued demos have been noted, together with songs that Hank Williams wrote or cowrote that were placed with other artists. Live recordings and transcriptions have not been logged even if they were issued on records, except for a series of recordings probably made at KWKH in Shreveport, La., in early 1949. They have been included because MGM treated them as regular (i.e., nonlive) recordings after their acquisition.

The dates of the overdub sessions have not been listed. Only the original session dates or approximate demo dates are included.

Only the original issues have been noted. Except where noted otherwise, all issues are MGM, the composer is Hank Williams, and the producer of the Sterling and MGM sessions is Fred Rose.

Bob Pinson of the Country Music Foundation is in the process of publishing a complete Hank Williams chrono-discography. Inquiries should be addressed to the Country Music Foundation, 4 Music Square East, Nashville, TN 37203.

MASTER NO. TITLE (COMPOSER[S])   *RECORDING NO.*

Demo recording or transcription made from WSFA in Highland Bridge Radio and Shoe Shop, Montgomery, April 7, 1942.
        I'M NOT COMING HOME ANY MORE   Polydor 847194 (LP)

Song registered with Library of Congress December 20, 1943. No surviving demo.
        (I'M PRAYING FOR THE DAY THAT) PEACE
        WILL COME*
* Recorded by Roscoe Hankins, 1951. Mercury 6337.

MASTER NO. TITLE (COMPOSER[S])	RECORDING NO.

Demos probably made for Acuff-Rose. Probably 1946/47.

GOING HOME	Arhoolie EP 548
MOTHER IS GONE	Arhoolie EP 548
A HOME IN HEAVEN	Arhoolie EP 548
IN MY DREAMS YOU STILL BELONG TO ME	Arhoolie EP 548
WON'T YOU SOMETIMES THINK OF ME?	CMF 07 (LP)
WHY SHOULD I CRY?	CMF 07 (LP)
CALLING YOU*	CMF 07 (LP)
YOU BROKE YOUR OWN HEART	CMF 07 (LP)
PAN AMERICAN	CMF 07 (LP)
I WATCHED MY DREAM WORLD CRUMBLE	
LIKE CLAY	CMF 07 (LP)
IN MY DREAMS YOU STILL BELONG TO ME	CMF 07 (LP)
WEALTH WON'T SAVE YOUR SOUL	CMF 07 (LP)
SINGING WATERFALL	CMF 07 (LP)
I TOLD A LIE TO MY HEART†	CMF 07 (LP)

* With Audrey Williams.
† Overdubbed with Willie Nelson for *Half Nelson*, Columbia
39990, 1985; undubbed on CMF-07.

Session December 11, 1946: WSM Studios, Nashville.

201-A CALLING YOU	Sterling 201
201-B NEVER AGAIN (WILL I KNOCK ON	
YOUR DOOR)*	Sterling 201
204-A WEALTH WON'T SAVE YOUR SOUL	Sterling 204
204-B WHEN GOD COMES AND GATHERS HIS	
JEWELS†	Sterling 204

* Misprinted as "Never Again (Will I Knock at Your Door)."
† Misprinted as "When God Comes and Fathers His Jewels."

*Session February 13, 1947: unknown location, probably WSM
studio.*

208-A I DON'T CARE (IF TOMORROW NEVER COMES)	Sterling 208
208-B MY LOVE FOR YOU (HAS TURNED TO HATE)	Sterling 208
210-A HONKY TONKIN'	Sterling 210
210-B PAN AMERICAN	Sterling 210

Session April 21, 1947: Castle Studio, Nashville.

47-S-123 MOVE IT ON OVER	10033
47-S-124 I SAW THE LIGHT	10271
47-S-125 (LAST NIGHT) I HEARD YOU CRYING IN	
YOUR SLEEP	10033
47-S-126 SIX MORE MILES (TO THE GRAVEYARD)	10271

Undated demo, possibly 1947.

HONKY TONK BLUES	CMF-06 (LP)

MASTER NO. TITLE (COMPOSER[S])   *RECORDING NO.*

Session August 4, 1947: Castle Studio, Nashville.

47-S-6004 FLY TROUBLE (Honey Wilds/Bunny
Biggs/Fred Rose)   10073
47-S-6005 HONKY TONK BLUES   Unissued/lost
47-S-6006 I'M SATISFIED WITH YOU (Fred Rose)   11768
47-S-6007 ON THE BANKS OF THE (OLD)
PONTCHARTRAIN (H. Williams/Ramona Vincent)   10073

Session November 6, 1947: Castle Studio, Nashville.

47-S-6018 ROOTIE TOOTIE (Fred Rose)   10124
47-S-6019 I CAN'T GET YOU OFF OF MY MIND   10328
47-S-6020 I'M A LONG GONE DADDY   10212
47-S-6025 HONKY TONKIN'   10171

Session November 7, 1947: Castle Studio, Nashville.

47-S-6021 MY SWEET LOVE AIN'T AROUND   10124
47-S-6022 THE BLUES COME AROUND   10212
47-S-6023 A MANSION ON THE HILL (Fred Rose/
Hank Williams)   10328
47-S-6024 I'LL BE A BACHELOR 'TIL I DIE   10171

Composition registered with Library of Congress November 30,
1948. No surviving demo.

IF I DIDN'T LOVE YOU (Hank Williams/Fred Rose)*
* First recorded by Rome Johnson, November 25, 1947. MGM 10810.

Undated demo, probably 1948.

LOST ON THE RIVER   CMF-06 (LP)

Session December 22, 1948: Herzog Studio, Cincinnati.

49-S-6057 LOST ON THE RIVER*   10434
49-S-6058 THERE'LL BE NO TEARDROPS TONIGHT   10461
49-S-6059 I HEARD MY MOTHER PRAYING FOR ME
(Audrey Williams)*   10813
49-S-6060 LOVESICK BLUES (Irving Mills/Cliff Friend)   10352
* Duet credited on label to "Hank and Audrey."

Composition registered with Library of Congress January 5,
1949. No surviving demo.

YOU'RE BARKING UP THE WRONG TREE NOW
(Hank Williams/Fred Rose)*
* First recorded by Red Sovine. September 1, 1949. MGM 10717.

Spring 1949: probably Johnnie Fair Syrup transcriptions,
KWKH studio, Shreveport, Louisiana.
Note: The following masters were acquired by MGM in a
batch, probably in 1955. They were recorded for radio shows,

MASTER NO. TITLE (COMPOSER[S])	RECORDING NO.

but were mastered and eventually remastered with overdubs by MGM for single and LP release, which is the reason they have been included here. The different sets of master numbers assigned to the titles have not been tabulated. All single releases are undubbed except where noted. It is very likely that a few of the performances below do not derive from the Johnnie Fair shows, but from other recordings made at KWKH.

PLEASE DON'T LET ME LOVE YOU (Ralph Jones)	11928
FADED LOVE AND WINTER ROSES (Fred Rose)	11928
THERE'S NO ROOM IN MY HEART FOR THE BLUES (Fred Rose/Zeb Turner)	12244
THE LITTLE PAPER BOY (Johnnie Wright/Jack Anglin)	Polydor 823695 (LP)
I WISH I HAD A NICKEL (Tommy Sutton/Sammy Barnhart)	12244
ROCKIN' CHAIR MONEY (Lonnie Glosson/Bill Carlisle)	E-3803 (LP)*
TENNESSEE BORDER (Jimmie Work)	E-3803 (LP)*
MY MAIN TRIAL IS YET TO COME (Pee Wee King/J. L. Frank)	Time-Life TLCW-01 (LP)*
THE DEVIL'S TRAIN (Cliff Carlisle/Mel Foree)	E-3850 (LP)*
THE SINGING WATERFALL	12332
COOL WATER (Bob Nolan)	E-3803 (LP)*
THE WALTZ OF THE WIND (Fred Rose)	12535
AT THE FIRST FALL OF SNOW (Lorene Rose)	12077
DIXIE CANNONBALL (Gene Autry/Vaughn Horton)	E-3803 (LP)*
I'M FREE AT LAST (Ernest Tubb)	E-3803 (LP)†
YOU CAUSED IT ALL BY TELLING LIES	Unissued/Lost
LEAVE ME ALONE WITH THE BLUES (Joe Pope)	12484
IT JUST DON'T MATTER NOW (Ernest Tubb)	E-3803 (LP)‡
SWING WIDE YOUR GATE OF LOVE (Hank Thompson)	E-3803 (LP)*
WE PLANTED ROSES ON OUR DARLING'S GRAVE	Unissued/Lost
THE OLD HOME (J. W. Earls)	E-3803 (LP)*
ALONE AND FORSAKEN§	12029
THE PRODIGAL SON ("Floyd Jones")‖	Unissued/Lost
THE TRAMP ON THE STREET (Grady & Hazel Cole)‖	Unissued/Lost
SOMEDAY YOU'LL CALL MY NAME (Jean Branch/Eddie Hill)	12077
THANK GOD (Fred Rose)	12127*
BLUE LOVE (IN MY HEART) ("Floyd Jenkins")	12332
ROLY POLY (Fred Rose)	12727*
THE BATTLE OF ARMAGEDDON (Roy Acuff/Odell McLeod)	12127

MASTER NO. TITLE (COMPOSER[S])   *RECORDING NO.*

WE LIVE IN TWO DIFFERENT WORLDS (Fred Rose)	12635*
WAIT FOR THE LIGHT TO SHINE (Hank Williams/ Charlie Monroe)	E-3850 (LP)*
NO ONE WILL EVER KNOW (Fred Rose/Mel Foree)	12535
WITH TEARS IN MY EYES (Paul Howard)	12484
ROCK MY CRADLE ONCE AGAIN (Johnny Bond)	E-3803 (LP)⁺
FIRST YEAR BLUES (Ernest Tubb)	E-3803 (LP)*
SUNDOWN AND SORROW (J. L. Frank/Pee Wee King)	E-3803 (LP)*

* Overdubbed.
† Overdubbed; undubbed on Polydor 825554.
‡ Overdubbed; undubbed on Polydor 827531.
§ First recorded commercially by Bill Darnel, March 1952.
Decca 27994.
‖ Version by Hank Williams that was issued derives from
Health & Happiness shows.
⁺ Overdubbed; undubbed on Polydor 825548.

Demo recorded unknown date/location, possibly ca. 1948.

SOMETHING GOT A HOLD OF ME (A. P. Carter)*	
	Polydor 831633 (LP)

* Duet with Audrey Williams.

Session March 1, 1949 (7:30–10:30 P.M.): Castle Studio, Nashville.

49-S-6030 DEAR BROTHER*	10434
49-S-6031 JESUS REMEMBERED ME*	10813
49-S-6032 LOST HIGHWAY (Leon Payne)	10506
49-S-6033 MAY YOU NEVER BE ALONE	10609

* Duet issued as "Hank and Audrey."

*Session March 1–2, 1949 (11:00 P.M.–2:00 A.M.): Castle Studio,
Nashville.*

49-S-6034 HONKY TONK BLUES	Polydor 823695 (LP)
49-S-6035 MIND YOUR OWN BUSINESS	10461
49-S-6036 YOU'RE GONNA CHANGE (OR I'M GONNA LEAVE)	10506
49-S-6037 MY SON CALLS ANOTHER MAN DADDY (Hank Williams/Jewell House)	Polydor 823695 (LP)

*Session March 20, 1949 (7:30–10:30 P.M.): Castle Studio,
Nashville.*

49-S-6038 WEDDING BELLS (Claude Boone)	10401
49-S-6039 I'VE JUST TOLD MAMA GOOD-BYE (Sunshine Slim Sweet/Curley Kinsey)	10401

*Composition registered with Library of Congress June 29, 1949.
No surviving demo.*

ON THE EVENING TRAIN (Hank & Audrey Williams)*
* First commercially recorded by Molly O'Day. April 4, 1949.
Columbia 20601.

MASTER NO. TITLE (COMPOSER[S])	RECORDING NO.

Undated demo. Composition registered with Library of Congress July 12, 1949. Demo probably recorded in Shreveport 1948/9.

WHEN YOU'RE TIRED OF BREAKING OTHERS'
HEARTS (Hank Williams/Curley Williams)*   E-3955 (LP)⁺
* First commercially recorded by Curley Williams. September
15, 1952. Columbia 21039.
⁺ Overdubbed on E-3955.

Session August 30, 1949 (2:00–5:30 P.M.): E. T. Herzog Studio, 811 Race Street, Cincinnati, Ohio.

49-S-6072 I'M SO LONESOME I COULD CRY	10560
49-S-6073 A HOUSE WITHOUT LOVE	10696
49-S-6074 I JUST DON'T LIKE THIS KIND OF LIVIN'	10609
49-S-6075 MY BUCKET'S GOT A HOLE IN IT (Clarence Williams)	10560

Compositions registered with Library of Congress November 25, 1949. Demos probably recorded 1949.

'NEATH A COLD GRAY TOMB OF STONE
(H. Williams/Mel Foree)*   Polydor 827531 (LP)⁺
NO, NOT NOW (H. Williams/Curley Williams/
Mel Foree)‡ §   Polydor (UK) 2391.519 (LP)
* First commercially recorded by Charlie Monroe. October 20,
1950. RCA 0417.
⁺ Full band performance, possibly from Shreveport.
‡ First commercially recorded by Curley Williams. September
11, 1949. Columbia 20633.
§ The demo features a fiddle and a second vocalist on the
refrain.

Composition registered with Library of Congress January 3, 1950. Demo probably recorded late 1949.

JESUS DIED FOR ME*   E-3955 (LP)⁺
* First commercially recorded by Roy Acuff. December 1949.
Columbia 20684.
⁺ Overdubbed; undubbed on Polydor 825551.

Session January 9, 1950 (2:00–5:00 P.M.): Castle Studio, Nashville. Supervision by Frank B. Walker and Fred Rose.

50-S-6003 LONG GONE LONESOME BLUES	10645
50-S-6004 WHY DON'T YOU LOVE ME	10696
50-S-6005 WHY SHOULD WE TRY ANYMORE?	10760
50-S-6006 MY SON CALLS ANOTHER MAN DADDY	10645

Session January 10, 1950 (2:00–5:00 P.M.): Castle Studio, Nashville.

50-S-6007 TOO MANY PARTIES AND TOO MANY PALS* (Billy Rose/Mort Dixon/Ray Henderson)	10718
50-S-6008 BEYOND THE SUNSET* (Blanche Kerr Brock/Virgil P. Brock/Albert Kennedy Rowswell)	10630

50-S-6009 THE FUNERAL* (Poem — P.D.; music Fred Rose)	10630
50-S-6010 EVERYTHING'S OKAY*	10718

* Issued under pseudonym "Luke the Drifter — with musical
accompaniment."

*Compositions registered with Library of Congress April 21,
1950. Demos probably recorded late 1949/early 1950.*

ALABAMA WALTZ*	Polydor 825554 (LP)
A HOUSE OF GOLD†	11707‡

* First commercially recorded by Bill Monroe. February 3,
1950. Decca 46236.
† First commercially recorded by Milton Estes. December 30,
1949. Coral 64031.
‡ Overdubbed. Undubbed demo issued Polydor 833752;
alternate demo issued on CMF-06.

*Composition registered with Library of Congress December 29,
1950. Demo probably recorded early 1950.*

HOW CAN YOU REFUSE HIM NOW?	11707*

* Overdubbed; undubbed on Polydor 833749.

Undated demo, probably early 1950.

HELP ME UNDERSTAND	CMF-06 (LP)

*Audrey Williams Session March 28, 1950: Castle Studio,
Nashville.*

76046 MY TIGHTWAD DADDY	Decca 46264
76047 MODEL T LOVE	Bear Family BFX 15346 (LP)
76048 HELP ME UNDERSTAND*	Decca 46275
76049 HOW CAN YOU REFUSE HIM NOW	Decca 46275

* Hugh Cherry duet vocal.

*Audrey Williams Session April 1, 1950: Castle Studio,
Nashville.*

76066 WHAT PUT THE PEP IN GRANDMA	Decca 46233
76067 I LIKE THAT KIND	Decca 46264
76068 HONKY TONKIN'	Decca 46233

*Session June 14, 1950 (noon–3:30 P.M.): Castle Studio,
Nashville.*

5-S-6064 THEY'LL NEVER TAKE HER LOVE FROM ME (Leon Payne)	10760
50-S-6065 HONKY TONK BLUES	Unissued/Lost

*Composition registered with Library of Congress August 16,
1950. No surviving demo.*

MASTER NO. TITLE (COMPOSER[S])   *RECORDING NO.*

HONEY DO YOU LOVE ME, HUH?
(H. Williams/Curley Williams)*
* First commercially recorded by Curley Williams. June 5,
1950. Columbia 20748.

Session August 31, 1950 (2:00–5:00 P.M.): Castle Studio,
Nashville.

50-S-6096 NOBODY'S LONESOME FOR ME	10832
50-S-6097 MOANIN' THE BLUES	10832
50-S-6098 HELP ME UNDERSTAND*	10806
50-S-6099 NO, NO, JOE (Fred Rose)*	10806

* Issued under pseudonym "Luke the Drifter — with musical
accompaniment."

Compositions registered with Library of Congress October 5,
1950. No surviving demo on "Rockin' Chair Daddy."

ROCKIN' CHAIR DADDY (H. Williams/Braxton Schuffert)*
A TEARDROP ON A ROSE*†   12029

* First commercially recorded by Braxton Schuffert (issued as
"Braxton Shooford"). February 8, 1950. MGM 10670.
† Overdubbed; undubbed on Polydor 833749.

Composition registered with Library of Congress October 7,
1950. No surviving demo.

NEVER BEEN SO LONESOME*
* Recorded by Zeb Turner. October 28, 1949. King 861.

Session December 21, 1950 (7:15–9:50 P.M.): Castle Studio,
Nashville.

50-S-6132 COLD, COLD HEART	10904
50-S-6133 DEAR JOHN (Tex Ritter/Aubrey Gass)	10904
50-S-6134 JUST WAITIN' (H. Williams/Bob Gazzaway)*	10932
50-S-6135 MEN WITH BROKEN HEARTS*	10932

* Issued under the pseudonym "Luke the Drifter — with
musical accompaniment."

Composition registered with Library of Congress February 7,
1951. No surviving demo.

THE LITTLE HOUSE WE BUILT JUST O'ER THE
HILL (H. Williams/Don Helms)*
* Recorded by Big Bill Lister. April 24, 1951. Capitol 1551.

Composition registered with Library of Congress March 10,
1951. Demo probably recorded early 1951.

JESUS IS CALLING (H. Williams/Charles Monroe)*   E-3850 (LP)†
* First commercially recorded by Charlie Monroe. May 6,
1951. RCA 0485.
† Overdubbed.

MASTER NO. TITLE (COMPOSER[S])   *RECORDING NO.*

Session March 16, 1951 (1:30–5:00 P.M.): Castle Studio,
Nashville.

      51-S-6027 I CAN'T HELP IT (IF I'M STILL IN
           LOVE WITH YOU)   10961
      51-S-6028 HOWLIN' AT THE MOON   10961
      51-S-6029 HEY GOOD LOOKIN'   11000
      51-S-6030 MY HEART WOULD KNOW   11000

Session March 23, 1951 (7:00–10:30 P.M.): Castle Studio,
Nashville.

      51-S-6012 LEAVE US WOMEN ALONE*   11083
      51-S-6013 IF YOU SEE MY BABY*   11083
      51-S-6014 THE PALE HORSE AND HIS RIDER†
           (Ervin Staggs/Johnny Bailes)   12394
      51-S-6015 A HOME IN HEAVEN†   12394
* Issued as Audrey Williams.
† Issued as "Hank and Audrey."

Composition registered with Library of Congress April 11, 1951.
Demo probably recorded late 1950/January 1951.

      THERE'S NOTHING AS SWEET AS MY BABY*   CMF 06 (LP)
* First commercially recorded by Carl Smith. January 30, 1951.
Columbia 20796

Composition registered with Library of Congress April 23,
1951. Demo probably recorded late 1950.

      WEARIN' OUT YOUR WALKIN' SHOES*   E-3955 (LP)†
* First commercially recorded by Tex Ritter. September 20,
1950. Capitol 1581.
† Overdubbed; undubbed on Polydor 833752.

Composition registered with Library of Congress May 24, 1951.
Demo probably recorded early 1951.

      SING, SING, SING*
* First commercially recorded by Charlie Monroe. October 20,
1950. RCA 48-0456.

Session June 1, 1951 (7:00–10:00 P.M.): Castle Studio, Nashville.

      51-S-6056 RAMBLIN' MAN*†   11120
      51-S-6057 PICTURES FROM LIFE'S OTHER SIDE*   11120
      51-S-6058 I'VE BEEN DOWN THAT ROAD BEFORE*   11017
      51-S-6059 I DREAMED ABOUT MAMA
           LAST NIGHT (Fred Rose)   11017
* Issued under the pseudonym "Luke the Drifter — with
instrumental accompaniment."
† Reissued under Hank Williams's name on MGM 11479.

Composition registered with Library of Congress June 20, 1951.
No surviving demo.

      A STRANGER IN THE NIGHT (H. Williams/Bill Morgan)*
* First commercially recorded by George Morgan. April 16,
1951. Columbia 21052.

MASTER NO. TITLE (COMPOSER[S])	RECORDING NO.

Session July 25, 1951 (7:15–10:35 P.M.): Castle Studio, Nashville.

51-S-6078 I'D STILL WANT YOU	11100
51-S-6079 LONESOME WHISTLE (Hank Williams/ Jimmie Davis)	11054
51-S-6080 CRAZY HEART (Fred Rose/Maurice Murray)	11054
CRAZY HEART	(alternate take) X-1014 (EP)
51-S-6081 BABY, WE'RE REALLY IN LOVE	Unissued/Lost

Composition registered with Library of Congress August 15, 1951. No surviving demo.
ME AND MY BROKEN HEART*
* Recorded by Carl Smith. June 8, 1951. Columbia 20862.

Composition registered with Library of Congress July 23, 1951. No surviving demo.
COUNTRIFIED*
* Recorded by Big Bill Lister. April 24, 1951. Capitol 1551.

Session August 10, 1951 (7:00–10:30 P.M.): Castle Studio, Nashville.

51-S-6111 I'M SORRY FOR YOU, MY FRIEND	Unissued/Lost
51-S-6112 HALF AS MUCH (Curley Williams)	11202
51-S-6113 I'D STILL WANT YOU	Polydor 823695 (LP)
51-S-6114 BABY, WE'RE REALLY IN LOVE	11100

Composition registered with Library of Congress November 21, 1951. Demo probably recorded fall, 1951.
I CAN'T ESCAPE FROM YOU*†   11574
* First commercially recorded by Rusty Gabbard. September 30, 1951. MGM 11110.
† Overdubbed; undubbed on Polydor 831634.

Composition registered with Library of Congress November 28, 1951. Demo probably recorded fall, 1951.
WEARY BLUES FROM WAITIN'*   11574†
* First commercially recorded by Ray Price. October 16, 1951. Columbia 20883.
† Overdubbed; undubbed on Polydor 825551.

Composition registered with Library of Congress September 15, 1952. Demo recorded October 25, 1951 (per Big Bill Lister).
THERE'S A TEAR IN MY BEER*†
* First commercially recorded by Big Bill Lister. October 26, 1951. Capitol 2148.
† Hank Williams's demo overdubbed with Hank Williams Jr. and group, 1988 (issued on Warner Bros./Curb 7-27584); Hank Williams's undubbed demo issued on Polydor 847194 (LP).

MASTER NO. TITLE (COMPOSER[S])	RECORDING NO.

*The following title was recorded on demo by Hank Williams at
the same time:*
ALL THE LOVE I EVER HAD   Polydor 847194 (LP)

*Session December 11, 1951 (10:00 A.M.–noon): Castle Studio,
Nashville.*

51-S-6128 I'M SORRY FOR YOU, MY FRIEND	11160
51-S-6129 HONKY TONK BLUES	11160
51-S-6130 LET'S TURN BACK THE YEARS	11202

*Composition registered with Library of Congress November 29,
1951. No surviving demo.*
I WISH YOU DIDN'T LOVE ME SO MUCH*†

* Recorded by Little Jimmy Dickens. July 12, 1951. Released
only in Canada on Columbia 1910. First released in USA on
Columbia LP FC 38905.
† Later rewritten and recorded by Hank Williams as "Why
Don't You Make Up Your Mind." See session July 11, 1952.

*Composition registered with Library of Congress December 19,
1951. No surviving demo.*
BAYOU PON-PON (H. Williams/Jimmie Davis)*

* Recorded by Jimmie Davis. October 14, 1951. Decca 46381.

*Composition registered with Library of Congress December 31,
1951. No surviving demo.*
FOREVER IS A LONG, LONG TIME (H. Williams/
Jimmie Davis)*

* Recorded by Jimmie Davis. October 14, 1951. Decca 46396.

*Composition registered with Library of Congress March 3,
1952. Demo probably recorded late 1951/early 1952.*
WHEN THE BOOK OF LIFE IS READ*   E-3850 (LP)†

* First commercially recorded by Jimmie Skinner. January 14,
1952. Capitol 1995.
† Overdubbed; undubbed on Polydor 825557.

Undated demo, probably early 1952.
JAMBALAYA   CMF-06 (LP)

*Session June 13, 1952 (10:00 A.M.–1:00 P.M.): Castle Studio,
Nashville.*

52-S-6059 WINDOW SHOPPING (Marcel Joseph)	11283
52-S-6060 JAMBALAYA (ON THE BAYOU)	11283
52-S-6061 SETTIN' THE WOODS ON FIRE (Fred Rose/ Ed Nelson)	11318
52-S-6062 I'LL NEVER GET OUT OF THIS WORLD ALIVE (Hank Williams/Fred Rose)	11366

MASTER NO. TITLE (COMPOSER[S])	RECORDING NO.

Session July 11, 1952 (1:45–3:45 P.M.): Castle Studio, Nashville.

52-S-6067 YOU WIN AGAIN	11318
52-S-6068 I WON'T BE HOME NO MORE	11533
52-S-6069 BE CAREFUL OF STONES THAT	
YOU THROW* (Bonnie Dodd)	11309
52-S-6070 PLEASE MAKE UP YOUR MIND*	11309

* Issued under pseudonym "Luke the Drifter — with instrumental accompaniment."

Composition registered with Library of Congress March 23, 1953; demo probably recorded fall, 1952.

IF YOU'LL BE A BABY TO ME*	E-3955 (LP)[†]

* First commercially recorded by Red Sovine. September 26, 1952. MGM 11567.
[†] Overdubbed; undubbed on Polydor 825557.

Undated demo, probably fall 1952.

YOUR CHEATIN' HEART	CMF-06 (LP)

Session called September 9, 1952 (10:00 A.M.–1:00 P.M.).
Canceled.
Session called September 19, 1952 (10:00 A.M.–1:00 P.M.).
Canceled.
Session September 23, 1952 (1:30 P.M.–3:40 P.M.): Castle Studio, Nashville.

52-S-6095 I COULD NEVER BE ASHAMED OF YOU	11366
52-S-6096 YOUR CHEATIN' HEART	11416
52-S-6097 KAW-LIGA (H. Williams/Fred Rose)	11416
52-S-6098 TAKE THESE CHAINS FROM MY HEART	
(Hy Heath/Fred Rose)	11479

Compositions registered with Library of Congress October 31, 1952. No surviving demos.

I LOST THE ONLY LOVE I KNEW (Hank Williams/Don Helms)*	
MY COLD, COLD HEART IS MELTED NOW (Hank Williams/Johnnie Masters)[†]	

* First commercially recorded by Ray Price. February 8, 1952. Columbia 21025.
[†] First commercially recorded by Kitty Wells. July 10, 1953. Decca 28797.

MASTER NO. TITLE (COMPOSER[S])   *RECORDING NO.*

Composition registered with Library of Congress December 2, 1952.

          ARE YOU WALKIN' AND A TALKIN' FOR THE LORD*†   E-3850 (LP)‡

* First commercially recorded by Wilma Lee and Stony
Cooper. February 17, 1953, Columbia 21131.
† A version of the song with band appears on Polydor 833749,
suggesting that the song was actually composed much earlier,
possibly while Hank was resident in Shreveport.
‡ Overdubbed.

POSTHUMOUSLY REGISTERED SONGS DEMO'D BY HANK WILLIAMS

These songs have been arranged in the order in which they were registered with the Library of Congress, which corresponds roughly to the order in which they were issued by MGM. The original recording dates are unknown. Only songs recorded on demo by Hank Williams have been listed. Since his death there has been a plethora of songs attributed to Hank Williams, or answer songs to his hits on which his estate receives part composer credit. In 1969 a miscellany of lyrics attributed to Hank Williams were set to music and co-copyrighted with Hank Williams Jr. These have not been included.

          READY TO GO HOME*   12438†

* Registered with Library of Congress March 5, 1953.
† Overdubbed; undubbed on Polydor 833752.

          YOU BETTER KEEP IT ON YOUR MIND
              (Hank Williams/Vic McAlpin)*   11675†

* Probably recorded in Shreveport ca. 1949; according to Mel
Foree, the second vocalist is Hank Snow.
† Overdubbed; undubbed on CMF-06.

          LOW DOWN BLUES*   11675†

* Registered with Library of Congress February 19, 1954.
† Overdubbed; undubbed on Polydor 831633.

          I AIN'T GOT NOTHIN' BUT TIME*   11768†

* Registered with Library of Congress August 17, 1954.
† Overdubbed; undubbed on Polydor 825548.

          ANGEL OF DEATH*   11861†

* Registered with Library of Congress December 18, 1954.
† Overdubbed; alternate demo issued on Polydor 831634.

          MESSAGE TO MY MOTHER*   11975†

* Registered with Library of Congress May 4, 1955.
† Overdubbed; undubbed with additional verses on Polydor
831634.

MOTHER IS GONE*   11975[†]
* Registered with Library of Congress May 4, 1955.
† Overdubbed. Demo possibly recorded in mid-1940s because
it appears in one of Williams's WSFA songbooks.

CALIFORNIA ZEPHYR*   12185[†]
* Registered with Library of Congress December 30, 1955.
† Overdubbed; issued undubbed on Polydor 825554.

WE'RE GETTING CLOSER TO THE GRAVE EACH DAY*   12483[†]
* Registered with Library of Congress April 23, 1957.
† Overdubbed; issued undubbed on Polydor 825557.

I'M GOING HOME*   E-3850 (LP)[†]
* Registered with Library of Congress October 31, 1960.
† Overdubbed.

LAST NIGHT I DREAMED OF HEAVEN*   E-3850 (LP)[†]
* Registered with Library of Congress October 31, 1960.
† Overdubbed; undubbed on Polydor 831633.

ARE YOU BUILDING A TEMPLE IN HEAVEN?*   E-3850 (LP)[†]
* Registered with Library of Congress November 7, 1960.
† Overdubbed.

THE LOG TRAIN*   Time-Life TLCW-01 (LP)
* Registered at unknown date. Demo reputed to have been
recorded in 1952.

FOOL ABOUT YOU*   E-3955 (LP)
* This song was registered in Hank Williams's name in 1962,
but it was actually written and first recorded by Ralph C.
Hutcheson. Hank Williams's demo was probably recorded ca.
1951. The undubbed demo was first issued on Polydor U.K.
2391.519.

A NOTE ON LPS

Only two Hank Williams LPs were issued during his lifetime. Since his death his recordings have been recycled onto hundreds, possibly thousands, of LPs, and individual titles
have appeared on as many more again. In addition to the endless duplication and overlap,
many LPs used recordings that had been overdubbed with additional instrumentation or
rechanneled into fake stereo. With the demise of the LP as a sound carrier, all of them have
been deleted, so it serves no good purpose to list them, and most should be approached
with caution.

The advent of the compact disc afforded a more or less clean slate. Polydor in England assembled a greatest hits collection that included all original (i.e., undubbed) versions. That collection was remastered for CD in the United States and is available as *40 Greatest Hits* (Polydor 821233).

Additionally, there is a series of eight LPs and cassettes (subsequently CDs) on Polydor that includes all the Hank Williams recordings known to exist as of 1987, with the exception of the titles on two LPs (subsequently one CD) issued by the Country Music Foundation. The Polydor series uses the original or, in the case of demos, the least dubbed version available. Those eight volumes follow:

Vol. 1: I Ain't Got Nothin' but Time (Polydor 825548)
Vol. 2: Lovesick Blues (Polydor 825551)
Vol. 3: Lost Highway (Polydor 825554)
Vol. 4: I'm So Lonesome I Could Cry (Polydor 825557)
Vol. 5: Long Gone Lonesome Blues (Polydor 831633)
Vol. 6: Hey, Good Lookin' (Polydor 831634)
Vol. 7: Let's Turn Back the Years (Polydor 833749)
Vol. 8: I Won't Be Home No More (Polydor 833752)

The demos issued by the Country Music Foundation on two LPs (CMF-06 and CMF-07) were reissued on one CD, entitled *Rare Demos: First to Last* (CMF-067D).

Three newly discovered Hank Williams recordings (the 1942 recording from Highland Bridge's Radio of "I'm Not Coming Home Any More" and the two titles from Bill Lister, "There's a Tear in My Beer" and "All the Love I Ever Had") were included in a 1990 three-CD/cassette set that included all of the singles issued under Hank Williams's name during his lifetime, entitled *The Original Singles Collection . . . Plus* (Polydor 847194).

In 1993, the eight *Health and Happiness* shows from October 1949 were issued complete and undubbed as *Health and Happiness Shows* (Mercury 314-517862).

All of Audrey Williams's Decca recordings are on *Ramblin' Gal* (Bear Family BFX 15346) (LP only). All of Molly O'Day's Columbia recordings are on *Molly O'Day and the Cumberland Mountain Folks* (Bear Family BCD 15565).

A selection of songs that Hank Williams wrote for other singers, specifically those who recorded for Columbia — including Ray Price, Molly O'Day, Roy Acuff, Curley Williams, Carl Smith, and Little Jimmy Dickens — are on *Hank Williams Songbook* (Columbia/Legacy CK 47995).

SINGLES RELEASED 1947–1953

By the end of 1953, only three studio masters remained unissued ("I'm Satisfied with You" and two duets with Audrey, "The Pale Horse and His Rider" and "A Home in Heaven"). Most of Hank's releases after the end of 1953 consisted of overdubbed demos, or reissued studio recordings that, in most cases, had been overdubbed.

Three country charts with fifteen positions were published by *Billboard* during Hank's lifetime: "Most Played Juke Box Folk Records" (renamed in 1949 "Most Played Juke Box Country and Western Records"); "Best Selling Retail Folk Records" (renamed "Best Selling Retail Folk Country and Western Records"); and "Country and Western Records Most Played by Disc Jockeys," a tabulation that started in 1949.

The Chart Peak Position column below derives from the research of Joel Whitburn, and the number shown is the highest position that the record reached on any of the three charts. A complete tabulation of all the positions on the three charts is available in Joel Whitburn's *Top Country Singles 1944–1988* (see Sources, above).

MGM 10434* 5/17/49 DEAR BROTHER
                         LOST ON THE RIVER
* Issued as "Hank and Audrey."

MGM 10461 7/15/49 MIND YOUR OWN BUSINESS   5
                       THERE'LL BE NO TEARDROPS TONIGHT

MGM 10506 9/9/49 YOU'RE GONNA CHANGE
                        (OR I'M GONNA LEAVE)   4
                        LOST HIGHWAY   12

MGM 10560 11/18/49 MY BUCKET'S GOT A HOLE IN IT   2
                        I'M SO LONESOME I COULD CRY

MGM 10609 1/27/50 I JUST DON'T LIKE THIS KIND OF LIVIN' 5
                        MAY YOU NEVER BE ALONE

MGM 10630* 2/24/50 THE FUNERAL
                        BEYOND THE SUNSET
* Issued as "Luke the Drifter."

MGM 10645 3/10/50 LONG GONE LONESOME BLUES   1
                        MY SON CALLS ANOTHER MAN DADDY   9

MGM 10696 5/19/50 WHY DON'T YOU LOVE ME   1
                        A HOUSE WITHOUT LOVE

MGM 10718* 6/16/50 EVERYTHING'S OKAY
                        TOO MANY PARTIES AND TOO
                        MANY PALS
* Issued as "Luke the Drifter."

MGM 10760 8/18/50 THEY'LL NEVER TAKE HER LOVE FROM ME 5
                        WHY SHOULD WE TRY ANY MORE   9

MGM 10806* 10/13/50 NO, NO, JOE
                        HELP ME UNDERSTAND
* Issued as "Luke the Drifter."

MGM 10813* 10/6/50 I HEARD MY MOTHER PRAYING FOR ME
                        JESUS REMEMBERED ME
* Issued as "Hank and Audrey."

MGM 10832 10/27/50 MOANIN' THE BLUES   1
                        NOBODY'S LONESOME FOR ME   9

MGM 10904 2/2/51 COLD, COLD HEART   1
                        DEAR JOHN   8

MGM 10932* 3/16/51 JUST WAITIN'
                   MEN WITH BROKEN HEARTS
* Issued as "Luke the Drifter."

MGM 10961 4/27/51 HOWLIN' AT THE MOON   3
                  I CAN'T HELP IT (IF I'M STILL IN LOVE
                  WITH YOU)   2

MGM 11000 6/22/51 HEY, GOOD LOOKIN'   1
                  MY HEART WOULD KNOW

MGM 11017* 7/20/51 I'VE BEEN DOWN THAT ROAD BEFORE
                   I DREAMED ABOUT MAMA LAST NIGHT
* Issued as "Luke the Drifter."

MGM 11054 9/14/51 LONESOME WHISTLE   9
                  CRAZY HEART   4

MGM 11100 11/23/51 BABY, WE'RE REALLY IN LOVE   4
                   I'D STILL WANT YOU

MGM 11120* 12/7/51 RAMBLIN' MAN
                   PICTURES FROM LIFE'S OTHER SIDE
* Issued as "Luke the Drifter."

MGM 11160 2/2/52 HONKY TONK BLUES   2
                 I'M SORRY FOR YOU, MY FRIEND

MGM 11202 3/28/52 HALF AS MUCH   2
                  LET'S TURN BACK THE YEARS

MGM 11283 7/18/52 JAMBALAYA (ON THE BAYOU)   1
                  WINDOW SHOPPING

MGM 11309* 8/29/52 WHY DON'T YOU MAKE UP YOUR MIND
                   BE CAREFUL OF STONES THAT YOU
                   THROW
* Issued as "Luke the Drifter."

MGM 11318 9/12/52 SETTIN' THE WOODS ON FIRE   2
                  YOU WIN AGAIN   10

MGM 11366 11/21/52 I'LL NEVER GET OUT OF THIS WORLD
                   ALIVE   1
                   I COULD NEVER BE ASHAMED OF YOU

MGM 11416 1/30/53 YOUR CHEATIN' HEART   1
                  KAW-LIGA   1

MGM 11479 4/24/53 TAKE THESE CHAINS FROM MY HEART   1
                    RAMBLIN' MAN*
* Reissue of MGM 11120.

MGM 11533 7/3/53 I WON'T BE HOME NO MORE   4
                  MY LOVE FOR YOU (HAS TURNED TO HATE)

MGM 11574* 9/11/53 WEARY BLUES FROM WAITIN'   7
                    I CAN'T ESCAPE FROM YOU
* Overdubbed demos.

MGM 11628* 11/53 CALLING YOU
                  WHEN GOD COMES AND GATHERS HIS JEWELS
* Reissue of Sterling cuts.

ACKNOWLEDGMENTS

This book is a cooperative effort. It was born out of a suggestion from Bill MacEwen, a community health worker in Prince Edward Island, who is one of the two or three most knowledgeable people about Hank Williams. As he was helping me on a series of Hank Williams reissues for Polygram Records, he put it to me that time was running out, and with every passing year the chance of getting Hank's story straight diminished. He introduced me to George Merritt, who lived in Montgomery during the '40s and has since become an authority on Hank Williams. This book is a combination of work that we have done separately and jointly. I took on the task of writing so that the book would have a uniformity of tone that is difficult to achieve with more than one set of hands on the wheel.

Our biggest vote of thanks goes to the Country Music Foundation in Nashville, an unparalleled resource center staffed by people who know about and care deeply about the music and, in a broader sense, the culture in which it exists. In particular, we wish to thank Bob Pinson for sharing his research with us. Paul Kingsbury, Ronnie Pugh, John Rumble, and Kyle Young were also helpful. Others in Nashville to whom we owe thanks include Joe Allison, Ari Bass, Richard Bennett, Kyle Cantrell, Ott Devine, Don Helms, Tommy Hill, Otto Kitsinger, Jerry Rivers, Dale Vinicur, Billy Walker, Kitty Wells, Johnnie Wright, Guy Willis at the American Federation of Musicians, and the staff at the *Nashville Tennessean* archive as well as the state, county, and municipal archives.

In New York, the Library of the Lincoln Center for the Performing Arts had predictably little on Hank Williams but much valuable data on the companies for whom he worked. Bill Levenson at Polygram and Dennis Drake at Polygram Studios made recording data available to us. The city archives were also useful in researching Sterling and MGM Records.

In Alabama we were helped by Freddy and Irella Beach, Country Boy Eddy Burns, Happy Hal Burns, Paul Dennis, Leaborne Eads, Ed and Marie Harvell, J. C. McNeil, Walter McNeil, Pee Wee Moultrie, R. D. Norred, Joe Penney, Erleen Skipper, Leila Griffin Williams, and Robert Williams. We are also grateful to the estate of Bob McKinnon for allowing us access to his archive. The mayor of Georgiana, Lynn Watson, and other people in the state as well as various county and municipal archives were also helpful.

Many people in Louisiana and eastern Texas helped us too, including Jim Boyd, Tillman Franks, Robert Gentry at the *Sabine Index*, Billie Jean Horton, Big Bill Lister, Horace Logan, Felton Pruett, Lum York and his daughter Kelly, and the staff of the archive at the Louisiana State University in Shreveport.

We'd also like to thank some of Hank Williams's band members in and out of retirement at various other points around the country: Jerry Byrd in Hawaii, Boots Harris in Mississippi, Bob McNett in Pennsylvania, Bernice Turner in Memphis, and Zeke Turner in Florida. Also, in no particular order, Dave Booth at the Showtime Music Archive in Toronto, A. V. Bamford, Bill England, Ed Guy, Murray Nash, Marvin Reuben, Robert Medley, and Richard Weize at Bear Family Records in Germany. We would especially like to thank Milton L. Brown of Bama Boy Productions for loaning us a copy of Hank's application for employment at the shipyards. And, finally, Lindsay Grater, who drew the map and heard more about Hank Williams than she ever wanted to know.

As ever, apologies to anyone we missed.

INDEX